SACRÉ BLUES

SACRÉ BLUES

*An Unsentimental Journey
Through Quebec*

Taras Grescoe

Macfarlane Walter & Ross
Toronto

Macfarlane Walter & Ross
An Affiliate of McClelland & Stewart Ltd.
37A Hazelton Avenue
Toronto, Canada M5R 2E3

Canadian Cataloguing in Publication Data

Grescoe, Taras
Sacré blues : an unsentimental journey through Quebec

Includes index.
ISBN 1-55199-048-2

1. Popular culture – Quebec (Province).
2. Quebec (Province) – Civilization.   I. Title.

FC2919.G733 2000   971.4   C00-931614-0
F1052.G83 2000

Macfarlane Walter & Ross gratefully acknowledges support
for its publishing program from the Canada Council for the Arts,
the Ontario Arts Council, and the Government of Canada
through the Book Publishing Industry Development Program.

Printed and bound in Canada

To Paul and Audrey, the editors of my life.

ACKNOWLEDGMENTS

This book couldn't have been written without the help of Georges-Hébert Germain and Jean Paré, veteran journalists who generously helped an anglophone colleague discover their *pays*. Thanks to Chantal Bouchard, of McGill, and Georges Dupont, for their kind comments and suggestions for improving the Ranch du Spaghetti chapter. And finally, thanks to Jennifer Wile for riding shotgun from St-Tite to the Charlevoix, and for offering support and inspiration during the two years it took to write this book.

Contents

Poutine Nation

Quebec, for much of the world, is a cliché. To the people of France, it will always be la Belle Province, where *les cousins canadiens* criss-cross the few acres of snow in front of their *cabane* in a horse-drawn *calèche*. For out-of-touch fundamentalists, Quebec is the priest-ridden province, a land of black-robed *curés* and stern nuns where steeples bristle like pikes from villages named for an army of saints. To the Québécois themselves, it is *un pays*, the core of an *Amérique française* that once stretched from Louisbourg to Louisiana, a flinty shard of six million francophones that even 250 million English-speakers haven't been able to dissolve in their nefarious melting pot. For anglophone Canadians, she is that other solitude, that distinct society – and lately, an insouciant, flighty, can't-live-with-her, can't-live-without-her, bitch. For European visitors, Quebec is all too American. For Americans, she is exquisitely European. Ah! That French *bonhomie*! That Latin *joie de vivre*! *Je me souviens! Vive la différence! Cherchez la femme!* Quebec isn't a province or a nation: it's a breeding ground for italics.

The clichés, of course, are half true; but like Sancho Panza's proverbs, there are so many of them, expressing so many contradictory propositions, that they cancel one another out. The visitor from the United States who comes to Montreal glimpses a couple of mansard roofs, an accordionist, and a girl with a baguette in her backpack, and goes home raving about Quebec's Old World charm. The European visitor, after seeing strip malls, fast food joints, multiplex theatres and in-line skaters, leaves complaining that Quebec – alas! – has been completely Americanized. An English-speaking Torontonian, in town for a summer festival weekend, soaks in the afternoon terrace sitting, the bars open till three in the morning, the women dressed in platform shoes and halter tops, and concludes that Quebec City is as hedonistically Latin as Rio de Janeiro. Should a Brazilian researcher show up for a conference in January, however, when faces are pale and spirits are undergoing their five-month winter lockdown, she'll return home with reports of a race of gloomy Nordics. Ultimately, the adjectives applied to Quebec are as revealing of the traveller's temperament and cultural background as they are of the place itself.

There are, thankfully, a few fundamental facts just about everyone can agree on. For example, in terms of square kilometres, Quebec is the largest province in Canada. Though it is nearly three times the size of France, 60 per cent of its 7.5 million inhabitants live in a narrow corridor within a few kilometres of the St. Lawrence River, that alarming notch crosscut into the heartwood of the continent. Quebec, long inhabited by Amerindians, was explored by Jacques Cartier in 1534 and settled in earnest by Europeans from the centre and west of France starting in 1608. An English victory on the Plains of Abraham in Quebec City in 1759 led to the withdrawal of French troops and the end of colonial New France. Under British rule, Irish, Scottish, and English immigrants, and later Loyalists fleeing revolutionary America, became an important component of the population. In 1867, Quebec, until then known as Lower Canada, became an equal partner in the creation of a new democracy, Canada. French-speaking Quebecers, who refer to themselves as francophone Québécois, now account for 84 per cent of the total provincial population and 20 per cent of the population of Canada. They control at least two-thirds of the economy of their province, have dominated provincial politics since Confederation, and as federal prime ministers and members of parliament have been responsible for establishing some of the key institutions of Canadian democracy. Quebec is a modern, dynamic society, unscarred in this century by warfare or famine, sharing a high standard of living with the other peoples of the richest continent in the world. One last detail: a significant portion of the population of Quebec has expressed its desire to form a new nation-state, independent from Canada. In a referendum in 1995, 49.4 per cent of Quebecers voted "yes" to a controversially worded question that asked if they were willing to negotiate independence from Canada. Those in favour of the move are usually called separatists, *indépendantistes*, or *souverainistes*; those against are referred to as federalists.

There; I won't bring it up again. Much.

Now that we've located Quebec on the globe and dispensed with almost half a millennium of history, let's get back to the real issues. Like, what's up with drivers here? As an English Canadian raised on the once courteous streets of Vancouver, I've tended to subscribe to the classic theory that the driving habits of the Québécois are proof positive of their Latin blood. As in Italy and France, walking the boulevards of Quebec's cities with less than maximum vigilance can be life-threatening. The cars of choice here are nervous little Honda Accords and Toyota Tercels, Renault 5s and Volkswagen Golfs, and there's no tradition of yielding to pedestrians or stopping at the province's rare crosswalks. Stooping to retrieve a coin while crossing the street is asking for trouble: you risk interfering with the guy in the jumpy Neon who, turning left into oncoming traffic, plans to complete the manoeuvre by leaving exactly three centimetres between his left fender and your retreating heel. On the road, popular tactics include tailgating, unsignalled lane changes, and pointless speeding towards a light already turned red. Then there's the Gallic technique that Parisians call the *queue de poisson*, in which a swifter vehicle passes you, then pulls into your lane and briefly decelerates, pausing like a mocking marlin administering a slap of the tail to a sea turtle. It is extremely French. It is extremely annoying.

Quebec accounts for 17 per cent of the North American sales of the Volkswagen Golf, a pug-nosed tamale of a car whose chief market is 18-to-34-year-old males and whose main selling point is its ability to accelerate rapidly. The 1995 ad campaign for the car included billboards that featured a hot-rodding kid in a red Golf exclaiming, "Tasse-toi, mon oncle!" (loosely translated, Out of my way, Pops!) Midway through the campaign, a 16-year-old Montreal driver sped out of control, crossed a highway divider, and was crushed to death, along with three high school friends, by an oncoming 18-wheeler. The car he was driving, naturally, was a red Golf GTI. (To make matters worse, the Radio-Canada news program that reported the accident was immediately preceded by a "Tasse-toi!" commercial.)

Is the Québécois penchant for speed just something in the air, or is it bred in the bone? Wherever it comes from, it's nothing new. When the American writer Henry David Thoreau visited Lower Canada in 1850, carrying his belongings in a bundle of paper, he watched the behaviour of drivers from the deck of his Quebec City–bound steamboat with bemusement. "I never saw so many caleches, cabs, charettes, and similar vehicles collected before, and doubt if New York could easily furnish more," he wrote of Montreal in *A Yankee in Canada*. "It was interesting to see the caleche drivers dash up and down the slope of the quay with their active little horses. They drive much faster than in our cities. I have been told that some of them come nine miles into the city every morning and return every night, without changing their horses during the day." Interesting – even before Canada was a country, the people of Quebec had a reputation for choosing potent, if undersized, horsepower. But, as Thoreau suggests, their need for speed may also have had a practical explanation: since they travelled long distances to work, their duties in town had to be accomplished with alacrity.

I suspect the latent Latinity of local driving habits is more cultural than genetic, generated by the restrictions imposed by Quebec's almost Napoleonic rules of the road. Apart from New York, Quebec is the only jurisdiction in North America that prohibits a right turn on a red light. When the light finally does turn green – traffic signals here are a dozen agonizing seconds longer than those in other Canadian provinces – drivers are often further withheld by an arrow until pedestrians cross. Since everybody here jaywalks, the crosswalk is generally still clogged with scampering pedestrians during the few seconds that remain to legally make the turn. Drivers respond by gunning their motors and none-too-gently nudging the foot traffic out of the way. No wonder that, when they're finally released from their confinement, they tend to peel out and accelerate like greyhounds in hopes of beating the light at the next corner. (There's a positive side to the traffic in Quebec: you can always count on drivers to act aggressively, and plan your jaywalking accordingly. In Vancouver, Calgary, and Toronto, there's now a dangerous mix of old-style British courtesy, nouveau riche aggressiveness, and New Canadian confusion, which means that you can't predict whether any given car will come to a full stop the minute you step off the curb, totally ignore you, or crush you like a bug.) After only a couple of hours of stop-and-start Montreal traffic, even I begin to act like Michael Andretti in a May Day *autostrada* pile-up – which means that either my Slavic father neglected to tell me about a couple of Latin branches in the family tree, or environment, not blood, determines driving behaviour. After all, when it comes to culture, it depends on which culture you're coming from. The Québécois will proudly tell you they drive like cowboys. Albertans, on the other hand, are pretty sure the Québécois drive like separatists.

As with the road, so with the dinner table. Depending on which restaurants you frequent, you could mistake Quebec for a gastronomic offshoot of Europe. Benedictine sisters in the Laurentian village of Mont-Laurier have been transforming goats' milk into *crottins* since the early sixties, and now 20 producers province-wide sell $6 million worth of Quebec goat cheese a year, typically and deliciously served as *un petit chèvre* – that is, warm, atop toasted baguettes on a bed of lettuce. When federal bureaucrats at Health Canada proposed a ban on such unpasteurized cheeses in 1996 on the grounds that they can carry *E. coli* and salmonella bacteria, 75,000 Quebecers added their signatures to a petition to protest the move. They won, and whole-milk chèvres and Oka cheese, as well as imported Reggiano Parmesan and Roquefort – illegal in the United States – can now be found on the shelves of local supermarkets. Like the French, Quebecers choose from a vast selection of dairy products, including quark, fromage frais, kefir, and flavoured butters. In much of the province, the topping of choice for french fries is not ketchup but mayonnaise. Quebecers also drink the most red wine in the country and eschew light beer in favour of high-octane Belgian-style brands.

One of the best-selling books in the province recently was a Québécois adaptation of a notorious high-protein, red-wine diet from France. In *Je mange donc je maigris* ("I eat, therefore I lose weight" – in France even the slimming programs are Cartesian), Michel Montignac, the former personnel director for a French pharmaceutical company, encourages his readers to consume as much chocolate mousse, Bordeaux, and foie gras as they want. The only condition, of course, is that they not mix these indulgences with "bad" carbohydrates in the form of refined flour, rice, and potatoes. Anglophone nutritionists called it another quack diet, but educated, middle-class Québécois have been eating it up. Chefs throughout the province, noticing gourmands showing up with photocopied tables of forbidden food combinations, suddenly started offering "Montignac menus," erasing starchy side dishes and carrots from their chalkboards. Popular television hostesses admitted to following the diet, and the Montreal bakery Première Moisson started nestling loaves of whole-grain Montignac bread among its buttery croissants.

In spite of such clearly Gallic gastronomic influences and the fact that you can eat like Louis XIV in Quebec for next to nothing (and now, without gaining weight!), English Canadians insist on typecasting the province as the land of low cuisine. It's true, Quebecers have some unique culinary proclivities. Poutine, that fat-laden clot of fries, gravy, and cheese curds served in roadside potato shacks, is the most notorious example. Kraft moves more boxes of Jell-O-brand jelly powder in Quebec than in any other Canadian province. Quebec's per capita consumption of barbecue-and-ketchup-flavour potato chips is the highest in the country (the rest of Canada reaches for the more British salt-and-vinegar variety), and Les Croustilles Yum Yum, the best-selling chips in Quebec, made a successful foray into co-branding with the St. Hubert restaurant chain by offering a barbecue chicken variety. High and low cuisine coexist contentedly here, and Quebecers are healthily ambivalent when it comes to junk food. A survey by pharmaceutical-and-food company Mead Johnson Canada showed that 88 per cent of Torontonians opted for taste over nutrition when choosing a snack food, whereas 90 per cent of Vancouverites preferred nutrition to taste. Montrealers were split down the middle, half reaching for the healthy snack, the other half going for empty calories. Quebecers also eat more fruit than other Canadians, making the province's grocery stores cornucopias of Lobo and McIntosh apples, blueberries, and cranberries. (This does not explain why local grocers insist on selling them sealed in plastic wrap.)

One thing is certain: when it comes to food, Quebec is the Duchy of Grand Fenwick of North America, a stubborn hold-out against modernity. For the Coca-Cola company, Quebec has long been the mouse in the corporate bottle, the only region in North America where Pepsi outsells the Real Thing. Part of the reason is historical: nickel Pepsi bottles once held 10 ounces, versus Coke's stingy six ounces (frugal francophones' preference for the former earned them the durable nickname "pepsis"). Another is Pepsi's canny marketing strategy: recognizing Quebec's unique character, the company has given comedian Claude Meunier, star of the wildly popular sitcom *La petite vie*, carte blanche to create surrealistic television ads involving a mop-haired character called Pepsi Man. Coca-Cola has countered with an ad campaign that contends Coke is "OK" – a slogan that has the distinction of being a bad rhyme in both of Canada's official languages.

The epitome of Quebec's culinary distinctness, however, lies in its pale margarine policy. A tub of margarine in most of North America contains a pat of vegetable oil emulsified with water or milk whose yellowish hue suggests the wholesomeness of butter. In Quebec, the same tub reveals an unappetizingly pale glob whose grey undertones suggest the toxicity of a petroleum product. For decades, the province's powerful dairy lobby has kept yellow dye out of margarine, arguing that it's a form of fraudulent camouflage; the product was banned outright until 1948. Then, under Premier Maurice Duplessis, dairy producers tried to introduce a law rewarding people who denounced neighbours for keeping ersatz butter in their fridge. Today, provincial bureaucrats in lab coats smear samples of suspect margarine on microscope slides to determine whether it violates the law, that is, "a colour that's not more than one degree and six-tenths, nor less than six degrees and five-tenths, of yellow or a combination of yellow and red," as measured by something called the Lovibond meter. The multinational company Unilever, manufacturers of Becel and Monarch margarine, complaining that it cost $1.2 million a year to supply tailor-made margarine to the Quebec market, forced the issue by shipping hundreds of tubs of butter-yellow Country Crock to a grocery store in Alma. Quebec inspectors confiscated the shipment from the shelves – but then, maddeningly, refused to lay charges. Unilever took its case to the province's Superior Court, claiming that Quebec was in violation of 11 federal and international laws and agreements. At the height of the controversy, Quebecers were treated to full-page ads in leading newspapers from both the margarine lobby and the dairy producers. As of early 2000, the decision is pending.

It would be wrong to interpret Quebec's legislative attack on margarine as a self-righteous Gallic refusal of all that is modern, North American, and vulgar. Vulgarity has nothing to do with it. Margarine was patented in France, by a certain Hippolite Mège-Mouriès, who in 1869 won a contest organized by Napoleon III, who was looking for a cheap form of grease to keep his soldiers marching. (Hippolite named his suet-and-skimmed-milk concoction after *margaron*, the Greek word for pearl, suggesting it was meant to be white in the first place.) The ongoing margarine debate is a signal instance of Quebec's unique status on this continent and a clue to why attempts to reconcile French and English Canada tend to butt up against apparently irreconcilable philosophical barriers.

"For consumers, the colour regulation is just plain silly," wrote anglophone columnist Jennifer Robinson in the Montreal *Gazette*, in an impassioned plea for more chemical additives. "It does not exist to protect consumers – it exists merely to restrict their choices." This kind of response is reflex for English-speakers, raised in an Anglo-American legal tradition that tends to favour the interests of the individual – or his capitalist proxy, the consumer – over those of the larger community. As in many European countries, a large proportion of the Quebec population believes that protecting collective rights (in this case, those of local dairy farmers) sometimes justifies infringing on the rights of the individual.

Beyond the margarine issue, this includes the idea that guaranteeing the survival of a language, a collective right, can supersede the rights of shopkeepers to put up signs in any language they want – or even those of French-speaking parents to send their children to English schools. This kind of talk upsets many North Americans. Among them are English-language-rights activists in Montreal, but also survivalists in Montana, who are adamant about their right to buy semi-automatic rifles and form citizens' militias. Americans profess surprise at how easily Canadians accept authority, how readily they are pushed around, how slow they are to stand up for their rights. But they'd be shocked at the situation in Quebec, where 70 per cent of the population believes the law should forbid citizens from possessing firearms (versus only 48 per cent on the Canadian Prairies). Once again, it's the good of society, not the rights of the individual, that takes precedence on key issues in Quebec.

How did we go from margarine to gun control? Ha! Get used to it. In Quebec, even the simplest issue tends to have philosophical implications whose roots can go back at least four and a half centuries – a phenomenon that often makes the province's policies inscrutable to outsiders. For example, in spite of all the clichés about conservatism and Catholicism, Quebec consistently shows itself to be the most tolerant and liberal society in North America. According to a 1998 CBC/*Maclean's* poll, 70 per cent of Quebecers strongly believe no one has the right to impose morality on others (versus 52 per cent in the rest of Canada), and 81 per cent strongly agree that people have the right to lead different lifestyles (in the other Canadian provinces, the figure is 59 per cent). Eight of 10 Quebecers believe abortion is a personal choice; and in practice, 29 per cent say they would support a 17-year-old daughter's decision to have an abortion (versus only 15 per cent in the rest of the country). Quebecers, 80 per cent of whom approve of openly gay or lesbian teachers, are also far more likely to say that an affair during marriage is acceptable, and far less likely to say that it's valid grounds for being thrown out of political office. Strangely, English Canadians and Americans, the most vocal defenders of individual rights, are more inclined to judge and condemn an individual who actually tries to assert her individuality. Quebecers, even though they boast the most rigid, Byzantine body of civil law and bureaucratic regulations on the continent, tend to suspend judgment and tolerate those who deviate from the norm.

Such a phenomenon, familiar to anyone who's visited the south of Europe, reposes on the rather pleasant gap between doctrine and life as it's lived day to day in places with a legacy of Catholicism. By all available measures, Quebecers are the most self-indulgent of Canadians: they're more likely to go to a play (the province boasts half of Canada's theatre companies), eat in restaurants, and take in concerts or movies. As in Barcelona and Marseilles, people in Montreal seem to wander the streets without much purpose (in Toronto it's called loitering); they make eye contact with strangers and smile (considered harassment on the West Coast); and they routinely start their weekends on Thursday night (grounds for dismissal in Calgary). In a country that breaks world records for lingering over sex, Quebecers make love longer than anyone else (the average sex act here lasts 45 minutes, with a half-hour of foreplay) and, at eight times a month, more often than anyone in Canada, with the curious exception of Newfoundlanders.

The explanation for such hedonism is simple: once you've accepted the premise that an inanely complex webwork of rules for living, administered by impossibly remote lawmakers, should be preserved for the sake of tradition and the long-term good of the community, everything becomes far more pleasant. You can then ignore these strictures, set about enjoying life together, and work on finding ways to get around the occasional cop, priest, or bureaucrat who shows up to enforce the rules. In societies with a Protestant legacy of individual moral responsibility, everybody becomes a cop. The Québécois have never bothered getting in touch with their inner patrolman.

Consider the local attitude towards smoking. Wherever you go in Quebec, you're rarely more than a dozen yards from a burning cigarette. In Montreal, some video stores put ashtrays on their shelves; I've seen city bus drivers smoking as they drive, and laundromat attendants with butts drooping from their mouths folding clients' towels. The province of Quebec is, in effect, Canada's smoking section. While 29 per cent of Canadians over the age of 15 smoke, 35 per cent of adult Quebecers are smokers, as are 30 per cent of the province's high school students. (There is even a political semiology of puffing in Quebec: people will tell you with a straight face that because the Player's package displays the colours of the Quebec flag and the Parti Québécois, it's the cigarette of choice of separatists. This makes glossy, Liberal red du Maurier, despite its Gallic name, a federalist smoke.) Over the next decade, Quebec's smoking laws are supposed to become the most restrictive in Canada, with cigarettes to be banned from taxis, restaurants, and offices, and penalties of up to $250,000 for merchants selling cigarettes to minors. Are these rules going to be obeyed? When France introduced anti-smoking legislation in 1992, threatening 1,000-franc fines for those caught smoking in public, the law was flouted, gleefully and unanimously. In Paris, I remember seeing people butting out their Gauloises on the brand new ESPACE NON FUMEURS signs, and when the rare nonsmoker complained at a place like the Brasserie Lipp, the waiters would stick him next to the toilets on the deserted upper floor. Expect a similar reaction in Montreal. Like the French, the Québécois have a talent for drawing up superb laws and then failing to enforce them.

The classic example is the French-inspired Civil Code, a corpus created in 1866, which regulates every aspect of private legal relations in Quebec. Drawing on a tradition dating back to the sixth-century Roman emperor Justinian, the French jurist Robert Pothier attacked the 360 distinct local codes of France (a nation that had about as many legal systems as cheeses), harmonizing them in the Code Napoléon, or Civil Code, of 1804. In contrast to English common law, which uses precedent to build up a body of law on a case-by-case basis, the French prefer drawing on general rules that outline appropriate behaviour in given situations. In short, the Civil Code is the rule book of a human community, a bit like a Catholic catechism of do's and don'ts. English common law, on the other hand, is the accumulated record of the real-life legal activity of a society, with every worshipper – judge and litigant – adding his or her own interpretation to an ever-growing body of scripture.

Early colonists in New France relied on a body of unwritten conventions called the Custom of Paris to settle civil matters. The British, after their victory on the Plains of Abraham, adopted an unusual, if not entirely selfless, policy. Under the Quebec Act of 1774, they allowed their new French-speaking subjects not only to enter public office, but also to maintain the Catholic religion, a seigneurial system of land holding, and their traditional legal practices. The Civil Code of Lower Canada, enacted a year before Confederation, drew on aspects of France's Code Napoléon and Louisiana's Civil Code (in force since 1808). In an early example of the Anglo-French syncretism that typifies Quebec, the Code was also heavily influenced by English common law, particularly when it came to commercial, maritime, and testate affairs.

In Quebec, if you shoot your husband, it's a criminal matter, and you will be tried under the provisions of the Criminal Code of Canada. If you only want to divorce him, however, you'll do so under the Civil Code of Quebec. A fully revised Code went into effect in 1994, suppressing many beloved clauses of the nineteenth-century version, such as the stipulation that "when pigeons, rabbits, and fish go into a neighbour's dove-cote, warren, or pond, they become the neighbour's property." Quebec's Civil

Code now consists of 10 books, whose 3,186 clauses set out, among other things, how property is inherited, how children are to be adopted, what constitutes evidence, and who is considered mentally infirm. Incidentally, the English version of the new Code, obviously translated by bureaucrats, has introduced some invaluable new words into the language. Quebec's Anglos can now while away the long winter evenings puzzling over the ominous portent of terms such as "exheredation," "resiliation," and "extrapatrimonial."

The Civil Code's more interesting provisions include an age of consent clause (Article 16), allowing teenagers older than 14 to have abortions without parental consent; a marriage clause (Article 393) that presupposes married women will keep their maiden names; and a family support clause (Article 585) that obliges all members of a family to support one another. (This last has led to grandchildren suing grandparents for child support their parents can't afford.) People brought up in Anglo-American traditions often bridle at the Code's intrusion into what they consider private matters. For example, Article 54 states that, if parents choose a name for their child that "invites ridicule" or "may discredit the child," the registrar of civil status can force the parents to replace the offending name with one of their own first names. Of the average 80,000 names submitted a year, the registrar's office questions about 20; it managed, for example, to reject the name Spatule, which means spatula, without provoking street rioting. The registrar's initial refusal of Tomás, whose acute accent was a tribute to his mother's Brazilian heritage, and Ivory, whose American parents insisted they were not thinking of the soap, turned out to be more problematic. As usual, the acerbic and thoughtful French-born editorialist of *La Presse*, Pierre Foglia, offered the most apposite comment on the issue: "It's an apparently trivial subject, but one that underlies two cultures, two outlooks, two models of society. One tries to guarantee individual liberties – [the right to] call a child 'C'est-un-ange,' wear the Muslim veil at school, pray in class, etc. The other model (sometimes called the model of the Republic) tries, for its part, to guarantee the common good." As one of the interzones between these two models of society, Quebec's Civil Code, now undergoing a lengthy harmonization process with federal laws, provokes surprisingly few such conflicts, largely because it is a fairly humane, liberal body of statutes. In 1999 the government amended the Civil Code, making it only the second jurisdiction in North America, after Hawaii, to give homosexual couples the same rights as common law couples. And a codified law book is really not all that alien a concept: after all, the Canadian Criminal Code is itself a vast rule book of community standards, also built on models dating back to Napoleon and Moses.

Now that they've got a new, duly itemized Civil Code in place, the people of Quebec can get on with their lives, which as ever involve ignoring, complaining about, and bending all manner of rules and by-laws, whether civil, criminal, or municipal. Montreal has the distinction of being the vice capital of Canada, a status it has cherished ever since the notion of Toronto the Good was invented. Lili St. Cyr, the stripper who cemented Montreal's reputation as the Soho of Canada in the forties and fifties, had a classic Quebec attitude towards the law. Working at the Gayety Theatre on St. Catherine Street in the late forties, she'd start her act at five minutes after Sunday midnight – striptease acts were naturally forbidden on the Lord's Day – by having herself wheeled onstage almost naked in a bathtub filled with bubbles. Since local statutes said you couldn't leave the stage with fewer clothes than when you came on, Lili would start her act half nude and get dressed in a languorous un-striptease. As William Weintraub recounts in his book *City Unique*, the police were accomplices to all this vice and vigorish. Patrolmen, for example, were routinely assigned to walk local madams to the bank to protect the neighbourhood brothels' weekly receipts. When priestly pressure got too bothersome, Premier Maurice Duplessis's Padlock Law, adopted in 1937 to allow police to close down any place suspected of producing Communist propaganda, was also applied to Montreal's dens of vice. But with a twist: when the cops stormed a barbotte gaming house, a brothel on De Bullion Street, or one of the city's many blind pigs, they would ignore the happily cavorting clients and slap a padlock on a broom closet or a rear entrance. They could then, in good conscience, report to the court that the premises were indeed locked up.

Quebec still deserves to be considered Canada's capital of sin, though the glamour of its convivial daiquiri-and-dice heyday is being supplanted by the seediness of video stores and video lottery terminals. Quebecers are the country's biggest spenders on government-run gambling, dropping an average of $348 a year on lottery tickets, the gaming tables of the casinos of Montreal, Hull, and Charlevoix, and the video lottery terminals found in nine out of 10 bars in the province (the highly addictive VLTs still haven't been approved in Canada's two other most populous provinces, Ontario and British Columbia, and are permitted in only 10 American states). Until the law was changed late in 1999, Quebec was one of the few jurisdictions that allowed teenagers to gamble; children routinely received Lotto 6/49 tickets as stocking stuffers, and tens of thousands of the province's adolescents showed signs of being pathological gamblers. Montreal's casino is one of the 10 largest in the world, and almost two thousand of its clients have voluntarily registered in a program that forces security staff to bar them from the premises. (They manage to sneak back anyway, and they get caught gambling an average of four times each in the months following their banning.)

The country's five biggest pornographic movie distribution companies are located in Montreal, selling 400,000 videos a year in Quebec alone. The city is filled with sex shops, their numbers somewhat limited by civic legislation that says they have to be placed at least 25 metres apart and 100 metres from a hospital, school, or church. Americans – most of whom can't legally consume alcohol and watch people take off their clothes – are particularly fond of Montreal strip joints like Wanda's, the Club Super Sexe, and Chez Parée, where a couple of banknotes buys a personal, table-top strip show. In 1998, one of the merchants in the peaceful if funky Plateau Mont-Royal neighbourhood was a suave Parisian transplant named Jean-Paul Labaye who quietly operated the Bar l'Orage on Rue St-Dominique. Swinging Montrealers paid $200 for a membership to his club, which allowed them free play on the club's third-floor mattresses, until the police barged in one night and interrupted a 22-person orgy. Labaye was denounced not by local parents, incensed by some outrage against community standards, but rather by a confrere – the owner of one of the neighbourhood's triple-X movie theatres – clearly worried about competition. Labaye was finally convicted of running a bawdy house, but it was under the Criminal Code of Canada, not any Quebec statute. (Montreal's admirably thorough undercover police visited the place seven times before making the arrest.)

If anglophones find the mores of the Québécois a little loose and insouciant, they might consider the advantages of living in a society that never bought into the hypocritical sexual morality and at-all-costs individual rights current in English-speaking North America. A newcomer to the

14

province who reads enough French to decipher the headlines in the tabloid *Le Journal de Montréal* or the true-crime weekly *Allô Police* might come away convinced that Quebec is not only a haven for Algerian terrorists, but also a dangerous place to live. It's true, the internecine wars between rival biker gangs the Hells Angels and the Rock Machine have produced impressive body counts. In the mid-nineties, there were so many firebombs going off in bars that the east end of Montreal and the Quebec City suburb of Beauport briefly became risky places to drink. But if you break the crime figures down, Quebec comes out as one of the safest places on the continent, if not in the world. There were only 133 murders in the province in 1998, and a quarter of them involved motorcycle gang members. In the same year, Baltimore, a city of fewer than a million, saw 300 murders – a homicide rate almost 20 times as high. Quebec puts fewer people in prison than virtually any other region in North America and now has the lowest youth delinquency rate in Canada. And in Montreal, the nation's second metropolis, you're far less likely to be assaulted than in more provincial cities like Calgary or Halifax.

If anything, Quebecers are noted for a proclivity towards crimes of derring-do, not mass murder. Local underworld legends revolve around people like Monica la Mitraille, Machine Gun Molly, the loyal mother of two who was gunned down in the streets of Montreal after holding up 20 banks. Meanwhile, in English-speaking North America, the killing sprees of Paul Bernardo, Ted Bundy, and Clifford Olson, the alienation of individualism taken to its pathological limits, are signs of a real social malaise. (Marc Lépine's massacre of 14 female students at Montreal's École Polytechnique in 1989, an event to which Quebec is still reacting, shows that the province is not entirely unaffected by such broad continental drifts.) You can still walk around virtually every part of Montreal without fear of aggression (except, of course, from the drivers). Like the sin industry in Amsterdam, vice in Montreal is old, institutionalized, and happens behind closed doors: weekend partiers buy cocaine in bars rather than alleys, johns phone up escort services or visit brothels, and compulsive gamblers lose their savings not to bookies but to the government, which pockets $1.1 billion a year on lottery and casino revenues. It's cynical, a little dismal, and quietly ruins a significant number of lives, but it has the marked advantage of minimizing collateral damage to the innocent passerby.

Newcomers raised in other traditions nonetheless find some aspects of the Québécois character hard to swallow, particularly their apparent self-interest. This is the Canadian province where people give the least to charity, an average of $127 a year per person versus $338 in Alberta. And in a continent with a long tradition of philanthropic social service, only 22 per cent of Quebecers volunteer their time, versus about a third of all Canadians and almost half of Saskatchewanians. Sociologists attribute this to the long domination of the Catholic church, whose system of orphanages, soup kitchens, hospitals, and asylums constituted a vast – and occasionally sinister – social safety net, one replaced, starting in the sixties, by the institutions of an equally omnipresent welfare state. (To this day, the front line of social aid in Quebec, including homeless shelters and street youth agencies, is largely Catholic.) In other parts of Canada, particularly the far less populous Prairies, government and church could never hope to create such a comprehensive system of social programs, and it fell to individuals, drawing on the best of the Protestant tradition, to assure the welfare of their neighbours. Quebecers, in contrast, were always pretty sure that if their fellow citizens were in serious trouble, some official organization out there would take up the slack.

The deep origins of this attitude probably lie in what the Greeks called autarky, an emphasis on the virtues of self-sufficiency, which was a survival technique in a land where five-month winters called for the amassing of huge stocks of food and firewood. In the case of the first French colonists, it was self-sufficiency on the material, not the spiritual, plane, which distinguishes it from the religious self-reliance and individualism of the Protestant tradition. The autarkic tendencies of early French-Canadian society, usually centred on an extended family, were counterbalanced by mass, saint's day parades, and the other highly collective and socializing rituals of the Catholic church. Though religious observance has long been in serious decline, Quebecers still have a tendency to do things en masse, living independently but periodically reasserting their membership in a larger community. This helps explain such puzzling and diverse phenomena as the rallying force of the St. Jean Baptiste Day parade, the staggering popularity of certain stand-up comedians and television shows, the record turnouts for elections, and the continuing attraction of one of the ugliest stretches of Florida coastline as a vacation spot.

It also helps account for one of Quebec's most bizarre ceremonies, the annual Moving Day ritual. Every year, a good percentage of the population of Quebec – at least 236,000 households, according to Bell Canada's phone reconnection figures – packs up and moves house the same day. On the island of Montreal, where 70 per cent of the population rents from a landlord, the situation is even more extreme, with one of every five apartments changing tenants on the first of July. This massive reshuffling of the civic deck is heralded, come spring, by the depletion of the city's stock of cardboard, as scavenger crews scour liquor stores and back alleys for stray moving boxes. Starting on April Fool's Day, when tenants intending to move are required to give notice, people in scarves and overcoats wander the streets looking for À LOUER – TO RENT signs. On the night of June 30, commercial moving companies double their rates to $150 an hour. Pirates with bizarrely worded contracts and taped-together vans temporarily set themselves up as small businessmen, professionals with the lifespans of mayflies.

If you're not changing apartments, it's best to stay home on Moving Day, because the streets of Montreal can be as treacherous as Pamplona during bull season. It doesn't help that the morning usually dawns with the mugginess of monsoon-time Bombay. Nor does Montreal's domestic architecture, three-storey triplexes with twisting, often rickety outdoor staircases, help matters. In the Centre-Sud, a poorer neighbourhood east of downtown and the site of Montreal's Gay Village, entire streets seem to move out at the same time, with couples and roommates – whose relationships obviously expired long before their leases – screaming at each other from behind sofas wedged in narrow hallways. People cram their belongings into taxis and shopping carts, and *Grapes of Wrath*-vintage half-ton trucks piled high with cradles and ping-pong tables leave a trail of teddy bears and bongo drums in their wake. Terrifyingly efficient teams of movers, with ominously tribal names (the presence of the rival Clan Panneton and Frères Panneton moving trucks suggests a history of family feuding), harness themselves up with moving straps, brace washing machines against quilted pads attached to their waistbands, and empty entire apartments as quickly as professional thieves, leaving their clients to detect the chips and fissures in favourite belongings in the weeks to come. In one of those Montreal traditions, as immutable as they are asinine, most flats here don't include refrigerators or stoves, so Moving Day also coincides with the sale, delivery, removal, and utterly pointless trading of thousands of heavy appliances. Pizza companies record their highest sales ever as exhausted movers, their kitchens still in boxes, opt for a large all-dressed – hold the anchovies – before collapsing on the sheetless futons in the middle of their new living rooms. In Quebec, North American record-holder for animal abandonment, the SPCA gets between 600 and 800 calls every year from people who discover a dog or cat in their new apartment, an unwanted gift from the previous tenants.

How to account for the Moving Day phenomenon? The British Broadcasting Corporation sent a camera crew and a team of amateur anthropologists here in 1998 to record the ritual and came up with some interesting answers. Interviewed in the documentary *Montreal Moving Day Madness*, Mayor Pierre Bourque advances the reasonable thesis that it was a legacy of the days when high birth rates forced ever-expanding families to seek out a more capacious apartment every couple of years (the recurring plight of Rose-Anna Lacasse in Gabrielle Roy's 1945 novel *The Tin Flute*). A Concordia University history professor points out that before 1974, when Premier Robert Bourassa's Liberal government changed the expiry date of leases to June 30, people used to move on May 1. In eighteenth-century Scotland, it was also customary to move on May Day – there called "flitting day" – and it's likely that the landlords of Montreal, a dispropor-tionate number of whom were Scottish, imported the practice. The provin-cial government changed the date to July 1, which coincides with Canada's national holiday, on the grounds that it would allow people to move when their kids were out of school and the weather was better. The practical result, of course, was that a significant portion of the population was too busy to celebrate the anniversary of the founding of Canada.

The documentary left a couple of fundamental questions unanswered. Why do so many Quebecers go stir crazy and decide to go through the trau-matic stress of packing up and moving, usually no more than a few blocks away? The Québécois call it *la bougeotte*, which means something like itchy feet. It's probably linked to the fact that Quebecers, more than other North Americans, are rooted to their corner of the globe by language and culture. While other Canadians can attend anglophone schools from Halifax to Victoria, and qualified professionals can pack up and work in their mother tongue in San José or Cincinnati, francophone Quebecers who haven't mastered English are more limited when it comes to relocation. (Quebecers, of all Canadians, make the fewest long distance calls: their relatives are far more likely to live in the same area code.) This doesn't mean, however, that they're unaffected by the natural human urge – particularly strong in endlessly mobile North America – to change scenery. It's just that their ambit is somewhat limited, so rather than migrate, they succumb to *la bougeotte*, a kind of monumental load shifting, a transitory agitation of the gopher colony after the winter thaw.

A second unanswered question goes to the heart of the Quebec character: Why set a common expiry date on leases at all? Why not, simply and logically, mark the month of the beginning of the rental as the starting point of the yearly lease? The answer that no one dares give is that Quebecers actually like mass movements – and in this instance, the masses literally are in movement, all at once. Even if van-clogged streets are undeniably ludicrous, there's something comforting in knowing you're in the same boat – the same unfurnished, five-and-a-half-room boat – as hundreds of thousands of your fellow citizens.

It's a reality English Canadians rarely grasp: Quebecers, in spite of their nominal attachment to Canada, have been used to considering themselves a coherent social unit, with their own distinct customs and institutions, for a long time. They have become masters of *survivance*, the unlikely survival of Gallic culture in a New World of more numerous Anglo-Saxons. If they're still around after close to five centuries, it's because at key points they've drawn together, asserted their identity, putting the common good above the individual. In a word, they think of themselves as a nation, a reality that shows up in thousands of day-to-day details. The provincial parliament in Quebec City, a Second Empire–style edifice studded with statues of French-Canadian heroes, is called the Assemblée nationale. The province's largest library – which receives two copies of everything published here, just like the Bibliothèque nationale de France – is called the Bibliothèque nationale du Québec. St. Jean Baptiste Day, whose parades sometimes end in riots and looting (most notoriously in 1968, when Pierre Trudeau, on the verge of becoming prime minister, was attacked), is commonly referred to as the Fête nationale – the national holiday.

Quebec has been collecting its own income taxes, and taxpayers have been filling out separate provincial tax forms, since the late sixties, and this is the only province that sets its own immigration policy. It has had its own flag, the fleur-de-lys, since 1948, when Canada's standard was still the Red Ensign, and its own Charte québécoise des droits et libertés de la personne since 1975, when Canada's Constitution was still in Great Britain. In English-speaking Canada, the Monday preceding May 25 is Victoria Day, the birthday of the late queen of England; in Quebec, the same holiday is known as Dollard-des-Ormeaux Day, after a soldier of New France who was killed by the Iroquois. It's quite normal for francophone Québécois, federalists and separatists alike, to refer to Quebec not as a province but as *un pays*, which, like the English word "country," denotes both a region and a nation.

They also refer to Quebec society as *la collectivité* – meaning a community bound by common goals and interests – a term that raises the hackles of many anglophones. Both Quebec-born novelist Mordecai Richler, one of Canada's greatest writers, and language-rights defender William Johnson, an intelligent and manipulative author with a thorough knowledge of Canadian history, inevitably use the expression with scorn when criticizing Quebec. For those born into English-Canadian or American culture (and Richler has always been an iconoclastic exemplar of individualism within the community-minded Jewish tradition), the term "collectivity" tends to conjure up images of sheep – duped peasants who too readily accept the words of paternalistic priests and political bosses. That said, for many raised in French traditions, whether in Europe or North America, the linked concepts of individualism, the primacy of personal rights, and multiculturalism suggest a relativistic, atomized society that sets career and material gain over collective identity, family, and community relationships – a culture, in other words, they have sound philosophical and historical reasons not to embrace blindly. Sometimes the contrast between these two outlooks feels so extreme that continued coexistence looks naive and pointless, a denial of traditions and cultures that are diametrically opposed. It's equally clear, however, that the history of Canada is so embedded in that of Quebec, and vice versa, that their long embrace may well be irreversible. The two entities are like a pair of bees with their stingers planted in each other's abdomens: it's hard to imagine how either could break such a buzzing clinch without tearing out its own guts in the process.

BIENVENUE AU QUÉBEC read the signs at Dorval airport. WELCOME TO CANADA, too. If living here sounds too complicated, too unworkable, like an unbearable tension that only masochists would subject themselves to, that's probably because you don't know the place. Politics, which permeates every issue in Quebec, somehow rarely comes up at the dinner table or in bars or restaurants. While feminism made greater gains in Quebec than in Europe, it never reached the extremes born on the paranoid campuses of the rest of North America, where femininity and flirtatiousness came to be demonized as the adjuncts of patriarchy. For better and for worse, few Quebecers give much thought to being politically correct. Although they sometimes trample on the sensitivities of other groups, they aren't too cowed by cultural relativism to express their own values, which means this is a society where there is still unembarrassed dialogue on important issues. Traditional social life, in the form of families, religions, and political involvement, is unravelling in Quebec as elsewhere, but people here don't fall as far or as hard into the extremes of alienated behaviour as they do on the rest of the continent. The near-absence of the Protestant work ethic – that macho, cellphone-clutching competitiveness that keeps the citizens of Toronto, Manhattan, and London treading water ever faster in their deepening sea of net worth – is one of Quebec's largely unsung pleasures, a social virtue low in glamour but surprisingly high in social and spiritual rewards.

And let's not forget the clichés, which, of course, are all partly true. There really is a part of this continent where you can bring your own bottle of Beaujolais nouveau to a smoke-filled bistro and watch casually graceful older women greet each other with doubled-barrelled *bisous*. You can skidoo to eighteenth-century bed-and-breakfasts, eat the continent's best bagels, and live bilingually. What's more, it's a society whose stubborn otherness suggests there's nothing absolute about a way of life most North Americans think is inevitable. This, perhaps, is the greatest value of Quebec's distinctness for all Canadians: it reminds us that there are, happily, other ways of looking at the world.

Squareheads and Other Strangers

A few days after my thirtieth birthday, I boarded a charter plane in Vancouver and touched down in Montreal, a routine cross-country trip that abruptly wiped away my identity. As soon as I stepped out of the terminal building at Dorval, underdressed in the frigid Laurentian wind, I became a minority. No longer simply a Canadian at home in Canada, I was now an Anglo in a primarily francophone environment, forced to guess whether my cab driver was Algerian or Egyptian, and which of Canada's – if not Quebec's – official languages would get me downtown faster.

Settling in the streets around Boulevard St-Laurent – an ethnically diverse neighbourhood that was once a Jewish buffer zone between the city's Protestant British west side and its Catholic French east end – I tried at first to resist the Anglo label. After all, though English was my first language, I felt more like a multicultural poster boy than an Anglo-Saxon oppressor: I was a western Canadian mongrel, a British Columbia–raised half-breed of Irish and Ukrainian descent. My adopted sister was black; I'd just left a six-year relationship with a Frenchwoman from Brittany; and I'd grown up in Vancouver, where Cantonese had become an unacknowledged second language. When travelling abroad, I was forced to concede to Delhites or the Madrileños that my passport was indeed Canadian; but having spent my youth among Sikhs, Hong Kong Chinese, expatriate Americans, native Indians, and the mixed descendants of every European nation, I was hard-pressed to explain exactly what Canadian meant. When pinned down, I dodged the question with a shrug and a stale quip: as a Canadian, I was simply an immigrant with seniority.

For the newcomer to Montreal, the issue of identity isn't so glibly side-stepped. The ethnic and religious labels that were once the chief markers of identity – Protestant versus Catholic, Canadian of British descent versus French Canadian – have given way to a new, but equally Manichaean, split. In the taxonomy of contemporary Quebec, two major linguistic kingdoms, the anglophone and the francophone, are supposed to subsume just about everyone. (The bilingual offspring of a marriage between a francophone and an anglophone is the acknowledged exception, the platypus that proves the rule.) Even immigrants are defined by sociologists as either francotrope or anglotrope, depending on whether they gravitate towards the language of Gaston Miron or that of Leonard Cohen. A four-year sojourn in Paris had left me capable of expressing myself in grammatical and fluent French, but according to the principal subdivision of the Québécois biome, my English accent made me, first and foremost, an Anglo. Period.

As a 20-minute walk through virtually any neighbourhood in Montreal will demonstrate, this Anglo-Franco dichotomy doesn't come close to describing the complex reality of contemporary Quebec. The allophones of Montreal, immigrants whose first language is neither English nor French, are now a significant presence in the city that accounts for half the population of the province. Outside the St-Michel metro station in the east end, Haitian teenagers dressed like gangstas from Compton listen to Dubmatique, a Montreal rap group that interlards French-language rhymes with American slang. (Are they francophone néo-Québécois or anglotrope Caribbean Canadians?) In the Caffè Italia near Jean-Talon market, a third-generation barman serves customers in patchy French, fluent English, and Sicilian-tinged Italian. (A trilingual allophone Quebecer?) During the Francofolies music festival, Central American fans of singer Lhasa de Sela line up for crêpes with Gaspésien admirers of Cajun accordionist Zachary Richard. (Hispanophone Anglo-Quebecers alongside Québécois francophones of French-Canadian origin?) In the thick of summer heat waves, when the traffic gets nasty, blunter terms are tossed around: immigrants get called "importés" (as though they'd been specially ordered from abroad to do menial labour); Italians are tarred with the sobriquet "gino" or "ginette"; Anglos become "blokes" or "têtes carrées" (squareheads); and Québécois francophones have to put up with "pepsi." In the category-straddling milieu of the immigrant-stoked Canadian metropolis, there's an endless choice of labels, from the politically correct to the vulgar. All of them, on some basic level, fail to describe Quebec's complex ethnic and linguistic makeup.

Only outside Montreal do the simplistic divisions still seem valid. Compared to even the secondary centres of English Canada – places like Victoria, Hamilton, or Winnipeg – Quebec's smaller cities look remarkably homogeneous. On the streets of Trois-Rivières, Quebec City, or Chicoutimi, there are virtually no native Indians, the English language is rarely heard outside the tourist season, and Vietnamese and Italian restaurants are the rare exceptions among businesses owned by Archambaults, Potvins, and Tremblays. Perhaps the old-stock Québécois have it right: seen from the indentations of the Saguenay fjord or the north shore of the Gaspé Peninsula, Quebec's chief split is between *nous autres* – the six million or so francophones whose ancestors were Catholic Canadiens, ethnically pure French – and *eux autres*, the province's 1.5 million Anglos, native Indians, ethnics, and immigrants, mostly concentrated in Montreal. In a word, the others – those who prevented the majority from forming a nation in 1995.

This much is true: the French were the first Europeans to establish permanent colonies in what is now Canada. After that, though, the pellucid waters of Quebec's mythological history start to get a little muddy.

At the age of 43, Samuel de Champlain, who was almost certainly born a Protestant in the predominantly Huguenot town of Brouage, married a 12-year-old girl and used her dowry to finance his expeditions to Canada.

On his early voyages, he travelled with a Scottish Protestant and Mattieu Da Costa, a free African fluent in Mi'kmaq who served as a trilingual interpreter. By the time Champlain died in 1635, a century of French exploration had established a community at Quebec City that funnelled the beaver pelts amassed by Indians back to the Bourbons but few other settlements of note. Only six years after his death, the entire French population of North America was less than 500, huddled precariously above 40,000 British and Dutch settlers and surrounded by almost as many Algonquins, Iroquois, and Inuit.

The young men of New France, who shared an ice-bound peninsula with five adult European women, were clearly not made of stone. From the start, Jesuits noted that the French had a passion for the *sauvagesses* – the Puritans to the south nicknamed them the Squaw Men – and later Louis XIV's minister Colbert urged the Canadiens to mingle with Indians to form "one people and one blood." Meanwhile, the founders of Acadia didn't need to be encouraged: ethnologists believe that by 1676, there was Indian blood in the veins of virtually all the French families of what is now Nova Scotia. On the St. Lawrence, it was the natives, more than the French, who underwent the consequences of *métissage*: Huron and Mohawk women, whose men had been killed by disease and warfare, adopted French-Canadian orphans and bastards, and after a few generations the Iroquois began to resemble the new arrivals. Quebec was no Latin America where miscegenation begot mestizos, mulattoes, and mustees; nor, however, was it British North America, where the conquerors favoured genocide over mixing of blood. Demographers believe that today, most Québécois families of French-Canadian origin have at least one Indian ancestor in their family tree.

Canada's first baby boom started in 1663. The arrival of 770 filles du roi – daughters of the king – mostly young, urban women who'd been sheltered in Paris's Hôpital la Salpêtrière, turned the colonists' eyes from the natives. Though immigration was sluggish throughout the French regime, the founding families were prolific: brides married young and averaged a child every two years, doubling the population from generation to generation. Over a century and a half, 27,000 French people passed through the colony, most of them poor, male, and single. In total, only 10,000 immigrants chose to remain and tough out a lifetime of winters in the new land.

If the population of New France – including the Acadians on the Gulf of St. Lawrence and Creoles on the Gulf of Mexico – eventually peaked at 85,000, it was mostly thanks to the commitment of comely, game girls from the poorer quarters of Paris.

When francophones describe themselves as Québécois *de vieille souche* or *pure laine* (pure wool), they are suggesting they can trace their family trees back to the 10,000 French, Catholic colonists who settled in New France in the century and a half before the Conquest. It's not an unreasonable claim. Most of the settlers did come from central and western France, particularly Normandy, Paris, the villages of Île-de-France, Poitou, Brittany, and the Atlantic islands of Ré and Oléron. But New France was not the homogeneous Catholic colony portrayed by early nationalist historians. Some scholars believe that, in spite of the 1627 ban on Huguenot immigration, as many as 2,000 Protestants lived the colony at various times. New France had a scattering of Swiss, Scots, Italians, Belgians, Germans, and Irish, including a Sullivan who was transformed into a Silvain and a John Leahy who magically became a Jean LaHaye. From skirmishes with New England villages, there were also captives, many of whom remained to found families. In all, 1,500 immigrants from 24 countries besides France helped populate the pre-Conquest French colony.

Nor were all the newcomers white. As historian Marcel Trudel brought to light in *L'Esclavage au Canada français*, the colony was also peopled by four thousand African and Indian slaves, owned by bishops and priests and bought and sold into domestic slavery in homes and shops from Detroit to Quebec. Indian slaves, many of them captured Pawnees, were branded with a fleur-de-lys if they were caught fleeing; most died, overworked and underfed, before the age of 18. Nonetheless, in the female-starved early days of the colony, 30 marriages between Canadiens and native slaves were recorded. As Trudel has emphasized, "Very rare are those Québécois today that can be described with the racist connotation of 'pure laine,' that is, who can draw a family tree in which their ancestors were always and only French, from France." New France was hardly a multicultural society – its non-French members were too thoroughly marginalized to call it that – but the complex threads that wove New World culture make a mockery of all notions of immaculate ethnic cloth. Early on, the apparent purity of the blue-and-white wool of Quebec was shot through with patches of red, black, and plaid.

Next came imperial crimson. The French lost their North American colonies to Britain in 1759, in a 20-minute battle on plains named after Abraham Martin, a Scottish ship's pilot who was a Protestant pioneer of New France. The first of the post-Conquest Quebecers were merchants who followed the British army – Scots, Englishmen, and Jews, impatient to profit from the fur trade and with a troublesome penchant for pressuring the new authorities to impose British law on the French majority. After the Revolutionary War, they were followed by the Loyalists, American colonists faithful to Britain, some of whom settled in Montreal, Sorel, and the Gaspé Peninsula (many were black, Scottish, German, or Mohawk). When the authorities decreed that freehold tenure, rather than the French seigneur-ial system, would prevail on a swath of arable land east of Montreal, as many as 15,000 Americans poured into the Eastern Townships, which came to resemble a northward protuberance of New England. (This idiosyn-cratic English enclave would eventually produce the scholar Northrop Frye, the silent comedy pioneer Mack Sennett, the frontier lawman Bat Masterson, and the newspaper tycoon Conrad Black.) By 1812, an English-speaking minority accounted for a tenth of the population of the vast ter-ritory now called Lower Canada.

Over the years, immigration increased this proportion to a quarter. Hundreds of thousands of Irish, Scots, and English, dispossessed by the Industrial Revolution or left idle after the Napoleonic wars, passed through Quebec City. The disastrous potato crop of 1846, which left close to half a million people dying of famine or disease, provoked a transatlantic tidal wave of Irish emigration to Canada. Of the almost 100,000 who came to British North America in the summer of 1847, 17,000 perished on the con-verted cargo boats dubbed "coffin ships," 5,300 died in quarantine on Grosse-Île, and a further 15,000 succumbed to cholera and typhus as they travelled west up the St. Lawrence.

Enough survived, however, to boost Quebec's anglophone population to its highest level in history. By 1861, there was an English-speaking major-ity in Montreal, the Eastern Townships, and the Ottawa Valley. Even Quebec City, today overwhelmingly francophone, was almost half British, as was a quarter of the Gaspé Peninsula (bilingual pop singer Kevin Parent, usually considered a *pure laine* francophone, is a descendant of these anglo-phone Gaspésiens). For the next century, an Anglo-Scottish aristocracy held economic power in Quebec and much of Canada, building railways, brewing beer, and controlling industry and trade. Demographically, the French could hold their own. Although immigration from France had stopped dead in 1759, rural families with a dozen children were not uncommon – eight was the average – and the French-Canadian population increased fourfold in 50 years. Such was their fruitfulness that they populated much of New England as well: close to a million French Canadians left their farms and *faubourgs* to look for work in such factory towns as Lowell, Massachusetts, and Lewiston, Maine. Their descendants today number five million, which means there are almost as many Franco-Americans as there are old-stock francophones in Quebec.

The French-Canadian population also proved adept at absorbing immigrants. A group of German mercenaries who had fought with the British army in the American Revolution settled in Quebec, and 600 of them married Lower Canada's women – who seemed willing enough to undergo an abrupt conversion to Protestantism. Orphans of the famine migration were adopted into French-Canadian families, and many of the Irish who'd worked in lumber camps with the French and attended mass at the same Catholic churches also started families with the Canadiennes. The village of Shannon still counts 800 Irish, who have retained their English over the generations in spite of living in the shadow of Quebec City. A surprising number of the icons of francophone Quebec have Irish roots: La Bolduc, one of the biggest French singing stars of the thirties, was actually Mary Travers, and Émile Nelligan, a turn-of-the-century symbolist poet in the vein of Verlaine and Baudelaire, was the son of an immigrant from Dublin. Politicians such as Daniel Johnson (*père* and *fils*) and Claude Ryan; Radio-Canada host Robert-Guy Scully; and singer Jim Corcoran – household names in French Quebec – all trace their roots back to Eire. Ethnologists estimate that 40 per cent of Québécois have Irish ancestors.

The nationalist historian Lionel Groulx called such racial mixing a "betrayal of the blood," a dilution of the pure French Catholic ichor that had coursed through the veins of Champlain (who, to repeat, was likely born a Protestant). If we are to fall back on the sanguine tropes of ethnic nationalism, then the average Québécois's bloodstream already contained at least a pint of admixed Iroquois warrior, Irish rebel, Protestant merchant, and Loyalist immigrant, as well as the odd drop of African slave and

German mercenary. Fortunately, the French-Canadian people never paid undue attention to their elites: while the Abbé Groulx and other priests preached xenophobia, the Canadiens tended towards peaceful coexistence with newcomers. In contrast, while the Presbyterians and Anglicans of Montreal professed tolerance, they encouraged a chilly form of social apartheid, segregating themselves in polite seclusion in the mansions of Westmount and the Square Mile.

From the Conquest, through Confederation, up until the Cold War, an English-speaking oligarchy put such a thoroughly British stamp on French Canada that it would have been possible to spend days in Quebec City – and entire weeks in Montreal – without noticing that most of the inhabitants were French. A well-heeled newcomer from Canada's second city, Toronto, could chase a natural history degree at McGill University, foxes on horseback as a participant in the Montreal Hunt, or debutantes as a guest at the annual St. Andrew's Ball without speaking a word of French. The most adventurous visitors might foray into middle-class Outremont or east of Boulevard St-Laurent, where they would have surely noticed that the words exchanged on the balconies and twisted outdoor staircases were French. Only political power, guaranteed by sheer force of numbers, wholly belonged to the French Canadians – and intellectuals dismissed postwar premier Maurice Duplessis as a "Negro king," playing the same game as African rulers in British colonies who, while mollifying the masses, kowtowed to real imperial power. The novelist Hugh MacLennan, borrowing a page from Rilke, in 1945 forever enshrined this geographic and cultural segregation as Quebec's *Two Solitudes*. He neglected another solitude, already well established by the end of the Second World War: the vital milieu of Jewish Quebec.

Montreal would be a poorer, more provincial place without its traditional Jewish neighbourhoods. Thanks to the recently arrived Hasidim, more than 6,000 of whom live in Outremont, parts of Montreal retain vestiges of life in shtetls, the tradesmen's communities of the Eastern European Jews, the Ashkenazim. In the neighbourhood of Mile End, smoke pours out of maple-fired bagel ovens, while the eternally busy Hasidim, wearing gabardine robes and black sable hats, stride gravely past crowded sidewalk café terraces, their side curls bobbing. Knife-sharpeners' trucks still ply Waverly Street, bells jingling, and Yiddish can be heard among the clients crunching on half-sour pickles and eating the grilled bologna-and-salami special at Wilensky's lunch counter. This is what many Jews in New York and Tel Aviv are talking about when they affectionately recall Montreal: the city celebrated by poet Irving Layton, where visiting New York saxophonist John Zorn once interrupted a concert to eat smoked meat sandwiches, delivered to the stage straight from Schwartz's Delicatessen on Boulevard St-Laurent.

The first Jews to settle in Quebec came with the British in 1760. Among them was Aaron Hart, a Trois-Rivières fur trader who packed kosher food in his canoe on expeditions among the natives and was eventually ennobled with the title seigneur de Bécancour. At Confederation, Canada's 500 Jews, most of whom lived in Montreal, tended to be as integrated into the Protestant elite, and as British in manner, as the English prime minister and self-described "ex-Jew" Benjamin Disraeli. These were the Uptowners, who would live in the mansions of Westmount and later own factories such as Grover Mills and Knit-to-Fit, where Quebec's first twentieth-century immigrants toiled. (The most notorious scion, and black sheep, of the Uptown community was songwriter and poet Leonard Cohen, whose family were late arrivals from Lithuania.) The Downtowners were Yiddish-speaking Jews who had left Europe after waves of anti-Semitic violence tore through Kiev, Warsaw, and Odessa. Between 1900 and 1925, 30,000 of them arrived in Montreal, few of them aware, at first, that Canada was much different from America – or that they'd landed in a province whose population was more French than British.

First settling north of the port in today's Chinatown, then moving over the ridge formed by Rue Sherbrooke into the narrow canyons of brick buildings that border Boulevard St-Laurent ("the Main" to anglophone Montrealers), these poor, Yiddish-speaking Jews were parochial Quebec's first true encounter with cosmopolitanism. When the city of Montreal finally opened its first public library in 1917, Jews had already been studying at their own Yidishe Folks Bibliotek for three years. Some stayed abreast of the radical political thought current in New York and Europe, and in 1912 they launched Montreal's first general strike (to the displeasure of the Uptown Jews, who owned many of the garment industry factories). Montreal's sophisticated Jewish literary scene produced such writers as A.M. Klein, Mordecai Richler, and Saul Bellow (the American novelist, Chicago's greatest booster, was born in the Montreal suburb of Lachine and lived on Rue Napoléon as a child).

During the Depression, the guttural language, the hints of foreign rituals behind the closed doors of synagogues, all the blintzes and borscht and blinis in the delicatessens elicited both fascination and suspicion. The city's population quadrupled to 820,000 in the first three decades of the century, and much of the growth came from francophones driven from failing farms to become day labourers, factory or construction workers, or, at best, landlords or small businessmen. For the newly arrived French Canadians, Montreal was already foreign enough, a city whose factories and institutions had largely been built by anglophones. When the Depression came, and with it joblessness for a third of the population, the Jews came to be cast in a nefarious light by Catholic ideologues. A skinny hate-monger with a Hitleresque moustache, blackballed *La Presse* reporter Adrien Arcand, got himself up in a blue shirt with beaver-and-maple-leaf badges and pontificated, arms flailing, to the 1,800-strong National Social Christian Party. (His newspaper, *Le Goglu*, scooped the world press with the news that Leon Trotsky was in reality the baron de Rothschild, a Jew, and that Lindbergh's baby had been kidnapped by rabbis, its blood drained for use in their fiendish rituals.) Editorials in major French-Canadian newspapers called for deportation and the end of Jewish immigration, and the anti-Semitic prime minister Mackenzie King invoked Canadien opinion when he imposed a virtual ban on Jewish immigration into Canada between 1933 and 1939, when European Jews most needed a safe haven.

This period, one of the most shameful in Canada's past, has recently become one of the most controversial in Quebec's history. Mordecai Richler, the author of such Montreal-based novels as *The Apprenticeship of Duddy Kravitz* and *Barney's Version*, brought international attention to the legacy of French-Canadian anti-Semitism in a 1991 article in the *New Yorker*. Drawing from the thesis of Esther Delisle, a Laval University doctoral candidate, he dwelt on the Abbé Lionel Groulx, the curé-cum-historian who in the twenties and thirties called Jews pornographers, fomenters of revolution, and enemies of the French race in Canada. Richler also decried the Depression-era anti-Semitic editorials in *Le Devoir* – still the leading daily of nationalist intellectuals – and the Jeune-Canada student movement, whose members lamented that it was "impossible to tread on the tail of that bitch, German Jewry, without causing yapping in Canada."

Richler subtly suggested that the racist nationalism of the thirties was omnipresent in the intellectual backdrop of nineties Quebec, particularly among those in favour of independence. Following the appearance of his article and his polemical book *Oh Canada! Oh Quebec! Requiem for a Divided Country*, the B'nai B'rith called for the renaming of Montreal's Lionel-Groulx metro station. Actor Jean-Louis Roux, after being appointed lieutenant-governor by the federal government in 1996, was forced to resign when the newsmagazine *L'actualité* revealed that he'd pencilled a swastika on his lab smock during an anti-conscription rally in 1942. Ever since, the people of Quebec have had to cope with the idea that, if ever realized, their aspirations to political independence – originally conceived by racist ideologues – would surely lead to pogroms and ethnic purification.

Curious to hear Richler's justifications for perpetuating the image of a Quebec that I have trouble believing still exists, I take a cab to Crescent Street, whose terraces are the scene of much hedonistic bar-hopping in summer. On this sleet-distressed April afternoon, however, it looks about as glamorous as the waterlogged pigeons huddled under the storefront eaves. It would be hard to find a more thoroughly anglophone enclave than the Sir Winston Churchill Pub, one of Richler's hangouts. The decorative motif is wood and bronze, there's Harp Ale on tap, and the mustachioed guy in a baseball cap at the other end of the bar is laconically defending the Reform Party and Preston Manning. "He's not as bad as people say. He's not a total fundamentalist. He wants to reduce government spending." The bored-looking drinkers let the monologist maunder, but his reflections trail off when Richler, clearly a celebrity here, walks through the door. With his rumpled demeanour, he brings to mind a hard-done-by basset hound that has been draped with a beige overcoat. He's also fighting jet lag. Though he has an apartment in Montreal and a house in the Eastern Townships, he spends the winter in England. From December to the end of April, his analysis of the Quebec *Zeitgeist*, regularly a feature of his weekly column in Southam papers, comes largely from his perusal of days-old Canadian newspapers in a London apartment.

We repair to plush, high-backed chairs in the corner, and a waiter with a French-Canadian accent brings Richler a long espresso. "I don't know what I can tell you here," Richler says a little impatiently, lighting a demi-tasse cigar. I say that, thanks to his articles in major magazines, many English-speaking North Americans have the impression that francophone Quebec is still anti-Semitic. "First of all, francophone separatists have enormously exaggerated my influence in America," he says, "which is very amusing to me. I'm not a representative of anybody but myself. I never accused Lucien Bouchard or René Lévesque of being anti-Semitic. I said their roots, their nationalist roots, are anti-Semitic. Without a doubt. The Bloc populaire. Lionel Groulx. *Le Devoir*. The history of *Le Devoir* is the history of a sewer. They have an outrageous history of anti-Semitism – a very primitive anti-Semitism. But I don't think that's the case now."

If that's so, I suggest, isn't it misleading to highlight the racism of the Quebec elite without mentioning that much of the Western world in the thirties, including English Canada, was guilty of anti-Semitism? "You weren't brought up here in those days. There was widespread anti-Semitism here. I remember it as a kid. I remember signs painted on the highway: À BAS LES JUIFS. I remember riots in the Laurentians."

But no one, I object, not even Québécois nationalists, is denying the anti-Semitism of the thirties. The point is that such racism plagued the entire Western world before the Second World War, a fact Richler barely mentions in his articles in the *New Yorker* and the *Wall Street Journal*. It's not out of place to remind the world that Quebec has a legacy of racism, but it's essential to put it in context. After all, there were anti-Semitic riots in Toronto, Asian exclusion leagues in Vancouver, official eugenics policies in Alberta. "Adrien Arcand had a much bigger following here than fascist groups had in English Canada," replies Richler. "The problem then was that it was a very church-ridden society, and the priests were not your educated or sophisticated Jesuits. They were backwoods preachers who probably thought the Jews had horned feet. I mean, they were really dumb and pathetic. And you had Duplessis's ministers standing up in the assemblies saying that Jews were relishing the naked bodies of French Canadians. I mean, it was primitive."

Even this brief sortie reminds me that I'm dealing with a man who, to say the least, has a way with words. Possessed of the rage of the Ancient Mariner, Richler can buttonhole his readers with forceful turns of phrase and vivid images, dragging them through his prose almost against their will. I show him a passage from his story "The Main." " 'My typical French Canadian was a moronic gum-chewer,' " I read aloud. " 'He wore his greasy black hair parted down the middle and also affected an eyebrow moustache. His zoot suits were belted just under the breastbone and ended in a peg hugging his ankles. He was the dolt who held up your uncle endlessly at the liquor commission while he tried unsuccessfully to add three figures or, if he was employed at the customs office, never knew which form to give you.' " It's good writing, a series of strong images that conjure up a devastatingly precise caricature. It also sounds like high-functioning hate literature, the kind of characterization that, if applied to Jews, Richler could cite as evidence of past anti-Semitism.

Richler hauls up the glasses hanging around his neck and peers at the words he wrote 30 years ago. "Yeah, but I was dealing with the stereotypes, the fact that there was no dialogue," he mutters, trailing off. "If you take it out of context, it sounds pretty brutal." That's my point: if you take the 60-year-old actions of the province's anti-Semites out of context, as he's done on the international stage, it makes Quebec sound pretty brutal, too. In fact, it sounds like a society so fatally flawed that any reasonable observer might feel justified in disparaging and combatting some Quebecers' long-standing aspirations towards independence.

In spite of flashes of intolerance expressed by nationalists during the 1995 referendum, Quebec – in a world riven by serious ethnic conflict – is a paragon of day-to-day racial harmony. I mention the Quiet Revolution, an episode that transformed Quebec into one of the more liberal and culturally vibrant societies on the continent. Richler isn't buying. "It's still backward. It's still parochial. It's still picayune. They're not open to the world. It's a closed, tribal society." I ask for some proof – certainly the young Québécois I know are well travelled and as plugged into world culture as other Canadians of their generation. "Do you think they're open to the world when they're marching down the street chanting 'Québec aux Québécois'?" he barks. Nor do I think Ontarians are being particularly open when they trample on the Quebec flag; nor western Canadians when skinheads beat Sikh elders to death. There are small-minded thugs and bigots in every society. Yes, a streak of xenophobia runs through the dinosaurs of the Parti Québécois, but a younger generation has little time for the old ethnic shibboleths.

Richler gives me another example, one closer to his heart. "There were 60 [Quebec] writers invited to France [for the 1999] Salon du livre, or whatever it was," he says. "I mean, you couldn't bring 12 from all of Canada and export them with any amount of dignity. Do you realize how funny that's going to be to the French? You don't think that's parochial and backward? Can you even name eight Quebec writers?" I start – Réjean Ducharme, Ying Chen, and Monique Proulx – but Richler cuts me off. "I haven't heard of her. But can you go to 60? Was it not discriminatory not to invite me? Not that I would have gone. I mean, being with 60 writers is my notion of a trip to hell."

With this, Richler signals that the interview is over; he's only in town overnight, and he's supposed to meet a friend at a bar across the street. Finally, he blows off the whole subject with a world-weary grunt. "I've reached a point where I just find the whole thing boring. I've had my say."

He certainly has. Thanks to Richler, the few Americans who can tell you anything about Quebec tend to tell you what a small-minded, anti-Semitic culture it is. (*The Columbia Journalism Review*, surveying major articles on Quebec in American magazines between 1977 and 1994, pointed out that half had been written by Richler.)

Leaving the pub, I walk past Seagram's offices and the buildings of McGill University, the dour greystone institutions of downtown Montreal. Since the fifties, when newly affluent Jews started moving into the early suburbia of Snowdon, Hampstead, and Côte-St-Luc, the Jewish community's marginalization, which gave Richler's early writing such self-righteous power, has been traded for hard-won mainstream social status. Seagram's scion Charles Bronfman is now the richest Quebecer alive; Moshe Safdie, creator of Habitat, is Montreal's best known architect – and one of the world's best known; Sonia Benezra has been a popular French-speaking host on the TQS television network; and Andy Nulman was until recently president of the world's biggest bilingual comedy festival. Jews have been chief coroners, rectors of McGill University, publishers of the *Gazette*; some, such as the controversial hospital administrator David

Levine, were even politicians for the Parti Québécois. In the last census, they had one of the highest per capita incomes of any group in Montreal. Richler's authorial stance as the plucky underdog, endlessly slugging it out against the vanished bluebloods and bigots of his youth, has produced some of the most passionate writing in Canadian literature. I can see, however, why it's a position that's easier to maintain from London and the Anglo pubs of Crescent Street.

In Pierre Anctil's office in downtown Montreal, the words *Toyre iz de beste sroyre* (Yiddish for "The Torah is the best merchandise") scroll across the screen saver of his computer. Anctil, one of the few goyim in the world who have taken the time to learn Yiddish, is neither Jewish nor Anglo. The tall, curly-haired anthropologist is a francophone from Quebec City – some might call him *pure laine* – but he's also an accomplished historian of Jewish culture, fluent in the fast-fading, expressive mélange of Middle High German and Hebrew once spoken by 11 million European Jews. Anctil translated Michel Tremblay's *Les Belles-Soeurs* into Yiddish – from another marginalized language, the working-class joual of Montreal's east end – and helped stage a well-received production of the play at the Saidye Bronfman Centre. It's hard to imagine where this urbane Québécois, who cites sixteenth-century rabbis while holding forth on the history of the bagel, fits into the cosmology of Mordecai Richler's anti-Semitic Quebec.

Trained at the New School for Social Research, a New York university founded by Holocaust survivors, Anctil doesn't deny the ravings of Adrien Arcand or the early editorialists of *Le Devoir*. "In the thirties, no question, there was anti-Semitism among the elites, which was very menacing verbally," he acknowledges. "But there has always been a rupture between the French-Canadian elite and the people, who have never been able to maintain a discourse of violence. It doesn't make any sense to them. Ordinary people continued to do business with Jews" – the Jewish-owned chains of Pollack department stores and Steinberg groceries thrived in spite of the attempted Achat Chez Nous boycott of the thirties – "and Jews could travel everywhere in French Canada without being attacked or threatened by the common people." The anti-Semitism of Quebec was picked up wholesale from right-wing intellectuals in France, automatically inculcated by the Catholic church and transmitted by rote, but somehow never translated into attacks on individuals. There were incidents – broken windows on St. Lawrence Boulevard in 1942, the desecration of a Quebec City synagogue after the Second World War – but these were crimes against property, not the kind of wholesale slaughter that occurred in Europe. Perhaps the gravest consequences were psychological: older Montrealers still recall hiding in their parents' apartments while students from the Université de Montréal, clutching bamboo canes, goosestepped up St. Urban Street chanting racist slogans.

Anctil insists, however, that "what existed in Quebec also existed in English Canada." In fact, English-Canadian racism was both more violent and more systemic than its Quebec counterpart. While there have never been laws against Jews, Asians, or blacks in Quebec, for years British Columbia's Chinese and Japanese were forced to pay head taxes, could not be elected to public office, and were prohibited from practising pharmacy or law (and subjected to the Asiatic Exclusion League's periodic rampages through Chinatown); the blacks of Ontario and Nova Scotia were forced into segregated schools; and the Doukhobors on the Prairies and in British Columbia were prohibited from voting in federal elections. For every Lionel Groulx or André Laurendeau in Quebec, there was a John Buchan (governor general and author of *The 39 Steps*), Stephen Leacock (the celebrated humorist), or Goldwin Smith (the prominent Victorian journalist and historian) – all mainstream Canadian anti-Semites.

"In Quebec, the French Canadians have never attacked the Jews," says Anctil. "There were a few broken windows, there were editorials in *Le Devoir* and *L'Action nationale*, but the people weren't really interested. Their religious and intellectual elite couldn't get them to move against the Jews." Meanwhile, in Toronto the Good, there was nothing the city's thugs liked more than a good anti-Semitic Donnybrook. During the summer of 1933, well-bred Torontonian members of the Swastika Clubs wandered the beaches wearing armbands, chasing off Jewish families who dared step on the sand. In August, they unfurled a Nazi flag at an amateur baseball game between a Catholic and a Jewish team, and the subsequent Christie Pits riots lasted six hours, as thugs armed with broom handles, fence pickets, and brickbats beat Jews until motorcycle cops broke it up.

In 1998, the B'nai B'rith recorded 20 anti-Semitic acts in Montreal – versus 123 in Toronto.

In retrospect, suggests Anctil, the Jews and French Canadians – urban workers, who shared second-class-citizen status and a folk tradition of mocking arrogant WASPs – might have found common ground in Montreal before the Second World War had they not been separated by language and religion. From 1869 to 1999, Quebec's schools were divided into Catholic and Protestant systems. The English-speaking Protestant schools reluctantly made room for Jewish children (who would eventually be the majority in high schools such as Baron Byng – the Fletcher's Field of Mordecai Richler's novels). However, in 1903, Jewish children were banned from Quebec's Catholic schools, roping off a significant terrain for potential entente. Gradually, a separate system of private Jewish education evolved. Today, 6,500 students attend 20 different institutions, making Jewish private school attendance in Montreal the highest of any such community in North America (the Quebec government nonetheless pays 55 per cent of the cost of running the schools). "For people like Richler and his generation," emphasizes Anctil, "there's a disappointment, a resentment, towards the French Canadians for not letting the Jews into their schools. And conversely, French Canadians have a grudge against the Jews for not learning French." For Montreal's Jewish community, social mobility would henceforth lie in fighting for reluctantly accorded space in discriminatory institutions – banks, department stores, insurance companies, McGill University's medicine faculty with its 10 per cent quota of Jewish students – controlled by the Anglo-Scottish oligarchy. (Hence a bygone dictum of Quebec Jewry: "Dress British, think Yiddish.")

At its worst, the relationship between Québécois and Jew was one of mutual suspicion and hostility. Too often, the French Canadians reproached the Jews as striving and materialistic, cynically casting their lot with the rich, the powerful – the Anglos. The Jews saw French-Canadian society as warm, tight-knit, family-oriented (values many of them shared), but also as a culturally impoverished dead end. Why bother learning the language or customs of these abject, lower-class Gentiles?

In spite of it all, Quebec's Jews – even those who have made the trip down Highway 401 to Toronto – tend to feel deeply attached to Montreal. While Jews in the United States became thoroughly integrated, powerful figures in the upper echelons of a society they'd radically transformed, many shed their religious identity altogether. Canadian Judaism tended to be more orthodox than its liberal American counterpart; and the French-Canadian matrix in which Jews had implanted themselves, while only occasionally perceived as hostile, certainly didn't offer the enticements or rewards of the American melting pot. Hence the extreme segregation of Montreal: the middle-class west end neighbourhood of Côte-St-Luc is the most Jewish municipality in North America, with 80 per cent of its residents claiming Jewish origins. (In Montreal, the Balkanization is institutional as well as ethnic: Westmount, Outremont, and the Town of Mount Royal are all separate municipalities near the heart of Montreal, with their own services and even security forces.) This is no accident of geography: excluded from the Catholic system, it made sense for Jewish families to live near community-run private schools.

Suspicion between Jews and Québécois of French-Canadian descent persists. Toronto – once seen as a WASP's nest, a cultural dead zone – is now the nation's largest Jewish city, thanks mostly to an exodus of young Jews from Montreal. Some of the 30,000 who left during the past 20 years, reducing the city's Jewish population to 92,000 (a quarter of them over 65), blamed the faltering economy. But many cited the election of the Parti Québécois in 1976 and laws that restrict the use of English while promoting the French language. The Jews who remain are becoming more bilingual (60 per cent now speak French), but ham-fisted slip-ups by Québécois nationalists and bureaucrats sent ripples of unease through the community in the nineties. In the 1995 "Matzogate" incident, the Office de la langue française removed kosher food from local stores – just as people were stocking up for Passover – because the labels weren't in French. The hermetic but highly visible Hasidim of Mile End still get called "les frisettes" – in spite of this eminently practical community's stated support of Quebec separation – and the people of Outremont have been known to gather signatures to prevent the Hasidim from building *sukkahs* (outdoor booths) on balconies of high-end condos for the seven-day feast of Tabernacles in October. It's reminiscent of the reaction to Sikh turbans in Canadian Legion halls and Chinese "monster houses" in Vancouver. At best, such reactions are the product of a certain parochial ignorance; at worst, they are interpreted as harassment, telltale incidents that bespeak deep incomprehension and fear.

There are signs of progress, however. The arrival of thousands of Sephardic Jews in the fifties (they now account for a quarter of Quebec's Jewish population) – mostly French-speakers from Morocco, who often felt more at home with francophones than with the anglicized postwar Ashkenazim – has bridged a significant chasm. The best hopes for rapprochement lie in the increasing bilingualism of the Jews who stay, and new generations of Québécois, including Pierre Anctil, whose minds are open to other cultures. Indeed, for Anctil, the presence of Jews is key to the province's future. "They were the first community in Montreal that were neither anglophone nor francophone, neither Protestant nor Catholic," he points out. "They made us ask ourselves, Can one be Jewish and Québécois? It's a fundamental question: Can one be Québécois without being one of the founding peoples? Now we see the consequences – there are immigrants who come from all over the world. It was the Jews who asked these questions for the first time."

In a society where immigrants are a growing presence, such questions urgently demand a response. Can one ever be fully Québécois without being ethnically French Canadian? Here's the official answer, courtesy of the Parti Québécois: As long as one lives in Quebec and makes an effort to speak French, one is Québécois. The prerequisites for belonging, for *appartenance* – in the province and potential nation of Quebec – are no longer racial, as in the days of Abbé Groulx, but cultural and territorial. It's a bit naive to take government professions of good will at face value, however (which may explain the long-running exodus of young Jews). So let's rephrase the question: Do recent immigrants think there's a place for themselves in business, government administration, and politics alongside the ethnic French Canadians who have dominated Quebec society for the past four decades?

In the last census, the allophones of Quebec (from the Greek *allo*, "other," for those whose first language is something other than French or English) finally outnumbered the anglophones. A visitor to Montreal is now more likely to meet Portuguese-speaking Brazilians, hispanophone Chileans, or Lebanese fluent in Arabic than old-stock English-speakers. A stroller on Victoria Street – where you can buy Jamaican rotis, Mexican quesadillas, Lebanese falafel, Vietnamese spring rolls, Ethiopian injera, and just about every other conceivable combination of flatbread and stuffing – might unwittingly hear dozens of the 110 languages spoken in Côte-des-Neiges, Canada's most multi-ethnic neighbourhood. During the summer street festivals, women in hijabs shop for inexpensive socks, and Latinas in halter tops browse for salsa tapes as the smell of roasting corn fills the air. At first glance, these could be scenes from the Punjabi Market in Vancouver or Kensington in Toronto: the kind of variegated *tableaux vivants* that boosters of multiculturalism delight in presenting to the world.

Quebec's immigrant population is actually rather small compared to Ontario's, where 26 per cent of the population was born outside the country, or British Columbia's, where the figure is 24 per cent. While an astonishing 2.7 million Ontarians come from abroad, there are only 660,000 immigrants in the entire province of Quebec, about the total foreign-born population of the city of Vancouver. Only eight per cent of Quebecers were born abroad, a situation akin to that in Germany or France, countries with highly restrictive immigration policies. Outside Montreal – where nine of 10 of the province's immigrants live – the contrast is even more dramatic: the proportions of immigrants in Quebec City (2.6 per cent), Trois-Rivières (1.7 per cent), and Chicoutimi (0.7 per cent) make those cities among the most ethnically homogeneous in the country. Although Quebec represents about a quarter of Canada's population, for much of the nineties it has attracted only 15 per cent of the nation's immigrants.

Since 1968, Quebec's Department of Immigration has set its own policy, maintaining officers abroad and in Ottawa. It was recently given exclusive powers over the selection of independent immigrants (those outside the family or refugee class). This partly accounts for the distinct nature of the province's ethnic communities. Those who stay tend to be francophone, mostly from France, Haiti, Lebanon, Vietnam, and Morocco. Latin Americans also favour Montreal, but the statistically important Chinese immigrants (classic anglotropes) stay away from Quebec in droves. Unlike in Vancouver and Toronto, no single immigrant group predominates in Montreal. As the Québécois demographer Jacques Henripin has pointed out, "Quebec does a rather poor job of retaining its foreign immigrants: 40 per cent leave within 10 years, 50 per cent within 20 years, and 60 per cent within 30 years. . . . We need to take in close to three immigrants in order to keep one."

What's more, Montreal has always been marked by high levels of residential segregation and ethnic retention. In other words, immigrants tend to stay in their own neighbourhoods and continue speaking their first languages, even a couple of generations down the line. The Italians in St-Léonard, the Greeks in Parc-Extension, the Portuguese around Rue Roy – the postwar Europeans kept to themselves and continued speaking the language of the Old Country. They also tended to attend Protestant schools and choose English over French as a second language. While their more thoroughly integrated contemporaries in English Canada have long since entered public life, Quebec's minorities are severely under-represented in the province's bureaucratic and political scene.

Poorly integrated minorities living in an ethnically homogeneous society with a legacy of anti-Semitism, nationalist violence, and cronyism: a recent immigrant might have good reason to worry about his future in Quebec. The official claim "Est Québécois, qui veut l'être" – anyone who wants to be Québécois (and is willing to learn French) is Québécois – sounds reassuring, but a series of astonishing faux pas before and after the 1995 referendum seemed to offer a glimpse into a Québécois heart of darkness. After the vote from Montreal killed the independence project, Premier Jacques Parizeau turned to the television cameras and lamented, "It's true that we were beaten, but, at bottom, by what? By money and ethnic votes. . . . The independence of Quebec remains the cement that binds us. We want a country, and we will have it." Earlier, Bloc Québécois MP Philippe Paré had bluntly stated, "Ethnic Quebecers shouldn't vote." After the referendum, Deputy Premier Bernard Landry buttonholed a Mexican-Canadian clerk behind a registration desk at a Montreal hotel and, while security cameras rolled, demanded, "Why do we open the doors to this country so you can vote No?" He became so aggressive that security guards had to be called. Landry is still in office, and though Parizeau resigned, his successor Lucien Bouchard lamented, "We're one of the white races that have the fewest children," urging Quebec's women to increase their birth rate.

The message an immigrant might take away is that this nation belongs to the *pure laine* Québécois – for whom we will always be *eux autres* – and those who interfere with its ambitions do so at their peril. Neil Bissoondath, a Trinidad-born novelist who came to Canada at 18, says he isn't alarmed by such incidents. After living for 16 years in Toronto, Bissoondath moved with his francophone wife to Quebec City, where he is one of the most visible of that city's tiny population of minorities. In the living room of a tidy bungalow in the quiet suburb of Ste-Foy, he admits being shocked by Parizeau's comments. "I regarded them with horror," he says. "I think they revealed that xenophobic, almost racist side that you find in any national-ist movement." But he hardly considers such outbursts representative of the opinions of all Québécois. "I think there's a battle going on for the soul of the nationalist movement in Quebec. It's generational to a great extent: people like Lucien Bouchard grew up with that racial vision of a white, francophone, Catholic Quebec. I think Jacques Parizeau, for one, feels threatened to the tips of his toes by immigrants – and may that long con-tinue." But Bissoondath also believes that such men are dinosaurs, hardly typical of an emerging Quebec, a place whose strong sense of self will allow it to accommodate and adapt to new immigrants.

In his 1994 book, *Selling Illusions*, Bissoondath argued that by encour-aging immigrants to maintain their cultures and languages, Canada's official policy of multiculturalism was creating immigrant ghettos and undermining the country's dwindling sense of identity. He held up Quebec's model as infinitely preferable. "While English Canada soon found itself adrift, with no sense of centre," he wrote, "Quebec redefined its own centre, strengthened it, sought to make it unassailable. . . . Simply put, then, while English Canada saw its defining Britishness dismantled, Quebec saw its defining Frenchness strengthened."

The Québécois have no truck with multiculturalism, which they see as an insidious strategy to reduce the culture of French Canada – a third of the population at the time of Confederation – to just another ethnic patch in a gaily coloured Canadian quilt. Quebec's official policy is interculturalism, which stresses the integration of cultural communities (as opposed to ethnic groups) into an environment where French is the common language of public life. To strengthen this position, the government has legislated that the children of allophone immigrants must be educated in French-language schools. The law has had only a modest impact on the number of immigrants who choose French. In the early seventies, about a quarter of the allophones who started speaking another language at home reported using French; today, the figure has increased to 40 per cent. In spite of extraordinary inducements, the majority of immigrants in Quebec still end up speaking English.

Bissoondath, who has enrolled his young daughter in a French-language school, doesn't find this astonishing; nor does he see the fact that many immigrants end up leaving as indicative of endemic racism. "I think Mordecai Richler provided us with the answer to this. Mordecai has asked, more than once, Why should people come to Quebec? They're coming to North America – to America. What's the language of success in America? It's not French. If the requirement under Bill 101 is that business be conducted in French, that kids go to school in French, I can see people being unhappy about that and leaving. And I don't think that's necessarily a loss to Quebec society, because those that stay accept the rules of the game. These are the ones who, somewhere down the road, will win."

But won't they have to sacrifice their cultural heritage to be accepted? "Quebec expects newcomers to integrate, not to assimilate, into the society," insists Bissoondath. "Integration, it seems to me, is engaging with society without ever losing your sense of personal identity and family history. Quebec has never surrendered its sense of self. I think the rest of the country becomes puzzled when demands are made; they will take absurd demands and treat them seriously, always afraid of being called intolerant. People in Quebec aren't afraid of being called intolerant, and they aren't afraid of speaking their minds. That to me is a society that takes itself seriously."

In the past, Quebec's "sense of self" had a troubling tendency to pit the *pure laine* against *eux autres*. This was mostly a question of xenophobia – which is different from out-and-out racism. As the novelist and filmmaker Jacques Godbout has emphasized, his compatriots most often manifest reactions of impatience and fear – the kind of unease that arises when people in a homogeneous society are confronted by otherness. Sometimes this xenophobia slides into racist reactions, and there have been unsettling incidents. The eighties saw a wave of racial brutality in which a virtually all-white police force several times shot unarmed black men and Indians. These days, there are signs of improvement. More and more minorities ride in the front seat of Montreal squad cars, and black teenage boys walk down east end streets arm-in-arm with francophone girls they've courted at high school dances. Artists like Lhasa de Sela – a francophone chanteuse of Mexican and American background who sings in Spanish – black writer Dany Laferrière, Shanghai-born novelist Ying Chen, and the Haitian-Zairean-Québécois rap group Sans Pression have all achieved mainstream success in a French-speaking milieu. Any hope for the future will come from this generation – the worldly, curious Québécois who have grown up, gone to school, and worked alongside Lebanese, Haitian, Jewish, and Vietnamese neighbours.

Bissoondath, who feels the people of Quebec City are unthreatened by immigrants (perhaps because, numerically insignificant, the newcomers can be looked upon as curiosities rather than forces of change), has decided he'll stick around even if Quebec becomes its own nation. "Merely Quebec becoming independent would not cause me to leave. This is where I've chosen to make my life." But he's willing to confess to a slight unease about life in a separate Québécois nation. "Parizeau talked about reducing the number of English radio and TV stations in Quebec. . . . If it's the Parizeau generation in power, I think it would be unpleasant. If Quebec ever does become independent, however, I think it will probably be a different generation."

Unfortunately, the ethnic nationalism of the older generation is not dead. St. Jean Baptiste Society president Guy Bouthillier still publishes essays in which he traces the history of immigration as an English plot to drown French Canada in a sea of foreigners. Raymond Villeneuve, the convicted FLQ militant, issued a call to halt immigration because "foreigners" and "enemies of Quebec" are blocking the Québécois *de vieille souche* from achieving independence. Nationalist politicians still cite Quebec's noble French, Catholic ascendance – wilfully omitting the Protestants, Hurons and Abenakis, Scottish navigators, Irish orphans, and enslaved blacks who make their *laine* such an intriguing patchwork. And immigrants still repress a shudder as Molson-swigging, mullet-haired loogans with fleur-de-lys painted on their bare chests march in the Fête nationale parade, chanting, "Le Québec aux Québécois!" Such tendencies exist everywhere: in the France of Jean-Marie Le Pen's Front national, in the lunatic fringe of western Canada's Reform Party, in the immigrants-out policies that former governor Pete Wilson pursued in California. Quebec is wrestling with its demons, and the debate is going on in public. On radio stations, in news-paper editorials, and on television talk shows, even nationalists are finally beginning to agree that *eux autres* can also be Québécois.

In coming to Montreal, unfortunately I became a member of one of the most strident, self-righteous minorities in North America. Most French-speaking Québécois will always consider me an Anglo, which means I sometimes get lumped in with one of the most paranoid bunches of loud-mouth buffoons on the continent. For every Bernard Landry, there's a Howard Galganov, the radio host whose 1996 field trip to New York to call attention to Québécois repression attracted exactly zero Wall Street bigwigs and opinion makers. Although Anglos are now a sad, remnant population, accounting for less than 11 per cent of all Quebecers, many older Brits still see themselves as mandarins among a sea of coolies. It's possible to over-hear Westmount matrons who will not address a word of French to shop assistants, or bumptious transplants from Ontario who always order their meal entirely in English – 'cause this is still Canada, goddammit. Whereas young francophone Québécois, raised on both Jean Leloup and the Tragically Hip, tend to be familiar with North American culture, their Anglo peers often draw blanks when names like Félix Leclerc or Richard Desjardins are mentioned. There's a word for such incuriosity about an entire society: arrogance.

Happily, there are signs that all this is changing. The majority of the half-million anglophones who have left Quebec since the early seventies have been of British and Jewish origin; they have tended to be unilingual and resistant to the changes sweeping society. Those who remained, many of Italian, South Asian, or mixed French and English background, are the kind of people Quebec needs: adaptable, multilingual citizens with an innate comprehension of complex identities. In the 1996 census, which counted 760,000 people who spoke English at home, it was found for the first time that Quebec's Anglos were more likely to marry somebody who spoke another language. What's more, 65 per cent reported they could speak French (versus only 40 per cent in the early seventies).

With their increased intermarriages with francophones, their higher enrolments in immersion schools, and their increasingly organic mingling with French-speakers at work or in ever-more-bilingual suburbs, Quebec's adapting Anglos are creating a far less combative linguistic atmosphere. The only place the old certainties persist, in fact, is in the greying heads of an older generation of Montrealers, for whom wealthy Brits will forever live in Westmount, and the French, in spite of all evidence to the contrary, will continue to cluster around the factories of the east end. Of the 4,100 members of the Anglo rights group Alliance Quebec, only seven per cent were under 30 in 1996, while 40 per cent were senior citizens. As the voices of the older generation of William Johnsons and Mordecai Richlers start to fade, the new breed of anglophone Québécois will undoubtedly help to attenuate the traditional polarizations.

My old friends in Vancouver suspect that, since I've taken to mocking the Anglos' complaints of oppression, I must be suffering from some pernicious Laurentian strain of the Stockholm Syndrome. But a few years in Montreal are enough to drive home the reality that even if Québécois are in the majority here, they have minority status in English-speaking North America (especially in summer, when American vacationers rub it in by asking, loudly and slowly, "Do – you – speak – English?"). A disgusted Anglo can always take Highway 401 to Toronto – or head south to New York, if the United States happens to value his university degree – with minimal cultural adjustment. For the people of Quebec, repatriation to France is no longer an option. Here is where French culture makes its stand in North America, and for some, *eux autres* have seemed to be the chief stumbling block to long-cherished dreams of independence. The older generation's xenophobia has been relatively restrained. The worst episodes of racism in this country's history, with its legacy of residential schools, sterilization of the Inuit, anti-Asian riots, and racial quotas on immigration, did not originate in French Canada. Younger Québécois are realizing that their best hope for survival (and fulfillment) involves acknowledging *les autres* in their past. It also involves accepting that today's others – whether immigrants, natives, or Anglos – are becoming, irrevocably, an integral part of the Québécois identity.

Two Chairs

It isn't even sundown, and the little village of St-Tite already looks like it's in for one hell of a hoedown. Couples in leather chaps and stone-washed Wrangler jeans wander the pedestrian-only streets, sucking beer from king cans of Milwaukee's Best. Greybeard bikers park their Harley-Davidsons next to the tent where Willy, the amazing two-headed pig, bobs forever in a jar of formaldehyde. Along Route 153, hovercraft-sized recreational vehicles decapitate dahlias as obliging townspeople surrender their front yards for a 20-buck parking fee. Next to the beer garden, a couple of good ol' boys in black leather cowboy hats have grabbed the corner of a porta-potty, and they're whooping as they tilt it back and forth, to the chagrin of its squawking female occupant. There are fiddles screeching and steel guitars twanging, horse manure in the streets, and the smell of pogos – deep-fried corn-dogs on a stick – in the air: all the ingredients necessary to put any red-blooded cowboy from Calgary to Nashville in pure country heaven.

Of course, this isn't Alberta or Tennessee: it's La Mauricie, an over-whelmingly French-speaking region north of Trois-Rivières, the celebrated Quebec heartland where Ovila courted Émilie in the popular television saga *Les Filles de Caleb*. The countryside around here, where log booms float past silver-steepled churches on the banks of the St-Maurice River, is pure, picture-postcard Quebec. In fact, if this town's 10-day Festival Western were any farther east, I'd be in an Atlantic fishing village. The whole St-Tite experience is somewhat surreal: you can eat a Breton galette in a crêperie where a sideways horseshoe stands in for the *c*, or watch campers in cowboy boots lobbing silvery French *pétanque* balls. It's a little disorienting, as though a bunch of dusty gauchos had taken it into their heads to hold the world's largest chamber music festival on the Argentinian pampas.

Launched in 1967 by local boot manufacturer G.A. Boulet, St-Tite's one-day, one-off festival gradually swelled into a bacchanal that now attracts 400,000 people every September, the largest country-and-western gathering in Canada outside the Calgary Stampede. And credit where credit's due: the Québécois have managed a convincing syncretism of borrowed cowboy culture and traditional French-Canadian rural life. You can watch steer-roping and bull-riding from capacious grandstands, or attend a *mariage western* in the twin-spired stone church in town, where this year Linda Faucher and Luc Gauthier are bound in holy wedlock to the strains of a trio belting out French hymns, country style. There's drama: a 1,600-pound Belgian steps on horse breeder François Tassé's foot as he attempts to harness it to a sled piled with thousand-pound blocks of cement. There's music: you can catch big-haired Gisèle Laliberté's show in the Country-thèque tent or just pause to listen to the old gent with a steel guitar sitting in a lawn chair, wailing, "Je suis triste, et je m'ennuie, de vivre toujours dans le passéééé." And there's kitsch aplenty: $129 ankle-length Australian coats for sale in stands on Rue Notre-Dame; ostrich steaks with a side of *fèves au lard*; plywood cacti and Lucky Luke cartoon cut-outs strapped to the porches of just about every two-storey house in the town centre. And, as at most any country fair, there are many people in fringe jackets getting extremely drunk. Only difference is, here they're whooping it up in French.

Oddly enough, a couple of hours' drive along the St. Lawrence – either downstream to Quebec City or upstream to Montreal – will have you feeling as close to Europe as you can get on the North American continent. At newsstands in the provincial capital, intellectuals flip through copies of Paris-based journals like *Le Monde diplomatique* and *Le Nouvel observateur*. At the Francofolies in downtown Montreal every summer, French performers such as Juliette Gréco, Arthur H., and rapper MC Solaar play to packed houses, while cinema luminaries such as Bertrand Tavernier, Claude Chabrol, and Gérard Depardieu routinely cross the Atlantic to promote their latest films. The French literary talk show *Bouillon de culture*, transmitted via satellite every Friday during prime time, keeps tens of thousands of sophisticated Québécois abreast of the latest novels of Françoise Sagan and J.M.G. Le Clézio. Getting to Paris from Montreal is frequently faster, and almost always cheaper, than flying to Vancouver. Even as it's becoming difficult to meet a middle-class Québécois who hasn't paid at least one visit to France, 2,000 French immigrants settle in Quebec every year, a phenomenon that keeps the province's liquor stores stocked with Burgundy and its restaurants serving the latest in New Wave bistro cuisine.

Between rodeos and Rodin, the Québécois are a people with, as the evocative French expression has it, their *cul entre deux chaises*, their ass between two chairs. One cheek is solidly planted on the American continent of cowboy kitsch, package getaways to Las Vegas, and major-league sports. The other is more delicately poised on the soil of the *mère-patrie*, the ancestral source of their *différence*: the French language, the traditions of haute cuisine and high culture, and a certain disdain for crude materialism in favour of intellect and sensuality. It's a form of cultural schizophrenia that divides classes, households, even individuals. Forged from Jacques Brel 78s and Elvis Presley singles, coquilles St. Jacques and Filet-o'-Fish sandwiches, boules and bowling balls, the Québécois personality is a fissile alloy of *francité* and Americanness. Occasionally alarmed by the neighbouring behemoth that sees foreign languages and local traditions as annoying impediments to free trade, Quebec styles itself as Astérix's village, a hardy Gallic enclave in a continent of business-minded automatons. Repelled by lingering colonialism, hidebound hierarchy, and formality, exasperated Québécois return from France with a new appreciation for the dynamic North American side of their identity. A people that defined themselves first as French, and then as Canadiens living under the heel of a foreign power, the Québécois now find themselves torn between the cachet of European culture and the potentially fatal attractions of American consumerism.

From Montreal, that Janus-faced city of Mies van der Rohe glass boxes and Gothic revival cathedrals, it has always been possible to look either way: back to the old centres of European civilization or ahead to the frontiers of the New World. More definitively than most, Joseph Ernest Nephtali Dufault, born in the Eastern Townships village of St-Nazaire-d'Acton in 1892, chose America, expunging all trace of France from his past. At 15, after hearing legends of the West from guests in the Montreal hotel where he worked as a bellhop, Dufault hopped a train with a bag of cookies in his hand and 10 dollars in his pocket. In the bunkhouses of Alberta, Wyoming, and Nevada, he picked up English with a convincing western twang while learning to ride mustangs, tend stock, and bust broncos. By the time he was arrested for rustling cattle in Utah in 1914, he had so thoroughly shed his francophone past that no one questioned his claim to be one Will R. James, a ranch hand from Montana.

Dufault/James never confessed to his habitant roots. Not in the auto-biographical *Lone Cowboy* – one of 24 classic books illustrated with impeccably observed bulls and broncs – in which he invented a father from Texas and a part-Scottish, part-Irish mother from California. Nor in his appearance in the Hollywood adaptation of his book *Smoky*, where his laconic drawl betrayed no hint of a French-Canadian accent. Living the cowboy legend to the hilt (far more so than oat-opera author Zane Grey, a dentist from New York), he bought the Rocking R ranch in his spurious home state and defiantly built campfires on the roofs of hotels when he sojourned in Los Angeles. In Jacques Godbout's documentary *Alias Will James*, members of Quebec's Dufault family say the only acknowledgment they got from their wayward relative – who died from alcohol-related liver problems in 1942 – was the occasional letter with a cheque for $800 stuffed in it. These days, Québécois singers such as Gildor Roy and Bourbon Gautier, both from the Abitibi region, reconcile the languages of Molière and Hank Williams on the province's country radio stations and on jukeboxes in hundreds of *bars westerns* from Trois-Pistoles to Cadillac. If nothing else, James/Dufault was one of the first to prove that it was possible (in his case, with a bit of mythologizing and a lot of binge-drinking) to come from Quebec and be American.

Like Will James, Louis-Bernard Robitaille hightailed it out of Montreal as an adolescent, but *La Presse*'s long-time correspondent in Europe followed Quebec's eastward gaze, renouncing America to settle permanently in Paris. As a novelist, radio commentator, and contributor to *L'actualité*, Robitaille has been interpreting all things French for readers in Quebec since 1972. His collection of essays and articles, *Et Dieu créa les Français*, was warmly received by both the *Washington Post* and the immensely influential *Bouillon de culture*. Published in English Canada in 1998 as *And God Created the French* and followed by a sequel in 1999, it's a vital primer for anyone who hopes to understand what distinguishes the French from their *cousins Québécois*.

I meet Robitaille in his dishevelled, skylit sixth-floor apartment on Rue Amelot in Paris. We thread our way through the Marais, where the boutiques of such couturiers as Azzedine Alaïa share the streetscape with synagogues designed by Hector Guimard. (The Orthodox Jews here, I note, speak far more French than their counterparts in Montreal.) Robitaille steers me towards the terrace of Ma Bourgogne, a restaurant beneath the arcades of the Place des Vosges. A little knot of teenage *beurs* (the term the French use for the children of North African immigrants) has formed outside the iron fence of the symmetrical square, and they're clownishly harassing comely passersby. It's a sunny fall afternoon in this 1,700-year-old capital, the waiter is rolling his eyes at tourists in the age-old way, car alarms are bleating, and piglet-like Renault Twingos are chasing pedestrians and pigeons onto the sidewalks. Ah, turn-of-the-millennium France: land of massive unemployment and ennui among the youth, where air pollution is so bad that cars are routinely banned from city centres. I have come, I realize, about as far from the cowboys of Quebec's St-Tite as I can without leaving the francophone world.

Robitaille starts on a *demi* of beer and a plate of salad sprinkled with rectangles of uncooked bacon. His leather jacket and suede cowboy boots make him look more outlaw American than his usual bookish European. Like many apparently *pure laine* Québécois, he has a little Irish in his family tree. With his long hair combed back over his ears, and his slightly crooked nose, he could play the lumberjack poet in a camp in the Gatineau backwoods. But Robitaille's voice is now completely Parisian, Belmondo after a couple of packs of Gauloises. "Parisians may say they find the Québécois accent charming," he says. "In fact, to them, it sounds like the way peasants talk. It's *très très mal vu*. It's the classic hick accent: almost like the Belgians – and there are two jokes a day on the television about the Belgians." After a quarter-century in France, this son of a Montreal lawyer has completely shed the joual of his Notre-Dame-de-Grâce childhood. "These days," he growls, "if people want to insult me, they call me a Parisien."

For Robitaille, the distinction between the Québécois and the French couldn't be more clear: in spite of superficial similarities, he believes, they live on different planets. "In France," he offers, "if you make the mistake of inviting people who aren't on the same social level to your dinner party, it's bound to be a catastrophe. Deathly silence for the entire meal. In Quebec, you can have a plumber, a lawyer, and a university professor at the same table, and everyone will drink and have a good time, in spite of their differences." For Robitaille, France is an uneasy confederation of widely different peoples: quick-tempered Corsicans, noncommittal Normans, arrogant Parisians, the virtually Teutonic Alsatians – all of whom look on each other with ill-disguised mistrust. "In France, it's really a case of 'friend or foe?' The Bretons hate the Niçois and vice versa. They may all come from the same country, but they feel absolutely no sympathy for each other." In Quebec, which largely drew its francophone stock from like-minded peasants of northwestern and central France, "people are favourably predisposed towards one another because there's a basic a priori: somewhere down the line, everyone's part of the same big family."

While the Québécois attributes of conviviality, bonhomie, and informality find distant echoes in France, too often they come into conflict with the dominant Parisian traits of snobbishness, hostility to outsiders, and obsession with hierarchy. A generation ago, points out Robitaille, this would not have been a problem. In the early sixties, when he arrived, most French people thought Quebec bordered on Louisiana, and the only French Canadians in Paris were a handful of diplomats and a couple of hundred students at the Cité Université. Today, however, it's hard to go for a five-minute stroll in Paris without stumbling across a fleur-de-lys flag, whether it's on the Fin du Monde beer ads at L'Envol, a Québécois bar in the fifth arrondissement, or outside Equinox, a chic *restaurant canadien* on Rue des Rosiers. On the boulevards, there are posters for Luc Plamondon's pop musical *Notre-Dame de Paris*, which has just opened at the Palais des congrès to dismissive reviews and sell-out crowds. I've noticed ads for the latest issue of the weekly magazine *Télé-Star* dangling from the ceiling of every metro car, hailing Lara Fabian – a Quebec-raised singer of Flemish and Sicilian parentage – as "La nouvelle star de la chanson française" after her triumph at the Olympia concert hall. Even Céline Dion has acquired enough social gravitas to be included in the latest edition of *Who's Who* in France. "Robert Charlebois, Diane Dufresne, Carole Laure – they're all still well known here," says Robitaille. "But you'll notice that the only aspect of Québécois culture that works really well in France is pop music."

This isn't completely true. The plays of Québécois dramatists such as Daniel Danis and Denis Marleau are received with enthusiasm at the Avignon theatre festival, and director Robert Lepage is now virtually an honorary European. Unfortunately, the fame of sentimental singers such as Roch Voisine and Lynda Lemay – and perhaps race car driver Jacques Villeneuve and comedian Michel Courtemanche – only tends to reinforce France's colonial condescension towards Québécois culture. In spite of the flood of Québécois authors of all ethnic backgrounds who received enthusiastic coverage during the 1999 Salon du livre in Paris – the one to which Mordecai Richler was not invited – the French tend to see Quebec as a backwater populated with wonderfully agile idiot savants. "Along with a Canadian accent," noted the Parisian daily *Libération* with lip-puckering tartness, "Céline Dion shares with her compatriots a tendency to bawl (Dufresne, Charlebois, Vigneault – the constraint of the wide open spaces, no doubt)." If writers such as Réjean Ducharme and Anne Hébert are known and read, they also have to compete with European talents of similar calibre. Meanwhile, in a France keen on exotica, hyperborean English-Canadian authors, particularly Robertson Davies, Michael Ondaatje, Margaret Atwood, and Neil Bissoondath, sell better in translation than their Québécois counterparts in the original French. The only recent exceptions have been Arlette Cousture's *Émilie* and *Blanche*, which sold hundreds of thousands of copies, largely because they appeared at the same time as the *Anne of Green Gables*-like series *Les Filles de Caleb* – a television program that had to be dubbed, notes Robitaille, because the French had trouble understanding the actors' Québécois accents.

The increased presence of Quebec in Paris can occasionally create the misleading impression that the former colony is just some exotic outcropping of France. In fact, the Québécois are now separated from the French by two revolutions (one *terrible*, the other *tranquille*), several global conflicts, and close to half a millennium of Laurentian winters. Robitaille, who has managed a transformation into a passable Parisian, confesses he's even developed a soft spot for the jaded European outlook. "There's a profound pessimism among the Europeans, because they've already lived through it all. In the twentieth century alone, there's been two world wars, the Spanish Civil War, Algeria. It produces this deep cynicism – which is often good-humoured. But deep down, they know that everybody could start slaughtering everybody else again. On the other hand, when there's the least bit of violence in Quebec, like at Oka, people just can't figure out what's going on. They're not used to it." Living on a continent where Basque terrorists and Balkan blood feuds set the journalistic agenda, Robitaille can be forgiven for stifling a smirk at the quibbling over the size of English-language characters in department stores.

A transatlantic transfiguration as dramatic as Robitaille's, however, is clearly the exception. For most Québécois, France remains a strangely familiar place, full of beguiling consonances of cuisine, gesture, and expression that, on closer inspection, proves a skein of decorum, conventions, and castes they can't fully untangle. "The Québécois may get the feeling," Robitaille has written, "after five or 10 trips, that they truly understand France, its customs and its codes of behaviour." Nothing could be more misleading. "The deep cynicism of French society – where a priori no one believes anybody, and where public statements are only taken seriously by the naive few – is a deeply ingrained reality that will always confound North American francophones." As Robitaille points out, Quebec can be just as confusing for the Gauls. "The average Frenchman, for his part, will never fully grasp that in Quebec society one is favourably disposed, from the outset, towards someone one doesn't know (as long, of course, as he is Québécois). And that in business or public life, people tend to say what they think and to be taken at their word."

After we settle our bill – these days the total is given in both francs and Euros – Robitaille looks at his watch in panic. Tomorrow morning *La Presse* has him crossing the Rhine to cover an election story in Germany. "You know what the biggest difference between France and Québec is?" he says as a parting shot, knocking back the last of his *express*. "It's that the French are 100 per cent European, and the Québécois are 100 per cent North American. Which means that there's practically no history, no weight of history, in Quebec. You can start your life from scratch there. In 1960, for example, the whole society started anew with the Quiet Revolution" – a society-wide transformation unthinkable in modern-day France, where every infringement on the acquired rights of teachers or railway workers sees a million and a half people marching in the streets. "On a personal level, in Quebec, you can quit your job, try something new, change your life, come back, get married, get divorced, look for another job. In France, what is noble, what is good, is to become a *fonctionnaire*, a bureaucrat, with job security for the rest of your life."

As Robitaille storms off in a clatter of cowboy boots on cobblestones, I reflect that what is noble and good here is now also virtually unattainable. I idly watch the same group of young *beurs* from the suburbs, still boldly teasing the well-dressed strollers behind the bars of the Place des Vosges as though harassing a cage full of particularly elegant macaques. French society has become so rule-bound and stagnant that, for many young people, Quebec is starting to look like a pretty good place to make a new start. When I talk to French people younger than, say, 35, they inevitably express interest in moving to Canada – which usually means Montreal – where founding a business, finding an apartment, or setting up an Internet account aren't the Sisyphean tasks they are in Paris. A 1998 survey showed that given a choice of countries in which to work abroad, half of French people would choose Canada, well ahead of the United States and Germany. That same year, at the Canadian embassy in Paris, applications to immigrate jumped by 50 per cent.

And therein lie the seeds of a problem, because the 60 million Français de France still treat their six million long-lost cousins with infuriatingly affectionate condescension. The explosion of cheap transatlantic package tours hasn't helped. A certain lingering colonialism, a durable belief in France's eternal glory and centrality in world culture allow the French to persist in denying Quebec's distinct history in North America. The Québécois have always responded with subversive humour, treating the teachers and restaurateurs who showed up in the fifties as *les sales Français* – the dirty French – after an apparent hygiene problem caused by the postwar European shortage of bathrooms.

In the collective memory, however, the French are just as often *les maudits Français* – the damned French – whose frivolous Bourbon king abandoned New France to the English. (Voltaire vaguely dismissed France's American colonies as a "few acres of snow" around Canada.) To the horror of the peasants and the remaining seigneurs on the banks of the St. Lawrence, the godless revolutionaries on the other side of the Atlantic then started burning their cathedrals and beheading their aristocrats. The Terror of 1793 was an indication of how thoroughly an increasingly republican and secular France had broken with a past that would linger in Quebec for many decades. For a while, the two countries got on with tending their respective gardens: the French cultivating the remaining outposts of their nineteenth-century *gloire*, the Canadiens retreating to an almost medieval rurality as an Anglo-Scottish elite took over Montreal. When Alexis de Tocqueville showed up on his North American tour in 1831, he expressed surprise at finding any French-speaking people left in Lower Canada at all. It wasn't until 1855 that contact with the old country was tentatively re-established, when the French frigate *La Capricieuse* sailed up the St. Lawrence, presaging the creation of France's first consulate in Canada three years later.

As if trying to make up for Voltaire's bons mots (not to mention several centuries of neglect), Charles de Gaulle spread his arms on the balcony of Montreal's Hôtel de Ville in 1967 and bellowed: "Vive Montréal! Vive le Québec! Vive le Québec libre!" (encouraging rebellion on the threshold of the United States, even as a vast corps of elite French troops crushed any nascent independence movement by local populations in colonial Africa). Since then, successive French governments have teasingly hinted they might formally recognize an independent Quebec. Lately, however, Jacques Chirac and his technocrats have noticed that, when you're trying to convince your own people to abandon their national autonomy in favour of a continent-wide economic union (and clamping down on Corsican and Breton independence movements in the process), it doesn't make much sense to encourage regional separatist movements abroad. When French prime minister Lionel Jospin visited Ottawa and Quebec City in 1998, he supported Canadian multiculturalism as a bulwark against American-led globalization, going so far as to intone a modest "Vive le Canada" – to the consternation of Québécois politicians. (A year later, Chirac scrupulously avoided the question of separation altogether, offering an impressive display of what the Québécois call *patinage* – the politician's knack for verbally skating around an issue.) The fact is, a long-lost North American colony can be of only marginal concern to a nation wrangling with a Europe that includes Northern Ireland, Catalonia, and Padania. To the extent that Quebec wishes to retain a certain cultural aloofness from America, however, the existence of France will always be a central psychological reality.

The analysis of national characteristics is an exercise the ill-advised attempt at their peril. Unfortunately, in the case of the French and the Québécois, it's also irresistible – and if you're an advertising executive, an essential part of the job. In 1978, the founder of Quebec's top advertising agency, BCP, published *Les 36 cordes sensibles des Québécois*, a book that broke down the character of his compatriots into six principal roots. For Jacques Bouchard, the key traits of the Québécois were their minority status, their connection to the land, and the fact that they were at once North American, French, Catholic, and Latin. (In only 20 years, the decline in the influence of Rome means that the Québécois – many of them descendants of the Normans, themselves Frenchified Vikings – are now Latin in language alone. It just goes to show that national characteristics are as malleable as modern borders.) In turn, each of these traits was linked to certain aspects of character: peasant earthiness, for example, made the Québécois lovers of nature, valuers of common sense, and shrewd negotiators. A minority status, on the other hand, left them with an inferiority complex, a parochial outlook, and a tendency towards envious gossip.

Québécois television admen who make the transition from Montreal to Paris report that they have to leave behind a freight car's worth of cultural baggage if they want to sell to the French. The openness, sincerity, and warmth that are featured values in Quebec's television commercials tend to be held in low esteem in France (an oft-repeated aphorism, usually delivered in rapid-fire Parisian, sums up the attitude: "Trop bon, trop con." In other words, if you're too nice, you're also too stupid.) In France, the emphasis must be put on sensual seduction (full, red lips suck on a Gervais ice cream bar), a nostalgia for lost glory (a Citroën flashes past castles on the Loire), and caustic verbal humour, where a *mot juste* puts a *prétentieux* in his place (an employee cunningly embarrasses his boss into giving him his France Télécom cellphone at the office Christmas party). The ideal French consumer is the sure-footed wit blessed with an ostentatious and somewhat cruel intelligence. What appeals in Quebec, by contrast, is the generous, warm-hearted boy-next-door whose common sense prevents him from becoming a dupe.

The most intriguing aspect of the *36 cordes* theory of the Quebec character, however, is the antinomy engendered by the entwinement of the French and North American roots. According to Bouchard, the Québécois' Gallic past has turned them into impractical chauvinists, torn between luxuriant sensuality and cold Cartesian rationalism. Living on the same continent as the Americans has made them self-promoting superconsumers and lovers of material comfort with a weakness for pink flamingos and Virgin Mary night lights. If these sound like the oversimplistic generalizations of a glib adman, keep in mind that Quebec's academics tend to agree. Yvan Lamonde, a specialist in the province's cultural and intellectual history at McGill University, would add that it's time for Quebec to mourn its severed French roots and fully assume its North American identity.

From his office in McGill's Peterson Hall, Lamonde has a view that's a constant reminder of how foreign influences shaped Quebec: the campus's dour stone buildings, built by British architects, are set against downtown Montreal's thicket of American-inspired glass-and-steel office towers. Taking me through the history of cultural influences, Lamonde emphasizes that Quebec's government is based on the British system of parliamentary democracy, which supplanted the French regime's absolute monarchy. "It's so obvious that we don't even think of it anymore," he says. Nor do people tend to recall the deep structural French influences, which go beyond language: "The fact that we have a constitutionally recognized French civil law, rather than British common law, isn't something people think about from day to day, when they're drinking a Coke." The vocabulary of public life, too, is largely borrowed from the regrettable bureaucratic lexicon of post-war France. Any Parisian would feel right at home if he heard that Quebec's Assemblée nationale had allocated more money to the INRS (the "national" scientific research institute) and the HLMs (public housing projects), and decided to rethink the administration of ZECs and ZACs (protected parks and hunting areas).

For Lamonde, however, Quebec's intellectuals and elites have minimized the historical influence of the United States. After all, they point out, the French Canadians greeted American troops, who came to Montreal in 1775 to provoke a continent-wide revolution, with benevolent indifference, opting for continued coexistence with the British. In the nineteenth century, the United States was demonized by Quebec's priests as the evil empire where rude egoism and materialistic instincts reigned – most memorably by the Abbé Henri-Raymond Casgrain, who saw the French race as the radiant source of morality, religion, and philosophy on a debased continent. "What a vulgar crowd!" marvelled the Abbé after one of his frequent sojourns in Florida. "Can you imagine a poet dressed as a Yankee?" At the same time, Quebec was leaking population from its farms – 900,000 French Canadians would permanently settle in New England between 1830 and 1930. For those who remained, the proximity of the United States transformed beach resorts such as Maine's Old Orchard or Florida's Hollywood into seasonal suburbs of Montreal. "Since the Second World War," Lamonde emphasizes, "Quebec has been a society of mass consumption. Cars, stoves, radios, tele-visions – you name it, we bought it. The kind of discourse popular a century ago – 'Look at those Americans, those mercantile materialists' – is impossi-ble now. We have almost exactly the same lifestyle."

The Québécois, commentators have observed, may sometimes be con-sciously anti-American, but they are almost always unconsciously pro-American. Between the Festival Western in La Mauricie and Elvis Presley conventions in the east end of Montreal, between Florida holidays and Nevada gambling junkets, the Americanization of Quebec is a deep-rooted, ongoing affair. Nor is it a recent one: the first stretch of Canadian railway track, the 1836 Laprairie–St-Jean, was built to link Quebec to the United States, as was the province's first modern highway. By 1889,

Montrealers could drink beer at the Parc Sohmer, a replica of Coney Island located near the current Radio-Canada tower. In the mid-twenties, almost all of the city's magnificent movie temples were controlled by Paramount, and 96 per cent of films shown in Quebec were being produced in the United States. While the gendarmes of postwar France were still rattling over the *pavés* on bicycles, their colleagues in the Sûreté du Québec were weaving between streetcars in Ford squad cars.

Whether it's the racks of tabloids in 24-hour chain stores or a Bruce Willis appearance at the opening of Planet Hollywood in Montreal, Americanization has most transformed Quebec on the level of popular culture. This is a worldwide phenomenon, of course, but the proximity of Quebec and Canada to the United States means they've borne the brunt of it, and for much longer than any European nation. "Pleading in favour of Quebec's Americanness doesn't mean blindly accepting Americanization," notes Lamonde. "It's a matter of recognizing that Quebec, like Canada, belongs to the North American continent, and to the New World as a whole."

I'm not convinced. Apart from a fad for tango clubs in Montreal and the fact that Mexicans on the beaches of Veracruz have taken to calling Québécois tourists "tabarnacos" (after their tendency to swear liturgically), Quebec's links to Latin America are pretty tenuous. But if Quebec's elites have long lived in a European cultural universe, its people are fully immersed in a North American biome of border-straddling trade unions, four-by-fours, and instantly dubbed Jim Carrey movies. "There's a profound social split," acknowledges Lamonde, "which is linked to income group and levels of education. France, generally speaking, has become a kind of deluxe cultural product: it represents Chanel, Dior, fashion, perfumes, champagne. And the popular classes don't have access – maybe they don't care about having access – to a bottle of Moët et Chandon that costs 75 dollars." Since most of Quebec's trade is with the United States, Lamonde sees the lingering cultural ties to France as out of touch with reality, mere remnants of a colonial mentality. "The principal effect of coming to terms with our Americanness will be to cut the umbilical cord with France. We no longer belong to Europe, and realizing this may mean kissing France goodbye."

On the streets of Montreal, certainly, America has long ruled. Case in point: the Howard Stern affair. From behind his microphone on the fourteenth floor of Infinity Broadcasting's building in midtown Manhattan, the

American "shock jock" celebrated his debut on Montreal airwaves in 1997 with one of his tirades – this one against everything French. In taxis cruising along Rue Ste-Catherine, in 99-cent pizza joints on the Main, in hockey rinks on Boulevard Pie IX, hundreds of thousands of Montrealers listened as Stern called the six million francophones of Quebec "scumbags and peckerheads." Gleefully conflating European and Canadian history, he accused the French of betraying the U.S. during the Second World War by collaborating with the Nazis. "These Quebecers want to preserve their culture?" he asked, incredulous. "What culture? For me, French is as insignificant as Yiddish. Everyone should speak English."

The reaction came quickly. *Le Journal de Montréal*, the city's popular true-crime-and-horoscope tabloid, smeared outrage across its front page: "Il nous chie dessus!" (He's shitting on us!) Even the middlebrow daily *La Presse* saw fit to resort to vulgarity: "From New York, Howard Stern promptly vomits on the francophones," read one headline. Two months later, Stern was the number one morning man in Montreal, making CHOM-FM the most listened-to radio station in Quebec. Though his ratings eventually fell, Stern's show was pulled a year after its debut because of new station-owner Shaw's concerns about a licence renewal, not because of any innate incompatibility with the Quebec market. After all, loud-mouth radio hosts are hardly unknown in Quebec: Montreal had long been tuning in to CKAC to hear the American-style rants of francophone after-noon man Gilles Proulx.

If Stern had been preaching only to Quebec's already converted anglo-phones, there would be nothing unusual about his popularity. But more than 65 per cent of CHOM's listeners were francophone. When informed, Stern didn't recant. "After all," he insisted, "you are Americans." Call it fluid backpedalling, but there's truth in Stern's retort: Quebec's working class tends to feel comfortable with its North American identity. In an ambitious province-wide survey undertaken by the multi-university Groupe de recherche sur l'américanité, though 54 per cent of the respondents said that they'd call themselves first Québécois, 80 per cent said they'd then identify themselves as North American or American rather than European. A further 44 per cent said they considered themselves only slightly, or not at all, different from the citizens of the United States. As Yvan Lamonde points out, there's no Québécois equivalent for *Ricain* or *Amerloque*, the pejorative terms the French use when they're lamenting the incursions of American imperialists.

Au contraire: America has often been perceived as Quebec's salvation. Patriote leader Louis-Joseph Papineau called for annexation to the United States, and the Québécois voted overwhelmingly in favour of free trade candidates in the 1988 federal election. (Three-quarters still believe NAFTA has had a favourable impact on Quebec's economic development.) It was the newly affluent kids of singer Robert Charlebois's generation, the baby boomers, who identified themselves most clearly as Americans, imitating Jack Kerouac and hitchhiking to California rather than repeating the Grand Tour of Europe of previous generations. In his 1972 "Complainte de Presqu'Amérique," Charlebois gave clear voice to this unconscious pro-Americanism: "Please take me to Broadway or Carnaby Street / Please let me in / I need to swing / I want to see what's happening / Let me cool before I freeze." When he comes back to Quebec, Charlebois fully expects to find his compatriots either already transformed into Americans or dead "for two steps of folklore / An inch and a half / Above the United States."

Given the experience of French-speaking Louisianans or the Franco-Americans in Massachusetts, an inch and a half above the United States is probably a minimum safe distance for any culture that wants to hold on to its language and traditions. One can only imagine how quickly Hollywood lobbyists would have Bill 109, which prevents English-language films from being shown unless dubbed French versions are also available, struck down if Quebec were just another American state. For Lamonde, however, the people of Quebec tend to draw a clear line at political union. "They may be willing to call themselves American when they're eating, when they're travelling, when they're talking about economic prosperity or work, but there's an area where they don't consider themselves American at all: in their willingness to allow greater state intervention, whether it's in health insurance or welfare, than in the United States."

To distinguish themselves from other North Americans, Quebec's middle class increasingly looks towards Europe. Even as France seems more present than ever in Montreal and Quebec City, the imprint of England is fast fading from Toronto, Halifax, and Vancouver. Though English Canada can't quite manage the official kiss-off, Britain's role as source of all things gleaming and glorious has long since been assumed by the United States.

The Queen may still grace the stamps, and afternoon tea may still be served on bone china in the Empress Hotel in Victoria, but these are increasingly empty symbols. In reality, sixties-vintage anglophilia has largely given way to Tarantino-and-*New Yorker* models of urbanity.

This British decolonization of Canada's anglophone urban middle-class culture has been matched by a Frenchifying of Quebec's bourgeoisie. In the late fifties, you could have spent much of the afternoon trying to chase down a month-old copy of *Le Figaro* in Quebec City; and thanks to enforcement of the Vatican's Index of Prohibited Books, Flaubert, Proust, Gide, and other such decadents could be obtained only through Montreal's English bookstores or through the mail from Paris. These days, newsstand chains keep the latest issue of *Paris Match* and *Géo* on the shelves, and every afternoon the widely watched cable network TV5 broadcasts the evening's news direct from France. In the spheres of publishing, academia, fashion, and cuisine, exchanges (many organized by the active Franco-Québécois Youth Office) are far more frequent with France than with the United States. A transatlantic voyage that would have been a bankrupting, once-in-a-lifetime excursion a generation ago is now less stressful than a drive to Ogunquit, Maine.

I'm on the corner of Montreal's Rue St-Denis and Avenue Mont-Royal, in one of those forgettable, neo-Italianate espresso joints where North Americans have been forced to spend much of the last decade. Compared to the Parisian café terrace where I met Louis-Bernard Robitaille, it feels as impermanent as a portable site office at a downtown construction lot, the kind of place that, with a couple of afternoons' work, could be dismantled and transformed into a video store. The women at the counter, however, have ready smiles, and I wasn't elbowed into the gutter with a curt "pardon" as I walked down the sidewalk. The New World has its comforts.

Mathilde and Anne sweep into the coffee bar, refulgent loci of energy on this dismal fall morning. They're old friends, freelance dancers with con-temporary dance troupes, both sophisticated women in their early thirties who have travelled widely in North America and Europe. Mathilde isn't tall, but she's so admirably sprung that I suspect she could outplay me on a basketball court; I've watched her cover a parking lot in a few bounds to greet her long-time boyfriend. Anne is all elegant punctuation: ponytail as question mark, high cheekbones underscoring dark eyes that form the umlaut over a black turtleneck. They're both Quebecers – Mathilde was brought up in Montreal by Swiss and French parents, and Anne was born to a francophone Irish mother and a francophile French-Canadian father – pure products of the mostly French-speaking upper-middle-class neighbourhood of Outremont. It's odd, I point out, that they often sound like they were brought up in the seventh arrondissement of Paris.

"*C'est normal*," says Anne, picking at the bran muffin that will constitute her lunch. "My father got his master's degree at the Sorbonne. He was fascinated by France. He wore us out talking about it." Nonetheless, on her first trip to France at the age of 21, she too succumbed to the charms of Paris. "*J'ai bien tripé*," she recalls. "I remember having dinner in a restaurant near the Folies-Bergères – the waiter was a real bastard. He was like, 'What do you want? *Vite!*' And I was saying, 'We've come to eat, relax.' But you get used to the Parisians – and if you stay there long enough, you end up becoming like them." I ask if she now uses French expressions when she's angry, or whether she still uses the Québécois swear word *calice*. "No, I tend to say *putain*, like they do in Paris. It just comes out by itself." Mathilde interjects, "You never really swore too much anyway." Anne thinks about this. "That's true. I've never said *tabarnac* in my life. Although a good *calice*, that comes in handy sometimes."

Anne seems to be undergoing a change of mind about all things French. For the past 10 years, she's dated men who are Français de France (the unavoidable Québécois qualifier for the French of France), but her current boyfriend is what she calls *un bon Québ'*, a good ol' Québécois. "The Québécois are a lot more relaxed," she believes. "They don't spend a lot of time worrying about how they're dressed when they go out. All my French boyfriends were very precious, very careful about their appearance. At heart, they were more concerned about form than content. The Québécois have more integrity: in general, they won't say things they don't believe, just to please." I point out that such qualities make the French pretty good at flirtation and seduction. "Yes, that's something I have to give the French, something I like. They are very sexual. The Québécois, on the other hand, tend to be a little afraid of women. They don't know how to court them.

They're very direct," she says, grabbing Mathilde's thigh with a wolfish lunge by way of demonstration. "A little too direct," she laughs.

I ask Anne and Mathilde whether they feel at ease in the rest of North America. "I used to go to Virginia Beach and Kennebunk when I was a teenager," replies Anne. "I've been to Miami, which I hated. It's too jet-set, too superficial. Los Angeles was the same. But I love New York and Maine. In general, however, I feel a lot closer to French culture than American culture." She pauses, looks around the café. "But I also feel American, too, because I live in a completely Americanized city." Mathilde gestures towards the huge signs for smoked meat and pizza slices on Rue St-Denis: "All that advertising! I understand why the Europeans who come here think we live in an American city. The first time I came back from a trip to Europe, I remember thinking to myself that Montreal was like a set for a Western movie. All the buildings were so low" – particularly compared to the six-storey buildings in Paris – "it all looked fake to me." Anne says, "At the level of culture, I almost never go to see American movies. I always loved French films." I tell her, if that's the case, then she's definitely not in the majority here. "Oui . . . ," she muses. "Perhaps I'm an exception."

Actually, both Mathilde and Anne are typical of at least one facet of contemporary Quebec. The Québécois aren't precariously seated between two chairs – instead, they're comfortably planted on both the American bar stool and the French tabouret. The United States in the age of the Pax Americana is beginning to look like a New Rome, capable of importing any great chef, artist, or director that it can't produce itself, or of perfectly reproducing a Parisian brasserie, down to the nicotine-clouded mirrors, in such trompe l'oeil eateries as Manhattan's Balthazar. Meanwhile, France, and Europe as a whole, will continue to style itself as a soulful Greece, its glory slightly faded but still boasting an uninterrupted tradition of high culture. Most societies play along with this modern dichotomy to some degree, but Quebec is particularly well placed to exploit the best of both worlds. Even as her economic exchanges with the United States increase, two-thirds of her wines come from France. And if her tan is Miami Beach, her Chanel is straight from Place Vendôme. Most important, gazing at the threadbare American social safety net, Quebec continues to draw a line at the 45th parallel, revealing a concern for social equality that, in spite of ongoing political attacks, could still be qualified as European. When the province's sociologists and policy-makers look abroad for new social ideas and programs, they inevitably compare themselves to such nations as Sweden and Denmark, not the United States.

It's this lingering sense of responsibility for fellow citizens, this recognition that untethered market forces marginalize and impoverish as much as they enrich, that makes the strongest outside influence on Quebec the one that's almost never talked about: the Canadian influence.

LE RANCH DU SPAGHETTI

It's lunchtime at Schwartz's on Boulevard St-Laurent, and the joint, as usual, is packed. Behind jars of pickled red peppers and the roasted chickens dangling from chains in the window, the countermen are shredding dark-rinded brisket, slamming stacks of hickory-smoked beef pearled with fat between ovals of rye bread, and handing plastic plates of the Spécial Combo Schwartz to harried, white-smocked waiters. Clients, hunched elbow to elbow and six to a table, are washing down their sandwiches with warm cherry cola. Most afternoons, you can tease words of Yiddish, Greek, Italian, and French from the convivial babble at Schwartz's, but English is clearly the language that works best in this 70-year-old landmark of Jewish Montreal. This is Quebec, which means that, thanks to laws in force since 1977, all signs must be predominantly in French. Schwartz's has dutifully translated the paper placemats that serve as menus; even so, they've received warnings from Quebec's so-called language police for refusing to make the French characters on their signs twice as big as the English equivalents. In 1998, a camera crew from the American news program *60 Minutes*, tipped off by Mordecai Richler, showed up to hammer home the more absurd excesses of the Office de la langue française. Look, said host Morley Safer with a smirk: the tongue troopers have even removed the apostrophe from good ol' Schwartz's, turning that sacrosanct delicatessen into Chez Schwartz Charcuterie Hébraïque de Montréal.

If *60 Minutes* had been concerned about balance, they could have gone a few blocks north to La Binerie Mont-Royal, another time capsule of an eatery. When Quebec's sign laws were instituted, the Office de la langue française inspectors didn't have to give La Binerie a second look. Since 1940, the clientele of this 18-seat lunch-and-breakfast counter has been working class, hungry, and predominantly francophone. In the morning, carpenters hang mackinaw jackets on wall pegs and sit down at a Formica counter spread with swallow-tailed syrup containers and spread-eagled copies of the tabloid *Journal de Montréal*. A required stop for campaigning Parti Québécois politicians trying to connect with the people, La Binerie is the kind of place where you could savour the all-protein breakfast no. 2 (eggs, sausages, ham, bacon, and pork-pâté *cretons*) every morning for the next decade without being troubled by the English language.

Well, almost. As I scan the list of dishes hand-lettered on a board on the wall, vainly looking for something light, I realize that any speaker of Parisian French would be clicking his tongue in disapproval, shocked at the anglicisms rampant in what's supposed to be a francophone environment. Forget that a request for a European breakfast of croissant and espresso would have every thick neck at the counter turning in disbelief. It's the vocabulary of this Québécois greasy spoon that's insidiously contaminated by English. Any European francophone would feel comfortable ordering the "bacon," "sandwich," and "Steak parisien" that are served up on pale-green plastic plates, but what would he make of the Sugar Twin next to the ketchup, or the menu's "12-once T-bone" and "saucisses wieners"? When I refuse the brown-smocked waitress's offer of a *breuvage* – the archaic word for what the French call a *boisson*, maintained in North America thanks to its similarity to "beverage" – she counters by offering me *un refill* for my coffee. The guy next to me is working on a bowl of *pouding chômeur* (unemployment pudding, a spongy homemade cake soaking in thin syrup), a term adapted from the English "pudding" in 1810. I finish with the specialty of the house, *fèves au lard*, simmered in a brick oven with pale chunks of pork for 18 hours, then slathered with maple syrup. Even these loose-skinned beans, an apparently immutable cornerstone of French-Canadian cuisine, are merely an adaptation of the recipe for Boston pork and beans jotted down by Louis-Joseph Papineau's father in the early 1800s when he was visiting the lumber camps of New England. What's more, everyone here calls them "*bines*," pronounced like the English beans. This makes La Binerie, that quintessential bastion of Québécois cookery, nothing more than a Frenchified beanery.

Quebec's infamous Bill 101, widely reviled in English Canada and mocked by Americans, was created in part to correct such pernicious linguistic confusion. Sure, making the predominantly English clientele of Schwartz's choose between smoked meat and *viande fumée* is slightly ludicrous – but at worst, courting arteriosclerosis in a French environment is only a nuisance. Confusing the French-speaking diners at La Binerie about whether they're eating *bines* (a deformed anglicism), *fèves* (a word current in Quebec, but an archaism in France), or *haricots* (the term used in Paris these days) is closer to being a cultural tragedy. When a minority tongue finds itself awash in the brand names, slang terms, and catch phrases of the world's most prestigious and omnipresent language – the steadily worsening fate of French in Quebec since 1759 – too often the only *mot juste* that comes to mind is an English one.

In the life of a language, two centuries is a long time to spend separated from the mother tongue. Though the spoken French of Quebec is no longer exactly joual, that infamous creole born in the English-dominated factories of Montreal, it's still far from the standard Parisian approved by the Académie française. A visitor from France, lulled into complacency by her first contact with the reassuringly international French of Radio-Canada's newscasters, is in for a shock when she hops into a cab or a city bus in Quebec. The Volkswagens and Renaults on the streets of Montreal aren't *voitures*, but *chars* – as though pedestrians were sent scuttling across the street by the aggressive behaviour of so many seventeenth-century horse carts. Proffering a chair, a polite host in Quebec City will say

"Assoyez-vous icitte" instead of "Asseyez-vous ici" – and when his girlfriend calls, he'll take his leave with the excuse that "Je vas jaser avec ma blonde astheur" instead of the modern Parisian "Je vais bavarder avec ma copine maintenant." Just as she's getting used to archaisms straight out of Rabelais, a well-dressed man in a cashierless store will ask aloud, "Y'a pas personne icitte?" (Ain't there nobody here?), a double negative guaranteed to set her gritting her teeth.

This is only the beginning. Shopkeepers, bus drivers, and waitresses will address her with the familiar "tu" and "toi" rather than the respectful "vous" she'd expect in similar situations in France. (And with a complete lack of consistency, they'll finish a sentence beginning with the informal pronoun "tu" with the formal "s'il vous plaît.") She hears words confined to the rural patois of Normandy and Poitou in the mouths of upper-middle-class *dames* of Outremont. A *livre* (pound) of *blé d'Inde* (corn) will set her back *une piastre* (one dollar) and 25 *sous* (25 cents), exotic terms that make the local *dépanneur* (corner store) sound like a pirate's cove in the Caribbean. Even the sound effects are different: a stubbed toe that provokes an "aïe!" in France elicits an "ayoye!" here; a messy baby's diaper that yields a "beurk!" in Chartres excites a "ouache!" in Chicoutimi. And then, most astonishing, the *sacres* – swear words – she hears shouted out of car windows in midsummer traffic jams: "Tabernacle! Bouge ton maudit char, calice! Hostie de chauffard de marde! Ciboire!" It's the architecture of the Eucharist, dismantled and re-erected daily on the streets in ephemeral rood screens of profanity. Before a couple of weeks have acclimatized her to all these anglicisms, archaisms, dialectalisms, solecisms, and blasphemies, our beleaguered Parisian visitor will probably be wondering, What the hell kind of language do they speak in Quebec, anyway?

The answer, of course, is French – but a particular variety of French, one coloured by its genesis in the peasant societies of the centre and the west of France. In the seventeenth century, the soldiers, day labourers, and tradespeople who left Normandy, Poitou, and the Atlantic coast islands of Ré and Oléron to try their luck overseas spoke local patois that could vary drastically from village to village. Philippe Barbaud, the Université du Québec à Montréal linguist who wrote a pioneering study of the early dialects of New France, believes that few of the early emigrants could even communicate with each other. "For example, if a colonist from Rouen, in

Normandy, met someone from Saintonge, which is south of the Loire River, then they would have had no chance of understanding one another whatsoever," says Barbaud, whose own parents emigrated from northern France to Quebec a half-century ago, when he was 10. "I trust my personal experience in this case. I know Normandy, and I've heard schoolchildren and peasants talking modern patois in small villages, and I can't understand anything." Herded by the hundreds into boats in such Atlantic ports as St. Malo, La Rochelle, and Nantes, the patois-speaking emigrants' first sustained encounter with the French language would have been through the shouted orders of ships' officers.

According to Barbaud, the docks of Quebec City in 1670 would have been a "real cacophony." Peasants from the southwest who spoke *langue d'oc* (where the word for "yes" was "oc") would have jostled Normans who said "men" and "ten" instead of "mon" and "ton," and Bretons who spoke a form of Celtic closer to Welsh than modern French. "They would have had to use interpreters," believes Barbaud. "It was fairly common practice in France at the time; someone who knew two different patois would serve as an intermediary." As the new arrivals settled in the seigneuries around Quebec City, they slowly swapped the idioms of their youth for the Parisian French spoken by the local nobility and clergy. In what would become a pattern in Quebec, it was the women who guaranteed the survival of the French language. More than half of them came from Paris, and they ensured that the language spoken at home conformed to the grammar, pronunciation, and vocabulary of the Île-de-France region, rather than the obscure patois of their mostly illiterate menfolk. "The women were in the minority," says Barbaud, "but they were better educated than the men. They knew how to count, keep books, and at least half of them knew how to write." After only three generations, the women of New France had woven the skein of local dialects that had tangled on the quays of Quebec City into a coherent language.

The colony on the St. Lawrence River came to be graced with a particularly lordly brand of French. At a time when only one in five of the inhabitants of France actually understood the language of the king – speaking instead Occitan, Provençal, Breton, or Alsatian – New France was a linguistically unified community. Much of the vocabulary and pronunciation that modern Parisians find alternately barbaric and charming (*si rustique!*)

is actually faithfully preserved aristocratic French of the seventeenth century, interlarded with the patois of western France. *Barrer la porte*, with its hint of dropping a plank over the cabin door to keep out the wolves and Iroquois, was the correct way to lock, or *verrouiller*, the door in pre-revolutionary France. Molière would have approved of the Québécois habit of following *eux* with *autres* to indicate "them," while Montaigne wrote *à cette heure* (meaning "now") exactly like modern playwrights working in vernacular joual: *astheur*.

What's more, the contemporary Québécois who says "frette" instead of "froid" would have passed for a well-spoken courtier in the Versailles of the Bourbons. Even that hallmark of lower-class *canayen*, the tendency to pronounce words like "toi" as "tway" and "moi" as "mway," would have been considered elevated diction in the court. "The way Montrealers roll their *r*s," says Barbaud, "and the way we say 'mway,' was the very best Parisian accent – back in 1670." During the Revolution, however, the French bourgeoisie set up the guillotine and lopped off many of the heads that said "mway" – which means that it's the phonetic habits of the Parisian riff-raff that now hold sway in the Elysée and the Opéra Bastille. If Louis XIV suddenly reappeared in the east end of Montreal, he would purr with approval to hear one of his former subjects say, "Mway, je vas souper avant de boire des liqueurs à la taverne." If, on the other hand, he heard a Parisian intoning, "Moi, je vais dîner avant de boire un cocktail au bar," he could only conclude that the rabble had taken over.

On the other hand, the Sun King might be puzzled by a relatively recent development among his long-lost colonists: their propensity to blaspheme like black popes. The French, like the Italians and the Spanish, tend to curse with what has long obsessed them: the inaccessible female, deconstructed into the *putain* (whore), the *bordel* (a brothel), the *con* (from a medieval word for vagina). The Québécois, on the other hand, still damn what long oppressed them: the *maudit* church, with its *hostie* (communion wafer) and its *ciboire* (the container that holds the wafers), not to mention its *tabernacle* (the niche at the altar in which the ciboire is housed) and its *calice* (the chalice in which wine is consecrated). Along with *Christ* and *baptême*, these are the *sacres* that, since at least the middle of the nineteenth century, have formed the core of Québécois malediction. Each morpheme serves as a nucleus around which various euphemisms and combined forms cluster.

Just as W.C. Fields turned goddam into Godfrey Daniels, a vexed school teacher can hobble the foul utterance *tabernacle* by rendering it a fey *tabarnouche* or *tabarouate*. Likewise, the sacrilegious Christ becomes *crisse*, which in turn yields the verb *déconcrisser*, as in: "Hostie! Je viens de déconcrisser mon maudit char, calinne!" (In other words, he just wrecked his damn car. By gosh.) I thought the local *sacres* looked fairly laughable on the page – no more threatening than 'struth or gadzooks – until I heard my landlord gleefully crafting endlessly varied litanies of damnation as he laid a hardwood floor. "Maudit tabarnac – crisse!" he groaned as a nail went in crooked. "Hostie de tabarnac de ciboire!" – he'd cut a plank too short. This was no Falstaff with a canker sore, all drat and zounds; my landlord sounded like a lumberjack wrestling with a moose.

With all the derived forms, a Université du Québec à Trois-Rivières study counted 890 distinct *sacres* in the French-Canadian lexicon, from the everyday *calinne de binnes* to such esoteric gems as the verb *contresaint-ciboiriser*. In a recent essay in *Le Devoir*, author Isabelle Gélinas exulted that "the *sacre* is to the Québécois what Notre-Dame Cathedral is to the Parisians." The analogy may call up images of dedicated teams of philologists on scaffolding, painstakingly restoring the gargoyle-like profanity *Simonacque*, but there's some truth in such hyperbole. The *sacre* is the linguistic trait that immediately sets a Québécois apart from a francophone in Geneva, Montpellier, or Dakar, and liturgical swearing is a direct inheritance of having survived a virtual theocracy. Just as the modern French language was emerging, with the founding of the Académie française and the appearance of the first dictionaries, the cord between France and its colony was definitively cut in the late eighteenth century. The educated nobility and the officers went back home, leaving the Canadien peasants in the hands of black-robed priests for the next 200 years. By the beginning of this century, the surest way to shock polite society in such a devout environment was to appropriate the church's most sacred words, using them in anger or scorn. Even now, when many churches are up for sale and the fearsome mother superior of yore tends to be today's frail octogenarian, a well-placed "sacrement" can still elicit an outraged glare from passersby in Quebec City.

For a while, using *sacres* was the most subversive literary act around. In 1964, a young and unknown author named Jacques Renaud realized there was something wrong with the sentence he'd just written. Speaking to interviewer Malcolm Reid years later, he recalled how he crossed out "Elle s'en fout" – which is the way they'd write "She doesn't give a damn" in Paris – and replaced it with "Elle s'en sacre," which is what he heard every day on the streets of Montreal. He then wrote *Le Cassé*, a depressing story about an unemployed drifter who kills a drug dealer in a gloomy Montreal, lacing the narrative and dialogue with *sacres*. It was the first novel written entirely in joual. Renaud's pioneering text gave other writers the courage to create a kind of joual pride movement, led by intellectual Jacques Godbout, singer Robert Charlebois, humorist Yvon Deschamps, and playwright Michel Tremblay.

Not everyone was impressed. A few years before Renaud's novel appeared, Frère Untel (Brother Anonymous), a young, reform-minded Marist brother teaching high school in the Saguenay region, had written: "To speak joual is to say 'joual' instead of 'cheval.' It is to speak as horses might speak if they hadn't chosen silence. . . . This lack of language that is joual is an example of our great French-Canadian nonexistence." In 1968, then federal justice minister Pierre Elliott Trudeau said that his compatriots should stop demanding more rights and work on cleaning up their "lousy French." In the Quebec of the Quiet Revolution, the outlines of a great debate were first traced: in one corner, populists such as Renaud, Tremblay, and the *joualisants*, brandishing syntactic aberrations and phonetic spelling as the symbols of Quebec's linguistic distinctness. In the other, earnest reformers like Frère Untel and the first contributors to the leftist journal *Parti pris*, who saw slang, lazy pronunciation, and anglicisms as symbolic of Québécois alienation.

According to Quebec's foremost dramatist, Michel Tremblay, the debate never really simmered down. "It's still going on!" he cries in consternation. "Thirty years later, the polemic is exactly the same." We're in his agent's office in a renovated mansion-turned-office-building on Sherbrooke Street, and Tremblay is fighting a late fall cold – Montreal's last-minute gift to its native son before his yearly winter-long flight to Florida's Key West. In 1968, Tremblay's play *Les Belles-Soeurs* debuted at Montreal's Théâtre du Rideau Vert. Fifteen actresses, decked out in curlers and cheap print dresses, gathered in a replica of an east-end apartment to help a lucky sweepstakes winner stick a million trading stamps into booklets. Even though the treacherous visitors end up stuffing their handbags with their neighbour's winnings, it's a generally affectionate portrait of working-class squalor. As Tremblay emphasizes, it was also a depiction of the world he grew up in: "I was born in 1942, on the corner of Fabre Street and Gilford, in a city where there were no men. They were all away fighting in the war. I was raised by five women. The first criticisms I heard of society came from female mouths." With owl-like glasses topped by a Salman Rushdie-esque brow, and a roundness of shoulder and belly offset by his height and erect bearing, Tremblay brings to mind one of his favourite joual words, *enfirouâper*. A direct borrowing of the English "in fur wrapped," it means "to seduce or trick someone with soft words." Tremblay himself gives the impression of being, literally, *enfirouâpé*: all fleecy outer eloquence, bound tightly around a long since petrified core of class resentment.

"I was a working-class kid with middle-class tastes," he says, squelching a sniffle. In his teens, he was obsessed with literature and music, and started composing fantastic novellas in the generic literary French of Paris. "In August 1965," he recalls, "when I was 23 years old, I went to see Pierre Patry's *Caïn* with a friend. Walking out of the theatre, we asked ourselves, Why did we hate that film so much? And we realized that, though it was a Québécois film, the characters were speaking in a kind of mid-Atlantic French. It was a language that no one had ever spoken – not us, not even the French themselves – and yet it was supposed to take place in our world, in our homes and apartments." Out of his disgust with this artificial language, Tremblay started to write scenes for what would later become *Les Belles-Soeurs*. For the critics who first saw the play in 1968, the most shocking thing was not the dead-on social realism but its language: the play, in pure joual, was a faithful transcription of all the tics of the Montreal French Tremblay had grown up with. In the mouth of a character such as Marie-Ange Brouillette, "je suis" becomes "chus," "moi" comes out "mway," and "pas du tout" is transformed into "pantoute." It wasn't the first time joual had been used on stage – in 1948, Gratien Gélinas had put similar words in the mouth of his character Tit-Coq – but it was the first time joual sounded that raw, that real. In Quebec, where middle-class theatre-goers were more used to seeing French-style boulevard comedies and Molière revivals, the reaction was predictable and swift: *Les Belles-Soeurs* was hailed as either a masterpiece or the most abominable atrocity ever to hit the boards.

Ever since, Tremblay has been responding to accusations that, by enshrining joual in literary texts, he's forever debased the quality of Québécois French. When a passage from one of his plays was included in a provincial high school exam recently, some teachers protested against being forced to expose their students to the very *sacres* they'd spent all year forbidding. "For these people, the ultimate argument is always, 'We're not about to show our children that we speak joual,'" says Tremblay, rolling his eyes. "As if the theatre existed to give French lessons! It's completely ridiculous. The people of France didn't speak in alexandrines in Racine's time, and not everybody speaks in joual today. I'm a witness to my epoch, and I reserve the right to repeat what I hear."

For Michel Tremblay, joual, with all its anglicisms and slurred pronunciations, is a part of the cultural history of Quebec. "When the peasants left the countryside to come to work in Montreal at the end of the nineteenth century," he explains, "the factories belonged to the English. The men would come home from work with all these English words. But the women, who tended to go to school a little longer than the men, wanted to remain francophone, so they created these magnificent neologisms by translating English words into French." For example, "the word for outdoor toilets, backhouses, was adapted into *bécosses*." As in the case of the earliest colonists in New France, "it's thanks to these women that we still speak French," says Tremblay. "I find it atrocious that anyone can claim to judge these people, and then go on to say that our entire society speaks poorly."

In the century of James Joyce's *Ulysses*, when Scottish authors such as Irvine Welsh and James Kelman can write Booker Prize–nominated novels composed in Scots (a sometimes impenetrable variant of working-class English), it should be obvious that literary masterpieces can be crafted out of even the most ungrammatical local vernaculars. Two decades after *Les Belles-Soeurs* was vilified by Montreal's francophile bourgeoisie, the play opened in Glasgow, translated from joual into Scots as *The Guid Sisters*. Tremblay was heralded as "the greatest playwright that Scotland never had" by the Manchester *Guardian*. "It was the first time that a play had been performed in Scots on the stage in Glasgow," marvels Tremblay. "The next day, the polemic in the newspapers was exactly the same. I could have been in Quebec 20 years earlier." In both cases, the negative reaction was a good barometer of a society's insecurities. The loudest protestors had been the kind of provincial elitists who like to consider their compatriots' vernacular a debased pidgin, and Oxford English or Parisian French the only valid norms. "To forget oneself, one's origins, just to please other people – I find that terrible," says Tremblay. "As long as Québécois literature was just an imitation of French writing, France wasn't interested in us. As soon as we began to give up this self-colonization, as soon as we started to resist, then they started to get interested." By then, of course, serious artists in Quebec no longer needed to look compulsively over their shoulders at France.

Three decades of defending joual have left Tremblay a little weary of the whole topic. His latest novels and plays have a variety of levels of language, and if some of his characters still say "chus" and "coudonc," others are just as comfortable with the imperfect of the subjunctive. "If, in writing *Les Belles-Soeurs*, I'd wanted to impose joual as some kind of national language," he sighs, "I would have been the worst asshole imaginable. I did it as a homage to the women who raised me." Tremblay is obviously looking forward to nursing his cold among the palm trees in Key West. I can't resist teasing him – fully aware of my status as a recently arrived Anglo – that anyone who spends five months in Florida is no longer one hundred per cent Québécois. "I hate it when people say that," he snaps, as if he's heard the reproach once too often. Ah well: a lifetime spent juggling the contradictions of being a nationalist *enfirouâpé* would make anyone a little touchy.

When a businessman from the City overhears a ticket agent in Paddington Station saying, "I already told you what bleedin' time it is, din't I?" he's unlikely to interpret this jargon as a sign of the imminent decline of the English language. And yet in Quebec, where joual is no more the linguistic norm than cockney is in England, ungrammatical speech still provokes endless teeth gnashing about the quality of the French language. Critics point to the 21 per cent of the population unable to decipher or compose a paragraph – the highest illiteracy rate of any province in Canada – as a sign of Quebec's linguistic marginalization. But this is a fast-fading demographic phenomenon. Since Quebec has had a widespread secular educational system only since the fifties, most functional illiterates are older people born when schooling was one of French Canada's lowest priorities.

Today, the Québécois are better educated than they've ever been. A growing elite of intellectuals, artists, and academics maintains a level of public discourse that, at its best, is as sophisticated as any in the francophone world.

And yet the critics of the quality of Québécois French persist, and they're taken as seriously as they were in the days of Frère Untel. Georges Dor, the most outspoken and persistent of these critics, is the author of a series of slim volumes that itemize the ongoing degeneration of the French language in Quebec. A singer and songwriter, his first linguistic essay was called *Anna braillé ène shot* (freely translated, "Anna bawled a lot"); the second was *Ta mé tu là?* (Or *Ta mère, est-elle là?* The equivalent in much of North America would be: "Yo' ma 'round?") After the appearance of the first volume, which execrated Québécois teenagers, newscasters, and sales clerks for tortured syntax, garbled pronunciation, and limited vocabulary, a team of academics shot back with a succinct rebuttal. According to linguist Marty Laforest and some of Quebec's most distinguished phoneticians and lexicographers, most of the abominations that Dor highlighted as deviations from Parisian French are in fact long-established historical characteristics of the language in Canada. For every teenager in Laval who says "chus" instead of "je suis," there's one in a Parisian suburb who says "chuis"; and if the Québécois are rather free with their "tu"s and "tway"s, it's because North American society is, in general, far less rigid than hidebound Europe.

In the third, and what he promises is the last, volume of the series, Dor has responded with an impressive roundup of 504 punctiliously numbered grammatical slips, culled from such television networks as TVA, TQS, and even the venerable Radio-Canada. It's a catechism of solecisms; taken together, they suggest that the French language in Quebec is in the hands of half-educated hicks who can barely babble a coherent thought. In the kitchen of his suburban home on the flats of Longueuil, a short metro ride south of downtown Montreal, I suggest to Dor that Parisian radio and television stations are also chock full of such abominations. He disagrees. "I watch the news from Switzerland, Belgium, and France on TV5 every day," he replies, "and I've never heard such syntactic horrors." True, I point out, but the French-language satellite network broadcasts only the top-line newscasts; smaller European stations, not available in Quebec, have their share of grammatical bloopers and gaffes. Dor isn't easily fazed. He

reminds me of a linguistic Napoleon in plaid house slippers – an association heightened when he jabs his hand into his black cardigan, rivets his
gaze on the middle distance, and launches into one of his monologues.
"The reproach that I make is that we Québécois suffer from a linguistic
laziness that reflects a broader intellectual laziness. Why should we refuse
the idea that we can improve ourselves?"

After all, Georges Dor himself has made the effort. Though he never
attended university, he now expresses himself in a grammatical, sonorous
French that betrays little trace of his working-class youth in Drummondville.
His experience as a songwriter in the sixties – he wrote Félix Leclerc–type
folksongs about lonely workers on northern dams – has left him with the
kind of rich, tobacco-scraped voice you'd expect to hear in a Left Bank
coffee house. "When the obsession with joual started in the sixties, some
people discovered a certain liberty of expression," he says, between puffs on
the Player's Filter wedged between the clenched fingers of his right fist. "A
liberty that soon gave way to self-indulgence and carelessness." For Dor,
writers such as Michel Tremblay made it acceptable to possess a limited
vocabulary and shaky syntax. "What bothers me is that people here aren't
able to express themselves in their own language, the French language.
They'll say 'c'est le fun!' but they can't explain what they mean by that.
There's also the question of mumbling. I call it our local *meneu-meneu*." He
believes that, though more people now go to university, standards in academia have fallen – as have standards in all areas. "This linguistic decay is
just the reflection of the decay of our society," he concludes, slamming the
table. "It's the refusal of all rules."

It's easy to dismiss the diatribes of Georges Dor and his ilk as the stodgy,
insecure rants of a certain generation of self-taught elitists, proud of a personal culture gleaned from a Paris that was the source of the only acceptable linguistic norm. After all, a Québécois who asks "Al a dzit ssa à tway?"
("Elle a dit ça à toi?") is using a regional pronunciation – one in vogue in
France in the seventeenth century – that's no more incorrect than a New
Englander who tells you she's from Baaaaston. Parisians complain that,
with all its diphthongs and *dzi*s and *tsi*s, Québécois French sounds like the
buzzing of a cheap, bashed-in car speaker. But then, Parisians say a lot of
things. They damn the Swiss and Belgians as being witless because of their
drawling speech, and automatically mock anyone with a Provençal, Breton,

or Picard accent who has the temerity to appear on a nationally televised game show. Meanwhile, many Québécois will now tell you that they can't stand the way the Parisians speak: the French accent sounds *pointu* to them (pointy or sharp) and it's really just too *cul de poule*. In other words, the French clip their vowels and purse their lips like a chicken's ass. Which only goes to show: an accent is just something the other person has, and a language – whether the Received Pronunciation of London or Île-de-France French – is merely a local dialect that has succeeded.

There's one point that all parties, from the *joualisant* Michel Tremblay to the francophile Georges Dor, agree on: the English language has had far too much influence on Québécois French, and for far too long. "One part of joual that I've always refused to use in my plays," Tremblay told me, "are those pointless anglicisms like 'j'ai ronné.' I always found that really stupid. If you're going to say 'I ran,' say it right: 'j'ai couru.'" The French of Quebec, even after the passage of language laws, is riddled with English and American terms, and in a way that's far more pernicious than in Paris, where people pick and choose from a small set of chic anglicisms.

Here's how it works. At an electronics shop in Montreal, a clerk diagnoses my defective CD player and writes on the repair slip, "Quand on presse sur open, ça fait un bruit weird." (In Paris, that would have been, "Quand on appuie sur 'ouverture,' ça fait un drôle de bruit.") At my gym, in a French-speaking part of the Plateau Mont-Royal, the weightlifters help each other out with "un spot pour le bench-press," enter their "weight in pounds" on an American-made stair-climbing machine, and listen to an English-language hard rock station. At a Blockbuster Video outlet, I overhear a francophone clerk explaining to two teenage clients, also French-speaking, that, in the dubbed film they're about to rent, actor Kevin Spacey "est framé" for a crime he didn't commit. When I ask whether the English "to be framed" could be replaced by "être victime d'un coup monté," he nods and looks a little abashed. "Terrible, non?" he says from behind his cheek microphone. "I've been working in anglophone neighbourhoods for eight years now. When I go back to Quebec City, my mother thinks it's awful that I can't remember the French words for anything."

This insidious linguistic interference is no longer a one-way street. Quebec is one of the few places on the North American continent where native English-speakers undergo the significant structural influence of a second language. It may not be surprising that an Anglo musician would stop by the *dep* (the *dépanneur* or corner store) and the *caisse populaire* (credit union) before going to jam at the *local* (an office or practice space). English-speaking Italians in the St-Léonard neighbourhood have long been setting off *patows alla masse* (firecrackers by the ton, from the French terms *pétard* and *en masse*), telling each other to close the lights (after the Québécois *fermer les lumières*), and putting *salad* in their *sangwiches* (the former is French Canadian for lettuce, the latter pure Montreal Italian). Since the passage of Bill 101, anglophone Quebecers have been living and working in a French environment, and they're starting to show the kind of scars their francophone neighbours have long borne. As the Oxford *Guide to Canadian English Usage* emphasized, it wouldn't be unusual for a Montreal Anglo to say "the choice of that animator was really determinant for the global success of the congress." What he means is that the conference's organizer had a decisive impact on its overall success, but a number of similar French words, prevalent in the day-to-day office environment, got in the way. I recently received a blank stare from a visitor from New York when I said I'd "go pay our note at the caisse." It took me a second to find the right words: I was taking the bill to the restaurant's cashier. There's nothing like the queasy unease that comes when you notice your vocabulary is slowly being replaced by another tongue. You begin to suspect that, day by day, word by word, someone is pilfering your very identity.

The francophones of Quebec have been experiencing this subtle soul-snatching since the Conquest. In *L'Homme rapaillé*, the late nationalist poet Gaston Miron described being stuck in a traffic jam on a highway in the Laurentian Mountains in 1955 and noticing that all the signs were word-for-word, unidiomatic translations from the English: GLISSANT SI HUMIDE came directly from SLIPPERY WHEN WET, and PARTEZ AU VERT was the equivalent of GO ON GREEN. He called such botched half-language *traduidu*, and saw it as the symbol of Quebec's linguistic marginalization. "I experienced a strange malaise," he wrote. "In this instantaneous, colonial bilingualism, I no longer knew how to recognize my signs, to recognize that they weren't really French. This rupture, this becoming a stranger to one's own language without realizing it, is a form of alienation." For Miron, a committed nationalist, the only hope for regaining some linguistic integrity lay in a definitive, political separation from Canada.

All languages borrow words, of course. The richest, most widespread languages can do it with impunity, only becoming richer in the process. But French is no longer the most prestigious tongue in a Europe-centred world, and the periodic attempts of francophones to purge themselves of English terms are generally perceived as a laughable manifestation of paranoid protectionism. Chantal Bouchard, a McGill sociolinguist who has studied the history of anglicisms in French, believes that though both Quebec and France started appropriating English words at about the same time, they tend to use them in completely different ways. "In France," says Bouchard, "they started borrowing from English in the eighteenth century, and the words tended to be fashionable terms, used by the most chic society. These days, it's in television, journalism, advertising that people borrow, mostly from the American." Hence, Marcel Proust would have written of a *snob* in a *smoking* (a tuxedo), riding to a Norman resort in a *wagon-lit* (a sleeping car); a contemporary French author would write a *best-seller* about a *self-made-man* and a *cover-girl*. "In Quebec, on the other hand," says Bouchard, "we tend to use English words for the day-to-day things, the completely prosaic material objects." While the French put their anglicisms in italics, the Québécois have left them in Roman characters, integrating them seamlessly into the language.

It's a dangerous practice. At the exact time the North American industrial boom put consumer goods (usually labelled in English) on French-Canadian shelves, millions of farming families migrated to the cities to work in English-owned factories. There are thousands of legacies of this bastardized language, what Miron called *traduidu*: a restaurant called Le Ranch du Spaghetti near the Vermont border, the signs on construction sites that read PAS D'ADMISSION SANS AFFAIRE (NO ADMISSION, EXCEPT ON BUSINESS). A recent survey of five major dictionaries produced a total of 4,227 distinct anglicisms in Québécois French. The world of the automobile in particular is deeply, nefariously anglicized. If your Econoline *vanne* happens to *faire un flat* on Autoroute 20, you'd better put on your *flasher*, *pull over*, and *jacker* the *tire*. Even the term *char* (in France, a centuries-old word denoting a horse cart) probably persisted in Quebec because of its similarity to the English "car." The same goes for *barbier* (barber), *coquerelle* (cockroach), and *itou* (me too), all archaic words that have survived thanks to English homonyms.

Such non-stop linguistic interference eventually makes people doubt their own words. "It ends up making the Québécois insecure about their own language," laments Bouchard. "We never know if the word that immediately comes to mind is really French or an anglicism that's been more or less masked by some kind of phonetic assimilation." The only consolation for Bouchard, and it's a small one at best, is that the French themselves are beginning to do the same. I talked to the linguist in Paris, where she's been spending an agreeable sabbatical year. "I've been here for five months now," she says, "and it's astounding how many anglicisms I hear. The French are starting to adapt English words into French morphology, just like we've been doing in Quebec for a long time. The other day, I heard that a certain actress was *coaché* [coached] by someone and that a rock group had just *splitté* [split up]. I must say I'm impressed," adds Bouchard, with a touch of sarcasm. Apparently, there's hope for the French yet.

The people of Quebec are crazy about dictionaries. In the province's bookstores, you can buy slapdash glossaries of joual, repertories of anglicisms (and ways of eliminating them), and nine-volume etymological concordances of the entire French language. The standard works tend to be twice as expensive as comparable editions of *Oxford* or *Webster's*; a three-volume boxed set of the paperback *Petit Robert* – perfect for Noël! – costs $94.95 at the Montreal bookstore Champigny. The lexicons published in Paris – *Le Petit Robert*, the *Hachette*, or the *Larousse* – cater to francophiles, lovers of Piaf, admirers of de Gaulle. Locally published dictionaries, such as the *Dictionnaire québécois d'aujourd'hui* or the *Dictionnaire du français plus*, are created by and for the so-called *aménagistes*, those in favour of a linguistic norm defined in Quebec (from the word *aménager*, to convert or adjust). These days, purchasing a dictionary in Quebec is a political act: it's a statement about whether the buyer sees herself as the speaker of a marginal dialect in a Paris-centred universe or an equal player in a varied, multi-polar francophone world.

At Montreal's Salon du livre, the annual book fair in the Grand Central Station–scaled Place Bonaventure, thousands of people are queuing in front of numb-wristed authors who are giving up a Saturday afternoon to sign everything from Belgian adult comics to ice-storm souvenir books. On one side of the cavernous hall, a couple of dozen people have gathered to hear a debate provoked by the launching of the latest Québécois dictionary, a scholarly etymological effort called the *Dictionnaire historique du français québécois*. The dictionary's creator, the dogged Laval University linguist Claude Poirier, is clearly on the side of the *aménagistes*, in favour of establishing a Quebec-centred lexicon. Curly-haired, straight-backed Marie-Éva de Villers, the creator of the popular *Multidictionnaire de la langue française*, is a notorious francophile – she's the scourge of *sacres*, anglicisms, and joual and a partisan of a norm that leans towards France. Through her involvement with the Office de la langue française and the editorial boards of leading magazines, this woman has had an inordinate influence on the way the people of Quebec speak and write French. Michel Therrien, the underdog seated between a Laurentian wolf and a Parisian poodle, is an author of grammar manuals and a former president of the provincial association of French teachers. He desperately wants to find a dictionary that will help him do his job here in Quebec.

The accusations fly: Poirier reproaches de Villers for putting disparaging labels such as "emploi fautif" or "anglicisme" on terms that have been common in Quebec (but not France) for centuries. "I'm not saying her dictionary is bad," he barks. "There's lots of good things in it. But the philosophy is unrealistic. When Madame de Villers talks about words that the Québécois use every day, they're always labelled separately. Unlike her, I don't consider the French of Quebec suspect." With measured tones, de Villers responds: "I don't necessarily think that Québécois words are suspect. But earlier dictionaries weren't accepted by the public because they inserted doubtful words, which belong only to the spoken language. For example, *lastique* [a slang term for elastic band] isn't really a word. It's of no use to include it." Finally, Therrien, the proofreader, can't stand the interminable dogfight anymore. "What about the word *souper*?" he asks. In Quebec, it's what everyone calls the evening meal, but in French dictionaries such as *Le Robert* – where the word *dîner* is preferred – it's dismissed as a regional usage. "It's a word our ancestors used," insists Therrien, "and the word the majority of Québécois use today. When we're creating a dictionary, do we have to justify ourselves for giving the Québécois meaning? It's the end of the nineties, and unfortunately, we're still obliged to buy several different dictionaries in order to find the words we hear in Quebec every day. Personally, I think that's unacceptable."

Neither of the lexicographers can account for the martyred dictionary-user's simple observation: at the turn of the century, there is no single work that describes the French language in Quebec. Hence, there is no recognized standard reference for Québécois French – and in the absence of a reference, schoolchildren and teachers turn to Paris-based dictionaries that exclude many of the 10,000 distinctly French-Canadian additions to the French language. The closest thing to an inclusive, descriptive dictionary of contemporary French in Quebec is the *Dictionnaire québécois d'aujourd'hui*, a college-level work first published in 1992 by the publishers of Paris-based *Le Robert*. It had only one real flaw: the editors deliberately decided not to label expressions that were particular to Quebec. They argued that since Parisian dictionaries didn't specify that champagne was French, why should they note that the traditional alcoholic drink caribou was Québécois? Such misguided political correctness is of no use to a teenager, who might be curious to learn that nobody from France, Haiti, Belgium, Switzerland, or Mali will have a clue what she's talking about when she refers to her boyfriend as a *chum*, rather than a *copain*. But for the critics, this was only a detail. The 40,000-word descriptive dictionary was violently torn apart for other, far more revealing reasons.

"We were attacked for including three words," says Jean-Claude Boulanger, the chief lexicographer of the ill-fated Québécois *Robert*. "The first was *astheur*, which means 'now.' The second was *tsé*, which means 'you know.' And the last was *coudon*, a reduction of *écoute donc*, which means something like 'look here.' People said these words didn't exist." In fact, you only need to read a half-dozen pages of any Michel Tremblay play and you'll come across all three. The most virulent attack came from an editorial in *L'actualité*, which accused Boulanger of attempting to create a new language, Québécois. "Ironically," points out Boulanger, "*L'actualité* is probably the most interesting magazine around for spotting *québécismes*. Jean Paré's article" – the magazine's editor excoriated Boulanger's dictionary in a scathing column – "contains at least 10 terms unique to Quebec. In other words, without the Québécois *Robert*, it would be impossible to decode *L'actualité*."

I have to agree with Boulanger. I find his dictionary useful precisely because it includes non-standard French usages such as *tabernacle* and *chum*. (If he'd stuck a little fleur-de-lys beside such *québécismes*, it would have been perfect.) As vulgar or English-derived as these terms may be, I read them in novels, hear them on the streets and on the radio. They exist. A dictionary that prescribes some idealized mid-Atlantic French, rather than describing the linguistic community around me, is useless. "Madame de Villers's dictionary says that we shouldn't use archaic terms," points out Boulanger. "Archaic? They're only archaic from the point of view of the French. I'm sorry, but when I go to Canadian Tire and pick out a *godendart*" – the Québécois term for a cross-cut saw – "I'm not buying an archaism. It's a perfectly contemporary word in Quebec." The same goes for anglicisms, sternly censured in most corrective dictionaries. "Some anglicisms are negative," acknowledges Boulanger, "but others have been a positive contribution to the development of the language. A phrase like 'La strappe du fan est lousse' is full of anglicisms, but it's a grammatically acceptable sentence in Québécois French. The fact is, we can't create a dictionary in Quebec without acknowledging the British part of our history."

I tell Boulanger that I'd be willing to buy a future edition of the *Dictionnaire québécois d'aujourd'hui*, but he says I'm unlikely to see one soon: the media feeding frenzy killed any hope of a third edition. "I now know the francophone world well enough," says Boulanger, "to say that the worst judges of Québécois French are the Québécois themselves – in particular those who swear by some kind of idealized international French that doesn't actually exist." An effort is currently underway at the Université de Sherbrooke, led by Pierre Martel and Hélène Cajolet-Laganière – the leading *aménagistes* – to establish a database of texts that will lead to a descriptive dictionary of French as it's spoken in Quebec. I'm not holding my breath: they say the project will take about five to 10 years, and it's already hobbled by as many objections from francophiles as Boulanger's *Dictionnaire québécois d'aujourd'hui*.

In the meantime, there's little doubt that Quebec's linguistic norm is changing rapidly. Since the seventies, the women of Quebec have been insisting on the feminization of their job titles, so that one now visits a highly recommended *docteure*, reads a popular *auteure*, and addresses

Madame as *la ministre*. (In France, the virtually all-male Académie still maintains that *docteur*, *auteur*, and *Madame le ministre* are the only acceptable forms.) That's not to say that everyone here now speaks like a bland Radio-Canada announcer; instead, there's an increasing consciousness of different levels of language. These days, someone weary of Céline Dion's ubiquity might moan to friends, "'Stie, chus tanné d'entendre les tounes de Céline en tout et partout." But he's also capable of switching registers, explaining to a Parisian in the same bar that "J'en ai marre de toujours entendre ses chansons."

Since 1828, Americans have been able to look up "dude" or "greenhorn" in *Webster's*, and English Canadians can confidently seek out "pogey" or "chinook" in the *Gage* dictionary. Hell, you can even find "shitkick" and "fuck that noise" in the latest *Canadian Oxford*, duly labelled coarse slang, North American. English-speakers have long accepted different geographical and cultural norms, and the Anglo-American lexicographical tradition tends to put the emphasis on describing the language as it's spoken and written. "I find that Canadian anglophones and francophones have intrinsically different attitudes," says Katherine Barber, editor-in-chief of the new *Canadian Oxford Dictionary*, launched with great success in 1998. "We don't have the problem with joual, for example. There's nothing analogous to anglicisms, all the things that cause people's hackles to rise in Quebec. And we certainly don't have their tradition of corrective dictionaries" – like de Villers's *Multidictionnaire* – "which are more like usage guides, written by fogeys."

On the contrary, "English Canadians are very interested to find out what's unique to their vocabulary," points out Barber. "It's not just knowing that one shouldn't say 'chesterfield' when in the United States. For us, it's a great affirmation of our culture and uniqueness, whereas traditionally, there's been this mindset in Quebec that if it's Quebec French, it's inadequate, or dialectical, or just not good French. They've been subjected to this attitude by English Canadians as well. How many times have you heard people say, 'Oh, I don't want to learn that Quebec French; it's just a dialect. I speak Parisian French.' And then they'll speak the most fractured, awful French you can imagine." As arrogant as we can be about the fortuitous political success of our language, at least English-speakers have long resisted top-down linguistic legislation and norm-setting. The French passion for setting up elaborate systems of rules, so apparent in Quebec's Civil Code, unfortunately also extends to that most organic of systems, language. In France, such an attitude is embodied by the Académie française, whose lifelong members are writers and scholars. In Quebec, the terminologists of the Office de la langue française, a vast bureaucracy, fill the same function – a situation that should make any sane person shudder.

I'm in what, for William Johnson and Howard Galganov, is undoubtedly the belly of the beast. For these outspoken defenders of anglophone rights, the Office de la langue française (OLF) headquarters, in a dignified brick building on Montreal's Rue Sherbrooke, can only be the equivalent of the Orwellian Ministry of Love. It's here, in the Room 101 of their nightmares (*'Scusez, Salle 101*), that they're tortured until they can conjugate the pluperfect of the verb *comprendre*.

Actually, it's a rather pleasant setting for the linguistic enforcement branch of what Johnson and Galganov would have the world believe is a totalitarian regime. The OLF has recently changed digs, moving from a downtown office tower into the turn-of-the-century neoclassical edifice, the former École des beaux-arts. Huge skylights pour sunlight over the cubicles of the bureaucrats, and there's a view of stately Rue Sherbrooke townhouses from the corner offices. There is a kind of desecration here, however. In the corridors where bohemian artists such as Fernand Leduc and Paul-Émile Borduas dreamt up the tenets of the *Refus global* manifesto, brittle little women with pinched mouths and fat dossiers now clatter over the tiles.

Gérald Paquette, a slick, stocky communications man in a double-breasted suit, keeps me waiting half an hour and then ushers me into a conference room. With felt marker in hand, he hurriedly outlines the various provisions of Bill 101 and the history of the Charter of the French Language. Bourassa's Liberals made French the official language of the province in 1974, in both government and commerce; the Charter was introduced by the Parti Québécois three years later. English and other languages were banned from exterior signs, and the public face of Quebec rapidly became almost completely French. In 1993, the Supreme Court of

Canada declared that certain provisions of the provincial legislation were in violation of the federal Charter of Rights and Freedoms, thus making it legal for signs in shops and businesses (but not public institutions) to be bilingual. As long as French is "markedly predominant" – Paquette underlines the words on the board – shops can now display signs in English. This means that the French characters must be twice as big as the English – hence the cliché of the OLF inspector combing the streets for offending signs with a ruler and notepad in hand. Paquette says fines range from $250 for a first offence to $7,000 for a particularly recalcitrant recidivist, though he's never seen the maximum penalty imposed.

I go over a few of the more notorious horror stories, some of which have been resentfully catalogued in the Montreal *Gazette* and Mordecai Richler's book *Oh Canada! Oh Quebec! Requiem for a Divided Country*. What about the pet shop owner who received a complaint that he was selling an English-speaking parrot? "That never happened," says Paquette. "We never received a complaint." The OLF's demand that a Jewish cemetery change its tombstones from Hebrew into French? "That was an April Fool's joke," he shoots back, "by a local radio station. The story made page one of the *Gazette*; our denial was buried on page 17." In that case, what about L. Berson & Fils Monuments, whose tombstone business on Boulevard St-Laurent was the object of a complaint about a 50-year-old sign whose Hebrew characters were larger than the French? "We did receive a complaint about that," allows Paquette, one of the between five and six thousand complaints they receive over their snitch line every year. "We sent an inspector down to take a photo, and Mr. Berson, the owner, came out and saw him. Of course, the first thing he did was to call the *Gazette*. We dropped the whole thing, because we found it ridiculous: the Hebrew words weren't a commercial message, they were the name of the shop."

On the other hand, Paquette defends what I consider the OLF's more absurd nitpicking. A hospital in the Eastern Townships was forced to remove English signs that – alongside French equivalents – said RADIOLOGY and MAIN ENTRANCE, even though a quarter of its clientele was anglophone. "Article 29.1 of the Charter clearly states that, in the area of public administration, French is the only language of public display," he shrugs. I tell him that this can only be perceived as petty meddling. Old and infirm people deserve clear indications, particularly in a hospital, a setting where public health is at stake. "Language planning means we have to put some messages across," Paquette shrugs. "And the message we want to send to francophones is, in Quebec you can work and be served in French. Anglophones have the right to their own institutions, but they have to know that French is the language of public interaction in Quebec."

If that's the case, there appears to be a double standard. American-owned chains such as Dunkin' Donuts and McDonald's – the latter has 12,000 employees in Quebec – aren't required to remove their apostrophes, while the lowly delicatessen Schwartz's is forced to become Chez Schwartz. Where's the logic there? "Simple," says Paquette. "When it's a trademark, like Burger King or Red Lobster, we accept it, because trademarks are the responsibility of the federal government." In the interests of making French omnipresent in Quebec, the OLF also imposes a program of francization – conversion into French as the language of business – on companies with more than 50 employees. But certain corporations with Montreal head-quarters, boasts Paquette, including pharmaceutical giants Burroughs-Wellcome and Merck Frosst, benefit from special agreements that exempt them from the francization program, allowing them to conduct their inter-national trade in English. This fosters business in Quebec, concludes Paquette. Here's another conclusion. A craven bureaucracy has latched on to technicalities that exempt multinational fast-food chains and pill companies from provincial laws while still allowing them to kick around voiceless merchants in the Portuguese, Chinese, Jewish, and anglophone communities. For the Quebec government – to adopt a little business-speak – it's a win-win situation.

Gérald Paquette takes me upstairs, to the francization department. I'm introduced to François Grou, one of the 45 OLF inspectors who supervise the transition of companies to a French working environment. Grou, a pale, balding man in an eggplant-coloured suit, tells me in a creaky whisper about his work. He's had to respond to trivial complaints, forcing an entirely French restaurant to alter its cash register slip, because the date on the receipt happened to be printed in English. He's also had to ensure that aeronautics companies such as Rolls-Royce, with its thousands of engi-neers, make French-language software mandatory for their often anglo-phone workers. Grou acknowledges that people aren't always happy to see the OLF's inspectors: if he recommends that a company's francization licence be pulled, the company can be fined or prevented from obtaining contracts with the Quebec government. He believes in his work, however. "I think we absolutely had to undertake the francization of corporations in Quebec," he says. "If you no longer need a language to get a job, suddenly that language becomes much less important, and it's more likely to disappear."

Like most Québécois – and an increasing number of anglophone Quebecers – Grou believes two decades of heightened visibility of French have had largely positive results. Mechanics are starting to say "les pare-chocs" instead of "les bumpers," and parents are encouraged when they hear their kids clamouring for "le poisson-frites" instead of "le fish-and-chips." French-speakers describe the relief of walking through a primarily French streetscape. It's no doubt troubling for the anglophone residents of Montreal to realize that their cityscape is a palimpsest, with BOULEVARD RENÉ-LÉVESQUE inscribed over the Dorchester Boulevard of their child-hood. Elsewhere, it must have been galling for Cuban plantation oligarchs to watch the Holiday Inn become the Habana Libre, or the North African colonial elite to see the preposterous transformation of Avenue Anatole France into Avenue Anatole Alger. Unlike in Cuba and Algeria, however, in Quebec the alteration of street signs symbolizes what has mostly been a war of words, rather than fighting in the streets. It's likely that, if Bill 101 hadn't been adopted and enforced, frustrated francophones would have by now gained independence by any means available.

Perhaps because of vindictiveness or just a certain punctiliousness, excesses still occur. Quebec continues to be mocked for its penchant for insecure hypercorrection. A Parisian can order a *hamburger*, pull up to a *stop* sign, or cash a *traveller's cheque* on the *weekend*. In Montreal, one eats a *hambourgeois*, comes to a stop at the *arrêt* sign, and buys a *chèque de voyage en fin de semaine*. The OLF is often responsible for inventing these new words. A few such coinages, like *dépanneur* (corner store), have actu-ally been adopted. Most recommendations, however, are snubbed by a population that, strangely, seems to have a will of its own. The rather effete-sounding term *grimpette*, the OLF's recommended term for the hand-holds on telephone poles, was not surprisingly rejected by the manly world of the urban high-rigger. But in this highly regulated society, the OLF has genuine influence: all government agencies are required to use the terms they recommend. And the OLF has been known to persistently fax Montreal electronics shops with recommendations to change the term "surround sound" to *système ambiphonique*.

At its worst, such bureaucratic meddling is a denial of history. François Grou unintentionally gives me an example. The OLF attempts to establish a Quebec-based linguistic standard by maintaining a gigantic computerized database of three million terms. When new technology, or a new concept, rears its head as an English word, the OLF tries to knock it back, searching for an existing equivalent or creating a French neologism in its place. On the Internet, e-mail becomes *courriel*, shareware becomes *partagiciel*, and a "smiley" – the little typographical happy face of colons and brackets – is an *emoticon*. Grou recalls working as a terminologist for the OLF in Quebec City. "In Quebec, we always used to call the people who build houses *briqueleurs*," he says. Leaning forward, as if confiding a dirty secret, he whispers, "Well, we discovered that *briqueleur* came from the English term 'brick layer.' So we recommended the adoption of the word that's used everywhere in France." In other words, Quebec's masons, who have been calling themselves *briqueleurs* since at least the nineteenth century, have been officially rechristened. According to the government bureaucrats, they are forevermore *briqueteurs*. If the OLF took this logic to its xenophobic extreme, they'd have to eliminate the word *brique* as well. The French borrowed it from the Middle Dutch word *bricke* in the thirteenth century.

The French language will continue to survive in North America, and a judicious application of Bill 101 will undoubtedly help it thrive in Quebec. But if a distinctly Québécois linguistic standard is to emerge, one that could eventually be described in a useful descriptive dictionary, Quebec would be better off dispensing with bureaucrats as arbiters of language. It should also stop heeding the provincial fogeys who look to Paris for approval and justification. Quebec's North American history is an integral part of its identity and its future. The French in the New World couldn't describe their environment if it weren't for the Indian words *tabagane, manitou, sachem* – not to mention the native terms "Quebec" and "Canada" themselves. In turn, the New World couldn't get by without its French, from prairie to butte, from Baton Rouge to Detroit. To eviscerate Quebec of its English past, through an Orwellian attack on language, is to rip out its roots. As the linguist Philippe Barbaud has emphasized, "the anglicisms you hear in European French are merely glamorous. In Quebec, they're the very heart of the language."

Many of the apparently *pure laine* Québécois mentioned in this chapter are a product of the province's complex experience in the New World. Georges Dor, that francophile whose standard is Parisian French, is the grandson of an Irish immigrant from Limerick County. The great-grandmother of the creator of the unjustly maligned Québécois *Robert* dictionary, Jean-Claude Boulanger, was also Irish. The maternal grandmother of Michel Tremblay was a Cree from Saskatchewan. In other words, if you remove the British and the native from the Québécois family tree, you're not just trimming: you're defoliating with Agent Orange. Likewise, the purists and correctors who, with erasers and dictionaries, attempt to extirpate English from Québécois French – and along with it words such as *enfirouâper*, *trappeur*, and *briqueleur* – aren't heroically making up for past injustices. They're committing an unpardonable crime, here and now, against the French language as it has evolved in Quebec.

(5)

Meet the Presse

It was just another instalment in the saga of the Olympic Stadium, an ongoing penny dreadful that's been helping move newspapers in Quebec for three decades. The Olympic Installation Board had just tossed another $37 million into Quebec's most notorious money pit – an elephantine sports arena in Montreal's east end – this time to replace a Kevlar fabric roof that could never quite be fully retracted. Then 40 centimetres of snow fell on southwestern Quebec in a single day, a record for the month of January. Employees on the floor of the stadium, setting up the displays for the 1999 International Auto Show, were told not to worry about the festering abscess forming in the blue fabric of the roof over their heads. Finally the boil burst, sending the panicked workers scrambling down ladders and hopping over tables as tons of accumulated snow and slush tore through the fabric, crushing a Subaru display.

For Montreal, this was a run-of-the-mill story. The journalists at Quebec's daily newspapers had long become used to covering mishaps at the 1976-vintage megaproject, which had been known to shed 55-ton steel girders onto the infield during the Expos' baseball season. Reporters will probably be covering embarrassing stadium mishaps well into this century, making this the classic Quebec news event and a perfect opportunity to take the pulse of the province's print media. *La Presse*, Montreal's workmanlike French-language daily, heralded the news with colour photos taken inside and outside the stadium, beneath the 90-point banner headline "La toile se déchire" (The fabric tears). On the television-screen-like cover of *Le Journal de Montréal*, Canada's largest-circulation tabloid, a colour photo of snow pouring through the gaping hole was emblazoned with the screamer "Catastrophe Évitée de Justesse" (Disaster Narrowly Averted) in red capital letters. *Le Devoir*, a dour intellectual broadsheet, featured black-and-white photos of concerned-looking officials reading out communiqués. In the analysis that followed, the populist *Le Journal de Montréal* presented three pages of photos, as well as a chart that broke down exactly what the stadium had already cost the people of Quebec. The capital's determinedly provincial *Le Soleil* emphasized that the roof's architect hailed from Quebec City, and *Le Devoir* featured a signed front-page "Perspectives" column analyzing the significance of the event. Meanwhile, the Montreal *Gazette*, the one remaining English-language newspaper in a town whose anglophone community could once choose among three major dailies, phoned up a demolitions expert and asked him how much it would cost to blow the provincially managed stadium to kingdom come.

Montreal has always been a great newspaper town. At certain times in the sixties, the city topped New York, with 10 different papers slugging it out for domination of a fiercely competitive, bicultural market. Even in an era of increasing uniformity and concentration of ownership, Montreal is still more abundantly served with newspapers than more populous Toronto. On a typical Saturday afternoon, you can collect enough newsprint at a Maison de la presse internationale newsstand to start a dropcloth for the Sistine Chapel: there are three French-language dailies, the English-language *Gazette*, and four substantial cultural weeklies. What's more, Quebec as a whole is magazine-mad. More than 475 titles, from women's glossies such as *Elle Québec* and *Madame au foyer* to celebrity catchpennies with titles like *Échos-Vedettes* and *Riches et Célèbres*, are sold at 10,000 newsstands – as many as there are in all the other Canadian provinces combined. Nor are these just French equivalents of popular English-language titles: the media in Quebec is shot through with a disorienting blend of European and North American influences. In Quebec's kiosks, broadsheets like *Couac!* a conscious echo of Paris's satirical *Le Canard enchaîné*, and *Le Devoir*, which recalls France's *Le Monde*, vie for space with the raunchy true crime weekly *Photo Police*, a sensational crime tabloid clearly nourished by the purest *New York Post* gutter-press tradition.

Perhaps it's no surprise, then, that the province has been the launching pad for some of North America's great media magnates: the late Pierre Péladeau of Quebecor, Conrad Black of Southam-Hollinger, and Paul Desmarais of Power Corporation all founded their newspaper empires in Quebec. Journalism, once a route to social influence in a province where the upper echelons of business were monopolized by an anglophone minority, is now a well-paid glamour profession whose practitioners are firmly integrated into Quebec's star system. Claude Poirier, a columnist for the true crime tabloid *Allô Police*, who has acted as a hostage negotiator for the police dozens of times since the seventies, has attained the supreme consecration of celebrity in Quebec, making a walk-on appearance as the trenchcoat-clad Inspector Poirier on the staggeringly popular sitcom *La petite vie*. When Gaétan Girouard, the young host of the TVA network's Friday-night investigative journalism program *J.E.*, hanged himself from the ceiling of his home in a suburb of Quebec City, *Le Journal de Montréal* devoted five pages of coverage to analyzing every aspect of the suicide. Four days later, a 32-page special edition of the magazine *7 jours* – packed with interviews, homages, and full-colour photos of his family – appeared in every supermarket in Quebec. In English Canada, it's hard to imagine the passing of a Peter Mansbridge or an Allan Fotheringham eliciting such an outpouring of popular grief.

Nor would it be easy to find an Anglo-Canadian equivalent for the notoriety of Pierre Foglia. Three times a week, this foul-mouthed, highly literate curmudgeon rages and rhapsodizes on page A-5 of *La Presse*, with a licence and influence unimaginable in English-language newspapers. His columns are often 1,200-word masterpieces, peppered with fucks and *crisses*, usually elicited by some familiar brush with the local brand of human folly: an asleep-at-the-wheel driver who sends him slipping through a snowbank in the Eastern Townships, a grammatical error on a sign in rural Quebec, or the invasive presence of advertising panels above the urinals in Montreal universities. His byline will suddenly issue from Havana (where he observed, "Cuba's principal tourist resource seems to be Hemingway. They've erected a monument to him on every corner where he's known to have pissed. And since that jerk pissed everywhere . . ."). Or Baghdad ("If anyone was afraid, it wasn't me; it was the people I encountered. Afraid that I'd talk to them. Sure, Baghdad is dangerous: for the Iraqis"). Or post-Soviet Georgia ("as different from Russia as Chibougamau is from Italy. But the Georgians aren't like the Italians. They're worse: they're like Neapolitans. To give you an idea, this is the first place I've been since I left home where I found myself thinking, Hmm, I could get to like it here . . ."). It's travel journalism in the tradition of Albert Londres, the globe-trotting grand reporter of twenties France, executed with a caustic intimacy that makes the most exotic destination immediately accessible to Québécois readers.

But for all his charm, Pierre Foglia is also a cruel bastard. His early literary influences include the misanthropic French genius Louis-Ferdinand Céline and the alcoholic American postal worker Charles Bukowski, tough-talking loners who swung uncompromising, often abhorrent words like sledgehammers, as if to clear a space for themselves in a world they found hard to stomach. Foglia is a sworn enemy of the New Age, the politically correct, the multicultural; but his is not the knee-jerk conservatism of power-worshipping English-language columnists such as Barbara Amiel and Andrew Coyne. On the contrary, Foglia was a Marxist as a young man, and a friend of Pierre Vallières, the separatist theorist who penned *White Niggers of America*. When a letter to the paper's astrology section was accidentally stuck into his box at work, Foglia replied to a mother wondering about which direction her Libra son's career should take: "It matters little whether he orients himself towards folkloric dance (via the Drummondville Festival) or Mecca (second stoplight, to the right). The most important thing is that he removes himself as rapidly and as far as possible from a mother stupid enough to plan her son's future with a horoscope."

It's thus with trepidation that I approach Foglia in his office on the third floor of the *La Presse* building off Rue St-Jacques in Old Montreal. Walking past rows of desks, laid out like printer's formes on the chase of the newsroom floor, I absorb the atmosphere of the self-proclaimed "largest French daily in America." (This front-page slogan is apt only in terms of square inches. The weekday circulation of the tabloid *Journal de Montréal* – more accurately decked "the No. 1 French daily in America" – is almost twice as high.) It's the standard-issue, fluorescent-lit, big city newsroom, 1959 vintage, with the usual couple of dozen reporters and scores of empty desks, a scene that suggests break-time at some privileged sweatshop. Foglia, however, is removed from the hoi polloi, in an office of his own. His bosses, realizing he'd take tens of thousands of readers with him if he ever left *La Presse*, are rumoured to submit to his most extravagant whims.

Foglia is tall and lithe, with closely shorn, greying hair and the most negligent of wardrobes: burnished green corduroys are wrapped around powerful cyclist's thighs, and he's pulled a washed-out black track suit jacket over an untucked knit sweatshirt. Apart from a blue-ink caricature of Lucien Bouchard on a wall board, the office doesn't look particularly lived in – Foglia does most of his writing at home in the town of St-Armand, near the Vermont border. His obvious athleticism is mitigated by a drunken forest of teeth jutting out beneath a pair of John Lennon–style circular bifocals. He brings to mind the goofy, approachable college pro-fessor who immediately puts his students at ease – and then marks their papers so viciously they leave the course feeling like they've been throttled.

Foglia announces, right off the bat and à propos of nothing, "Me, I'm a bit of a separatist." There's a pause, and we exchange poker-faced stares. Once this unsolicited avowal is out of the way (for many baby boomers whose youth was spent in the ideological pressure cooker of the Quiet Revolution, this ice-breaker seems to be a matter of form), the conversa-tion can move on to more important things. Like, for example, has Foglia read any good books lately? Suddenly animated, he pulls a French transla-tion of Rohinton Mistry's *A Fine Balance* out of his backpack. "Have you read it? Millions of Americans are saying it's the best book they've ever read." I point out that the author is a Bombay-born Canadian, and that the novel was first published in Toronto. "He's a Canadian? *Tabarnac!*" says Foglia with what looks like consternation and surprise. I ask him if he's ever written fiction himself. "No. I'm not an artist," he replies quickly. "On the other hand, I've got a particular talent for writing short texts. But I've always needed the proximity of news, of information, in order to write." I ask him about his name, which he pronounces "Fol-lia." "My parents were Italian immigrants in France," he explains. "My mother was a housecleaner and my father was a bricklayer." Foglia himself started in journalism as a typographer in Paris before serving in France's brutal colonial war in Algeria. He emigrated to the New World in the early sixties to join his sisters in California but ended up marrying a woman from Quebec. "People think they know my whole life story," he observes, "because they've been reading my columns for 20 years. But what do they really know? They know that I've got a fiancée. They know that I've got cats. They know that I like to travel. They know that I ride a bicycle. But that's it! No more than they might know about one of their cousins. I never write anything very personal. Perhaps they know I've got a sister, who's stupid. But everyone's got a stupid sister – or brother-in-law."

Not everybody, however, gets to call his brother-in-law stupid in the pages of the "largest French daily, etc." In Quebec, Foglia's renown is such that if he casually mentions enjoying a translation of an obscure American detective novel, the head buyer at the bookstore Renaud-Bray orders copies by the dozen. An endorsement by Foglia can mean overnight cult success for a book in Quebec, or turn a family-run restaurant in the Laurentians into an instant hangout for the Montreal jet set. In a recent survey, he was the first of the handful of print journalists francophone Québécois could name spontaneously. One of Quebec's leading authors, Monique Proulx, dedicated a short story to him in her collection *Les Aurores montréales*. (Try to imagine Alice Munro, say, penning a tribute to *National Post* columnist David Frum.) In the story, a lovelorn suburban housewife is seduced by the power of a local journalist's style. "He was insolent and cruel," Proulx writes of the fictional scribe. "He had a way of expressing himself, without really saying anything, that inevitably left someone or something ruined in its wake." Her modern-day Madame Bovary invites the newspaperman to her home – a visit he endures with polite indifference – only to see herself viciously mocked in the following day's column.

"It didn't happen like that at all!" objects Foglia excitedly. One summer, he admits, in an attempt to get closer to the daily life of his readers, he appealed for invitations into their homes. "People did invite me, but most of them had only one thing in mind: to show me some manuscript they'd been working on. When that had happened four or five times, I said, '*Wô! Tabarnac!* This has to stop, right now!' But it wasn't true what Monique Proulx wrote. If she wanted to dedicate something to me, using my name, she should have at least respected certain facts." Foglia concedes, however, that his penchant for the massively authoritative ad hominem attack has caused him regret. After writing a devastating portrait of the tackier aspects of the Québécois tourist world in Miami, he was asked to lunch by the employee of a nearby bank. "She sat down and said, 'Monsieur Foglia, that was my mother and my father, the ones you called tacky. We saved our money to send them south – they'd never been farther than Longueuil in all their lives – and they were happy in Florida.'" Foglia assumes an air of contrition. "I realized that I could start treating people with a little more humanity. Maybe stop looking down on things from on high." No easy task, when you're more than six feet tall, a perfectionist, a lover of great litera-ture, and a world traveller. I ask which continent we can hope to see his dateline coming from next. "*Justement,*" he replies, eyes blazing, he's been talking about that with the boss. "I want to go do the Balkans. But not the Balkans as in the war zone. I'm thinking Romania. I'm thinking the Middle Ages, Moldavia, Bulgaria, the Black Sea, Prague, that kind of thing. With a knapsack on my back . . ." Picture a comic-book-cum-travelogue entitled *Tintin Goes to Timisoara* as drawn by Ralph Steadman, and you'll have some idea of what's in store for the readers of Quebec.

A phenomenon like Foglia – a highly influential journalist drawing on European and North American reportorial traditions – is hardly an anomaly in Quebec. From the start, journalism in francophone Canada was a blend of French and American sources. The first printing presses, banned in New France, had to be dispatched from Philadelphia by Benjamin Franklin, who saw them as propaganda tools of nascent American democracy in the monarchist north. William Brown, a Scottish-born American, founded the bilingual weekly *La Gazette de Québec* in 1764, and Fleury Mesplet, a printer from Lyons inspired by the iconoclastic writing of Voltaire, ran off the first copies of Montreal's *Gazette* in 1778. The journals that followed – 125 news-papers would appear before 1850, from the Patriotes' *Le Canadien* to the reformist *La Minerve* – were mostly short-lived, four-page bulletins affiliated with political parties or religious groups. Encouraged by improved postal service, rotary presses, and the telegraph, Hugh Graham's

1869 *Montreal Star* was the first Quebec newspaper to adopt the techniques of the modern city daily: the latest news off the wire, delivered the same day, sold for next to nothing.

A French-language equivalent was soon born in Trefflé Berthiaume's *La Presse*, which by the turn of the century was gleefully adopting the worst excesses of the yellow journalism practised by William Hearst's *New York Morning Journal* and Britain's Sunday papers: screaming headlines, spectacular illustrations of fires and train crashes, and an obsession with bloody murder. (An early coup involved ferrying a corpse to *La Presse*'s editorial offices to be photographed, and then returning it to the murder scene before the arrival of the police.) Condemned by the clergy for such Anglo-American excesses, *La Presse* nonetheless flourished. With a circulation of 150,000, it was reaching virtually every French-speaking household in southern Quebec by the end of the First World War.

Populist, American-inspired papers like the *Star* and *La Presse* never completely supplanted the nineteenth-century, European-inspired tradition of high-minded political and religious journalism. Quebec City's *Le Soleil*, created by Sir Wilfrid Laurier in 1880 as "the organ of the Liberal Party," only gradually became the hard-news daily it is today. *Le Devoir*, founded by Henri Bourassa in 1910 to further the interests of French Canadians, was from the start an anachronism, an old-fashioned tribune for high-minded pamphleteers and essayists, rooted in the Catholic faith (one editor-in-chief, André Laurendeau, spent most of the fifties feigning a recurring Sunday-morning migraine to hide his agnosticism). Bourassa labelled *La Presse* Montreal's "prostitute of the Rue St-Jacques" – which would have made his *Le Devoir* the Virgin of the Rue St-Sacrement – thereby creating the whore-Madonna dichotomy in the Quebec media that's never truly disappeared. Though the most influential francophone journalists owed much to the literary, polemical style current in France, many – including pioneers Olivar Asselin and Honoré Beaugrand – had learned the trade in the francophone communities of New England, early on developing a taste for scoops and hard news.

This tension between cold fact and hotly expressed opinion often pro- duced a kind of complacent stasis in the Quebec press. The situation was exacerbated in the postwar years by the muzzling of dissent during Premier Maurice Duplessis's 15-year autocracy. By the early 1950s, Quebec City

Press Gallery reporters would describe Duplessis's Friday-afternoon press conferences as virtual *dictées*; inaccurate transcribers could count on being expelled from the next week's session. The publisher of the *Star* was a friend of Duplessis and had been known to receive cartons with $100,000 in banknotes from the office of Le Chef before elections; thanks to such cronyism, society-shaking strikes in Quebec were virtually ignored. In a period when alcoholism was a valued prerequisite for a low-level career in journalism, $45-a-week reporters were happy to accept 20-buck bribes from the cronies of Montreal mayor Camillien Houde.

"It was a very Damon Runyon kind of world in Montreal," recalls Peter Desbarats, a career newspaperman and former dean of the University of Western Ontario's Graduate School of Journalism. "I started at the age of 17, with Canadian Press and the *Gazette* in the mid-fifties, during the dark Duplessis years. I learned all the wrong things about journalism back then," he chuckles. "I remember being pulled out of a car completely drunk at three o'clock one morning in Montreal by a cop. I whipped out my press pass" – a gesture that today would guarantee the bum's rush to the drunk tank in most cities – "and he ended up taking me around the corner and buying me a cup of coffee to make sure I felt all right."

As yeasty a milieu as Quebec could be for a cub reporter, it was hardly a haven for good investigative reporting. There were exceptions. The *Gazette*'s Jacques Francoeur (later the head of the UniMédia newspaper chain) wrote exposés of brothels and barbotte gaming houses that led to sweeping City Hall reforms. *Le Devoir*'s Gérard Pelletier covered the 1949 police-led bludgeoning of striking miners in the town of Asbestos, earning the paper Duplessis's undying enmity. Le Chef punished such betrayal by raising the price of newsprint or restricting lucrative government printing contracts. "The *Star* and the *Gazette* simply never criticized Duplessis," recalls Desbarats. "When I left Montreal to go to the Winnipeg *Tribune*, I discovered a totally different kind of journalism, one that was clean and competitive. I spent my first year covering the provincial legislature, looking for all the corruption. It took me a while to realize that Manitoba actually had a clean government."

By the end of the fifties, however, journalists began to train their flashbulbs on the murkier corners of the Great Darkness. In June 1958, *Le Devoir* broke the natural gas scandal story, accusing four of Duplessis's

Union Nationale ministers of netting $20 million speculating on Hydro-Québec's sale of its gas distribution network. The *Gazette*'s management finally made it official policy to stop accepting bottles of whisky in exchange for favourable coverage. In the pages of *Le Devoir*, editorialist André Laurendeau brazenly started referring to the premier as a "Negro king." With Duplessis's death in 1959, the journalists of Quebec seemed to shake themselves out of a long torpor (it was a journalist, *Toronto Star* correspondent Bob Mackenzie, who coined the term "Quiet Revolution" to describe the changes that swept French-Canadian society as a whole). Jean-Louis Gagnon remade the drab *La Presse*, opening bureaus in Lac St-Jean and Trois-Rivières, and even sent a journalist to Havana to provide first-hand coverage of Castro's anti-imperialist revolution.

The readers of francophone Quebec were briefly privileged with an unprecedented – and unrepeated – golden age of investigative reporting. In their style, Quebec's journalists of the late fifties and early sixties were anticipating the highly subjective New Journalism that would later take hold in the United States. *La Presse* editor Jean-Louis Gagnon took 30 of the paper's most enterprising journalists to found *Le Nouveau Journal,* a short-lived daily heavy on politically committed reporting. Many reporters so identified with the reforming goals of Jean Lesage's Liberals that they spent short spells working for the government, often as press secretaries or for the newly created Ministry of Education.

But the end of the union-busting Duplessis days also brought a series of crippling strikes, in which long-underpaid reporters turned their energy to improving their own lot in life. Over the next two decades, Quebec's newspaper landscape radically changed. At *La Presse*, the end of the century-long reign of the dynasty founded by Trefflé Berthiaume was preceded by the firing of the much-respected editor, Gérard Pelletier. The paper's 1967 buyout by Paul Desmarais, founder of the aptly named Power Corporation, has often been interpreted as a federalist takeover of a newspaper whose young reporters were becoming increasingly separatist. When *La Presse* management locked out typesetters a year after the October Crisis of 1970, 12,000 union members marched in solidarity with the striking pressmen, violently clashing with Montreal policemen. The Toronto-based owners of the *Montreal Star* – a paper long in serious denial about the rising power of francophones – decided to close shop. After an eight-month strike that saw traditional second fiddle the *Gazette* sweeping up tens of thousands of *Star* readers, the 110-year-old institution permanently locked its doors. Meanwhile, at least a half-dozen journalists had taken office in the Parti Québécois, among them Radio-Canada's Lise Payette, Québec-Presse veteran Gérald Godin, and *Le Devoir*'s Jean-Pierre Charbonneau. (Charbonneau was celebrated for writing a series of exposés of the Montreal Mafia in 1973, which inspired an associate of underworld chieftain Paolo Violi to walk into the newsroom and shoot him in the arm.) By the end of the seventies, the two most important political officers in the province were veterans of journalism: Premier René Lévesque was a former Radio-Canada foreign correspondent, and the Liberal opposition was led by long-time *Le Devoir* director Claude Ryan.

An unexpected consequence of the political and labour unrest among the serious dailies was the rapid and triumphant rise of the populist tabloid. Pierre Péladeau, the manic-depressive owner of a Montreal cabaret and a minor community weekly – and a Hitler admirer who kept a bust of Mussolini on his desk in the fifties – launched *Le Journal de Montréal* during a 1964 strike at *La Presse*. Péladeau's success depended on what he called his three-S formula: *sexe, sang* (the reporting of bloody crimes), *et sports*. *Le Journal* was an innovator in Canada: it steered clear of politics, boasted no editorial page, and included a bikini-clad pin-up seven years before the first Sunshine Girl graced the pages of the *Toronto Sun*. The real key to Péladeau's success, however, may have lain in his exemplary treatment of journalists. Aware that a metropolitan daily in search of readers couldn't afford a strike, Péladeau made sure that his reporters were the best paid in Canada. Higher wages attracted popular sports writer Jacques Beauchamp – and tens of thousands of his readers – from the rival *Montréal-Matin*, and Péladeau convinced both René Lévesque and Robert Bourassa to become occasional contributors. The 1971 lockout at *La Presse* made *Le Journal* the second-largest paper in the Montreal market, and a strike at *Le Soleil* six years later helped Péladeau establish a capital-city clone, *Le Journal de Québec*.

Péladeau didn't conjure his success out of the ether. Since the turn-of-the-century *La Presse* struck it rich with a sulphuric blend of sensationalism and muckraking, Quebec has been mining an apparently inexhaustible vein of yellow journalism. The fifties in particular were a golden age for the gutter press. Michael Rosenbloom, a St. Urban Street boy, transformed the sleazy weekly *Montreal Midnight* into a hugely successful tabloid in the Oprah Winfrey's Celebrity Sagittarius Diet genre. (With 1.1 million readers, the *Globe*, now based in Boca Raton, is the third most widely read supermarket tab in the United States.) It should come as no surprise, either, that the Canadian edition of *Hustler* magazine is published out of an office in St-Jérôme, Quebec. Today, for $1.99 a week, Québécois track the slightest moves of *vedettes* (stars) such as Roch Voisine, Céline Dion, and Kevin Parent in tabloids with names like *Allô-Vedettes*, *Show Biz*, and *Vedettes 2000*.

Also available at virtually every *dépanneur* in Quebec, next to the bags of rubbery cheese curds, are weekly newspapers that have no counterpart in the rest of North America. If you're looking for photos of illegal stills being hacked apart in Thetford Mines and amateur photos of root vegetables in the body orifices of Laval housewives, look no further than *Photo Police* ("Le No. 1"). If, on the other hand, you're interested in graphic shots of the bloated torso of a biker being fished out of the St. Lawrence River, or of the bloated chest of the fourth runner-up in the Miss Nude Canada contest, you might opt for *Allô Police* ("Le Vrai No. 1").

Regularly found in raids of Hells Angels clubhouses, diligently clipped by career criminals to add to bulging scrapbooks, the "judicial" tabloids are a parallel press with a long history in Quebec. Bound into volumes and stacked in the rare book department of McGill University, the leprous pulp paper of the first issue, from 1953, sets the tone. The jaggedly lettered *Allô Police!* logo emerges from the open mouth of a wide-eyed woman clutching a phone to her ear. Inside, the opening editorial solemnly promises that this newspaper will never become one of those "rags, often 'imported,' that delight in the shameless exploitation of the lowest instincts of humanity." The next issue opens with a photo of a woman lying on a morgue table, her throat rent by a gaping knife wound.

"Those macabre photos, phew," recalls Georges-André Parent, a 30-year veteran of *Allô Police* who got out of the business when the crime tab started its slide into down-market pornography. "As journalists, we were more than a little uneasy with that." Seated in front of a colour-coded map of Montreal, sporting a wrinkled long-sleeve shirt, a tie, and a salt-and-pepper mustache,

Parent looks more like a cop than a reporter. The impression is reinforced by the fact that we're sitting on the third floor of police headquarters, on the northern edge of Old Montreal. Parent has definitively crossed over to the other side, using his master's degree in criminology to become a salaried statistician for the city police's planning department. He started, however, as a $30-a-week reporter at *Montréal-Matin*, the now-defunct daily that was virtually the house organ for Duplessis's Union Nationale in the fifties. After being reprimanded for writing an unflattering story about a priest who kept a photo of Hitler next to the crucifix in his classroom and forced his students to shout "Heil Christ!" every morning, Parent decided in 1964 to take a slightly less thankless job at *Allô Police*. "It might sound pretentious, but at least at *Allô Police* we were doing a form of investigative journalism," he says. "If there was a murder somewhere out on the Gaspé Peninsula, I could hop in a car with a photographer and spend three or four days talking to the neighbours, the witnesses, the police. We were very free and very well paid."

It took official Church condemnation for *Allô Police* to became a true success. "In Rimouski, the bishop banned the newspaper," recalls Parent, "and they threw the distributor in jail for selling it." Sales shot up to 200,000 copies a week. "The Catholic hierarchy was saying, 'Ah Quebec! This beautiful land, chosen by God . . .' And here we were, saying, 'Yoo hoo! Look! There was a murder here! And another over there! Quebec has its bandits, criminals, and killers too.' They didn't want to admit that." With a staff of 20, *Allô Police* covered every murder in Quebec – all two dozen of them, in most years – with excruciating exactitude. Crime historians say it can be a more complete source of information than police archives (particularly if you want to know exactly how many feet the model's severed head rolled). Competition, first from Péladeau's *Journal de Montréal*, then from the seedier, sex-oriented *Photo Police* and tabloid television shows, finally started to gnaw at circulation. By the time Parent left for good in the mid-nineties, *Allô Police* was selling far fewer than the 100,000 copies it distributed to grocery stores and had taken to including centrefolds to boost circulation.

In other words, when the standard of the mainstream media drops to tabloid level, the raunchier tabloids are forced to lower their standards. (The trend is not limited to Quebec; the *National Enquirer*'s circulation has taken a significant hit since tabloid TV became a network staple.) Fortunately, there's always *Le Devoir*, the ever-suffering Virgin of the Quebec press, looking increasingly anemic among the raddled hussies beckoning from every newsstand. This is a newspaper whose pages have never been sullied by comic strips, crosswords, or Jo Jo Savard's Horoscope. With its black logo, sober layout, and near-absence of advertising, the 16-page weekday edition of *Le Devoir* might be mistaken for the pamphlets Marxist-Leninists hawk outside metro stations. With a Monday-to-Friday circulation of 26,000 and a cover price of a dollar, the paper that's long aspired to be a Québécois version of *Le Monde* now sells fewer copies than Chicoutimi's *Le Quotidien*. An editorial staff of only three dozen means that *Le Devoir* can no longer claim to cover the entire province or even most of Montreal. Nonetheless, when its reporters do tackle a topic, the standard of journalism is high; the editorial pages rarely pander; and the broadsheet's weekend cultural supplement and book review section is by far the best in the province.

As an elitist, independent cultural institution sworn to upholding the interests of French-Canadian Catholics in Canada, *Le Devoir* has been buffeted by the shifting currents of twentieth-century ideologies. Until 1940, its editorialists fervently fought against granting the women of Quebec the vote. They opposed Jewish immigration and supported fascist regimes in Europe during the thirties, and approved the anti-Semitic policies of Marshal Pétain in Vichy France. Then, after supporting Duplessis early in his reign, *Le Devoir* became a *journal de combat* under director Gérard Filion, covering strikes and corruption stories no other paper dared touch. Since the sixties, a largely separatist staff has worked under a variety of directors: the federalist Claude Ryan, the unconfirmed Benoît Lauzière, and until recently, the separatist intellectual Lise Bissonnette. The director of *Le Devoir* (once nominated by a board of shareholders, he or she becomes both editor and publisher and is granted 50.1 per cent of the shares and near-dictatorial powers) has always set the tone. Under Bissonnette, a talented if humourless editorialist, *Le Devoir* regained some of the moral authority it had lost in the eighties, becoming the only major daily to support separation in the 1995 referendum. Three years later, however, Bissonnette stepped down, amidst muttering about patronage, to accept the top job at Quebec's new Bibliothèque nationale from friend and Parti Québécois cultural minister Louise Beaudoin.

In its current incarnation, under the direction of former managing editor and 25-year veteran Bernard Descôteaux, *Le Devoir* is wan and thin. "Yup, *Le Devoir*'s looking pretty feeble these days," agrees Konrad Yakabuski, a young *Toronto Star* veteran and *Globe and Mail* correspondent who worked as the social-justice reporter during Bissonnette's reign. We're sitting in Yakabuski's office in the *Globe*'s Quebec bureau, on the eleventh floor of a downtown Montreal tower. It's clear that I've stumbled into an outpost of multicultural, urban English Canada: the ethnic mix in the *Globe*'s offices overwhelms the uniformly French-Canadian newsrooms of *La Presse* and *Le Devoir*.

Yakabuski himself is of Polish and Irish descent, a small-town Ontario boy who fell in love with Quebec and mastered French through sheer force of will ("It was sort of an obsessive thing"). Keeping one eye on the television above his desk (tuned to the French news network RDI), he says, "You have to understand that *Le Devoir* has been kept alive by institutions of Quebec, Inc., like the Mouvement Desjardins, the Quebec Federation of Labour's Solidarity Fund, and Quebecor. It's received a lot of charity, and its board is made up of former Hydro-Québec employees and chairmen." Nonetheless, reporters, including Yakabuski, were shocked when Lise Bissonnette announced she was hiring an environmental reporter whose $50,000 salary would be paid by Hydro-Québec. The reporters' union attacked the sponsorship as an attempt to buy favourable coverage; in the wake of the controversy, the subsidy was never received. "A lot of people felt that Bissonnette was very vindictive in how she reacted," recalls Yakabuski. "She withdrew the privilege from *Le Devoir* reporters – which is still very common in Quebec journalism – to take paid trips as long as you declare the sponsorship." For some, it raised questions about whether, in an increasingly corporatist society, a newspaper funded by corporate welfare can truly be considered independent.

The issue also hints at some of the deep structural differences between the press in Quebec and English Canada. The union militancy of the sixties won Québécois journalists privileges their English-language counterparts can only dream of. Marvels Yakabuski, "A reporter with five or six years' experience at *Le Journal de Montréal* can easily be making $75,000 a year, base gross salary, without overtime. And that's for a four-day work week." (Senior reporters at even the largest national and Ontario dailies make about $60,000 for a 35-hour week.) While editors at English papers routinely change the "lede" – the first paragraph – and even the focus of a news story, the collective agreements Québécois reporters negotiated in the seventies prevent editors from touching their articles. "At *Le Devoir*," recalls Yakabuski, "we basically didn't have copy editors. There were *relecteurs* [re-readers] who checked for spelling mistakes, but only two of them for the whole paper. Overall, I'd say the English media is editor-heavy, and the French media is writer-heavy. In English papers, there's more discipline as to the structure of the story, and less individuality and analysis on the writer's part; it tends to be more hard news. It's a much less disciplined métier on the French side, in terms of checking sources and covering your bases. I find people will run stories based on nothing, on unsubstantiated rumour."

Yakabuski stresses another distinction: the historically high social status of journalists in Quebec. In Montreal, metro stations are named after journalists such as Henri Bourassa and Honoré Beaugrand, and the upper echelons of the province's intelligentsia have been dominated by editorial-ists like *Le Devoir*'s André Laurendeau, *Cité libre*'s Pierre Trudeau, and *La Presse*'s Gérard Pelletier. "These people weren't reporters like me," points out Yakabuski. "I think journalism in Quebec was an esteemed profession for a long time. It was an intellectual domain."

All these differences make perusing a Québécois newspaper a slightly disorienting experience for an anglophone reader. Papers such as *Le Soleil* and *Le Devoir* seem to value analysis over fact, often placing signed editorials on the front page alongside hard news stories. As in France, columns are often followed by footnotes, and references to books are cited. It's rare to see a Québécois reporter on an Indian reserve, in a prison, or on an army base, bringing an issue to life by telling a vivid human story. (Foglia and magazine writers such as Georges-Hébert Germain are exceptions, and they've been recognized for their feature writing with National Newspaper and Magazine Awards.) As a historian of Canadian journalism, Peter Desbarats sees this as nothing new. "The virtues of objectivity, the five Ws, that sort of Associated Press style of reporting were transmitted to English-Canadian papers through the Canadian Press. The whole emphasis on short, Hemingway-type sentences, factual reporting, with the reporter's personality absent from the story, was never a really strong influence in French Canada. Journalism there has always been more personal and political." These days, the Quebec press seems to be dominated by highly opinionated columnists, often reacting to the same press releases and government dictates, without the vital raw material of decent journalistic legwork. (The national dailies, with their growing stables of bombastic freelance columnists, are leading English-Canadian journalism down exactly the same path.)

Many attribute the triviality and lack of investigative reporting on both sides of the linguistic divide to the increasing corporatization of media. Newspaper ownership in Quebec, as in Canada as a whole, is now concentrated in the hands of fewer than half a dozen major players. In 1965, Quebec's 14 dailies were owned by 14 publishers; today, the 11 remaining dailies are owned by three chains, with only *Le Devoir* remaining nominally independent. (Saskatchewan, where all the dailies are owned by Southam, and New Brunswick, where the Irving family controls all five English-language papers, have it a lot worse.)

For one reason or another, Quebec has served as the launch pad for some of North America's biggest press barons. Montreal-born Conrad Black, who owns 41 per cent of Canada's newspapers – as well as the *Jerusalem Post*, the *Chicago Sun-Times*, and England's *Daily Telegraph* – started his empire in Quebec's Eastern Townships. Using part of a $200,000 inheritance to buy the struggling Sherbrooke *Record*, he anticipated his future "demanning" technique by firing half the paper's staff. Mortimer Zuckerman, who owns the *Atlantic Monthly, U.S. News and World Report,* and the *New York Daily News*, is a Montreal-born McGill graduate. Pierre Péladeau's Quebecor, run by his young sons Pierre-Karl and Karl since his death in 1997, bought out the Sun Media chain, giving the conglomerate control of a fifth of all the daily newspapers in Canada, including the *Toronto* and *Ottawa Suns*. Quebecor, the world's largest printer, now owns Quebec's two major tabloids. Black, meanwhile, owns Quebec City's *Le Soleil*, Chicoutimi's *Le Quotidien*, the Montreal *Gazette*, and the Sherbrooke *Record*.

No one seriously doubts that the corporate ownership of newspapers has affected editorial content; the only question is the extent to which editors alter news and opinion to satisfy publishers. Power Corporation's four Quebec papers – Montreal's *La Presse* and dailies in Trois-Rivières, Granby, and Sherbrooke – are staunchly federalist, consistently offering editorial support for a united Canada. This shouldn't be surprising, since Paul Desmarais was a friend of Lester Pearson, a confidant of Pierre Trudeau, an employer of Brian Mulroney, and is now an in-law of Jean Chrétien. His son, André, is not only president of the board of directors of *La Presse* but also the husband of Chrétien's daughter. When the paper's chief editorialist Alain Dubuc and columnist Chantal Hébert criticized Chrétien's gaffes during the 1998 Quebec provincial election, they were reprimanded, and Hébert was offered a new, nonpolitical beat. "If you ever saw the series *Scoop*," says Raymond Brassard, managing editor at the *Gazette*, "it's completely based on *La Presse*." In the popular Québécois television drama, a meddlesome owner wielded inordinate control over the paper's content. "If the powerful publisher says, 'Put a doggy-doo story on page one, because I have a friend who sells doggy-doo scoops,' I think they do. That's the kind of mentality they have at *La Presse*."

The *Gazette*, of course, has its own powerful publisher, Black, and since he's often busy in London, the paper's editors have had to learn to censor themselves. "I know what Conrad Black thinks," says Brassard, who owes his flattened New England vowels to a Franco-American upbringing in Lowell, Massachusetts. "But I can honestly say that he has never said, 'You must do this.' He didn't have to. You know what he thinks, you know what he feels, and you watch what you do. And I don't think that's bad." Maybe not; but trying to second-guess a notorious ultraconservative, the approving biographer of the freedom-squelching Maurice Duplessis, and a man who called investigative journalists a bunch of "swarming, grunting jackals" might make you think twice about publishing too many articles that question the corporate status quo. A Simon Fraser University analysis of 4,000 items from Southam-Hollinger papers showed that when Black buys a newspaper, coverage of labour, women's issues, and native affairs almost completely drops off the front page, while business and crime reporting increase significantly. Black's *National Post* illustrated an article on a brain drain of Canadian talent to the United States with a front-page photo of Pamela Anderson Lee in a bikini. The British, who read Black's *Daily Telegraph*, have dubbed his approach to news "tits and analysis."

That said, in a province where investigative journalism never really took hold, Black's Montreal *Gazette* is still the one place you can find decent feature writing and thoroughly researched inquiries. "Unfortunately, I think that's true, by default," concedes Roderick Macdonell, a 15-year *Gazette* veteran and the paper's resident swarming, grunting jackal. "There's nobody out there fighting with us." With co-workers William Marsden and Andrew McIntosh (who was lured away by the *National Post*), Macdonell has broken stories the *Gazette*'s French competitors wouldn't touch. In 1993, for example, he wrote an award-winning series showing that the huge delays in cases before Montreal's municipal courts were caused by the salaried judges' habit of spending their afternoons sunbathing, enjoying long lunches, and relaxing at their cottages. Macdonell says he works five days a week, and sometimes 16-hour days. "There have been times when I knew we didn't have to worry about the heavy hitters coming out with the same story," he says. "They're working a four-day week, and I know the day the news breaks they're just not going to be in the newsroom." (There are aggressive, highly competent exceptions, such as novelist-cum-journalist André Noël at *La Presse* and *Le Devoir*'s excellent environmental reporter, Louis-Gilles Francoeur.)

Many francophone commentators, particularly the ones who remember the glory days of energetic French-language investigative reporting in the early sixties, tend to agree. "A real journalist doesn't work a four-day week," spits Jean-Claude Leclerc, long-time *Le Devoir* editorialist and a founder of the Canadian Centre for Investigative Journalism. "He works an eight-day week. A real journalist works all the time, like an intellectual. Unionization might have actually done harm, in winning work conditions that were too good; it's favoured a lazy, fat-cat journalism."

These days, reporting in Quebec resembles what journalism has long been in France: a privileged trade, where high salaries, a vast old boys' network, and a deep-seated fear of the consequences of overturning institutions leads to a complacent acceptance of political corruption. In France, the recent rise of the *fouille-merdes*, the kind of shit-disturbing journalists who broke the story of the Greenpeace bombing and the contaminated blood scandal, suggests there's some hope for Gallic journalism. In the meantime, the Quebec press, so well placed to combine European analysis with the best aspects of aggressive Anglo-American journalism, seems content with triviality. "Last Saturday, the headline on the front page of *La Presse* was 'The price of bubbly is about to go up,'" ruefully notes Pierre Godin, a career journalist and the respected biographer of René Lévesque. "In the seventies, we might have written an article about champagne, but we would never have put it on the front page. The press is now like it was in the fifties, with the accent on trivial news items and official communiqués, this or that declaration from a politician." Godin adds, "And maybe that's appropriate, because, on the level of ideas, the Parti Québécois under Bouchard is beginning to look more and more like the Union Nationale under Duplessis."

The usual dodge is to blame the tabloid press for lowering journalistic standards. The runaway success of Péladeau's tabloids in Montreal and Quebec City, the argument runs, has forced *La Presse* and *Le Soleil* to focus on accidents, biker feuds, and sports. In reality, Quebecor's papers have a great stable of energetic reporters, the province's best photographers and sportswriters, and thoughtful political columnists such as Michel C. Auger and Pierre Bourgault. Commentators in Ontario, however, have long dismissed the papers as the lowest gutter strainings. Diane Francis wrote in the *National Post* that "Quebecor publishes truly trashy tabloids, like the *Journal de Montréal* . . . for people who move their hips when they read." As Florian Sauvageau, a professor of journalism at Laval University, emphasizes, "*Le Journal de Montréal* has economic and international news; it's a real, complete newspaper, not a version of the *National Enquirer*. And when I happen upon the *Ottawa* or *Toronto Sun*" – with their array of bigoted columnists and the semi-clad Sunshine Girl – "I realize that *Le Journal* is a monument of culture." (Since Quebecor's purchase of Sun Media, Ontario-born expressions of scorn for Quebec's tabloids have noticeably declined.)

While Quebec's tabloids are far better than their English-Canadian counterparts, its mainstream broadsheets can't rival the resources and writing of Canada's national dailies, which are being spurred to new aggressiveness by the competition between the *Globe and Mail* and the *National Post*. *Le Devoir*, the last avatar of a venerable tradition of independent commentary and reporting, is now an etiolated wraith, occasionally conjured back to life by an $800-a-plate dinner for corporate investors. Meanwhile, the conglomerate-owned dailies have surrendered to the triviality and toothlessness of boilerplate journalism. "If Céline Dion has won another award," mutters the *Globe and Mail*'s Konrad Yakabuski, "you can bet it's going to be on all the front pages."

What's more, Quebec's voracious star system has turned the journalist from intellectual into pundit, endlessly consulted in radio, television, and magazine guest appearances over whatever political peccadillo or sex scandal happens to be obsessing the province's chattering classes. "People don't really get warm and fuzzy about Peter Mansbridge," points out the *Gazette*'s Rod Macdonell. "I can't think of any Canadian journalist who really has a comparable status to, say, Pierre Foglia or Lysiane Gagnon in Quebec." These days, it's hard to get through an evening of talk shows without coming across the trademark pompadour of editorial cartoonist Serge Chapleau, the baby-faced sneer of *Voir* editor-in-chief Richard Martineau, or the sparkling eyes of *La Presse* columnist Nathalie Petrowski. "I love Nathalie," says Yakabuski, "she's a good friend of mine, but even she would agree she's overexposed. These people are so entrenched as the stars of their respective domains that it becomes a bit tiring." Quebec's journalists, once thundering, patriarchal opinion makers, are increasingly entertainers and lifestyle specialists. The phenomenon, though acute here, isn't limited to Quebec: the North American intelligentsia, it seems, isn't as intelligent as it used to be.

The Quebec media recently lost one of the last of the serious, old-time thinkers of the Quiet Revolution. In his mid-sixties, Jean Paré, looking relaxed and a couple of decades younger than his years after a Christmas spent with family in the Eastern Townships, has handed over the reins of the newsmagazine *L'actualité* to a new editor. Calm and suave, nattily dressed in a herringbone jacket, Paré is the polar opposite of the excitable, carelessly arranged Pierre Foglia: half a head shorter, with the irreproachable good looks of a fifties leading man, Paré is all well-rehearsed repertoire, as opposed to thrashing improv. In a corner suite of Maclean-Hunter's offices in downtown Montreal, I feel I could ask this translator of Marshall McLuhan's works the most off-the-wall question and get a response that would indicate he'd already given the issue abundant thought.

Jean Paré founded *L'actualité* in 1976, approaching the publishers of *Maclean's* magazine with a proposal to create a Quebec-centred news-magazine that would combine elements of *Newsweek* and France's *Le Nouvel observateur*. Over the years, it has grown into a solid, highly original reflection of Quebec society, with far more personality than the bland, just-the-facts uniprose that tends to dominate *Time* or the latter-day *Maclean's*. Criticized as federalist in outlook and mired in an eighties vintage business-oriented vision of society, *L'actualité* is also admired for its vivid, people-oriented feature writing. As one of the few serious outlets for good journalistic storytelling in Quebec, it's consistently the biggest French-language winner in the National Magazine Awards.

L'actualité was also a pioneer in Quebec's thriving magazine market. Those who click their tongues over the decay in newspaper readership would do well to note the concomitant mushrooming of magazine titles and sales. Quebec's feminine press boasts impressive circulation figures: between *Coup de pouce* and *Clin d'oeil*, *Elle Québec* and *L'Essentiel*, one million Québécois pick up a copy of a woman's magazine every month. More than three million free *hebdos* (from the word *hebdomadaire*, or weekly), including cultural city guides such as *Voir* and *Ici*, appear on news-stands every week, providing one of the few entry points for young writing talent. The leading magazines, such as *Châtelaine* and *Sélection du Reader's Digest*, have more than 200,000 readers each; *L'actualité* weighs in at close to 190,000. Not bad, I suggest, for a market of only six million. "Especially," emphasizes Paré, "when you consider that *Maclean's* has a paid staff of 40 full-time journalists, *L'Express* in France has 250, and *Time* has 300. At *L'actualité*, we have only four."

The relatively small francophone community in Canada is a frustration for Paré for other reasons. "Quebec is like a tiny bowl," he says. "Somebody says something, and we talk about it for six months; we start to choke on our own recirculated air." This is why, Paré explains, in *L'actualité*, unlike other French-language publications, you're likely to see datelines that issue from Vancouver, Whitehorse, and other Canadian cities. With the exception of *La Presse*'s recently established business reporter in Toronto, coverage of the rest of Canada tends to stop in Ottawa. I point out that the same isn't true in English Canada: the columns of Benoit Aubin, Lysiane Gagnon, Chantal Hébert, Josée Legault, and Paré himself are frequently published on the editorial pages of national English-language papers. Paré agrees, but believes that the English-Canadian reporting on Quebec is superficial and tends to be limited to politics. "Their coverage is usually twisted, approximative, wide of the mark. *Maclean's* parachutes somebody in, and he never leaves [Montreal's] Crescent Street. Their guys have typically talked to Mordecai Richler and Mr. Montreal" – the late Montreal *Gazette* columnist Nick Auf der Maur – "and they think they have the story."

For Paré, Quebec's size also explains the lack of hard-hitting investigative reporting. "I'd like for my journalists to be a little more aggressive. In the United States and English Canada, I've noticed that reporters make it a point of honour to cover their walls with the stuffed heads of the politicians they've brought down. A good journalist is one who's exposed 15 corrupt municipal politicians." It's certainly not the case in Quebec. "Because this is a small society, reporters don't like to write extremely aggressive articles. I'll suggest a portrait of a politician, and the journalist will reply, 'No, not that guy, he's a jerk.' In that case, I say, do the portrait of a jerk! But the writer is afraid of being prevented from doing his job in the future. He thinks that by writing something negative, he'll incur the deep hostility of half the people he'll run into for the rest of his life." It's a good point. A reporter who ends up on too many shit lists in Edmonton can always try his luck in Vancouver, Toronto, or Halifax (unless, of course, the list he's on happens to be Black). The French-language world in North America being highly circumscribed, many battles have to be fought on the spot, often over decades. Being impolitic with the wrong people can have long-term consequences. "There's always this fear about acting in a self-destructive manner," says Paré. "For a journalist, that means not doing things to destroy his own government, his own institutions. It's extremely frequent among minority populations."

In the end, the varying quality of journalism in Quebec is more influenced by the social climate than by any deep French or North American reportorial traditions. Investigative journalism flourished in the late fifties and early sixties, when the collective action of toppling the Duplessis government and supporting Lesage's Liberals involved essentially constructive investigations of sclerotic social institutions. These days, well-paid journalists are more inclined to identify with a class of politicians and corporate leaders whose power is best served by keeping all news trivial and all debates inconsequential. This is why, in Quebec, we're not likely to see serious coverage of issues that would threaten political and corporate power. A society-wide debate about proportional representation, the quiet surrender of natural resources and economic autonomy to international corporations, the dangers of media monopoly, or the long-term social consequences of downsizing and globalization have no place on the two-dozen-word cover of *Le Journal* or the front page of Power Corporation's *La Presse* – or, for that matter, in Conrad Black's Montreal *Gazette*.

Not when the price of champagne is about to go up.

6

THE BLUE GLOW

Crisse! It's *Hockey Night – La Soirée du hockey – in Canada*, the Habs are playing the Leafs, and it's as though a giant gearworks is grinding through downtown Montreal, drawing the phalanxes of beer-stoked Torontonians in Maple Leafs jerseys away from the strippers at the Calèche du sexe, down Rue Ste-Catherine, finally dumping them in churning bunches before the precipitous walls of the Molson Centre. I feel like my sleeve has been caught in some invisible cogwheel, dragging me inexorably towards the turnstiles and that unmistakable odour of Canadian popular joy: potatoes frying in tired fat, undercut by flattening beer.

The failing hands of an elderly doorman tear my ticket, and I'm burped into Montreal's soulless new coliseum. Inside, the machine grinds on, drawing me up escalators, past the $125 seats in the Red section, past the suits eating smoked salmon in plush corporate suites, past the skinny guys in short-sleeve shirts barking "Cold beer – bière froide!" finally to deposit me in my seat in the Grey section, a finished sports product, packaged, delivered, and ready to consume. So close to heaven, so far from the ice.

The Montreal Canadiens, variously known as Les Habitants, the Flying Frenchmen, La Sainte-Flanelle, Nos Glorieux, and lately Les Boys, have won 24 Stanley Cups since they were founded in 1909, the most successful hockey team in the history of the sport. Their closest competitors, the Leafs, have picked up 13 such trophies, and the dynasty-spanning rivalry of hockey's two oldest clubs is as central to the mythology of Canadians as the antagonism between Athens and Sparta was to the Greeks. Even the table-top hockey set I got one snowless Vancouver Christmas pitted flattened Habitants against crew-cut Maple Leafs. But since the last of their Cup wins in the late seventies, the Canadiens have managed only two championships, and those largely thanks to a goaltender – Patrick Roy – now playing for Colorado.

Once the elegant representatives of French-Canadian élan, men with nicknames like the Rocket, the Flower, and Boom-Boom played their trademark firewagon hockey on teams that were 98 per cent Canadian. In this, the 1998/99 season, 40 per cent of the NHL players are European or American, the best French-Canadian talent has been scattered to the four corners of the continent, and the Habs routinely lose to teams with such subtropical monikers as the Tampa Bay Lightning and the Nashville Predators. When a semicircle of 19 Habs pours onto the ice, I count only five French-Canadian surnames among the Dawes and the Zubrus – and it turns out that one of these apparent Canucks, Scott Lachance, hails from Charlottesville, Virginia. Even though they're playing hockey in the town where the game was invented, the Canadiens are now just another multicultural franchise in a league of 27 teams playing in heartless, over-amped stadiums.

Things were different when the game was played at the Forum, the no-frills arena on the English side of downtown Montreal that was the world's leading temple of hockey between 1924 and 1996. In his novel *The Loved and the Lost*, Morley Callaghan describes the crowd gathered one Saturday night in the late forties: "They came from all the districts around the mountain; they came from wealthy Westmount and solid respectable French Outremont and from the Jewish shops along St. Catherine, and of course a few Negroes from St. Antoine would be in the cheap seats. There they were, citizens of the second biggest French-speaking city in the world, their faces rising row on row, French faces, American faces, Canadian faces, Jewish faces, all yelling in a grand chorus; they had found a way of sitting together, yelling together, living together." In the heat of the game, Jim McAlpine, a history professor and aspiring journalist, can temporarily forget about his troubled love affair with the girl sitting next to him: he's transported by the performance of a Canadiens centre who fakes out the Rangers defence and then calmly lifts the puck over the goalie's prone body into the net. Between periods, McAlpine chats with a bony-faced French-Canadian priest about right-winger Maurice Richard's knack for single-mindedly charging the goal. After a referee's bad call, the disgusted crowd toss rubber overshoes onto the ice, and the evening ends with a Canadiens victory that sees hundreds of felt fedoras soaring onto the rink. The florid man next to McAlpine, writes Callaghan, "slapped him on the back and hugged him, and the French-Canadian priest burst into eloquent French. Everybody was filled with a fine laughing happiness."

It's hard to imagine the Canadiens arousing such ebullient camaraderie tonight. When the Montreal defence lets a Toronto defenceman slip past to score the Leafs' second and last goal of the night, the teenage Québécois boy next to me leans forward and shouts: "Maudit' gang de pourris!" – joual for "Bunch of rotten bastards!" When I lean over to mutter that Montreal should consider pulling the zombielike Igor Ulanov off the ice, I'm interrupted by a thundering chorus of the Rolling Stones' "Start Me Up," nipping any cross-cultural bonding in the bud. That's the problem with this high-tech stadium: the hockey experience is mediated by four giant screens, which tells fans when and even what to cheer. (The traditional "Les Canadiens sont là là là!" has been replaced by the more succinct "Go Habs Go!" apparently for reasons of brevity. Naturally, the Toronto fans behind me respond with a mocking chorus of "Go Frogs Go!") With our field of vision dominated by the scoreboard, a Janus-faced hexahedron hovering over centre ice, and our senses numbed by a non-stop sound-and-light show, there's no risk of any spontaneous gestalt in the crowd.

Most eyes are on the ever-active screens. Cameras scour the arena, pausing occasionally to dole out 15 seconds of stardom. A row of college boys behind me bare their hairless chests, each painted with a blue letter to form the word L-E-A-F-S, a bid to attract the camera's eye. The cameramen instead pick out a big-breasted girl who's braless beneath her Habs sweatshirt; when she realizes she's onscreen before thousands of people, she begins a jiggling belly dance. Even the hockey players seem more interested in the screens than the ice. When a camera zooms in to catch Shayne Corson's reaction to a penalty, he's not muttering to himself in frustration; he's staring upwards, blank-eyed and open-mouthed, watching himself on the scoreboard.

After a scoreless third period, filled with the hooking and interference that are hallmarks of the modern game, the Habs manage to win. It's an anticlimax: the Leafs are going to the playoffs anyway, leaving the home team to lick its wounds over the summer. And really, tonight's victory belongs to the behaviourists – with its all-seeing cameras, the Molson Centre is a giant panopticon, a triumph of multimedia crowd control more suggestive of Orwellian dystopia than McLuhanesque global village. These days, we're not likely to see the kind of riot that wrecked downtown Montreal in 1955, as French Canadians set off tear gas and smashed street-car windows to protest Maurice Richard's suspension by anglophone league managers. Somehow, though we've all met in the same big room, we've done so without meeting one another's gaze.

Ever since Canada's first television station, CBFT, started broadcasting in Montreal in the early fifties, the most significant communal experiences in Quebec – a society so enthusiastic about television that everybody, eventually, gets to be a star – have been mediated by the small screen. Hockey owes its reputation as the quintessential Québécois sport to television: the beginning of the most glorious seasons of Nos Glorieux coincided with the appearance of that first station. Before 1952, the Canadiens, with only five Cup victories to the Leafs' seven, were just one of six major hockey clubs playing a sport invented by British soldiers, codified by McGill University students, and run by English-Canadian and American businessmen. Then, as Radio-Canada broadcast its first *téléromans* and hockey games, stars like Maurice Richard and Jean Béliveau came into their own, and a sophisticated, Canada-wide amateur recruiting network started paying dividends. The vision of the beetle-browed, helmetless Rocket skating 20 feet to score a goal, even though two grown men were hanging off his shoulders, was captured by the cameras, making him the sport's first major star.

By the time the Habs had won their fifth championship in a row, in 1960, the Stanley Cup parade had become an annual civic event, as predictable as the St. Jean Baptiste Day procession. *La Soirée du hockey* was Quebec's most popular show, attracting an average 1.5 million viewers on Saturday nights, denying theatres and cinemas weekend custom, leaving thousands of taxicabs idle. (Hockey still has a measurable sociological effect: during a 1994 NHL lockout, police in the suburbs of Montreal recorded a huge leap in the number of men arrested on Saturday night for domestic violence. Likewise, a sociologist found a sharp increase in male suicides in Quebec in the years the Canadiens were knocked out of the playoffs.)

Before hockey shacked up with television, mass culture in Quebec didn't get much beyond Catholic pageantry, American vaudeville, and poorly attended plays staged by a handful of intellectuals. "There was no culture in Quebec before television," the writer Guy Fournier states bluntly in an introduction to a directory of major Québécois series. "There was folklore, which is completely different. A few writers – five or six; a handful of opera singers – who made their living abroad; a few painters – who we ignored; a single, semi-professional theatre troupe, Les Compagnons de Saint-Laurent, that performed plays – from France."

Today, thanks largely to a popular culture nourished and reinforced by television, the Québécois sense of shared identity and history is one of the strongest in North America. Canadian elitists mock the province's pop culture. This is a parochial France, they say, whose more memorable cultural exports have included disco gerbil Mitsou, wrestler Mad Dog Vachon, and big-haired psychic Jo Jo Savard. They point out that when France devoted a major retrospective to one of its beloved comic book characters, it was Paris's Musée des arts et traditions populaires, not the Louvre, that played host to the Astérix exhibit. In Quebec, the plucky Gaul spent his soujourn in Montreal's Musée des beaux-arts – the province's oldest and most prestigious art museum.

This is not only giving France – where leather-trousered Johnny Hallyday, a Eurotrash Elvis, is a national icon – far too much credit; it's also being unfair to Quebec. True, this is not one of the world capitals of high art; but unlike other Canadians, the Québécois actually like their own television shows, pop songs, and movies, which means their imaginary unconsciousness hasn't been entirely colonized by Nashville, Los Angeles, and New York. Get on a city bus in Quebec, where people listen to the radio 22 hours per week, the most of any Canadians, and you'll notice not only that the driver has the right to listen to the radio, but also that she's cranking the wheel to one of Ginette Reno's torch songs. Nor is Québécois culture merely local anymore: no matter what you think of the Cirque du Soleil, Luc Plamondon, Céline Dion, or Jacques Villeneuve, they've triumphed in circus tents, concert halls, and racetracks around the world. Quebec's hyperactive star system is no longer a quaint regional idiosyncrasy; it's a global phenomenon whose biggest *vedettes* can make English Canada's stars look like mid-list local heroes.

Modern Quebec was born with the *tivi* (the folksy French-Canadian diminutive for what Parisians call the *télé*), and the demands of this relentlessly productive popular industry – which per capita churns out two and a half times as many series as the American networks – have made for an impressive culture of celebrity. If Europe's identity is literary, America's cinematic, and English Canada's radiophonic (the ethereal static of the CBC on the Trans-Canada), then Quebec's is televisual. This is a *tivi* nation. If you're not watching French-language television in Quebec, on a fundamental level you're just not getting the place.

Some statistics. Francophone Quebecers are Canada's television-watching champions, tuning in an average of three hours and 48 minutes a day (versus Albertans' two hours and 54 minutes). The top 30 television shows in Quebec this year were all made in Quebec; in the rest of Canada, the Nielsen charts belonged to the Americans, topped by *E.R.* and *Ally McBeal*. When an English-Canadian program attracts a million viewers, in a market of 23 million, it's considered a heartening triumph for Canadian content. If a miniseries rates that badly in French Canada (with only seven million potential viewers), it may well get the axe. Quebec's biggest hits, shows like *Les Filles de Caleb*, *Lance et compte* and *Scoop*, have captured half the entire French-speaking population of the country. On a single winter evening, 4,098,000 francophones tuned in to an episode of the series *La petite vie*, breaking a world record for marketplace penetration previously held by the immensely popular *telenovelas* of Brazil. In other words, on the night of March 20, 1995, about two-thirds of Quebec's six million francophones were in front of their sets, watching a character called Moman ironing a shirt still attached to the clothesline.

"That blue glow," chuckles Louise Cousineau, television critic at Montreal's *La Presse* for more than 20 years. "At 7:30 every Monday night, whether you're in the heights of Outremont, or the depths of St-Henri, you're going to see the same blue glow, and it's coming from the same show. In a way, we owe our social cohesion to television." We're sitting in La Croissanterie on the edge of Outremont, one of the few Montreal cafés that – thanks to the ersatz-baroque decor inside and the Hasidic Jews outside – can fool you into thinking you're sipping an *express* in Paris. A rotund woman with chubby cheeks and a voice abraded by tobacco, Cousineau looks as though any early asperities have been eroded by thousands of hours of professional couch sitting. "This neighbourhood is full of stars," she says. "Montreal, when you think about it, is a small town. There are maybe 12 very good restaurants here – like L'Express, Toqué!, Chez Lévêque on Laurier – so you're bound to see someone famous if you go on a weekend. It's curious – nobody hassles them, but you can feel an electricity in the air. Everybody knows they're there; they watch what they order." I tell her that in English Canada, we tend to snub any local celebrity foolish enough to venture out into public. Cousineau deadpans, "Stars? Then you have some stars?" I consider constructing a sentence that involves Jim Carrey, Alanis Morissette, Bryan Adams, and the expression "world-class," but can't quite work up the energy. "You English Canadians have such a puritan, Protestant ethic," she scolds. "You're not supposed to express your emotions, to show you're successful or famous."

Much as I resent being lumped in with all the other squarehead prudes, Cousineau has a point: a season of idle channel-hopping has convinced me that Québécois popular culture is a world unto itself. The basic francophone cable channel package – available just about everywhere in the province but Montreal's West Island – allows viewers to choose from two major public networks (Radio-Canada and the provincial government's educational channel Télé-Quebec), two private networks (TVA, recently made available on cable across Canada, and TQS, an aggressive upstart), and 11 specialized stations. I've watched an Italian gangster on Radio-Canada's trilingual crime drama *Omertà* kick a rival mobster out of a limousine with the words, "What the fuck are you waiting for? Get the fuck out!" as subtitles at the bottom of the screen helpfully translate, "Dehors, hostie!" I've gaped at the inexplicable *Dieu reçoit* on TQS, a high-concept talk show in which God, played by a toga-wearing, Jack Daniels–sipping actor, interviews local comedians in front of a studio filled with angels. I've even caught a few glimpses of a current of disturbingly retrograde xenophobia in Québécois comedy. In the 1998 *Bye Bye*, Radio-Canada's hugely popular New Year's Eve countdown show, host Daniel Lemire showed a picture of rosy-cheeked Mi'kmaq leader Ronald Jacques and snickered, "You only have to look at his nose to understand that the monsieur likes his firewater" – to which the well-dressed studio audience responded with delight. I suppose some English Canadians might have laughed at such a quip, too, if they were fans of *The Wayne and Shuster Show*. And if it were 1972.

I tell Cousineau I'm surprised at such jokes, as well as the lack of minorities, on the Québécois screen, but she doesn't find it a mystery. "You know, the authors of these shows are often suburbanites who don't come to Montreal often. They drive around in their cars, they don't ride mass transit, so they just don't see immigrants. They're sheltered, I think, from the new realities." Even more surprising is that in a few months of casual channel-hopping, I've seen more bare breasts in mainstream miniseries, and more pubic hair and writhing buttocks in such nightly porn shows as *Aphrodisia* and *Phantasmes*, than I've seen in a couple of decades of frequenting European art house films. Québécois television is comically, exaggeratedly, hot. In leading series like *Omertà* and *Caserne 24*, you can count on a fairly explicit sexual encounter of the nipple-and-buttocks variety every couple of episodes. "*C'est assez soft*," pooh-poohs Cousineau. "And the porn shows are on late at night. The children are already in bed by 11 o'clock."

For the *La Presse* critic, who was educated by nuns, television has replaced Catholicism as the source of all pageantry in Quebec culture. "The problem with the church was that it was always the same spectacle," she says, "whereas TV is always changing: it's never exactly the same show twice." In Quebec, it's glib pop sociology to claim that Catholicism has been replaced by dam-building, major league hockey, New Age cults, separatist politics – just about every social phenomenon that can get more than a dozen people into the same room. Television has a better-than-average claim to being a surrogate church, however: in the vast social vacuum left by the absence of such rituals as weekly mass, saint's day processions, and confession, *tivi* offers a gathering place that reinforces shared values through comforting, regularly scheduled morality tales.

Atop Mount Royal, a 10-storey-tall cross tastefully outlined by white lights – the enduring symbol of Montreal's piety – shines forth bravely over the St. Lawrence Valley. Since the early sixties, however, it has been dwarfed by an even loftier spire: the transmission tower of CBFT. The Catholic church, usually exquisitely sensitive to such symbolism, apparently saw the airwaves as too incorporeal to meddle with. Quebec's love affair with communications technology started early and continued untrammelled into the television age. The nation's first radio licence had been issued to the Canadian Marconi Co. in 1919, and Montreal's XWA became one of the first stations in the world to offer regularly scheduled broadcasts. By 1960, nine of 10 Quebec households had plugged in a television set, compared to only eight of 10 in English Canada. French-speaking television immediately galvanized the people of Quebec. While anglophones were being lured away by American competition, in the form of *The Jackie Gleason Show* and *Amos and Andy*, Radio-Canada's French programming attracted huge audiences to Canadian-made shows. Transmitting only nine hours a day for much of the fifties, haughtily refusing to broadcast Saturday-night Canadiens games until 9:30 p.m. – when the match was already well into the second period – Radio-Canada nonetheless mustered 1.5 million francophone viewers for its most popular shows.

"The emergence of television in '52 – for me, that was our cultural revolution," Gérard Pelletier told the journalist Pierre Godin in the early eighties. "It was an extraordinary magnet, the television. The cinemas in Montreal emptied out completely. The theatre almost perished, at least to begin with. People stayed home! Nobody went out any more! We couldn't even keep up meetings of associations – nobody came. It was a massive social phenomenon." Produced on the federal terrain of CBC's Montreal studios, beyond the grasp of Premier Maurice Duplessis, television offered a secure pressure cooker for intellectuals such as Pierre Trudeau and Jean Marchand, who were quietly concocting the Quiet Revolution. (The non-telegenic Duplessis, perhaps sharing Richard Nixon's repugnance for the cameras, refused to grant live interviews.) In the only surviving episode of the astonishingly engaging international affairs program *Point de mire*, an intense René Lévesque, his voice already gravelly, takes a camera to the streets of Paris, where he solicits French opinion on the Algerian independence movement. Many historians consider television's early days the gestation period of Quebec's separatist movement. The Montreal producers' strike of 1959 – a clash over job security and creative freedom that has been mythologized into a French-Canadian uprising against Anglo authority – permanently politicized intellectuals, including Lévesque, confirming them in their nationalism.

By showing Québécois families in recognizably modern settings, in the same box in which up-to-the-minute Americans and English Canadians appeared, television proved to Quebec that it could become a full member of modernity. The leading vehicle for this was the *téléroman* (the television-novel), a form that has no exact counterpart in world television. Generally centred on a single extended family, the Québécois *téléroman* isn't exactly a soap opera: unlike the ongoing American shows *General Hospital* and *Days of Our Lives*, those never-ending sagas set in parallel worlds, the *téléroman* eventually comes to an end. Nor are they familial sitcoms like *Leave It to Beaver* or *The Brady Bunch*, neatly resolved in half-hour episodes. The closest equivalents in world television have been *Peyton Place* (which was written by a New Englander of French-Canadian origin, Grace Metalious), *Coronation Street* (created, according to some accounts, after BBC researchers came back from a mid-fifties fact-finding mission to Quebec), and the family sagas of the Brazilian *telenovelas*.

But nothing really comes close to *La Famille Plouffe*, the prototypical *téléroman* that introduced Canada to the archetypal modern Québécois family. In the third-season opener in 1955, the author, Roger Lemelin, a dapper devil in a thin-lapelled suit and striped tie, warns viewers that the Plouffe family has moved into a new building. Gesturing with a burning cigarette to a photo of a classic Montreal triplex, with its facade of brick and balconies, Lemelin tells us that Madame Plouffe – a roly-poly woman, perpetually fussing about her children – and her husband have moved into the second-floor apartment. Their daughter, Cécile – the image of the strong-willed, if somewhat neurotic, urban wife – lives below with her bus-driver husband. Monsieur Plouffe, a rather ineffectual, overalled busybody perpetually playing with his tools, has set up a plumbing shop with his burly son Napoléon in the basement. The show itself is full of tiny dramas: the frugal Cécile wants to rent a room in her apartment ("$60 a month and no dogs!"); Napoléon puts on a suit and proposes marriage to his girlfriend; and the family mounts an ingenious periscope-like pipe on the wall so they can communicate with Cécile in the kitchen below. An inter-kitchen shouting match develops after Napoléon calls Cécile a tomboy, and he finally shuts her up by dropping a glass of water down the pipe. Then everyone calms down, and the credits roll as the family shares a basket of grapes at the kitchen table. And so it went for a total of 194 episodes, little half-hour dramas in which nothing much happened. But for the people of Quebec, *La Famille Plouffe* was a revelation: it was like a picture window into the kitchen of the family next door.

At his tastefully renovated home among the blocks of three-storey townhouses in Montreal's Rosemont neighbourhood, any one of which could serve as the set for a revival of *La Famille Plouffe*, Jean-Pierre Desaulniers, a Université du Québec à Montréal professor of the anthropology of communications, draws a parallel between the history of modern Quebec and the fates of the Plouffe children. "Ovide is the intellectual," he says, using the corner of a Camel package to point to actor Jean-Louis Roux in a cast photo. "He'll end up being a top-ranking civil servant in Quebec City. Cécile's obsession is money; she eventually dies, but not before becoming rich. Napoléon, the young entrepreneur, is a plumber who starts his own company. And Guillaume, the hockey player, goes into public relations. The four pillars of the Quiet Revolution – political ideology, feminism, small business, and communications – are present in the children of the Plouffes." For Desaulniers, watching the gradual, week-by-week transformation of a family of factory workers into middle-class prosperity enabled Quebec's dramatic entry into modernity.

In other early *téléromans*, characters subtly challenged the social order: *Le Survenant*, a handsome outsider with a fondness for fringed-leather jackets, shows up in the village of Chenal-du-Moine, undermining the traditional authority of the priests by his very presence. "Like the coureur du bois, the *survenant*" – an unexpected guest – "had absolutely no responsibility to the social order," says Desaulniers. Poetic and independent of spirit, a look-alike of the contemporary folksinger Félix Leclerc, "he was extremely disconcerting for people, who couldn't imagine they could think for themselves."

The exact opposite of a character in another *téléroman*, Séraphin, the Scrooge of Quebec, whose name is still local antonomasia for oppressive stinginess. In *Les Belles Histoires des pays d'en haut*, which set a Quebec longevity record between 1956 and 1970, Séraphin Poudrier – a greasy-haired miser, the kind of guy who uses a rope to hold up his pants – came to symbolize all that was wretched and benighted about the Great Darkness. The mayor of a small town during the nineteenth-century colonization of the Laurentians north of Montreal, he makes life miserable for squatters and jealously tyrannizes his beautiful young wife, the slender, blond Donalda.

For Desaulniers, there are clear parallels between Séraphin, a local despot bent on maintaining his personal fiefdom in a rural backwater, and Maurice Duplessis, premier until 1959. "Séraphin was the embodiment of all the conservative forces of the time. What's more, he wasn't some alien invader – he was the chief, which meant that all the evil came from within the community, from his authority." Over 15 seasons, the colonists gradually learn to marginalize the tyrant, killing him with scorn and ridicule – the fate much of Quebec has reserved for the memory of Duplessis. "The stake in this battle is Séraphin's wife, who's completely oppressed," says Desaulniers. "For the viewers, it was clear that they had to stop being like her, to stop blindly accepting and obeying authority." When Donalda was forced by her husband to sew with cheap, white thread, Radio-Canada's Montreal studios were deluged with crates of coloured yarn, sent by credulous fans. "The more miserable you are on earth," says Desaulniers, "the happier you will be in heaven. 'Il faut gagner son ciel' – that was the message of Catholicism in Duplessis's Quebec. If the sixties saw the disappearance of the whole religious movement, as if in a gust of wind, it was because the *téléroman* had long combatted those kinds of ideas."

Decade after decade, these cheaply produced, slow-paced melodramas engaged the imagination of millions of francophone Quebecers, reflecting and enabling incremental social change through their thousand tiny dramas. While the fifties saw modest challenges to the authority of paternal figures like Séraphin, the sixties and seventies were all about emancipation and changing roles, particularly for female characters. In *Rue des Pignons*, set near Montreal's port, working-class families struggle with breakups and rebellious children but ultimately realize that love and satisfaction with life's simple pleasures are the answer. Desaulniers sees one of today's biggest hits, *Omertà* – in which a pair of marginal cops become reintegrated into the force by going undercover among the bikers and Mafiosi of Montreal – as equally reflective of the decade's *Zeitgeist*. "It shows a kind of will towards reintegration into the community," he says, "without sacrificing one's own individuality, which has been a marked theme of the nineties."

All this might sound like the overanalysis of pop academia (we are, after all, talking about a bunch of TV shows, the filler between ads for Vachon Snack Cakes and Volkswagens) if it weren't for the prodigiousness, popularity, and frequent high quality of Quebec's television. "When Lord Durham wrote in his famous report [in 1839] that we were a people without literature," says Jean-Pierre Desaulniers, "it was true. This was a society of peasants." Up until the 1940s, the history of fiction in Quebec is a rather barren one, punctuated by the occasional earnest historical novel celebrating "la race" and "le sang." In contrast to the bookish Français de France, whose conversational style tends to the Cartesian catechism delineating what is and isn't socially acceptable, the *cousins du Canada* earned a reputation as impassioned storytellers. As the songwriter Gilles Vigneault put it, the Québécois were "gens de parole," people of the spoken word, with a taste and talent for the enthralling tall tale. Such nineteenth-century oral traditions slid seamlessly into the electronic media of the twentieth century: there's not a huge leap, after all, between spending a night around the stove in the *cabane* listening to Grandfather's entertaining lies, and gathering around the *tivi* in a five-and-a-half-room apartment to watch the familiar follies of the family down the street.

It helped, too, that some of French Canada's most talented novelists and playwrights, many of whom had been cutting their teeth on the similarly episodic *radio-roman*, had few prejudices about trying their hand at the *téléroman*. Writers' names still appear prominently before each episode, and fans have learned to look for the signature of Lise Payette, Guy Fournier, or teams like Anne Boyer and Michel D'Astous. (Major American series are written by teams of up to 10 screenwriters, and often overseen by several script editors.) If Honoré de Balzac were living in Quebec today, *Lance et compte* creator Réjean Tremblay once declared, he'd probably be writing *téléromans* for broadcast TV.

In fact, there are indications that a kind of Laurentian Balzac is alive and well, and hard at work in a small town called Trois-Pistoles. Victor-Lévy Beaulieu, whom Pierre Foglia has called "Quebec's greatest living author," writes stylistically sophisticated family epics whose recurring characters recall the diachronic social portraiture of *The Human Comedy*. An iconoclastic separatist who's notoriously disdainful of group-think – particularly the Montreal sovereignist intelligentsia who tended to support the free trade agreement with the United States in 1989 – Beaulieu is a cultural industry unto himself. He's the director of the influential publishing house Éditions VLB, which is publishing his complete works, 54 volumes printed on high-quality paper.

The respected literary author also writes *téléromans*. *L'Héritage*, which Radio-Canada ran for three seasons in the late eighties, went like this: In a small town north of Quebec City, a rural patriarch has a passionate incestuous relationship with his daughter, who then flees to Montreal to have their child. Fifteen years later, Miriam returns to inherit the family farm from her dying father, who has cut her brother – his first son – out of the will. No moralizing, no easy answers, and definitely no *Days of Our Lives*: a *téléroman* by Victor-Lévy Beaulieu is to the soap opera what *Oedipus Rex* is to *Jurassic Park*.

Beaulieu isn't surprised to hear that many English Canadians consider television an inherently minor form. "From the start, some of Quebec's best *téléroman* writers were also novelists," he says. "It's a phenomenon that doesn't exist in English Canada – I can't imagine Margaret Atwood writing a series for television, for example. I think English Canadians subscribe more to the traditional myth of the author as a man or woman exclusively of books. It's the same in France – if you ask a French author to write a television drama, he's likely to say, 'Write *feuilletons* for the *télé*?'" – Beaulieu imitates the fluty tones of a Parisian bourgeois taking umbrage at the mention of TV serials – "'Who do you take me for? *Voyons, donc!*' I'm more on the side of Jean-Paul Sartre, who said that the writer should occupy all available fields of discourse – including radio and television." Beaulieu acknowledges that more pragmatic forces are at work as well. It's possible to make a living in France and English Canada writing fiction, but Quebec's biggest best-sellers seldom reach the 40,000 mark, and it's rare for an author to sell movie rights to Hollywood.

"There aren't many authors in Quebec who really make a living from their pen. Perhaps Michel Tremblay, who's a phenomenon unto himself, and Antonine Maillet [the Acadian author, winner of France's prestigious Goncourt prize in 1979]. But it's such a tiny market."

In many ways, *téléromans* are the popular literature of Quebec, a canon of overlapping, inter-referential fictions that have established lasting, resonant archetypes in the collective consciousness. The name Jean-Paul Belleau, for example, a Lothario from one of Lise Payette's series, has become a Québécois byword for the aggressive cruiser. "The *téléroman* contributed to making Quebec a kind of homogeneous whole," argues Beaulieu. "We now share the same spirit, the same speech, the same hopes, the same pains. In the final analysis, television has given us a grand period in our popular literature, like the literary *feuilletons* of the last century." Though the more bookish of the intellectual elite still dismiss *téléromans* as mass-market opium, many academics have started recognizing them as worthy of study. The Musée de la civilisation in Quebec City recently hosted an ambitious, 14-month-long exhibition devoted to the history of the *téléroman*. Beaulieu himself is opening a permanent television museum near his home in Trois-Pistoles.

It won't be the province's first such tourist attraction. In the Mauricie region north of Trois-Rivières, sites like the Village d'Émilie – which recreates the sets of the *téléroman Les Filles de Caleb* – seem to appeal more to the local imagination than vestiges of turn-of-the-century Mauricie itself. There's something a little pernicious about televised fiction standing in for history in the public mind. Québécois high school students are taught as much history as those in the rest of Canada – almost none at all. (English and French Canadians finish high school with 300 hours of history instruction, whereas Californians get 700 hours, Italians 900 hours.) If francophone Canadians' familiarity with a legendary past seems higher than anglophones', it's because there's barely an episode in the history of Quebec that hasn't been turned into a popular *téléroman*. Through miniseries like *Les Forges de Saint-Maurice*, *Maria Chapdelaine*, and *Duplessis*, the people of Quebec have been exposed to a televisual survey course of their history in seasonal semesters of 13 episodes. Laden with the usual anachronisms – the impossibly feminist pioneer schoolmistress is a recurring character – these mini-series have consistently set ratings records in Quebec.

The absence of the nineteenth century from the scripted history doesn't much surprise anthropologist Desaulniers. "The more that century appears arduous and martyred, the more modernity seems like a real liberation," he says. "In Quebec, we want to preserve the nineteenth century as the period when the English oppressed us. It wasn't true! Not at all! When the Conquest happened, the francophones here said: 'Bravo! We're finally free of those damned Français de France. We're going to have a real King of England, not some homosexual walking his poodles in the gardens of Versailles.'" One historical series, film director Charles Binamé's lavishly costumed *Marguerite Volant*, sympathetically portrayed a love affair between a handsome British officer and a Canadienne heiress after the Conquest. It was a gorgeous, expensive flop.

In a society with a love of inversions and exaggerations, full-bodied reality has always seemed a little flat next to the fabrications of the television screen. When the outbreak of the Gulf War interrupted a key episode of *Les Filles de Caleb* – the *téléroman* was then followed by 3.5 million francophones – Radio-Canada's star newscaster Bernard Derome himself excused the intrusion and promised that the show would resume with the briefest possible delay. Local *téléroman* actors, unshielded by Hollywood bodyguards, tell stories about strangers in restaurants and supermarkets greeting them by the first names of their fictional characters as if they were old friends. When a roguish character in Lise Payette's series *Dames de coeur* started beating his wife, the abuse the actor got on the streets of Montreal forced him into a months-long exile in the Eastern Townships. Many Québécois couldn't help but see Jean-Louis Roux's forced resignation as lieutenant-governor of Quebec in 1996 as the long-awaited comeuppance of Ovide, the highbrow son he'd played decades before on *La Famille Plouffe*.

Such confusion of fiction and reality isn't that surprising, given the Québécois *téléroman's* tendency to convince viewers it's about the people next door. While recent English-Canadian series like *Night Heat* and *Urban Angel* take place in some generic, vaguely American-looking big city (a role interpreted effortlessly by Toronto), Quebec's shows are precisely situated on familiar streets. *Jasmine*, about a black policewoman, was filmed using real Montreal police cars and uniforms in the streets around Poste 35. The children's puppet show *Passe-Partout*, produced by Quebec's Ministry of Education when there was talk of introducing a dubbed version of *Sesame Street*, showed shaggy-haired seventies moppets playing hopscotch in front of Montreal's twisting outdoor staircases.

Meanwhile, growing up in British Columbia, I got to watch an imported Grouch in a streetside garbage can interacting with black and Hispanic kids on a set out of Brooklyn – when the kids in my neighbourhood were Japanese and native Indian. (To this day, I maintain a clear grasp of the legislative divisions of the American government, drilled in by the educational jingles of an oft-repeated animated cartoon sequence called "Schoolhouse Rock.") Later, I got to watch SCTV, basically a team of Canadian comedians spoofing American programs such as *Love Boat* and *Days of Our Lives*. Kids in Quebec got to watch *Rock et Belles Oreilles*, also a send-up of TV series – but virtually all of the shows parodied were Québécois.

Television writer Fabienne Larouche was a product of this rich televisual culture, and spent her youth torn between Donalda on *Les Belles Histoires des pays d'en haut* and Samantha on *Ma Sorcière bien aimée*, the dubbed *Bewitched*. A childhood of assiduous television-watching led to a scriptwriting career in Montreal, and Larouche is now the author of *Virginie*, a *téléroman* about a high school teacher that attracted an average 1.2 million viewers four nights a week. In the windowless conference room of Aetios, her new production company in a suburban Laval office tower, Larouche has the squirming demeanour of a hyperactive child at 10 minutes to three on the first day of spring. "I come from Lac St-Jean," she says. "I'm *pure laine*. At the same time, I eat at McDonald's, I vacation in Ogunquit, and I'm crazy about New York. When I go to a Broadway musical, I don't understand half of what they're saying. *Pas grave*. I trip out on it anyway. At the same time, my heritage is French: my characters cite Cocteau, Prévert, they sing 'Le Temps des cérises.'"

With her tightly cinched, wide-lapelled black leather jacket, a black miniskirt that's constantly riding up over black stockings, and the black-and-gold sunglasses poised above her hairline, Larouche presents herself very much as a francophone *à l'américaine*. "Me, I'm 40 years old," she informs me, "so I've spent a lot more time watching television than I have reading." This is the kind of all-inclusive non sequitur only a convinced member of the Pepsi Generation could make, and Larouche's cultural references are all late baby-boom. *"Gilligan's Island, I Dream of Jeannie, Hawaii Five-O –* I liked American television, quick edits, lively, straight to the point. But I also watched *Rue des Pignons* – my influences are very Québécois too." After teaching high school in the suburbs north of Montreal in her early twenties, Larouche took a job at *La Presse*, where she met sports writer Réjean Tremblay, who was then working on the hit hockey saga *Lance et compte*. They became a team – professionally and romantically – and the Tremblay-Larouche credit would appear on *Scoop* (set in a newsroom transparently modelled on *La Presse*), *Urgence* (a knock-off of the American series *E.R.*, in the fictional Montreal hospital Coeur-de-Jésus), and *Paparazzi* (a celebrity photographer drama that debuted shortly after Princess Diana's death). All were fast-paced, big-budget miniseries, which even managed to one-up the sexiness of the American series they were imitating by throwing in some distinctly French sex.

Now divorced from co-writer Tremblay, Larouche is writing and producing *Virginie*, a more traditionally Québécois *téléroman*. The series centres on an attractive 30-year-old teacher at a Plateau Mont-Royal high school. The choice of character allows Larouche to relate not only the amorous adventures of a rather libidinous gang of teachers but also the problems of their teenage students, netting a loyal – overwhelmingly female – audience across every age group.

Since this is Quebec, *Virginie* can get away with addressing themes that wouldn't fly in the same seven o'clock time slot in English Canada. In one episode, Quebec watched in delight and surprise as the school's resident sixties-issue Marxist-Leninist takes up Virginie's 90-year-old grandmother's invitation to give her a full-fledged French kiss. (The Québécois verb for giving tongue, or *frencher*, is arguably the ultimate example of just how anglicized joual can get.) In another episode, a violent cop, after breaking up a teachers' strike, is forced to go into therapy for beating his wife; we learn he was a member of the Front de libération du Québec in the sixties. "So, all of a sudden," says Larouche, taken with her own audacity, "at seven o'clock, we can talk about the FLQ in Quebec." Thirty years after the fact, of course, and in rather oblique fashion, but it's far more relevant than the English-Canadian equivalent, *Degrassi Junior High*.

Television, a middle-of-the-road medium, makes a good barometer of where a society stands or how far it has allowed debate to go on key social issues. A continuing conflict in Larouche's fictional high school involves Raïcha, an Iranian student who wears a hijab, the headscarf of Muslim purdah, to class. When I ask Larouche about Virginie's ongoing difficulty in accepting the headscarf, her response is passionate. "When I see a girl wearing the hijab in the street, I'm in shock. It's true, we have to find a way to live together, but for me, the hijab represents fear, submission. And I'm not a submissive woman. I'm a rebel, I'm a fighter! And the hijab is something that I'd be willing to take up arms against. Because – I don't understand it. And what it suggests to me isn't anything pretty."

Larouche is also the product of ethnically homogeneous Lac St-Jean, and her teaching experience in a small town called Ste-Thérèse in the early eighties brought her into contact with very few immigrants. Like many *téléroman* writers, she lives in the predominantly white, francophone suburbs of Montreal. Yet her show is set in a high school in downtown Montreal, a city where Haitian, Asian, South American, and North African students fill the halls. *Virginie*, like many Québécois series, still presents superficial portraits of immigrants as social problems to be dealt with, rather than as new realities changing society.

If Quebec occasionally acts as if it's threatened to the core by the idea of accepting cultural difference – in the form of the Muslim hijab, native languages, or the ideograms of Chinatown – the explanation usually lies in failures of imagination rather than out-and-out racism. After all, no matter what you think of the male-imposed hijab as a disturbing symbol of spreading Muslim fundamentalism, it's foremost a symbol of individual religious expression. If those who objected to the wearing of the hijab in the schools of both Quebec and France also forced every female student to remove the Catholic crosses and Jewish Stars of David hanging around their necks, their arguments might carry more force. They don't dare, of course – and this hints at the xenophobia at the root of the issue, whatever the self-righteous appeals to collective rights. In the fifties, the *téléroman* revealed Quebec's tendency to remain closed to the world. A few series, such as *Jasmine, Ces Enfants d'ailleurs*, and *Le Polock*, about a Polish family, have dealt with non-French-Canadian Québécois. In general, however, the television landscape is striking for the near absence of minorities, except in caricature, as Mafiosi or exemplars of social problems. The current crop of *téléromans* betrays Quebec's hesitancy about opening to a world that can't help but change it.

Nowhere is this ambivalence better captured than in *La petite vie*, an often hilarious situation comedy – and the highest-rated show in Canadian history – that serves as a catalogue of a half-century of *téléroman* clichés. The absurdly idyllic opening sequence, which shows the dysfunctional Paré family emerging from the orifices of their brick triplex, is played out to a tinkling piano line based on the theme for the seventies *téléroman Rue des Pignons*. As in *La Famille Plouffe*, most of the action takes place in the kitchen, a Day-Glo nightmare of polka-dot curtains and chrome furniture. The bearded patriarch, Popa, played by the show's creator, Claude Meunier, takes Monsieur Plouffe's interest in his tools to an absurd limit, obsessing about garbage bag technology as a way to avoid all physical contact with his wife. (The launch party for Meunier's best-selling book about the world of *La petite vie* was held not in a bookstore but in a Canadian Tire outlet.) The Paré family are determinedly lower middle class, xenophobic, and utterly indifferent to anything beyond lottery tickets, recipes for *pâté chinois* (a kind of shepherd's pie with corn), and their perpetual squabbles. When their cousins from France come to visit, they turn out to be filthy boors with bad teeth who travel with a mould-covered, scurrying Camembert that can be lured back into its box only when they bare their Brillo-like underarms. Disgusted to learn that they've won an all-expenses-paid voyage to Hong Kong in a raffle, Moman and Popa trade it for 100 trips to Plattsburgh – a New York State border town 45 minutes from Montreal.

La petite vie sends academics into paroxysms of postmodern ecstasy. "Meunier has his own genius, which is spectacular," enthuses the anthropologist Jean-Pierre Desaulniers. "As much as *Rue des Pignons* and other *téléromans* of the seventies are based on the idea that 'we all love one another,' *La petite vie* starts with the premise that 'we all hate one another.' At the level of a distinctly Québécois symbolism, it's the first time we're witnessing a critique of the entire literary current represented by the *téléroman*." Some commentators suggest that *La petite vie*, now in its sixth season, actually signals the death of the *téléroman*. The genre seems to have weathered Meunier's critique with ratings intact, however: in the 1999 season, relationship *téléromans* like *4 et demi . . .* and *Un gars, une fille* continued to pull in audiences of close to two million.

Though far from being a world centre of high art, Quebec is an incredibly fertile source of television shows, pop songs, and movies. In the sixties, the only American program to draw a significant francophone audience was *The Ed Sullivan Show*, but it was quickly supplanted in the ratings by *Music Hall*, a Radio-Canada variety program developed to showcase and encourage Quebec talent. Locally produced movies, such as *Cruising Bar*, *La Florida*, and *Les Boys* – the gross of the third, $6.8 million, is second only to *Porky's* in Canadian movie history – have actually set all-time box office records in parts of Quebec, outperforming Hollywood blockbusters like *Titanic* on local screens. For every aspect of Québécois pop culture that is derivative – talk shows that rip off *David Letterman*, sitcoms that are shameless burns of shows like *Cheers* – others have been innovative enough to inspire imitation abroad. *Louis 19*, a $3-million film about an obscure Montreal television salesman who allows a camera crew to film his life, was remade in 1998 as *EDtv* by director Ron Howard with a budget of $45 million.

On the world stage, Quebec's most identifiable icons are agile circus people, impressionists, and race-car drivers, powerful singers, and brilliant choreographers: performers and athletes whose talents aren't verbal or intellectual but rather visual, physical, spectacular. On a continent with only seven million French-speaking Canadians, making a pop culture breakthrough on a North American scale often depends on honing one's nonlinguistic skills, which has made for lively, if decidedly nonintellectual, culture. Here as elsewhere, the *neuvième art*, as the French call comic books, is an ill-paid ghetto, but Quebec has a talented crop of *B.D.* – or *bandes dessinées* – artists, including Julie Doucet, Fidèle Castrée, and Sophie Cossette. What's more, the best French comic books are reviewed alongside novels and essays in the weekend culture supplement of *Le Devoir*. Quebec's underground death metal scene, including bands like Cryptopsy, Gorguts, and Necrotic Mutation, relies on a low-throated, language-neutral growl.

Actually, it sometimes feels like there's too much pop culture on display, particularly in the midsummer festival season. I've seen too many mediocre videos on Musique Plus – say, an anguished half-hippy/half-headbanger with a goatee moaning "Tu m'aimes-tuuu?" while a crow flaps in slow motion behind his billowing hair. Besides the world's largest comedy and jazz festivals, there are 240 official *fêtes* and celebrations in Quebec. It can all get a bit absurd. Not long ago, I noticed that a framing shop on Boulevard St-Laurent was hosting the world-renowned, bilingual Festival du laminage de Montréal – the Montreal Laminating Festival.

In the Holy Trinity of Quebec stardom, the Fathers are the Montreal Canadiens of seasons past, the Son is Jacques Villeneuve (heir to the Formula One victories of father Gilles), and the Holy Ghost is Céline Dion. The Habs of the fifties weren't just a hockey team: they represented the aspirations of the entire French-Canadian race against a vanishing class of Anglo overlords. Jacques Villeneuve isn't just a race-car driver: he's the future of Quebec, a cosmopolitan figure who unsettles every nationalist intellectual and politician who would limit identity to language, tribe, and nation. And Céline Dion isn't just a pitch-perfect singer: she's the ghost of Quebec past and future, a rake-thin child of the land who, torn from her home by a magnificent destiny, has been cursed into barrenness for abandoning her native soil.

If you want to know the kind of person you're dealing with in Quebec, ask him what he thinks of the province's reigning diva. Unless he's an elderly, unilingual, Cantonese-speaking immigrant with a horror of music, he'll know who you're talking about: a recent poll showed that 99.3 per cent of Quebecers knew Céline Dion's name, more than recognized Premier Lucien Bouchard. Francophones over the age of 55 can rarely find a bad thing to say about her: even if they're tone deaf, they seem to believe speaking ill of "notre Céline nationale" represents cultural apostasy. City dwellers in their twenties and thirties tend to be split on Dion: some are refreshingly cynical; others admit an affection for her, in the same breath assuring you that her French albums are really much better. Cab drivers of any age, who have undergone a ruthless, *Clockwork Orange*-style exposure to Céline on their dashboard radios, are notoriously irreverent, with a marked penchant for quoting Howard Stern's mockery of her "bony, sweaty ass." And the anglophones of Quebec – well, let's just say the two solitudes persist in certain domains.

When *La Presse* television critic Louise Cousineau, a big fan, heard Céline's voice on a transistor radio in Kampala, Uganda, she broke down and cried. For her, it was the triumph of not only the little girl from Charlemagne, but also Québécois culture around the globe. I had a similar reaction when I heard "All by Myself" on a rooftop radio in Havana. There's nowhere in the world, I realized – not even Castro's Cuba – where you can escape that big, English-speaking voice, as strikingly bland, technically accomplished, and fundamentally empty as anything in American culture.

By now, after at least nine biographies and tens of thousands of articles, just about everybody in Quebec can recite the fairy-tale life story of the world's pop diva. Here's the sugar-coated version, as told to *People* magazine and her authorized biographer. Born into a family of fourteen brothers and sisters, in the truck-stop town of Charlemagne, Céline grew up the cherished youngest child in a poor but close-knit family. Her father, Adhémar, had worked 18-hour days to save the money to buy the land for their house, which her mother, Thérèse, helped build, climbing ladders even when pregnant with her seventh child. Although there was only one bathroom for all 16 of them, they were happy, because they loved music. Little Céline started singing Barbra Streisand songs in the Vieux Baril, the family piano bar, stunning the locals with her voice and classy moves. When Céline was only 12, her mother left a ribbon-wrapped cassette of one of her daughter's songs in the office of a prominent manager. This suave older man, former Baronnets singer René Angélil, instantly recognized a world-class voice and became not only her manager but eventually her lover – a worldly Willy to Céline's Colette – a relationship that culminated in a spectacular wedding in Montreal's Notre-Dame Basilica. Since then, life has been all glamorous triumphs: Academy Award performances before audiences of a billion; 11 albums, which have sold 100 million units; the mansion in Florida; the duets with Pavarotti and even – supreme triumph! – with her childhood idol Barbra Streisand. In spite of her fame, however, Céline has never forgotten her roots in Quebec. When she appeared on the local music industry's Félix Awards, she delighted everyone by wearing the shower cap of the character Moman from *La petite vie*, and she showed up at the Molson Centre wearing a Canadiens jersey, with Maurice Richard's number nine emblazoned on the back. To quote her official biography, Céline is "free, autonomous, in love, in good mental and physical health, solid and supple."

Here's a cynic's version of the fable, with details gleaned from some of the nastier, scandal-mongering biographies. Born the spoiled youngest daughter in a huge family, Céline proved unable to relate to her peers. Only happy when she was being showered with mindless adulation, this friend-less girl cultivated a singing talent that brought her to the attention of a local promoter, a Syrian who had performed with a derivative band recy-cling American pop songs. Twenty-six years her elder, chubby and bald, with a penchant for gambling, René Angélil divorced his wife – who would call her barely postpubescent rival a "home-wrecking Lolita" – to gain total control over what looked like a sure thing. Homely, long-toothed Céline – whom the local media had dubbed Canine – got a new face, a trip to the Berlitz language school, and caps for her terrifying incisors. Her wedding was a fiasco which even B-list stars such as Jay Leno, Mariah Carey, and Michael Bolton failed to attend, and 3,000 fans were left standing in the December cold outside near-empty Notre-Dame. Though she tries to act like one of the family when she comes back to Quebec, no one is fooled: not surprisingly, she was booed when she dared to wear a Canadiens jersey in Montreal. After all, this is a Québécoise who agreed to drop the accent from her first name and now sings almost exclusively in English. She manages to get her sprawling family off her back by giving them jobs in her chain of Nickel's restaurants – a "family" eatery where a nickel gets you a second plate of spaghetti – and the occasional cheque for 100 grand. Obsessed with adding to her collection of 500 shoes, so stressed-out and cadaverous she had trouble starting a longed-for family, Céline is another sad, rootless victim of North America's mindless culture of stardom. If her official biog-rapher had been frank, he might have written: here is a young woman shackled by celebrity, locked into a cynical, loveless relationship, emaci-ated, insecure, and materialistic.

Wherever the truth lies, Dion's stardom has become key to Quebec's sense of self. Bloc Québécois MP Suzanne Tremblay in 1999 thundered, "In her soul she is neither a Quebecer nor a Canadian. Her songs reflect nothing of what Quebecers experience," proving herself once again a Laurentian Pierre Berton, one of those hard-headed Canadian nationalists who see anyone seeking success abroad as a betrayer of the homeland. During the 1990 Félix Award ceremonies, the Quebec music industry pointedly named Céline Dion the "anglophone artist of the year," a prize she ruefully turned down.

In his 1999 book, *Céline Dion et l'identité québécoise*, Université Laval graduate history student Frédéric Demers took the opposite approach, arguing that, through her modest origins, her use of popular language, her fidelity to values of land and family, Dion "is a character who is absolutely central to the collective memorial novel that the Québécois are writing in their quest for a new identity." At the same time, she's redefining "the Québécois identity by personifying the archetype of the modern Being who is capable, entrepreneurial, profitable, effective, and hard-working." *Travail, famille, patrie* is how they phrased it in Vichy France – and if it all sounds a bit like Roland Barthes in the service of Marshal Pétain, the essay's straight-faced conclusion is unbelievable: "With Céline Dion at the controls, majestic and wreathed with a glory that never stops growing, Quebec can feel itself ready to face the challenges of the twenty-first century." Céline Über Alles!

"If you say something against Céline Dion," says Richard Martineau, with just a touch of bitterness, "you're a snob, a damn snob. If you attack Céline Dion, you're attacking all Quebecers. You have to love Céline Dion." I've met Martineau in the Montreal offices of the newspaper *Voir*, and we've taken our bilingual conversation down the street to the tightly packed tables of a nearby café. The editor of Quebec's major cultural weekly is known for his vitriolic columns – columns that have brought him mailed packages filled with human excrement – in which he denounces parochial group-think, encouraging his compatriots to open their minds to other cultures. In his late thirties, he's often cast as the Generation X iconoclast to older intellectuals like Jacques Godbout, with whom he co-authored a book of essays called *Le Buffet*, and separatist movie director Pierre Falardeau. Dressed in loafers and a bomber jacket, with a neatly trimmed beard and piercing eyes in a broad, angular face, he could pass for an assistant director on the set of a Quentin Tarantino film.

"Quebec is like a big family," says Martineau. "You always have to show you're part of the family. When Céline Dion comes back here, elle parrrlle comme çcça," he says, rolling the *r* and aspirating the *ç* in the manner of rural Québécois. "She plays the timid little sister. After she'd been to a big banquet with Princess Diana, she told a talk show host here that she was so embarrassed, she didn't know which fork to use. In fact, she knows perfectly well how to behave in public! But when you're in Quebec, you can't act like you're better than anybody else. You have to pretend you're still part of the family."

If Martineau is critical of such parochialism, he also understands the cause. "A friend of mine who lives in Toronto says, How come everything is so cheesy in Quebec? I mean, it's true, it's Elton John paradise here. The thing is, there are only six million of us. In the United States, you can aim at five per cent of the population and make a living – you can be a David Lynch or a David Byrne. Here, you have to appeal to young people, their aunts, their fathers, mothers, and uncles. That's why everything is so middle of the road."

As impatient as Martineau can sound with the limits of local pop culture, he's no elitist. Growing up in the Montreal neighbourhood of Verdun, where anglophone factory workers lived alongside working-class French, he remembers seeing his grandfather getting dressed up in a suit and tie to watch television and politely replying "Bonsoir, Monsieur" when the newscaster addressed the camera. Martineau has written documentaries for television, and his 1993 book *Pour en finir avec les ennemis de la télévision* is an attack on intellectuals who use the medium as a scapegoat for society's ills. But he's frankly more attracted by other countries' TV – he also listens to Frank Sinatra, the Sex Pistols, and Culture Club on his car stereo – and he's notoriously impatient with nationalists who say he should confine his interests to local culture.

"Historical series like *Les Filles de Caleb* took us back to the time when everyone was white and spoke French, where there was the mother, the father, and the 13 kids," he says. "The good old days. In reality, Quebec is exploding outwards – there are people who speak different languages, lots of different ethnic groups. There was an ad campaign by the provincial government that showed a black guy, and it said, 'My skin is black, but my heart is Québécois.' It's like, my black skin can't be Québécois, only my heart can be truly Québécois. We want immigrants to change, to integrate, to become like us – as in, 'He may be Chinese, but he plays hockey.' When we watch television, we're reassured, because it takes us back to the old face of Quebec, when it was more homogeneous, more closed. I think we're insecure about globalization in Quebec. People say that I'm too individualistic, too cosmopolitan, that I've lost my roots." Martineau shrugs. "But that's basically my generation. We don't know if we're European, we don't know if we're North American. We're split between French and English. I think this is so great! For a long time we saw this as a weakness, but I think it's Quebec's greatest strength. The future will belong to people who have various identities."

Like Jacques Villeneuve, winner of the Formula One World Championship in 1997. Born in Quebec, he went to school in Switzerland and has spent much of his life in Monaco. Flamboyant but calm, worldly but clearly Québécois, Villeneuve is a new kind of role model. In the book *Le Buffet*, Martineau quotes *La Presse* columnist Pierre Foglia: "Jacques Villeneuve is our first modern hero. [He] is Québécois, BUT NOT TOO QUÉBÉCOIS. He takes us beyond Quebec, instead of keeping us glued here like our traditional heroes. . . . Maurice Richard or Guy Lafleur were even 'purer,' better forms of ourselves, even more Québécois than us in their courage, their tenacity, their pigheadedness. . . . Not Jacques Villeneuve. He's Québécois – yes, very well, but not only Québécois. Québécois with other influences. He takes us elsewhere precisely when we've never had a greater need to go beyond ourselves."

Villeneuve's father, the reckless Gilles, killed on a Belgian racetrack in 1981, liked to drink Molson beer after he'd won a race. His son is more partial to champagne. He acknowledges the hometown crowd but rarely panders to it. "Villeneuve appeals to a younger generation," enthuses Martineau. "I'm a big fan of his. I like the way he handles himself; I like what he's saying about Quebec. He's very intelligent." I agree. People can confront, and even conquer, the world while maintaining their complex, ever-changing, but still Canadian or Québécois identities. Too many, unfortunately, submit to the reigning global banality and then neurotically pander to the hometown crowd to convince them that they're still the same old loveable hicks. Villeneuve has never bothered.

Too bad that television, with its sound bites and quick edits, has an aversion to conveying such complex identities – or any complex idea at all.

True, television has the potential to be a great educator, an awesome tool of communication. But it's not. It's almost inevitably utter crap. I've been left square-eyed and vapid by too many hours of hypnotism, vaguely aware that I've lost an evening of my life to mediocre storytelling, superficial journalism, debased public debate, and the usual volleys of repetitive advertisements, to spend any time defending this medium. Programs with real literary merit – like the early *téléromans*, or Victor-Lévy Beaulieu's *L'Héritage* – though not unheard of, are as much an exception in Quebec as elsewhere. And for all the pious, nonjudgmental, all-inclusive celebration of the medium's potential for creating consensus and identity, there's something a little eerie about that blue glow that emanates from living rooms in this province. It's like the hockey game in the modern arena: all seeming to share the same experience, never quite meeting one another's gaze.

7

Q Is for Qulture

Aurore, Quebec's child martyr

On a winter's day in 1920, a gruesome autopsy is carried out in a Catholic church in a tiny village near Trois-Rivières. The local doctor notes 54 wounds on the corpse of an emaciated girl, among them a blackened eye, whip marks, burns, and a contusion on the forehead. The parents, Télesphore Gagnon and his second wife, Marie-Anne Houde, are immediately arrested and charged with the murder of their daughter. Little Aurore Gagnon lived only 10 years, but her long career as Quebec's most notorious martyr has just begun.

The whole province follows the trial with morbid fascination. The pregnant stepmother is led into the courtroom and peers through a black mourning veil as the prosecutor brandishes the curling irons, pokers, and ropes used to torture her helpless victim. The Quebec City judge has to scold the predominantly female crowd into silence; many have brought bagged lunches, for fear of losing their seats and a single second of the riveting testimony. After only 18 minutes' deliberation, the all-male jury condemns Marie-Anne Houde to death by hanging on the strength of the testimony of her own son. When Houde gives birth to twins shortly after the trial, her sentence is commuted, and she serves 15 years in Kingston Penitentiary. Her husband, who was seen beating the girl with horsewhips and axe handles, is convicted of manslaughter but serves only five years of a life sentence.

Somehow, the story of Aurore, a classic tale of Catholic suffering, continues to resonate even in a modern, irreligious Quebec. In the twenties, a Montreal theatre company turned the story into a shamelessly tearjerking melodrama, and it was performed six thousand times in the next three decades, often to packed houses. The story has been the subject of at least half a dozen novels, and there have been several radio and screen adaptations, including a 1994 TVA network courtroom drama.

But the most compelling re-enactment remains the 1952 film *La Petite Aurore, l'enfant martyre*. Embellishing freely, director Jean-Yves Bigras deepens the stepmother's wickedness by having her murder Aurore's natural mother with a forcefully administered dose of heart medicine. Free to torment the only witness to her crime, she pushes Aurore's head into a nettle bush and cuts off her long, flowing hair as the girl cries, "Pitié, Madame!" Then the real tortures begin. As incessant organ music swells, the skinny but resilient Aurore is battered with an axe handle, thrown down the attic stairs, and burned with a curling iron. ("It smells like grilled pork here," sniffs a nosy neighbour.) As punishment for confessing to the local curé, Aurore's tongue is then scorched with a red-hot flatiron.

Why this durable fascination with what, anywhere else, would have been simply a tragic case of child abuse? Scholars see Aurore as a metaphor for post-Conquest French Canadians, deprived of their real mother, France, and subjected to the humiliations of a new parent, England, under the complicit paternal gaze of the church and elected officials. In a 16,000-word article in the *Canadian Historical Review*, Université de Sherbrooke historian Peter Gossage argues that "the wicked stepmother story continued to reinforce prescribed notions of domestic morality in twentieth-century Quebec," which would account for its resurgence in the nineties, when Quebecers are seeking new models for ruptured families. By showing the most negative imaginable model of motherhood in a reconstituted family, Gossage believes, the story of Aurore actually reinforces the virtues of paternal authority and maternal love.

Whatever the explanation, the martyr-child is now so familiar that she's become part of the Québécois vernacular: mothers can still shush a theatrically whimpering child with a sharp, "Fais pas ton Aurore!" (Stop acting like Aurore!)

Boys, Les

The top-grossing Canadian production of 1998, and the most successful film in Quebec history, was a good-natured comedy about a garage hockey team triumphing against a gang of ex-NHL thugs. Filled with one-dimensional characters – an in-the-closet gay lawyer, a mindlessly violent Montreal cop, a rocker who does lines of cocaine between periods, and a team owner who's staked his sports bar on his boys' victory – the movie was predictably lambasted. For reviewer Odile Tremblay of *Le Devoir*, the comedy was proof of the philistine conformity of Québécois culture. "Whoever doesn't like *Les Boys* gets called an elitist and an intellectual. . . . Do you know any other society today where the word 'intellectual' is the equivalent of pariah, where any suggestion of elitism has the same stink of sulphur emitted by commie frequentations in the McCarthy era?" In retribution, director Louis Saïa wrote a ridiculous, poodle-like reporter called Odile Tremblette into the script of the sequel. Filmed in the Alpine village of Chamonix, packed with predictable jokes about cramped French hotel rooms, *Les Boys 2*, like the original, grossed well over $6 million. Even the soundtrack song, in which goateed rocker Éric Lapointe utters the phrase "Les Boys" over and over in a constipated growl, went platinum.

Its success suggests the analysts were missing the real significance of *Les Boys*. Sure, the characters played by Patrick Huard and Rémy Girard are a gang of louts. True, the triumph of broad humour doesn't bode well for any new equivalent of *Mon oncle Antoine*, the kind of understated gem Quebec excelled at producing in the seventies. But if *Les Boys* has succeeded, it's probably because lately the Canadiens have sucked. Only producer Richard Goudreau put his finger on the truth. "Timing is a key part of *Les Boys*' success story," he told an interviewer. "Les Nordiques [of Quebec City] are gone, and they were a team that people here really liked. The Montreal Canadiens are not the team of old, with heroes like Guy Lafleur and Patrick

Roy. There are no stars like that now. I think *Les Boys* came along and re-created those good old days." In other words, the 450,000 Quebecers who reportedly play garage-league hockey have turned en masse to a fictional version of the Canadiens legend, which was always about a bunch of love-able, raggedy-ass underdogs triumphing against big-league adversity.

Chouinard, Marie

In England, she's known as the choreographer who dared to reinterpret Stravinsky's *Rite of Spring*. The *Times* of London raved, "This Québécois choreographer has found a completely new way of treating one of this century's greatest scores." In Brussels, New York, and Paris, critics eagerly await her latest works, which tend to be aesthetically stark (but themati-cally rich) pieces centred on the female body. In English Canada, however, Marie Chouinard will be remembered as the dancer who came onstage and pissed into a bucket.

For most of the past decade, Montreal has been a recognized capital of modern dance, with 50 incorporated companies. The artists who in the seventies threw themselves – occasionally naked – around cold lofts and rock venues, creating a highly energetic, equilibrium-defying style of dance, are now international stars, often with companies of their own. Jean Grand-Maître, who supported himself as a butcher in Montreal in the eighties, is now one of Europe's foremost choreographers, producing shows for the Ballet de l'Opéra national de Paris and, most recently, a stun-ning *Madame Bovary* in the Munich Opera House. The muscular, dread-locked Louise Lecavalier, who has her own fan club in Japan, only recently announced her retirement from La La La Human Steps. Ginette Laurin of O Vertigo, Edouard Lock of La La La, Paul-André Fortier of the Université du Québec à Montréal – all are Montreal choreographers with worldwide reputations for original, highly physical dance.

None has been more innovative than Marie Chouinard. In a retrospec-tive in Montreal's Musée d'art contemporain in 1998, four young women showed why Chouinard's solo work is important. In the unforgettable "Dimanche matin, mai 1955," dancer Lucie Mongrain appears bathed in a bell-shaped bubble of scarlet light. As the sound of thunderous cathedral bells shakes the room, she leaps wide-eyed on the spot, like a leprechaun in a mason jar being jiggled by some perverse child. The 1987 solo that gave birth to Chouinard's acclaimed *Rite of Spring* has a flattened satyr lurching across the stage, its saccadic movements climaxing when it penetrates a pillar of light with a thrusting red strap-on. Many scenes are like kinetic tableaux vivants from circles of Dante's Inferno, nightmare glimpses of figures condemned to an eternal war with their own bodies.

Finally, a thin woman in a white slip walks onto the stage, metal pail in hand, profile to the audience. She puts down the bucket, crouches over it, and a thin stream of what is undeniably urine clatters on the tin. In context, the gesture is simple, dignified, and moving (not to mention an impressive triumph of muscles over nerves). An overly mystified human function is stripped to simplicity on the stage – something Nijinsky himself might have dreamt of doing in Paris in 1912.

Cirque du Soleil

When *La Presse* reporter Nathalie Petrowski went to New York to produce a National Film Board documentary on the Cirque du Soleil, she asked the clowns, contortionists, and gymnasts – then performing in Manhattan's Battery Park – whether they feared they'd lose their soul to the Americans. Denis, a brilliant clown who calls himself a Québécois nationalist, replied, "I've always sensed an arrogance on the part of Americans, in wanting to impose their culture. This is like our counterattack." Cofounder Guy Laliberté, a former fire-eater, cited the bottom line: "Our survival depends on our capacity to develop the American market." By the end of the documentary, the Cirque has won the hearts of the tough Manhattan crowd – and the nationalist clown has married a girl from New York City.

A decade later, Cirque du Soleil is a leading entertainment multinational. In Las Vegas, this troupe of street performers from Quebec, renowned for acrobatics rather than trained seals, fills 1,500 seats twice a night at $100 a pop. The organization boasts 460 performers, has offices in Amsterdam, Las Vegas, and Singapore, and generates annual revenues of more than $200 million, simultaneously running seven shows on four continents. They've opened a permanent theatre at Walt Disney World (their partnership with Disney will last until at least 2010) and are producing their first large-format IMAX film. Traditional European circus owners, who have seen some of their best artists stolen by these show-biz-oriented upstarts, accuse them of being the "McDonald's of circuses" – implying that the Québécois turn out their shows on an assembly line and treat their stars like burger flippers. Canadian nationalists sigh that they're yet another world-class act who have auctioned off their talent to Mammon.

All of which is grossly unfair. From the start, Cirque du Soleil was a North American version of a European circus, presenting traditional clowning and trapeze work to a rock-video rhythm. As for selling out, in 1996 they opened a $40-million office in the Montreal neighbourhood of St-Michel, and today it's an impressive centre for rehearsals, set design, and management that serves as the private company's worldwide headquarters.

The Cirque debuted the show *Dralion*, in a big top outside its corporate headquarters, in the spring of 1999. Hundreds of taxis deposited the cream of the Quebec media and entertainment industries in what was once a desolate no man's land. The route to the main ring led through smaller tents where employees sold $375 leather jackets, Cirque du Soleil albums, and computer mouse pads emblazoned with the smiling-sun logo. Inside the main tent, the names of corporate sponsors – Air Canada, Culinar, Wyndham Hotels – encircled the bleachers. The performance was, as usual, spectacular. A Ukrainian juggler in a G-string allowed volleys of balls to dribble precisely over a body straight out of a Calvin Klein underwear ad. A male singer in a Louis XIV–epoch gown screeched like the castrato Farinelli, haughtily wandering the stage as Chinese acrobats leapt through hoops, juggled umbrellas, and were borne aloft by a horizontal ring that descended from the ceiling.

These days, fewer than a third of the Cirque's performers are Canadian. That night, the artists came from Brazil, France, the Ivory Coast – and yes, the United States. In spite of it all, however, the local crowd didn't look particularly betrayed by the Cirque du Soleil's definitive transformation into what Americans call the "Ceurk dou Soley." After all, these jet-setting funambulists have made Montreal their pied-à-terre, bringing some of the world's best talent back home with them.

Desjardins, Richard

On a winter night at the Spectrum, a concert hall on Rue Ste-Catherine, it looks like every bearded and hennaed baby boomer in Montreal has made it downtown. It's the fiftieth anniversary of the signing of the Declaration of Human Rights, and tonight's $25 ticket price will benefit a variety of worthy organizations. We've already heard from an elderly Tibetan monk, imprisoned for 30 years by the Chinese, whose long series of thank-yous is laboriously translated into English by his interpreter, and then into French by the evening's master of ceremonies, Rhino Party candidate François Gourd. Periodically, local celebrities stand up to recite one of the 30 articles of the landmark 1948 United Nations document. It's the kind of evening when middle-class hippies feel obliged to applaud everything, with a kind of self-congratulatory earnestness that makes one long for an irruption by the local Hells Angels chapter.

Then Richard Desjardins steps on stage. Tall and slender, round wire-rimmed spectacles poised on a beakish nose in the centre of a bird-of-prey face, Desjardins has the caustic edge that made Bob Dylan transcend all the lame folkies who followed him. Acoustic guitar plastered against a long-sleeved black shirt, Desjardins calls to mind a rural schoolmaster (in fact, he taught among the Inuit) whose May '68–vintage convictions are tempered by a refreshing capacity for irony.

Born in Rouyn-Noranda, northwest of Montreal near the Ontario border, Desjardins sings in an impassioned nasal twang, his thick joual peppered with English slang. (When he performed at the Théâtre de la Ville in Paris in 1992, he good-humouredly pulled out one of those digital subtitling machines they use at operas, translating his Québécois lyrics into standard French.) Squarely in the tradition of the politically engaged troubadour singer-songwriters of Quebec, he also owes something to sophisticated European lyricists Boris Vian and Jacques Prévert, as well as blues-and-country-influenced folkies like John Prine. But he's rougher around the edges: in Pierre Falardeau's 1989 film *Le Party*, a condemnation of prison conditions, Desjardins plays a tattoo-covered prisoner who belts out a song called "Le Screw" to a crowd of roaring convicts, detailing exactly what he's going to do to the guards' cars and wives when he's released.

Desjardins goes farther than his chansonnier predecessors in social engagement, too. Interviewed in 1996, he emphasized, "I'm mostly worried about our natural resources. Guys like [Gilles] Vigneault and [Félix] Leclerc were always singing about their beauty. But me, I have to stand up for them. These days, a feller-buncher can tear down 15,000 trees in a week. Let's just say that it's the kind of thing that can change your perspective on the forest." Subsequently, he spent two years making a National Film Board documentary about Quebec's $10-billion-a-year forestry industry. *L'Erreur boréale* caused a scandal (and won a Jutra award) when it appeared early in 1999. Desjardins used interviews with retired loggers and engineers to show how government-approved forestry practices were pushing the edge of the forest ever northwards. To the driving rhythm of Desjardins's guitar, a helicopter-borne camera shows the 100-metre strips of green that forestry companies have been careful to leave on either side of the province's major roads, camouflaging lunar landscapes of clear-cuts.

Desjardins's reputation as Quebec's foremost *homme engagé* is bolstered by the originality of his voice and his twisted and frequently impenetrable word play. Here's a sample from "Charcoal," a song whose reconditeness even unilingual anglophones should be able to appreciate (though it helps to know that *capote* means condom, and *bander* means to have an erection): "Je suis le bonhomme minimum / l'accident d'Occident, le Act of God / Je suis Al Capote au temps de l'inhibition. / Oui je vous le dis 'James Bande encore' . . . / La compagnie du no future / Charcoal, demain la guerre, yes sir."

Brilliant. But please don't ask me – or anyone else in Quebec, for that matter – to explain exactly what it means.

Érable, sirop d'

In late March, after a sufficient number of cold nights and warm sunny days, the sap in the maple trees of the Beauce region south of Quebec City, which accounts for half the production of the province that supplies most of the world's syrup, starts its rise. Local maple groves are transformed into sylvan blood donor clinics, as watery liquid leaks through notches cut into the bark, and then into blue tubes that snake through the maple groves and into the sugar shack. The thin serum thus collected is then boiled down, 40 litres of sap decocted into a single litre of maple syrup. Sold in corrugated cans that look like old-fashioned containers of motor oil, poured over thin, rubbery crêpes or baked beans, maple syrup is to Quebec what the mussel is to Belgium, what paprika is to Hungary: the star ingredient in an earthy, if occasionally maligned, local cuisine. In a good year, Quebec produces 36 million kilograms of the stuff. Most gets exported to the United States, Japan, and Germany, much of it plonk. (Unlike the stuff sold in Quebec groceries for about six dollars a pint, the export variety is a mixture of various grades, akin to a run-of-the-mill vin ordinaire or a blended Scotch.) The Québécois disparagingly dismiss Aunt Jemima's glucose-thick treacle as *jus de poteau* – the sap you might expect to collect from a wooden telephone pole. The best syrup is clear and light, the lowest grade is amber, and batches are further labelled with letters, AA being the best and C the worst. If it's collected too early in the year, maple syrup has an aftertaste of rotting wood; but when it's captured at just the right time, it's nectar, the essence of the north woods.

The quintessential Québécois winter experience is the cabane à sucre, where stir-crazy urbanites welcome spring by gorging themselves silly on maple taffy. The most original of these sugar shacks is set up every year outside Montreal's Insectarium, a museum devoted to the insects of the world. During the annual bug tastings every February, when toque-topped chefs bear platters filled with mushrooms stuffed with crickets, dessert is served outdoors: steaming maple syrup is ladled into a trough full of snow, where it congeals over an inert mealworm. Children line up to press wooden sticks into the resulting bug-sicle, a rather chilling gastronomic synthesis of habitant tradition and the foodstuff of a Malthusian twenty-first century.

Ferron, Jacques

One of the most intriguing voices in the sophisticated literary canon that emerged during the Quiet Revolution, Jacques Ferron remains underappreciated by English Canadians. Born in 1921, the son of an earthy notary and an upper-middle-class society lady in dot-on-the-map Louiseville, Ferron was educated by Jesuits at the Collège Jean-de-Brébeuf in Montreal. For Ferron, this brush with gentry and clergy was an unhappy time, which might account for his lifelong antipathy to fellow alumnus Pierre Trudeau and the historical writings of Abbé Lionel Groulx. After serving as a doctor in New Brunswick during the Second World War, he set up a private practice in Longueuil, across the Jacques Cartier Bridge from downtown Montreal. In *The Shouting Signpainters*, author Malcolm Reid's survey of the Québécois left wing in the sixties, Ferron is presented as a kind of Louis-Ferdinand Céline, the brilliant doctor-writer of the Parisian backstreets whose compassion for human suffering unfortunately didn't extend to Jews. In fact, Ferron, who had been a Communist in Duplessis's Quebec, dismissed Céline as a lout in the service of the ultimate lout, Hitler, and cited instead Victor Hugo, Jack Kerouac, and Charles Dickens as authors more worthy of admiration.

Strangely, in his plays, novels, and essays (Reid called him "the world's greatest writer of letters to the editor"), Ferron recalls none of these prolix influences. His best works are pithy morality tales that leave haunting echoes. *La Nuit*, about a bank clerk's nocturnal foray into the brothels and bars of a slightly askew Montreal, chauffeured across a stygian St. Lawrence by a cab driver named Alfredo Carone, uses striking imagery to turn a middle-aged fugue into a densely layered odyssey. The architecture of the suburbs is "humbly pretentious, proudly shabby"; a jar of quince jam takes on echoes of the madeleine of Proust. Ferron's work never crosses the line into gratuitous surrealism, however, and *Papa Boss* and *Contes du pays incertain* rank among the best fiction written in Quebec.

Like the other outstanding novelists of the era – including Hubert Aquin, who in 1969 turned down a Governor-General's Award for *Trou de mémoire*, and André Major, author of *Histoires d'un déserteur* and lately a Radio-Canada producer – Ferron was committed to politics. He ran as a candidate for the Rassemblement pour l'indépendance nationale, the separatist party that preceded the Parti Québécois, and helped negotiate the surrender of FLQ terrorists during the October Crisis. His taste for the absurd, handled with restraint in his fiction, took full flight in his public life. Inspired by a news item that said disgusted voters in São Paulo had elected a hippopotamus to office, he founded the Rhinoceros Party in 1963, explaining that the rhino was "the perfect symbol of the Quebec federal member of Parliament – myopic, clumsy, and thick-skinned, indeed somebody who loves to wallow in mire but who is quick to sense danger and run from trouble."

Ferron died in 1985, but the Rhino Party lived on, an enduring reification of a novelist's fertile imagination. It soon became a nationwide phenomenon, endearing itself to politician-weary Canadians with its promises to pay off the nation's public debt with an American Express card and move the Israeli embassy to Schwartz's Deli in Montreal.

Girard, François

With his *Thirty-Two Short Films about Glenn Gould* (1993), this handsome young director from the remote Lac St-Jean region instantly became a name to be reckoned with on the international festival circuit. Its numerology derived from the number of keyboard exercises and arias in Bach's *Goldberg Variations, Thirty-Two Short Films* was like a series of intellectual rock videos (Girard had spent much of the eighties doing work for artists such as Céline Dion), varying from 45 seconds to several minutes long, soberly partitioned by brief blackouts. Gould was a reclusive telephone addict who successfully dabbled in mining investments, retired from the concert stage early in his career, and made sound documentaries about the Canadian North for national radio. With such a Rubik's Cube of a subject, Girard's choice of narrative structure, which allowed him to meditate on irreconcilable facets of Gould's life, was inspired.

Another Québécois directing star, Robert Lepage, convinced pop singer Peter Gabriel to hire Girard as the director of his concert film of a five-continent world tour. Girard used multimedia software to produce the illusion of Yo-Yo Ma playing Bach cello suites within the walls of an eighteenth-century prison designed, but never built, by the Italian architect Piranesi. And he directed an acclaimed version of Stravinsky's *Oedipus Rex* for the Canadian Opera Company in 1997. By the time Girard was in his early thirties, his trophy cupboard included Emmys, Grammys, and Genies.

Girard's most recent film, *The Red Violin*, continues his obsession with music. Written with Don McKellar, the Toronto-based writer and director, it follows the story of a perfect instrument that is melodramatically varnished by a master Italian violin-maker, on the night of a full moon, using the blood of his dead wife. The violin passes through the hands of various owners – a child prodigy in an Austrian monastery, a priapic golden boy in nineteenth-century England, a Chinese classical musician during the Cultural Revolution – finally turning up in a Montreal auction house. Gorgeously filmed by Québécois cinematographers, boasting an international cast that featured *Pulp Fiction* hitman Samuel L. Jackson, *The Red Violin* picked up eight Genies at the Toronto-based film industry awards and nine Jutras at Montreal's equivalent.

Though he's consistently refused offers from Hollywood, Girard is nonetheless dismissed as too cosmopolitan by Québécois nationalists, who consider him a rootless, if undeniably talented, individualist. This parochial reaction nonetheless contains a hard core of truth. Film is the perfect medium for attaining the universal by delving ever deeper into the particular, whether through François Truffaut's day-by-day depiction of the life of a Parisian delinquent or Claude Jutra's evocation of a mining town on Christmas Eve. The films Girard cites as inspirations, including Wim Wenders's *The State of Things,* Jean-Luc Godard's *Contempt,* and David Cronenberg's *Crash,* are stylistically sophisticated exercises that demonstrate their directors' chilling and durable detachment from the human race. Girard is Quebec's best-known movie director these days, and one of the most technically gifted. Fortunately, he's hardly the most typical.

Gratton, Elvis

Created by the cantankerous director Pierre Falardeau in 1981, incarnated by the beer-bellied actor Julien Poulin, Elvis Gratton is a movie character who has become a byword for the materialistic, Budweiser-swilling vulgarian who opposes separatism because it might threaten his bungalow in the suburbs. Mindlessly satisfied with his vacations in the tropics, Elvis Gratton above all loves his upholstered van, his rec room shrine to the King, and the pro-business, American branch plant status quo of Quebec in Canada.

Falardeau brings to mind early Woody Allen: stale slapstick involving sticky beach chairs, obvious political gags, and a rather sorry run of jokes about midgets and women with braces. The film is saved by Poulin's over-the-top performance as a strutting amateur Elvis impersonator and garage-owner, whose triumph at a talent show wins him a week in the El Colonial hotel on the island republic of Santa Banana. The movie's best moment comes when a seatmate asks the southbound Gratton where he's from. Bumptiously proud, then increasingly perplexed, he replies: "Me, I'm a Canadien, Québécois." But that doesn't sound right, so he adds: "A Français, canadien-français." Still not quite right. "A French North American . . . a francophone, Québécois-Canadien . . . We're Canadian Americans, francophones from North America . . ." For many young Quebecers, the monologue epitomizes what they see as their absurd lack of identity on the world stage.

For separatist Falardeau, the only possible response to such a question would be "Québécois." Though he's proved he's an able filmmaker, Falardeau is still working with a political consciousness and sense of humour mired in the sixties. For him, Quebec remains a colony of English Canada, and the business and political leaders of the province are like the co-opted governors of a pre-independence African nation. He makes this explicit in a 14-minute-long film, the notorious *Le Temps des bouffons*. The short manipulatively contrasts 1957 footage of Ghanaians dressed in safari-wear, drooling and rolling their eyes in a trancelike parody of their white colonizers, with scenes of the festivities at the 200th-anniversary dinner party of Montreal's Beaver Club. What's really troubling is the hateful tone of Falardeau's gravelly voice-over; as the camera lingers on the faces of the revellers, he gleefully catalogues the objects of his scorn: "Little cunts who give head to get to the top, rotten lawyers, ass-lickers who take themselves for artists." He describes the Québécois bureaucrats in the crowd as "bilingual collaborators, dutiful French Canadians dressed up as bicultural Negro kings." Since Falardeau uses the techniques of propaganda at their most blatant, I'll point out that Hitler devoted similar energy and imagery to describing Jews in *Mein Kampf*. Though Falardeau's audiovisual rant switches the parameters from race to class and culture, the hateful timbre of the discourse is exactly the same.

The sequel to *Elvis Gratton*, released in the summer of 1999, shouldn't be confused with *Les Boys 2*, *Ding et Dong*, or other minor comedies that occasionally make it onto the low-powered radars based outside la Belle Province. With Falardeau, entertainment is always accompanied by polemic (most of it heavy-handed), which might explain the federal government's three-year delay in giving him funding for his latest project, a fictional retelling of the aftermath of the Patriotes' rebellion of 1837. After benefit concerts and a letter-writing campaign turned its initial refusal into a *cause célèbre*, Téléfilm Canada, that antidemocratic organ of our notorious police state, finally coughed up half a million dollars for the film.

Needless to say, Falardeau's acceptance of the cash should in no way be taken as an indication he's joined the other colonized ass-lickers who take themselves for artists in this oppressive banana republic.

Jutra, Claude

What is it with Quebec's most talented filmmakers? They burst on the scene with lyrical movies that tantalizingly suggest we'll enjoy a career's worth of ever-more-sophisticated works. And then they go and die, flaming out like James Dean in his Porsche (or Gilles Villeneuve in his Formula One).

Claude Jutra (1930-1987), who as a young man went to France to collaborate with François Truffaut and Jean Cocteau, came back to Canada to work for the National Film Board and in 1970 made the gorgeous *Mon oncle Antoine*. The simple story of a Christmas Eve calèche ride through asbestos-mining country in 1950, the film shows us in a single sequence everything we need to know about life in Duplessis's Quebec: an arrogant anglophone factory owner rides through town on a sleigh, dropping gifts in the middle of the road, like a sahib scattering rupees to Calcutta untouchables. Jutra made other films, but after his masterpiece he seemed to go into a decline. By the eighties, he was reduced to directing CBC documentaries in Toronto. One night, he wandered away from his Montreal home; his body was found six months later on the shores of the St. Lawrence. Jutra was one of the first identified victims of Alzheimer's Disease, a syndrome that until then didn't even have a name.

Francis Mankiewicz (1944-1993) was born in Shanghai after his father, a young judge, wrote a book denouncing the Nazis and was forced to flee Germany. As an infant, Mankiewicz lived in Los Angeles, where his family had relatives in the movie industry (most notably Joseph L. Mankiewicz, writer and director of *All about Eve*). The family moved to Montreal, and Mankiewicz went to French schools, eventually coming to think of himself as a francophone Québécois rather than an anglophone Quebecer. Before he died of cancer at 49, he had become an accomplished television director, making such acclaimed English-language films as *And Then You Die* and *Conspiracy of Silence*. In Quebec, he's remembered for *Les Bons Débarras* (1980), an intense gothic tale of a preadolescent girl's obsessive love for her mother. Réjean Ducharme's story of marginal outcasts, set among the opulent chalets of the Laurentians, was perfectly complemented by Mankiewicz's understated direction, producing a challenging, unsentimental portrayal of the limited horizons of childhood.

Judging from *Léolo* – at once his second, best, and last film – Jean-Claude Lauzon (1953-1997) was destined to become one of Quebec's most individualistic directors. The semi-autobiographical story of a kid who escapes from the sordid, everyday sexual obsessions in Montreal's Mile End neighbourhood by creating an elaborate fantasy world for himself (Lauzon opened the film with a shot of the facade of his family's Rue St-Dominique triplex), it had echoes of Fellini's *Amarcord* and Truffaut's *400 coups*. But it was a lot seedier than either of them – more reminiscent of *The Tin Drum* of Günter Grass than *The Tin Flute* of Gabrielle Roy – with sequences involving incest, cat torture, and an unforgettable scene of artificial insemination in which actress Ginette Reno has an intimate brush with a spunky tomato. A truly distinct Québécois cinematic vision was stifled when Lauzon, a bush pilot, crashed with his girlfriend, former child star Marie-Soleil Tougas, on their way back from a hunting trip to northern Quebec.

Lepage, Robert
Born in a poor neighbourhood of Quebec City in 1957, Robert Lepage has a brother and sister who are English Canadian, adopted when his parents lived briefly in Halifax (he once told a *Maclean's* writer, "My family is a strange metaphor for Canada; I have this strong impression we're of the same flesh, even if it's not the case"). At five, he was afflicted with alopecia – a hyperactive immune system causes the body to reject its own hair – and his baldness, which he covered with a baseball cap, eventually sent him into a deep adolescent depression. (He now wears a convincingly tousled wig, but the absence of eyebrows gives his face a strangely unfinished look.) It was the stage that helped bring him out of his severe funk, in the form of a particularly theatrical show by the rock group Genesis, which confirmed the 15-year-old's interest in staging. (He would pay his debt to prog rock, a durable and regrettable influence in Quebec theatre, by collaborating with François Girard on the design of singer Peter Gabriel's Secret World Tour.) He's bisexual, quadrilingual (with a working knowledge of Japanese and Russian), and multitalented, an actor in his own one-man adaptation of *Hamlet*, the director of three personal, Quebec-centred movies, and the creator of a body of plays that have been acclaimed in Paris, London, and Berlin. Yet he prefers to live in Quebec City, a conservative bureaucrats' town that in his films becomes as mysterious as Prague, where his troupe Ex Machina creates new plays in a completely renovated firehouse. Though he has offered vague support for independence, he also committed the heresy of mocking FLQ terrorists as bumbling clods in his meta-farce, the 1998 film *Nô*.

Perhaps the best way to get to know the contours of his genius is to watch *Le Confessionel*, his first film. Gliding seamlessly between 1952, the year of Alfred Hitchcock's visit to Quebec City to make the Montgomery-Clift-as-preacher vehicle *I Confess*, and 1989, when a young man just returned from China tries to come to terms with his adopted older brother, a tortured homosexual, the movie is a crash course in the major Lepagean motifs. Adoption, suitably Hitchcockian false accusation (Lepage himself was a suspect in the murder of his best friend, an episode that would become the focus of his second film, *Le Polygraphe*), the ritual of confession, fiction and theatre as inextricably bound to reality – it's all there, in a narrative as involving as a good film noir.

Québécois critics tend to be hard on Lepage, in the same way that the hometown media are the most savage detractors of the Canadiens hockey team. When his play *The Geometry of Miracles*, an exploration through dance of Frank Lloyd Wright's architecture, debuted in Toronto, local critics accepted its rough edges as a work in progress, while Québécois reviewers tore it apart. At an Ontario press conference, Lepage diplomatically declared, "Quebec is a closed, insular, incestuous society that I'm very proud to be part of."

Miron, Gaston

In Quebec, *rapailler* means to pick up and gather diverse and often unrelated objects. Gaston Miron, often referred to as Quebec's national poet, saw himself as an uneasy alloy of ill-assorted identities, a characterization he emphasized by choosing *L'Homme rapaillé* as the title for his most important book of poetry.

Born among the Laurentian Mountains north of Montreal, Miron worked for a soft drink delivery company before founding Éditions de l'Hexagone in 1953, a publishing house that has since printed the work of Quebec's best poets. Nonetheless, for much of the Quiet Revolution Miron himself went unpublished, allowing his reputation as Quebec's Pablo Neruda to grow among the separatist left. When *L'Homme rapaillé* was finally released by another publisher in 1970, it was immediately recognized as a masterpiece. That same year saw Miron jailed for two weeks, along with Roch Carrier, at the height of the October Crisis. Miron would always retain his separatist ardour, but he didn't blindly scorn English Canada. At the Chez Temporel coffee house in Quebec City, he read aloud his translations of the poems of Dennis Lee (best known for his children's book *Alligator Pie*), and he gladly accepted the Canada Council's $50,000 Molson Prize in 1985.

Miron's sense of alienation from his own land, exacerbated by the American tourists who came to frolic in the mountain playground where he grew up, was felt most acutely on the level of language. He conveyed this estrangement brilliantly in *Monologues on Raving Alienation*, translated by Marc Plourde in 1980: "Now I am in the city of plenty / great St. Catherine Street clops and gallops through a *Thousand and One Nights* of neon / while I cringe, walled up inside my cranium / with my kinship and language depoetized / decentred and disoriented in my convergences / memory and flesh." Miron's was one of the most important voices in forging a dignified, passionate, and clearly Québécois poetics, midway between anglicism-infiltrated joual and the international French adopted by the writers of Gabrielle Roy's generation. Miron was the afflatus of separatism, but he was already middle-aged by the time the radical writers of the Quiet Revolution were hitting their stride. A video of him reading "Le Marche à l'amour," a love poem set in Montreal, shows a man who looks more like a rural accountant than a poet, his ample belly contained by a button-down shirt. Yet Miron's words, declaimed with a rumbling, country accent that lingered on the *r*s, betray the passion of the lifelong bohemian.

Before he died of cancer in 1996 at 65, Miron was feted by dozens of poets and politicians at the Bibliothèque nationale, where the crowd was reminded that he'd been awarded the prestigious Prix Guillaume-Apollinaire by the Académie française. Fittingly, one of the most moving speeches that night was given by Camille Laurin, the creator of Bill 101. The stuck-together man lived to see his language, at least, take the place of English on the neon signs of Rue Ste-Catherine.

Nelligan, Émile
These days, it's hard to see the poetry for the legends surrounding the thin corpus of Émile Nelligan. It's even harder to glimpse the life of the poet for the myth making around the national symbol: Nelligan, a fin-de-siècle Montreal symbolist in the style of Paul Verlaine and Gérard de Nerval, is more often invoked than read. His life has been the subject of a movie (*Nelligan*, by Robert Favreau, 1991), a romantic opera (libretto by Michel Tremblay, 1990), several novels (including one by Réjean Ducharme), and even a ballet (by choreographer Ann Ditchburn, 1976). One of the few existing photos of the young poet, a slightly worried-looking kid with a

heavy brow and an impressively bohemian head of wavy hair, has become as emblematic of youthful romance as the only known photo of Rimbaud. While the French have been able to construct a complete bohemian mythology around Baudelaire, Verlaine, Lautréamont, and dozens of other decadent versifiers, the Québécois have had to pile their romantic impulses on the frail shoulders and airy stanzas of a lad who never wrote more than a hundred poems.

Émile Nelligan really did live – from 1879 to 1941, according to the tombstone in the cemetery on the slopes of Mount Royal. His Irish father was a post office worker who married a French-Canadian woman, and the family lived in upper-middle-class comfort in Montreal. To his parents' dismay, Émile, an unexceptional student, left school to write poetry, under the influence of Baudelaire and Rodenbach, before becoming the youngest member, at the age of 16, of the École littéraire de Montréal. Like Rimbaud (famous for "Le Bateau ivre," 1871), the French poet who blazed debauched through Paris after leaving a provincial home and a doting mother, Nelligan completed his entire oeuvre before he was 20. Again like Rimbaud, who finished his life in obscure and silent exile as a trader in North Africa, Nelligan lingered on earth after his period of greatest productivity. In 1899, he was diagnosed with dementia praecox, an incurable form of schizophrenia, and he spent the remaining 42 years of his life in asylums.

In fictional versions of the poet's life, particularly Michel Tremblay's opera and Robert Favreau's film, Nelligan is portrayed as a martyr, caught in an oedipal triangle with a brutal, philistine father and an unhealthily doting mother. The Québécois twist in this *poète maudit* saga lies in his father's refusal to speak French. Favreau's film opens with a scene of a haggard Nelligan towards the end of his life, clutching his skull and screeching, in English, "My head is bursting!" as a shirtless midget bangs the dripping wall beside him. According to Tremblay's libretto, it's his father's insistence that he speak English that finally drives Nelligan mad.

Nelligan was a fine poet – worlds beyond any of the Scottish poetasters who were stiltedly versifying in Victorian English Canada – the creator of stanzas so dependent on an inherently French-language assonance that their fragile essence evaporates in translation. One can't help grinning at the francophile juvenilia of his early poems, however, which tend to be filled with images of Baudelaire's tomb and Watteau's paintings. Nelligan would never actually make it to Europe, and one imagines it was hard to track down much opium or hashish in Montreal, then a pipe-tobacco-and-Scotch kind of place. His contemporary Louis Dantin wrote: "Nelligan was never a perfectly authentic bohemian . . . his beastliness was too studied, too conventional, too derived from reading and imitation. It mostly consisted of tousled hair, a rumpled frock coat and ink-stained fingers." Fortunately, Nelligan the myth is now so unassailable that it can withstand any hints that Nelligan the poet was a bit of an adolescent poseur.

Plamondon, Luc

Instantly identifiable with his black sunglasses, full head of wavy, greying hair, Riviera tan, black suits and $100 T-shirts, Quebec's most successful songwriter sounds as bad as he looks. Most of what is commercial, soulless, and insipid in Quebec pop music can be attributed to his influence over the past three decades. Plamondon's hits say it all: "Dans ma Camaro" (his first success in 1971, performed by Steve Fiset); "La Chanteuse straight" (by Diane Dufresne); "Coeur de rocker" (by Julien Clerc); and "Piaf chanterait du rock" (Piaf would sing rock), which gets my vote as the most pandering song title of the twentieth century. In fact, Plamondon's lazy reliance on *l'anglicisme sexy* is the only valid argument for the extension of Quebec's language laws to the cultural sphere. "I'm more interested in form than in content," he once told *L'actualité*, a memorable understatement. "One day I made baby doll rhyme with *idole*; Gainsbourg never managed to pull that one off." Serge Gainsbourg wouldn't have bothered trying. The French singer-songwriter, whose sophisticated, sensual word play made even Brigitte Bardot sound like a genius, would certainly have rejected such a lame rhyme.

In 1976, Plamondon wrote a rock opera called *Starmania*, whose soundtrack sold five million copies throughout the francophone world. His latest, *Notre-Dame de Paris*, is an adaptation of Victor Hugo's Gothic romance, with a couple of minor changes: the hunchback is a relatively good-looking Québécois hunk, the action takes place in modern times, and the cathedral is occupied by illegal immigrants from Africa. The press in France, bless their cynical hearts, trashed the musical. "A musical score that takes no account of new currents in music," marvelled *Le Monde*. "No hip-hop, no techno, just elaborate exoticism and a hyper-outdated classicism. . . .

Notre-Dame de Paris is a catalogue of clichés." At last count, the soundtrack had sold three million copies, mostly in Europe; by the end of 2000, the $10-million show itself will have been performed 270 times, in France, Belgium, Switzerland, and Canada.

Plamondon makes between six and seven million dollars a year on the project. Since the show relies entirely on prerecorded songs, working musicians in Quebec aren't making a penny. This means that *Notre-Dame de Paris*, in spite of its multimillion-dollar budget and the $115 ticket price, is essentially a karaoke megamusical, *Cats* with canned music. It's one we'll have to live with for a long time to come – particularly since an English version recently opened in London.

Poutine

The New World meeting of the famine-fleeing Irish and the frites-fancying French made it inevitable: the national dish of Quebec had to involve the potato. The etymology of the word "poutine" can be traced back to at least *poutingo*, a Provençal word that appropriately means "bad stew." In Quebec, the word was long applied to a kind of bread-based dessert – also called *pouding* – probably because of its consonance with the English word "pudding."

Surprisingly, the history of what we now know as poutine, that artery-choking meal of french fries covered with gravy and melted cheddar cheese curds, only goes back to the fifties. The scholarly *Dictionnaire historique du français québécois* cites several creation myths, including the version that has poutine being invented by an employee in the cafeteria of a Victoriaville taxi company. The most aggressive claimant for the title of the Edison of poutine, however, is Fernand Lachance, now in his seventies, who says he dropped a few cheese curds into a paper bag full of fries while working at the Café Ideal in the town of Warwick in 1957. It was a customer who dubbed the gooey result a "maudite poutine," and the rest is – maybe – history. In the nineties, poutine became something of an international fad, served in restaurants from Venezuela to New England, briefly available across Canada in restaurants in the A&W burger chain.

A typical plate of poutine contains about 700 calories and 60 grams of fat, which makes it pretty much the worst junk food imaginable, a heart attack on a plate. A restaurant in Quebec City devised an upscale version that consisted of cubed potatoes delicately fried with *fines herbes*, smothered with hollandaise sauce, and covered with grated mozzarella and a poached egg – the latter presumably to boost the cholesterol count to fatal levels.

Refus global

In 1948, a professor of drawing and decorative arts at Montreal's École du meuble deposited 400 copies of a thin, mimeographed pamphlet at the Henri Tranquille bookstore on Rue Ste-Catherine. Signed by painters, photographers, dancers, poets, a well-known psychiatrist, and a window decorator at Birks jewellery store (16 people, seven of them women, a group the local press would dub "les automatistes"), the manifesto titled *Refus global* would briefly provoke a scandal among the elites of Quebec. The ringleader, Paul-Émile Borduas, was an acolyte of painter and church decorator Ozias Leduc. In a society the intellectuals of the day referred to as the only theocracy north of the Rio Grande, daring to call Quebecers "a little people huddled against the skirts of a priesthood seen as the sole trustees of faith, knowledge, truth, and national wealth" – as the manifesto did – was a risky proposition. In the ruckus that followed, the window dresser was reprimanded by her boss, two of the signers committed suicide, and Borduas, fired from his teaching post, left Quebec for New York and then Paris, where he died in 1960.

When *Refus global* was published, it went virtually unnoticed by the population at large, but five decades later, post–Quiet Revolution Quebec celebrated the manifesto as one of its founding documents. In 1998, the *automatistes* definitively came home: major retrospectives of the canvases of Marcel Barbeau, Jean-Paul Riopelle, and Fernand Leduc were launched at Montreal's two leading museums, and poet and manifesto co-signer Claude Gauvreau's surrealistic play *Les Oranges sont vertes* was staged at the mainstream Théâtre du nouveau monde. Even Canada Post got into the act, announcing a series of commemorative stamps.

Then the counter-reaction began. Manon Barbeau, the daughter of Marcel Barbeau, a painter and manifesto co-signatory who now lives in Paris, made a film called *The Children of Refus global*. In it, she tracks down the dysfunctional kids of the *automatistes*: Borduas's son, a rake-thin beach bum with a gap-toothed grin, is living in a shack in the Dominican

Republic. Barbeau's own brother turns out to be a schizophrenic who was institutionalized in Quebec City for much of his life. There's a shocking interview with Jean-Paul Riopelle – the once dashing bohemian looks like a picture of Dorian Gray executed by Goya – in which he declares his disgust with art and the world, muttering, "There's nothing of any value in life."

Manon Barbeau's film is a courageous attempt to understand the complex social and personal factors that led to the explosion of her family. Her father, like many of the *automatistes*, was deeply troubled, a man who'd fought severe depression all his life. A conservative current in the media, however, interpreted *The Children of Refus global* as a demonstration of cosmopolitan bohemians' getting their just deserts. By seeking – and gaining – recognition abroad, the talk show hosts suggested, these self-indulgent artists had betrayed not only their children but also the whole of Quebec.

A reading of *Refus global* – it's a scant six typewritten pages – goes a long way to demystifying the discourse that's grown up around it. In the tradition of the surrealist manifestos that preceded it (the automatic writing espoused by André Breton was a clear inspiration for the Canadian *automatistes*), the pamphlet is filled with such lapidary appeals to self-liberation as "The frontiers of our dreams will never be the same" and "Make way for magic! Make way for objective mysteries! Make way for love!" *Refus global* is anti-church, anti-politics, anti-reason. One senses that, in an impossibly stifling society, the *automatistes* were trying to clear a space for themselves, the better to engage in artistic play. There's no hint, however, that they were interested in creating a new country. In fact, Borduas was firmly antinationalist. Since liberty was a precondition for creativity, he was suspicious of any group that preached the subordination of individual freedom to the needs of nation building. In a society whose goals have often been collective, Borduas preached the heresy of artistic self-fulfillment, as avant-garde artists the world over had before him. During the October Crisis of 1970, radical leftists, anticipating the imminent creation of a nation, decided they wouldn't allow the traitorous Riopelle to return to a sovereign Quebec.

Fortunately, when they're dead or inactive, even the most radical artists can be conveniently incorporated into the national pantheon. Hanging

on the walls of Montreal's Museum of Fine Arts and Musée d'art contemporain in 1998, the works of the *automatistes* looked curiously inoffen-
sive. Borduas's later Parisian impasto work, black-and-white canvases
reminiscent of patches of snow on a ground cover of wet leaves. Riopelle's
paintings looked like more tightly wound abstract impressionism, Jackson
Pollocks with Miró's gift for calligraphy. Easy to slot into other twentieth-
century schools and movements, they are hardly threatening, even for the
most conservative corporate sponsors.

"Decadence became pleasant and necessary," the *automatiste* manifesto
lamented half a century ago. "It allowed us to strait-jacket mighty rivers as
a prelude to the wilful destruction of our planet." The paintings can now
safely appear on the walls of the Museum of Fine Arts, whose president,
former Lavalin CEO Bernard Lamarre, had built one of the world's largest
engineering firms precisely by straitjacketing the rivers of Quebec.

Sol

Marcel Marceau meets Charlie Farquharson? Actually, that's not quite fair.
The Québécois clown Sol, alias Marc Favreau, is less precious than the
famous French mime and far more subversive than the punning bumpkin
interpreted by Don Harron. Now in his early seventies, Favreau first
appeared as Sol on television in 1958, in a Radio-Canada kids' show called
La Boîte à surprise. Through the sixties, he had a variety of partners: Bim,
Bouton, and finally – and most famously – Gobelet, who played the sneaky
clown to Sol's good-natured naïf. In 1973 Sol went solo, making the transition from television to stage when he plopped his trademark garbage can
on the boards of Montreal's Patriote theatre.

Favreau dresses as the classic vaudeville bum (more akin to Charlie
Chaplin than Farquharson's swaggering hayseed): overalls, loosely knotted
rag-tie, headpiece more holes than hat, face painted with Blutoesque
eleven o'clock shadow. The physical comedy of his early television shows
has long since given way to slippery puns, meaning-laden Freudian slips
reminiscent of the wordplay of Raymond Queneau (the French author of
Zazie dans le métro) or the gargantuisms of Rabelais. Sol is a precocious
clown-child whose linguistic reach far exceeds his grasp, but when ill-
formed neologisms slip from between his lips, they tend to undermine
dominant clichés.

In a monologue published in 1982, Sol complains of his obnoxious neighbours, who come over to forcefully offer him their monkey wrench, or *clef anglaise* – literally, their English key. Initially reluctant to take it, he realizes that his new *clef anglaise* opens all doors. Without it, you're bound to remain a "petit exployé" – a minor, exploited employee. With it, you can go into a department store, where you're sure to be the "first to be serviled"; it's almost like having a "credulity card." Sol imagines himself a businessman, "très imposable" (he means very imposing, but it comes out "very taxable"), making full use of his *clef*: he'd probably have a "déceptionniste" (a deceitful receptionist) who'd "répondre à l'anglophone" (rather than answer the telephone). Finally he sees himself a press baron, a "manipulpateur" of pulp paper, the friend of the "rétracteur-en-chef "(or *rédacteur-en-chef*, editor-in-chief, who becomes the head retractor).

The politics of Sol? He refused to make a television ad for Robert Bourassa's Liberal Party in 1970, but then he's refused all offers to sell soap flakes or ideology, making his living instead off his shows and sales of his monologues in book form. Nonetheless, Favreau has gone on the record saying that he's in favour of independence. Does that make Quebec's national clown a jesteratist?

Têtes carrées

Here's a classic Québécois joke, translated into English: An Anglo with winter motor problems goes into a Canadian Tire in Quebec City and asks for a block heater. The employee hands him a tuque. Funny, non?

The word "block" – an anglicism widely used in francophone stores – is pronounced like "bloke" in Québécois French; and "bloke" is local slang for an Anglo. Hence, a head-warming tuque is a bloke heater.

A more advanced reading of the joke would take into account the persistence of *tête carrée*, or squarehead, as a slang term for Anglos. In the popular phrenology of racial stereotypes, people of British descent are seen as having more rectangular skulls than those of French ancestry. (There may be some truth to this; I'm accustomed to the pleasing *rondeur* of Gallic faces, while increasingly disturbed by my Anglo compatriots' resemblance to Max von Sydow.) Part of the joke's appeal lies in the mental image it elicits: that of a striped tuque stretched around the rectangular, engine-block-shaped head of the befuddled Anglo.

A number of certified *têtes carrées* know enough French to swap jokes with their fellow citizens, a talent that seems to have earned them the unofficial title of Honorary Francophone in Quebec.

Among them: bilingual Montreal-lover Josh Freed, humour columnist for the *Gazette* and author of *The Anglo Guide to Survival in Québec* (and the sequel, *Anglo 2*) – even though he admits he doesn't understand the appeal of the sitcom *La petite vie*. Pop singer Corey Hart, whose long-standing relationship with Québécois singer Julie Masse means he can be interviewed on Musique Plus without the VJs' having to translate his responses. Ray Conlogue, a former Montreal correspondent for the *Globe and Mail* and the author of *Impossible Nation*, whose deep appreciation for local culture endeared him to francophone Quebecers (his Irish ancestry didn't hurt, either). Phyllis Lambert (née Bronfman), head of the Canadian Centre for Architecture, also makes the cut, possibly because she looks like the long-lost twin of another severe-looking knuckle-rapper, Lise Bissonnette. The most bizarre of the Frenchified blokes is surely British-born David Payne, member of the national assembly for the Vachon riding and the only anglophone member of the Parti Québécois. (It's as if British Columbia's historic Asiatic Exclusion League had nominated a Chinese treasurer.)

The title of Honorary Francophone entitles its bearer to at least one major profile in *L'actualité*.

Unibroue

Beer was always the drink of choice in Quebec. The first real industry in New France was the Brasserie du Roy, founded in 1668 by the colonial administrator Jean Talon. British orphan John Molson founded his brewery in Montreal in 1786. A year before Confederation, this honest little ale had made Molson so many friends that he was literally given a licence to print money: the Molson's Bank, a Second Empire–style wedding cake of a building that still stands on St. Jacques Street, briefly issued its own Molson money, an early prototype for Canadian Tire banknotes.

Molson's became the cornerstone of a nationwide, Anglo-controlled vice industry: Imperial Tobacco, Seagram, General Cigar – if it was addictive, its head office was probably in Montreal. In English Canada, a beer belly is known as a Molson muscle. In Quebec, the beer itself was adopted into joual, the stubby little bottle affectionately Frenchified as *une p'tite molle*.

The market stranglehold of big brewers across North America has lately been broken by microbreweries, whose triple-refermented-nut-brown creamy-acorn ales can now be found in convenience stores. Quebec was never much of a wine-producing society; not infrequent May snowfalls put an early end to any dreams of a local industry boasting its own unpretentious little Côtes-du-Saint-Laurent. The Québécois are Latin in the same way the Belgians or Bretons are Latin – that is, not very Latin at all, really. They drink 87.8 litres of beer per capita a year, second in the country only to Newfoundlanders, but only 12.9 litres of wine, behind British Columbians, who down 14.3 litres. The recent burgeoning of francophone breweries specializing in Gothic doomsday beers is proof positive of a Viking streak in the Québécois soul.

Take La Fin du Monde, for example, a delightful, coma-inducing beverage Leif Ericsson might have appreciated. Brewed in the Trappist style by Unibroue (a company that might be the locus of more nationalist pride if one of its chief shareholders weren't singer Robert Charlebois, notorious for hobnobbing with Liberals such as Paul Desmarais and Jean Chrétien), it's been noted for its hints of gooseberry and yeast, and likened to stewed apples and freshly baked muffins. London's *Independent* newspaper, which usually only notices Canada when the country is about to disintegrate, devoted a special feature to La Fin du Monde, declaring, "It is one of the most exciting beers ever to emerge from Canada, and certainly the best from that country to reach these shores." Its alcohol content is also nine per cent, almost twice the Canadian average and three times the percentage in American brews.

Other major Unibroue products include Maudite – an eight per cent beer whose label features coureurs du bois in an airborne canoe guided by a grinning Satan – and 1837, a seven per cent wheat beer whose name and label commemorate angry French-Canadian peasants marching with pitchforks towards the English oppressors. (It should come as no surprise that this particular Unibroue product is only available in Quebec.) The names of other Quebec ales – L'Infidèle, Eau Bénite (Holy Water), Illégal – are all designed for maximum sin appeal, and the labels look like the kind of van art you might have seen if they'd been making Chevys in the Middle Ages.

Vorilhon, Claude

It's a balmy summer evening, and a late sunset is pinkening the faces of a group of francophones gathered outside the Salle Gesù, a venerable pile of cut stone in downtown Montreal. It's an unusually convivial and touchy-feely crowd, even for Quebec: there are shouts of recognition, lingering hugs, affectionate rubbing of shoulders and biceps. Most of them are beautiful, too: buff, tanned men in ribbed white T-shirts, and striking women, apparently from every continent, staring newcomers like me in the eye.

This is a gathering of the Raëlians, an organization whose members believe that the fact that the human race was created by extraterrestrials shouldn't interfere with hedonistic enjoyment of sex. In the lobby, women dressed in white are passing out pamphlets for UFOland, a kind of alien amusement park in the Eastern Townships ("Exact replica of a UFO! World's biggest building made of bales of straw! World's tallest replica of DNA!"). The Raëlian Movement isn't, I've been assured, one of those Solar Temple–style death cults. It's a good thing, because, judging from all the beatific smiles and unconditional love around me, I get the feeling I'm one of the few non-Raëlians in the building tonight.

I enter the auditorium and sit next to a tall, blond woman, in a white halter top and tight white pants. She turns to me, fixes me with baby blue eyes as round as saucers, and asks, in heavily accented French, where I first heard the message. "Boulevard St-Laurent," I deadpan – which is where a Raëlian on in-line skates handed me a pamphlet for tonight's conference on human cloning. Ivana tells me she heard the message from her brother, and left her native Warsaw to be near other Raëlians in northern France. I ask whether she lives in a community, but she shakes her head. "We're free to come and go as we please, you know." She moved to Quebec about five months ago to be near Raël and is making her living as a dancer. This being Montreal, dance capital of the universe, I reflexively ask her what troupe she's with. "No," she says, looking at me as though I'm a bit of a dunce. "I dance in the clubs." *Riiight.* I'd heard that a disproportionate number of Raëlians come from the exotic dance community. Every few minutes, Ivana interrupts our conversation to hiss ineffectually at a toddler in a print dress running rampant in the aisles. "Isis!"

The Raëlians claim about 35,000 members worldwide, and though only 4,000 are French Canadian, the fact that Raël himself now lives here has made Quebec the organization's de facto headquarters. He's found fertile material for recruiting in la Belle Province. There are now 800 sects and religions to choose from in the Montreal area alone. Quebec's more notorious New Age religions have included the cult of Roch "Moses" Thériault, a Seventh Day Adventist who one day saw the light, declared himself Oint de l'Éternel, and took his brood to the remote Gaspé Peninsula, where he oversaw amputations, castrations, disinterments of rotting corpses, and brawls among the survivors. Then there's the infamous Order of the Solar Temple, a cult founded by a Belgian homeopath, whose local branch boasted the former mayor of Richelieu, several journalists, and a Hydro-Québec vice-president – before they committed mass suicide, embarking on that long voyage to Sirius.

The Raëlian Movement, thankfully, seems to demand less of its followers. Raël is actually Claude Vorilhon, a former French automobile journalist, who explains in his book *The True Face of God* that he was taken to the planet of the Elohim in a flying saucer in 1975, where he was introduced to Jesus, Buddha, Joseph Smith, and Confucius. The Elohim, small human-shaped beings with pale green skin and almond eyes, were apparently the original inspiration for the Judeo-Christian god. They informed Vorilhon that he was the final prophet, sent to relay a message of peace and sensual meditation to humankind under his new name of Raël, before the Elohim would return to Jerusalem in the year 2025. They didn't, however, oblige him to give up race-car driving, and Raël spent much of the eighties and nineties whipping around the world's racetracks in his beloved Mazda RX 7 Turbo. The theme of tonight's lecture, cloning, seems to be linked to Raël's conviction that the human race was created in the laboratory from the DNA of aliens 25,000 years ago.

As extraterrestrial religions go, the Raëlian Movement International seems to be fairly benign. In the 1995 book *The Gods Have Landed*, Susan Jean Palmer, a Dawson College expert in what sociologists call New Religious Movements, has found little evidence of nefarious activity among the Raëlians. Recounting one of the monthly Sunday meetings at Quebec's Holiday Inns, Palmer described the style of feminine dress ranging "from elegant *Paris Match*, to punk, to (apparently unconscious) parodies of

Brigitte Bardot in her St. Tropez heyday." Certainly enough to keep the stray bodybuilders of the me generation coming back for more. Like the Rajneeshi of Oregon, a movement that also attracted baby boomers, the Raëlians are essentially members of a lifestyle cult. In increasingly irreligious Catholic societies, Raël's success seems to derive from offering a structured environment for decadent behaviour: he offers a no-guilt playground for hedonism and sexual experimentation.

Ivana's interest in me has waned since she's learned that I don't really have the fundamentals of the "message" down, and her gaze wanders to the elaborately muscled men milling in the aisles. After several guest speakers, an MC announces the arrival of "the prophet of the Third Millennium," and Raël himself strides out on stage. Short, with a receded hairline and the remains of his curly black hair drawn up into a topknot, he looks a bit like a Samurai warrior crossed with the Man from Glad. He's wearing a white shirt with huge shoulders, baggy white pants, and white slippers, and sports the heavy silver medallion I've seen around many necks tonight, a Star of David filled with swirls. Somehow, I have trouble convincing myself I'm in the presence of a god. Raël's accent sounds like he's trying to dislodge a wad of phlegm — or a mussel — caught in the back of his throat, which makes me suspect that he's actually a Belgian.

Raël paces around like a seasoned stand-up comedian, working the crowd. After taking a couple of shots at the Pope ("The difference between me and Jean Paul II is that, every year, everything that he says is proved to be false, and everything I say proves to be true!"), he turns to the main theme of the evening. He doesn't want to encourage human cloning to create lots of little replicas of himself. He wants to clone himself so he can live forever! "Do you want to die at the age of 35?" he asks. "No!" is the resounding reply from the audience. Judging from the youthful appearance of everyone in the room – the baby boomers here are glowing with health – I'm beginning to suspect that I've stumbled onto some kind of sect inspired by the seventies science film *Logan's Run*, where the old are vaporized. And as an Anglo writer in a room full of French-Canadian hedonists, I feel like I'm thirtysomething going on 70.

What's more, I'm blatantly scribbling in a notepad just as Raël is having a go at the journalists. Distancing his religion from the Solar Temple, he confesses his disgust with reporters. "I used to be one myself, you know. But why do the journalists always call me when there's a collective suicide? I don't want to die! I want to be around to piss them off for a long time!" The crowd responds with roars of delight.

Ivana, I've noticed, is eyeing my dancing pencil. In spite of myself, an image straight out of the remake of *Invasion of the Body Snatchers* springs to mind: Ivana leaps to her feet, points at me in a rage, and the word "Journalist!" issues from her inhumanly twisted mouth. A circle of toned and tanned bodies inexorably closes in on me, and the scene fades to black as I disappear beneath a pile of writhing lap dancers.

The Raëlians have a very nice little religion, I say to myself, gathering up my journalistic impedimenta and making a quick exit. They might even be fun to hang out with for a summer, practising a little sensual meditation with a United Nations panel of strippers – if only it weren't for all that UFO stuff. The problem is, my pleasure would be ruined by the knee-jerk curiosity inculcated by my own sect, the Newsman cult. Too many questions are already springing to mind: What happens if you neglect to pay Raël his 10 per cent tithe? If the Elohim created humans from their own DNA, who created the Elohim? And – most important – what happens to Raëlians when they get old?

The Wolf

Francophone Quebecers have long been more inclined to canned disco and spacey progressive rock than original pop music, a trend that continues in Montreal's belated but enthusiastic embrace of reheated techno and rave culture. The real indigenous folk music of Quebec, the kind you hear in the Lac St-Jean region or La Mauricie, is all reeling fiddles and clicking spoons, an indication that hillbilly culture, like the Appalachian range itself, extends all the way from Georgia to the Gaspé. A few young performers, such as Mara Tremblay and Fred Fortin, are attempting to fuse Québécois folk with the energy of punk rock. In general, however, the Quebec sound has been a depressingly lame one: New Wave disco hippies such as Men Without Hats and Mitsou, heavy metal freak shows like the Killer Dwarfs and Voïvod, and retrograde stoner groups, notably Grimskunk and Les Colocs, which have persisted long after their godfathers the Red Hot Chili Peppers faded into merited obscurity.

Fortunately, there's the Wolf, or Jean Leloup as he's known to his compatriots. Though he was born in Quebec City in 1961, his father's teaching career gave him the gift of an African childhood, and the young Jean Leclerc (his real name) learned to play the drums in Togo and the guitar in Algeria. By the eighties he was back in Quebec, where he landed a role in Luc Plamondon's musical *Starmania* and studied French literature at the Université Laval before scoring a huge hit with the song "1990." A catchy, semi-rave dance tune that has a bored Leloup making love to his girlfriend while the Gulf War rages on the television set, it was a smash throughout the francophone world. A career-stalling flirtation with hard drugs followed, but Leloup has recently come back with *Le Dôme* and *Les Fourmis* – two rocking albums – and he can easily sell out a week's worth of shows at the 2,000-seat Metropolis. These days, the darkly handsome singer can be seen striding guitar in hand through the streets of the Plateau, distractedly humming a tune.

Leloup is a natural fit in France, where performers like Mano Negra, les Négresses Vertes, MC Solaar, and the Little Rabbits have used Arab and Spanish melodies, traditional *chanson*, gangsta rap, and English-language garage punk to create a cosmopolitan new sound. At home, he's closer to the hybrid anglophone-influenced scene. The city's ever-changing group of freefloating English-Canadian bohemians have either formed underground bands – including godspeed you black emperor! and Molasses – or merged with local francophone musicians to nourish the thriving, jazz-influenced *musique actuelle* scene showcased every summer at an international festival in rural Victoriaville.

Montreal is no northern Nashville, but the city's linguistic, cultural, and musical cross-breeding means that the genuine musical talents it does produce tend to be one-of-a-kind. Which explains Leonard Cohen, scion of an upper-class Jewish family, setting his poetry to country and western music. Or James DiSalvio, son of an Italian restaurateur (and a director of Leloup's early videos), who founded Bran Van 3000, a group whose black and white members jadedly rap in French and English about reading *Paris Match* in Laval doughnut shops. Not to mention such adolescent turntable wunderkinder as A-Trak and Kid Koala, or Rufus Wainwright, the gifted son of American draft dodger Loudon Wainwright III and Quebec folksinger

Kate McGarrigle. A gay opera buff and pianist, Wainwright does Gap commercials, stays at the Chelsea Hotel in New York, and sounds like the love child of a maudlin Liza Minnelli and a tipsy Tom Waits.

But perhaps the most extreme example of Montreal *métissage* is Lhasa de Sela, a Mexican American born in New York's Catskill Mountains who has resolved the language issue in her adopted Quebec by singing in Spanish, against a background reminiscent of tormented Romanian gypsy melodies. Endorsed by the francophone press – *L'actualité* referred to her as "Un melting pot nommé Lhasa" – she has broken thousands of hearts in Quebec by announcing that she's moving to Europe.

X, or Réjean Ducharme

In 1966, a 24-year-old Montreal cab driver and proofreader with a couple of manuscripts in his desk, frustrated by a rejection letter from a Québécois publishing house, packaged them up in a brown envelope and mailed them to Gallimard, a prestigious publisher in Paris. To the consternation of Quebec's literary world, the house that had (at first) rejected Marcel Proust accepted all three of Réjean Ducharme's novels – including *L'avalée des avalés*, later translated as *The Swallower Swallowed* – and the name of this young *prétentieux* appeared on the distinctive buff cover above Gallimard's colophon, elegantly bordered in red and black.

If this instant ascent to literary Parnassus weren't galling enough, Ducharme refused to step into the spotlight, turning down journalists' requests for interviews. A photographer in the bushes outside Ducharme's house managed to snap two pictures – they show a nondescript young man in a sweatshirt with an arm folded defensively over his belly – but they would be the last unauthorized glimpse the world got of Quebec's most famous faceless author. For more than 30 years, Ducharme has been a cipher: no literary talk shows, no signings at bookstores, and only the rare interview, which inevitably leaves the journalists and the public unsatisfied.

Rumours about his identity circulated immediately. The photos of Ducharme, according to the French newspaper *Minute*, were actually those of a dead student; the real author was a diplomat – undoubtedly a Frenchman – who naturally valued his anonymity. No, the counter-rumours went: he was in reality the Québécois politician and poet Gérald Godin or, more absurdly, Cardinal Paul-Émile Léger. To this day, the real

Ducharme hasn't emerged from self-imposed obscurity, except in 1994, when he issued a 10-year-old, full-length portrait with his dog Blaise, too indistinct to reveal any facial details.

While the output of his American counterpart, Thomas Pynchon, has been sporadic, Ducharme is rather prolific. Apart from writing some of the best Canadian novels of the past three decades, a series of absurdist plays, and the extraordinary screenplay for Francis Mankiewicz's movie *Les Bons Débarras*, he has also, under the name Roch Plante, exhibited idiosyncratic sculptures made of garbage collected during his nocturnal strolls through Montreal's Little Burgundy. And he's a remarkable song-writer, the author of both "Je t'haïs" for Robert Charlebois and "Je vous aime" for Pauline Julien. When Charlebois was accused of being so indiscriminating that "he'd even sing the phone book if you asked him to," Ducharme wrote him a song that used the local directory as a rhyming dictionary, creating a strangely touching catalogue of Bédards and Pouparts, of Sansregrets and Forgets.

Ducharme's wilful anonymity has meant that the literary establishment hasn't been able to commodify his authorial image (even if the mystery has been a decided selling point). His reputation is entirely founded on the quality of his texts. The Ducharmian style tends towards a taut first-person narrative centred on a marginal figure who is guided by deep movements of the soul rather than appearances and words. Ducharme's first novel, *L'avalée des avalés*, tells the story of Bérénice Einberg, a moody adolescent who lives in an abandoned abbey on an island in the St. Lawrence. She's obsessed with her beautiful mother, a Polish Catholic (such maternal monomania would form the basis for Ducharme's screenplay for *Les Bons Débarras*), and alienated from her cold, Jewish father. Einberg, hardly a typical figure in Québécois fiction, goes on to become an infantrywoman in the Israeli army. Ducharme's 1994 *Va savoir* deals with the travails of Rémi Vavasseur, who has exiled himself to the Quebec countryside when his wife takes off on a trek around Europe and Africa after a miscarriage. As all his efforts to restore a decrepit house succumb to bursting pipes, Vavasseur attempts to entwine his roots with those of the locals: an exotic dancer whose boyfriend is in jail, a lonely anglophone woman whose husband is dying of cancer, a pool-shooting handyman. His stories are told in playful — but never loose — language that is distinctly, self-confidently

Québécois. Most often, everyday entropy conspires to deny his characters the state of grace they seek. As in the plays of Samuel Beckett, Ducharme's heroes tend to end up on the scrap heap.

In the unlikely event that Ducharme will suddenly decide to tell it all, we should console ourselves with the information contained in the succinct autobiography that accompanied a recent paperback edition of his first novel:

> Réjean Ducharme was born in 1941 in Saint-Félix-de-Valoix (Comté de Joliette). He's hitchhiked, driven hack, hoofed it, and marched on the spot. He has written nine novels, staged four plays, and scripted two films. He is currently looking for work.

Zeitgeist

Zurich in the teens. Paris in the twenties. New York in the fifties. Prague in the nineties. Turn-of-the-century Montreal. . . which is, sad to say, just wishful thinking. Though Montreal does have one of the vital prerequisites to become a world bohemian capital – low rents – the cafés show no signs of becoming havens for impassioned expatriates spilling wine and concocting the ultimate subversive artistic movement. A good bohemia thrives on the disorientation that keeps expatriate artists gliding harmlessly over the surface of the host society, the kind of blissful disjunction that allowed Gertrude Stein to live in France for 43 years without learning to converse effectively in French. Montreal is a little too friendly, familiar, and unpretentious to allow visiting artists a convincing illusion of impenetrable exoticism.

For those in search of the frisson of ethnic conflict, the danger-tourists who thrive on the Basque Country or Belfast, Montreal is a disappointment. Canadian cities tend to be rather boring exemplars of racial harmony and equality, places where the anger of gangsta rap usually looks like laughable suburban posturing. Even stinking rich Manhattan has more palpable tension than Montreal; it is, after all, a city of wealthy white people who pretend not to notice that they are almost entirely served by blacks and Latinos. Any hope for a *coup d'état* in Quebec – pipe-smoking Habitant against kilted Anglo overlords – was squelched when francophone bureaucrats and businessmen took over. The late German director Rainer Werner

Fassbinder, visiting Montreal in 1981, was so impressed by the peaceful co-existence that he marvelled, "Montreal seems to me the highest point of hope for culture in the Western world." O noble Montreal! O yawn! This was a polite way of warning other Germans: This place is boring. Go to New York instead.

And yet culture in Quebec thrives. The theatre season, which never truly ends, is a cosmopolitan gallimaufry of intriguing playwrights, often performed in translation: plays by George F. Walker, David Mamet, Boris Vian, Fernando Pessoa, and Eugène Ionesco were all staged in 1999. If Luc Plamondon isn't in town, the Montreal stage is also blissfully unsullied by the megahit musical tripe that dominates the Strand and Broadway. The major art institutions – the Museum of Fine Arts and the Musée d'art contemporain in Montreal, the Musée de la civilisation and the Musée du Québec in Quebec City – show everyone from Jeff Wall to Claude Monet. And Montreal still profits from a European connection that eludes Toronto, drawing in francophone talent from Belgium, France, and Switzerland. A group of five Canadian-born Hollywood movie directors have announced that they're setting up shop here in order to "give something back to Canada" (more likely, to take advantage of cheap locations and labour).

Maybe no city will again achieve the status of Situationist Paris or Surrealist Madrid, but it's nice to imagine that some world capital will attain the state of grace – encouraged by agreeable living and inexpensive liquor and cigarettes – that fosters new thought and aesthetics. Perhaps Canadian creators are just too heavily subsidized to remember what subversion is. Too bad, because Montreal has all the ingredients: cheap food and housing, sidewalk cafés and unused theatres, lots of slackers on the dole, and a full range of the most modern vices.

Come to think of it, Montreal *is* like Paris in the twenties. The talent just hasn't noticed yet.

8

THE NATIVES ARE RESTLESS

It's an idyllic midsummer afternoon in the little community of Oka. Carloads of Montrealers, who have made the half-hour drive north to one of the few decent beaches in the area, stop to stuff picnic baskets with Oka cheese and nut-filled fudge purchased from a cassocked monk at the La Trappe monastery's outlet store. On the Lac des Deux-Montagnes, a lacustrine widening in the Ottawa River, hundreds of Mohawks are gathering in an oval clearing near the Kanesatake band council office. They're here for the annual powwow, a kind of relaxed rural rodeo where fancy dancing, rather than livestock abuse, is the main event. Elders wearing *kastowahs*, Mohawk headdresses topped by eagle feathers, begin a stately procession to the middle of the field, accompanied by a parade of flag-bearers. A crew-cut marine stiffly holds aloft a black ensign commemorating American prisoners of war, followed by the blue standard of the border-straddling Iroquois Confederacy, a red United States Marine Corps flag, and the colours of the United Nations. It's a startling display of international allegiances from which the fleur-de-lys of Quebec is pointedly absent. A slight woman in an old-fashioned summer dress asks for a warm welcome for these "veterans of all the wars, including Kanesatake, 1990" – an allusion to the legendary siege of Oka by the Sûreté du Québec (the SQ) and the Canadian army – and the circle of spectators bursts into enthusiastic applause.

It's hardly a surprising reaction. This is, after all, Mohawk Territory, whose citizens, among them members of the militant Warrior Society, travel on their own passports and consider themselves members of a sovereign nation. A few miles down the road, in a little stand of pine trees, Debbie Etienne, a round-faced Mohawk mother of two, has agreed to take a little time from the powwow to tell the story, yet again, of one of the most notorious armed conflicts in recent Canadian history. Eight years ago to the day, the Warriors of Kanesatake traded shots with assault-rifle-brandishing officers of Quebec's provincial police force. "The SQ got out of their blue panel truck over there," says Etienne, gesturing towards a tree-shaded stretch of Highway 344, "and like little Nazis they started lining up in a row, with their guns locked and loaded." Along with other protestors, this easygoing but doughty Mohawk woman had been camped out in the pine forest since March 1990, attempting to block the municipality of Oka's expansion of a private nine-hole golf course.

Emerging from her dew-covered tent on July 11, Etienne was confronted with the massed force of the tactical intervention squad of Quebec's provincial police. "Talk about a Prozac morning. I remember I was wearing a quilt, and my teeth were chattering. The SQ looked like the army – their faces were even painted green. They started throwing concussion grenades, which made the ground quake." Tear-gas canisters followed, and the jittery police stormed a flimsy barricade of dirt and logs, provoking an exchange of gunfire with Mohawk Warriors hidden in the woods. The 23-second gunfight left SQ corporal Marcel Lemay dead – a .223-calibre steel-tipped bullet had burrowed through his bulletproof vest – and kicked off a summer-long standoff that saw the Canadian army, under orders from Quebec premier Robert Bourassa, move in with tanks, helicopters, and armoured troop transports. Ever since, the memory of Oka's Indian summer has profoundly queered relations between Quebecers and natives.

As mosquitoes surge from the underbrush and settle on our arms, Etienne points to sap-plugged scars where the Sûreté du Québec's investigators cut bullet holes from the slender pines – "to get rid of the evidence that a lot of the shooting came from the SQ side, from the road," she insists. Etienne spent much of the summer behind the lines, braving police and army roadblocks; she speaks defiantly of repeatedly kicking a Canadian soldier after he'd pressed the muzzle of an M-16 into her prone daughter's head. "This place is so sacred," she says, looking around. "Our medicines grow here, in the Pines. Our people are buried here. It's ours, plain and simple. And [Oka mayor] Ouellette wanted to make a golf course parking lot out of it."

I follow Debbie Etienne's big American sedan back to her home, past a shirtless Mohawk teenager with a Mohawk haircut slumbering outside the Mohawk gas station. Oka is better known to local Mohawks as Kanesatake, a patchwork of native-owned properties, all that remains of a once-vast seigneury. In 1717, Sulpician priests promised Etienne's ancestors that, in return for leaving the island of Montreal, they would be given a deed from the king of France to a large tract of land on the Lac des Deux-Montagnes. The Mohawks crossed the river, but the deed never followed, and over the next two centuries the priests gradually sold the promised land to French-Canadian settlers. In spite of constant petitions, a transatlantic ambassadorial mission to King Edward VII, and a disgusted mass conversion to Protestantism, the Mohawks watched the four hundred square kilometres pledged to them whittled down to only four. Although much of the prime property has long since been occupied by white landowners, Kanesatake still has a distinctly Indian feel. When I'm briefly tailed by one of the ominous black cruisers of the newly established, all-native Kanesatake Mohawk Police (the Sûreté du Québec have been personae non gratae here since the siege), I make sure to come to a full stop at a trilingual sign that reads: ARRÊT – STOP – TÉSTA'N.

In Etienne's living room, beneath a wooden plaque that reads DEPT. OF CAUCASIAN AFFAIRS, we flip through photos from that long summer. What looks like a Sûreté du Québec wallet card falls from the album. I read it aloud: "The SQ are looking for a few stupid lame Frenchmen. Be a coward among cowards. Vive le Dunkin' Donuts libre." Etienne chuckles. "Before the siege, the SQ called us *maudits sauvages*. They'd say: 'Who do you think you are? This is Quebec! You're not special.' These days, they're more cautious, they're watching their p's and q's." In spite of her French name, another gift from the Sulpicians, Etienne, like most Mohawks, is thoroughly anglophone. She's quick to point out, however, that she grew up with French-speaking kids in Oka, hanging out in the same restaurants, chipping in with them to buy cases of beer. Though many francophone villagers sympathized with the Mohawks, even smuggling food past police lines, she heaps opprobrium on French authority. "The French people are like the rude neighbours who moved in. The English are more polite. On a political level, they recognize our status; they realize they are the outsiders who arrived late. The French are low. They consider us immigrants. Us!" She yelps with disbelief. "*We* were uncivilized, *we* were savages, they were going to save our souls."

It's jarring to hear such ardour from a placid mother in her early forties. But the Mohawks, the most militant members of the Iroquois Confederacy, have long been noted for the unstinting assertion of their identity in the face of ruthless encroachment. When members of the radical American Indian Movement swam to Alcatraz in 1969, occupying the former prison for 19 months, a Mohawk, Richard Oakes, was at their head. In the seventies, 150 Mohawks from Quebec, many of them Vietnam vets, crossed the border into New York State and seized a mountainous patch of land, finally forcing Governor Mario Cuomo to grant them 2,300 hectares of forest in the Adirondacks. Many francophone Québécois consider the Mohawks a powerful criminal underground involved in smuggling, arms sales, and drugs – as bad as any biker gang. They point to the illegal casinos and the Radio-Canada reporter who was roughed up after he revealed the location of 10,000 marijuana plants growing in Kanesatake, and tell prospective visitors they're taking their lives into their hands when they step onto Mohawk Territory. After all, according to only recently supplanted history books, these are the very Indians who slaughtered soldier Adam Dollard des Ormeaux, the same *sauvages* who roasted the still-twitching heart of Father Jean de Brébeuf.

Debbie Etienne, descendant of fearsome Iroquois warriors, wants to get back to the powwow so she can sprawl on the grass with her friends, drink lemonade, and watch the smoke dance. Before we part, I ask her when the siege at Oka finally ended for her. She looks at me with steady brown eyes, waits a beat, and replies, with a daunting absence of irony: "It's *still* not over."

In less than a generation, the number of natives in Quebec has doubled. They account for only one per cent of Quebec's population (versus 10 per cent in Manitoba and Saskatchewan) but have laid claim to significant swaths of Quebec's territory. Glancing at a map of the province, a Canadian of European descent might imagine a vast and mostly empty land reaching from the American border to the hydroelectric projects of the North. Quebec's natives, however, see a quilt of overlapping hunting grounds, traplines, villages, and burial sites, some of which they've used for millennia. Iroquoia, the homeland of the Mohawks and five other Iroquois nations, starts in Pennsylvania but stretches north to encompass the entire metropolitan area of Montreal; one reserve, Akwesasne, lies athwart the territories of Quebec, Ontario, and New York State. Nitassinan, the traditional land of the Innu, extends from the coast of Labrador to the Saguenay River, abutting, in the west, Eeyou Istchee, the vast homeland of the James Bay Cree. For many of the natives of the east, the Gaspé Peninsula is just the northern part of Mi'kmak'ik, an ancestral home arbitrarily trisected by the borders of New Brunswick, Quebec, and Nova Scotia. Nunavik, the land of the Inuit, stretches from the 55th parallel to the northern crenellations of the Ungava Peninsula.

Altogether, some 72,000 natives, belonging to 11 nations, lay claim to almost the entire area of modern Quebec. To the delight of English-Canadian opponents of Québécois sovereignty, almost half of them use English or native tongues rather than French, and their leaders mockingly echo the slogans of the early separatist movement to advance their claims. The Crees demand recognition as a distinct society – a society *more* distinct than Quebec – and the Mohawks point out that they have never given up their claims to sovereignty or their aggressive pursuit of self-determination. Anglophone firebrands such as Matthew Coon Come, grand chief of the Crees, portray the Québécois as technocratic conquistadores, arrogant imperialists whose 35 years of exploitation of the North have been no better, and often much worse, than the 200 years of economic control an Anglo-Saxon elite exercised over French Canadians.

Before the 1992 Charlottetown constitutional talks, Zebedee Nungak, then head of the Inuit's Makivik Corporation, held up a map of Quebec that stopped well below the treeline. With the subtraction of his homeland of Nunavik, he pointed out, a third of the province's land mass would be neatly lopped off. Lucien Bouchard – then leader of the Bloc Québécois – responded angrily, "There is no way that any Quebecer would accept that a square inch of that territory be extracted from Quebec." While indigenous leaders worldwide, increasingly conversant in international law, become sophisticated adversaries of their former colonizers, the dialogue in Quebec is still primal, fraught with ultimatums and terse pronouncements. What's more, since Oka, they are often issued from armed camps.

The sources of this durable polarization can be traced back to the first encounter, in 1535, between the French and the Iroquois. Jacques Cartier's crew – sailors from the epidemic-gripped town of St. Malo – not only kidnapped 10 Iroquoians from Stadacona (nine of them would later die in France), but also left the people of Hochelaga, on the island of Montreal, with what was probably smallpox. In the early 1600s, Samuel de Champlain gunned down the first Mohawks he met on what is now Lake Champlain, and then puzzled over the disappearance of Hochelaga, which his predecessor Cartier had described as a palisaded village of more than a thousand Iroquois. For an explanation, he need have looked no farther than his festering handkerchief. European germs, more surely than internecine warfare, accounted for the mysterious disappearance of the St. Lawrence Iroquoians (the survivors were probably absorbed by the Hurons, Mohawks, and other neighbouring tribes), which was just a local episode in a pan-American hecatomb. In a little more than a century, the original population of North America was reduced to a tenth its pre-contact level of 18 million.

The area that is now Quebec (from an Algonquian word that means "narrowing of the waters") had already been inhabited for 8,000 years when the first French appeared, throwing hitherto stable native societies into lasting turmoil. Many tribes of the Iroquoian language group – sedentary people who lived in large villages and grew corn, squash, and beans, like the natives Cartier met on the St. Lawrence – were annihilated by waves of epidemics and the famine and warfare that ensued. The Huron, fur-trading allies of the French, originally numbered 30,000, until they were routed by Mohawks and Seneca armed with Dutch muskets in 1649. Only three hundred survivors took refuge among the Jesuits near Quebec City, whose policy of allowing only baptized Indians to buy guns contributed to the destruction of Huronia. The Mi'kmaqs and Innu along the St. Lawrence, among the first to meet European explorers, bore the full brunt of famine and heightened warfare brought on by bouts of smallpox. Of the area's three major linguistic groups, only the Inuit speakers of Eskimo-Aleut, out of reach in the Far North, were spared European influence for any length of time.

War refugees who settled in the St. Lawrence Valley – the Mohawks who became the "praying Indians" of Kahnawake, the Hurons at Lorette, the Abenakis at Bécancour – were inculcated with both religion and disease by Ursuline nuns and the "black robes," the stern Jesuit missionaries. The culture of these settled Indians was steadily diluted by métissage, Catholicism, the French language, and the natives' willingness to adopt the abandoned illegitimate children of the French.

To give the French their due, they may be marginally less responsible than the British and Spanish for one of history's most abrupt genocides. The McGill anthropologist Bruce Trigger has emphasized that racist ideas about Indians tended to be strongest among Americans. "They were described as savages so their lands could be appropriated," he explained in an interview in *Le Devoir*, "but racist ideas about Indians only came to Quebec in the 1930s, and they were reflections of ideas circulating in the United States and English Canada. Up until then, Quebec had a relatively good history with the Indians, something I think hasn't been said often enough."

During the time of New France, this was probably a matter of realpolitik: the numerically weak French needed the Indians more than the Americans did. Until the Conquest, shifting alliances with Hurons and Algonquins allowed the French to resist the burgeoning English colonies to the south and to fight off hostile Iroquois tribes, particularly the Mohawks, who were the bane of New France. Sometime after Cartier's arrival, the Onondagas, Cayugas, Mohawks, Oneidas, and Senecas (later joined by the Tuscaroras) banded together in a sophisticated Iroquois confederation whose egalitarian principles, including significant political power for women, would later inspire the admiration of Karl Marx and Friedrich Engels. (Benjamin Franklin deemed the Iroquois Confederacy a good model for the English colonies, and the arrow-gripping eagle on the United States shield was a direct appropriation of Iroquois iconography.) Uniting to strike out at common enemies, the Six Nations terrified and tortured French soldiers and settlers. Following Louis XIV's 1664 order "totally to exterminate" the Confederacy, 1,500 warriors descended on the settlement of Lachine and massacred 24 of its inhabitants. The canny Iroquois' decision to side with Britain in 1759 produced an alliance that helped end France's colonial aspirations in the New World.

Under British rule, the demographic balance of the newly united Canadas shifted towards the Europeans and away from the natives. Many Mohawks found themselves forced from the United States to settle in Montreal and southwestern Ontario, where they were obliged to petition the government for steadily diminishing land and rights. The French had meddled with their souls and blood, telling them their nature spirits were actually demons and adopting an official policy of métissage to make them indistinguishable from the Canadiens.

The English found it more expedient to legislate the Indians out of existence. Though almost a third of the text of the Royal Proclamation of 1763 was devoted to natives, acknowledging their ancestral rights to lands not already ceded to the Crown, subsequent practice focused on eliminating the "Indian problem" through assimilation. Thanks to the 1876 Indian Act, natives were accorded the same legal status as minors, women, and "mental defectives." Democratically elected council leaders, supported by the federal government, were given authority over hereditary chiefs – a guarantee of internal dissent, which to this day pits traditionalists against band councils.

The twentieth century wasn't good to Canada's aboriginal peoples: infantilized by racist laws, denied the vote until 1960, sterilized by Arctic doctors, punished for speaking their languages in residential schools, and driven off their land by forestry, mining, and farming, natives were the victims of de facto cultural genocide. By 1950, only 18,000 of Quebec's original inhabitants were left to remind people that the word "Canada" came from the Huron term for "village." In Quebec, the Quiet Revolution looked like a hopeful sign for many natives. The newly powerful Québécois, of all people, should understand the pain of oppressed minorities struggling to maintain their cultures in the face of arrogant colonialism. Parti Québécois leader René Lévesque, for one, appeared sympathetic to native causes: "The fact that our native populations have inhabited the territory since the earliest times," he told the Assemblée nationale, "and were here before any of us, gives them particular status and rights that we should inscribe . . . in the fundamental laws that govern Québécois society."

Under successive governments, the emphasis was indeed taken off legal marginalization. In its place came nationalist swaggering, economic imperialism, and police brutality. In 1977, the government flew riot police to northern Quebec to break up Inuit protests against Bill 101's imposition of French in the North, where the second language, after Inuktitut, has traditionally been English. In 1981, 300 Sûreté du Québec officers and 90 wardens in helicopters, squad cars, and boats descended on the Mi'kmaq of Restigouche, whose reserve lies at the root of the extended tongue that is the Gaspé Peninsula. The Mi'kmaq had been warned by Quebec's Department of Fisheries to stop traditional night fishing because it threatened fish stocks. Natives responded that they'd been spearing salmon on the Restigouche River since time immemorial, and that the entire Atlantic aboriginal fishing harvest amounted to only 22 tons while sport fishermen – wealthy Americans and Montrealers who hired native guides – took 870 tons a year. To no avail: the SQ beat protestors with night sticks and arrested 12 Mi'kmaq; provincial wardens conducted a house-to-house search and cut fishing nets with knives. Fishing, hunting, and recreation minister Lucien Lessard appeared on the reserve and dismissed the Mi'kmaq's objections that they too were a distinct society: "To be a sovereign nation, you have to have your own language and culture" (unconsciously paraphrasing Lord Durham's much-resented 1839 dismissal of the French Canadians as "a people with no history and no culture"). Interviewed by native filmmaker Alanis Obomsawin, Mi'kmaq councillor Michael Isaac denounced Quebec: "Here's a government that's crying about sovereignty, that's crying about discrimination, that's been discriminated [against] by the rest of Canada. And here's the same government that's doing the same thing, only worse – they're using guns!"

Such irony tends to be lost on Québécois politicians and technocrats. In spite of the egalitarianism of Quebec society and its increasing tolerance and liberalism, the policies of the province's elites ape the more Jacobin elements of France's government, blusteringly attempting to impose a homogeneous national culture. Quebec's social and economic power, after all, was built on hydroelectricity, in turn made possible by the quasi-legal appropriation of vast swaths of native land. The 1971 flooding of 1,300 square kilometres of black spruce forest in Labrador, without the approval of the 40 Innu families whose hunting grounds and burial sites it affected, was the first such megaproject. Churchill Falls, one of the world's most potent dams, eventually put $14 billion into Quebec's coffers, allowing the provincially run Hydro-Québec to turn its sights on the untamed rivers that drained into James Bay. The province's James Bay Development Corporation, after noting in its project outline that most of the land to be flooded lay "in the so-called Taiga zone, characterized by a forest made up of non-commercial black spruce," suggested that for the Cree Indians the project could only be beneficial. "In reality," the report claimed, "many a Cree already has adopted some of the ways of modern society. His children attend modern schools. He has given up the dog team in favour of the snowmobile. He listens avidly to radio programs. . . . The development of James Bay opens a fascinating vista for the James Bay Indians. It provides them with a choice: to continue to live off hunting and fishing and/or to become part of a new lifestyle which some of them already have experienced in Montreal."

Not all Cree were ready to opt for the Montreal "lifestyle." To the surprise of the corporation, already building roads to project sites, a Quebec Superior Court judge took a petition of Cree and Inuit hunters seriously. In 1973, Justice Albert Malouf granted an injunction against the project on the grounds that it would "have devastating and far-reaching effects" on the natives of the North. The stymied provincial government was forced to negotiate and, in the first treaty ever signed with Quebec's natives, they granted the Cree and the Inuit $225 million, payable over 25 years.

Since then, the Cree have been criticized for surrendering their aboriginal rights and allowing thousands of square kilometres of their best hunting land to be drowned (a significant contingent of dissident Inuit had refused to surrender their rights). The Cree respond that they negotiated under duress: Quebec was already building Phase I of James Bay while talks were underway. Nonetheless, as apologists for the provincial government point out, the James Bay and Northern Quebec Agreement has been a boon for the indigenous peoples of the North. The Cree were able to establish the first constitutionally based Indian self-government in the country, as well as their own airline, Air Creebec, and the Cree Company, a major employer in the northern construction industry. Meanwhile, the Cree on the Ontario side of James Bay, who in 1905 signed away their lands for cash compensation of $4 a head per year for eternity, are living nine to a house in communities without running water.

That said, the Cree of Ontario, unaffected by one of the largest earth-moving endeavours in history, can still recognize the land they grew up on enough to hunt and fish. The Quebec Cree watched as 10,000 caribou drowned when a single dammed river rose to record levels, and saw wetland habitat for geese and ducks disappear and the fish in their rivers turn belly-up after being poisoned by methylmercury. With shorelines and rivers subjected to the artificial control of technicians in Montreal, the stock of traditional wisdom that allowed hunters to read the land was forever undermined, exacerbating the move to settlements like Chiasibi, where alcoholism and unemployment were endemic.

The tendency to see the North as a vast, blank space free for the taking, while hardly confined to Quebec, has found a ready host in an ambitious proto-nation anxious for economic autonomy. The Inuit in particular express exasperation with distant statesmen who scrawl lines across their homelands. In 1670, the Inuit became Rupertlanders when King Charles of England granted much of the North to the Hudson's Bay Company, naming four million square kilometres of taiga and tundra after his cousin Rupert. In 1870, they became Eskimos of the District of Ungava, as the British Crown handed their northern peninsula over to the new Dominion of Canada. In 1953, Prime Minister Louis St. Laurent, worried about American military movements in the North, had seven Inuit families transported from Northern Quebec to barren Resolute Bay ("They dumped us like dogs," one of the Inuit later observed) in order to establish a Canadian dot on the map in the High Arctic. In this century alone, the Inuit and Cree have been citizens of New Quebec, then Nouveau-Québec, and finally Nunavik and Radissonia.

Forty years ago, there were no Québécois in the North at all. For the Inuktitut- and English-speaking Inuit, francophone Quebecers are the Ouiouititut (after their ready impulse to answer "Oui, oui" to every question), callow newcomers on land natives have inhabited for 4,000 years. More than other indigenous people, the Inuit have come to see themselves as Canadian: they live in villages rather than reserves, and, since they aren't administered by the Indian Act, vote in federal elections and pay taxes. Many of Quebec's 8,600 Inuit belong to the Canadian Rangers, a corps of volunteers created during the Second World War to patrol the northern coastline. The government of Quebec now builds and maintains Nunavik's public housing and administrative services, at a cost of up to $120 million a year. The Inuit, however, pleading weariness with arbitrary territorial divisions, have said that in the event of Quebec separation they'd rather remain part of Canada. The James Bay settlement has given them a measure of self-sufficiency: Nungak's Makivik Corporation now runs three airlines and controls an investment portfolio of more than $100 million, much of it in blue-chip U.S. stocks.

The so-called Conquest of the North helped create the first substantial Québécois middle class, but it came with a price tag: the lasting alienation of the original inhabitants of two-thirds of the land surface of Quebec. Along the way, it has also done profound damage to Québécois governments' reputation abroad. In the early nineties, Hydro-Québec started the second phase of its occupation of Cree territory, the damming of the Great Whale River. In a series of sophisticated public relations moves, Matthew Coon Come, grand chief of the Crees of Quebec, then in his mid-twenties, accompanied Robert Kennedy, Jr., on a whitewater rafting trip down the threatened river – with a CNN camera crew in tow. Coon Come then had a $40,000 full-page ad taken out in the *New York Times*, announcing the impending "Catastrophe at James Bay." He helped drag the *Odeyak*, a hybrid Inuit and Cree canoe, over the ice of Hudson Bay and paddled it down rivers in Quebec and Vermont, arriving in New York City in time for the cameras gathered for Earth Day celebrations. (An assemblyman in Albany confided, "I don't know who the PR brains behind this were, but they made corporate Hydro-Québec look like lead-footed dunces.") Finally, the young grand chief watched in satisfaction as New York State, embarrassed by the international attention, cancelled plans for a $19-billion contract with the utility.

As the deal fell through, Lise Bacon, then Quebec's energy minister, spluttered to the television cameras, "The campaign that the Crees have had in the States and Europe, all over the world, maybe they were success-ful at it, or not. But are they Quebecers or not? . . . Their territory is still ours. We haven't given it up yet. I blame them for discrediting Quebec all over the world." Not surprisingly, "Quebecers" is the last thing Crees – and most other natives – would call themselves. In plebiscites before the 1995 referendum, 96 per cent of the Cree and 95 per cent of the Inuit voted to remain in Canada in the event of Quebec's separation. The Innu of the Côte-Nord, on the northeastern shore of the St. Lawrence, appeared before a working group of the United Nations in Geneva in 1997 to declare sover-eignist leaders "racist" and "neocolonialist," and to insist, "We have a lan-guage and a culture distinct from Quebec's."

For many francophone Quebecers, such resentment came as a sur-prise. The Innu, also known as the Montagnais, tended to speak French and had long been portrayed as "good Indians," a foil for the anglophone Crees and the truculent Mohawks. But such an outburst was a long time coming. The Innu, whom some anthropologists consider the most cultur-ally and materially intact First Nation left in North America, are appar-ently finished with suffering incursion, whether from Canada or Quebec, in silence. On Quebec's Côte-Nord, the heart of the Innu homeland, the fresh waters of rivers such as the Moisie, the St-Jean, the Mingan, and the Natashquan spill into the brackish currents of the St. Lawrence Estuary. By the time the Hudson Bay Company started setting their nets across river mouths, the Innu had been catching salmon on these rivers by torchlight for at least 2,000 years. Using the *negog*, a rock-maple spear with spread-ing jaws and a central barb, they stood on linked canoes and pounced on darting fish, catching and smoking enough salmon in a few nights to sustain them on winter-long treks in search of caribou on the inland taiga.

American boats started to visit in the 1850s, sending barrels of salmon down to Boston and New York. Meanwhile, elite anglers banned spear fishing as a barbarous abomination, and private clubs gained exclusive rights to 60 rivers in Quebec and New Brunswick. At a time when Innu were dying of starvation because they'd been barred from fishing, the governor general of Canada boasted of catching 200 salmon on a single fly-fishing visit to the Côte-Nord.

Some Innu survived by guiding American anglers. Others continued to fish, often to be labelled poachers on their own land. In 1977 the bloody corpses of two Innu, Achille Vollant and Moïse Régis, were found near a badly battered canoe after the young men had been warned to stay off a river leased by an American fishing club. Another Innu had nearly been drowned when his canoe was rammed by the guardians of the privately leased Natashquan River. In an attempt to regain control of the rivers, a delegation of Innu went to Quebec City in the early seventies, returning with a signed document that allowed them to fish on a 15-kilometre-long section of the Natashquan – only to find that the provincial government had unilaterally crossed out the paragraph that gave them priority to renew the lease on the river after two years.

Barred from their rivers, the Innu began to unravel. The priests who'd come to make the Innu give up the diabolical "shaking tent," a ceremony in which natives asked spirits to reveal the location of game, also gave permission to hydroelectric companies to build dams on the Betsiamites River. The enormous Manic 5, the largest dam in North America at the time, was built on their territory, and Alcan harnessed their rivers to produce aluminum, making it impossible for salmon to reach their spawning grounds. The American-owned Quebec North Shore Paper Company, which supplied newsprint to the *Chicago Tribune* and the *New York Daily News*, started cutting down coniferous forest and kicking back stumpage fees to the Quebec government. The province sold mineral rights to American mining companies – which made no effort to hire Innu workers. In Labrador, the hunting camps of families on the taiga were overflown by Belgian and German NATO fighters, hugging the ground and spewing radar-confounding aluminum strips of "chaff" to practise low-flying bombing techniques. Those Innu who finally surrendered to encroachments that had made their nomadic lifestyle impossible, settling in such villages as La Romaine, Sept-Îles, or Davis Inlet, were mocked as "pizza Indians" or pitied as unemployed alcoholics.

Lately, however, the Innu have fought back. In 1997, they occupied the Voisey's Bay construction site of Inco, the world's largest nickel company, pelting Mounties with valuable core samples snatched from trailers. Lucien Bouchard shouldn't have been surprised when a persistent band of Innu stymied his meeting with Newfoundland's Brian Tobin in the spring of 1998. The two premiers flew to Labrador to announce the $12-billion sequel to Churchill Falls – with a $1.4-million press conference – only to have their van blocked by a hundred women and children shouting "Go home!" The Innu angrily pointed out that, apart from not being consulted over the second phase of the project, they'd never been compensated for the drowning of their lands two decades before.

The sight of dignitaries in cashmere overcoats backpedalling along slippery ice could be savoured as pure slapstick, but such events, frequent in the nineties, also exposed how alienated the natives had become from the Québécois majority. The contrast with the rest of Canada is immediately evident: while English Canadians share their streets and neighbourhoods with natives – whether the Dene in Edmonton, the Cree in Toronto and Winnipeg, or the Sto:lo in Vancouver – a Quebecer can spend days in Montreal or Trois-Rivières without glimpsing a single native. Partly it's because Quebec has proportionately fewer aboriginals, but it's also a question of made-in-Quebec institutional Balkanization. The same phenomenon that keeps Montreal's Jews close to private schools in Hampstead and Côte-St-Luc sees Mohawks of Kahnawake shunning French-only public schools in favour of their own Iroquoian-language Survival School. (As with European immigrants, there's a flip side: retention of ancestral languages is higher among natives here than in any other province in Canada.) Whatever the causes, the result is an unusual degree of alienation between Quebec's francophone and its native peoples.

In 1990 a solitary Oji-Cree, clutching an eagle feather on a backbench in the Manitoba legislature, shook his head when asked to provide the unanimous consent necessary to approve the federal government's new constitutional agreement. By rejecting the notion that Canada had only two founding races, the French and the English, Elijah Harper helped kill the Meech Lake Accord, which would have recognized Quebec as a distinct society. (Phil Fontaine, then head of the Assembly of Manitoba Chiefs, said that natives had no problem with the distinct society clause itself, "but if Quebec is distinct, we are even more distinct. That's the recognition we want, and will settle for nothing less.") The defeat of Meech Lake, which was perceived as an aboriginal undermining of Québécois ambitions, was followed a month later by the summer-long siege of Oka. Forced to take a three-hour detour around the blockaded Mercier Bridge, Quebecers started hanging effigies of natives from traffic lights.

A decade later, the fallout from Oka and Meech Lake is still settling. Today, Quebecers are more ignorant of native cultures and less sympathetic to their claims than other Canadians: 28 per cent are unable to name a single First Nation, most believe native household incomes are higher than the Quebec average (Indians are among the poorest residents of the province), and two-thirds think their land claims are unreasonable.

In fact, says Georges Sioui, a francophone Huron who grew up near Quebec City, many Québécois express surprise that there are any real natives left in Quebec at all. "The common people of Quebec are just not able to see us," he laments. "I remember many instances, being out in the countryside or at a sugar shack, where people would say, 'The Indians? What are you talking about? There's still such a thing as those people around?' Even as I was telling them that I was a Huron! The psyche of Quebecers is still very much soaked in old religious doctrines, which ingrained the belief that Indians were no longer around and whatever survived were descendants whose spirituality and ideology were no longer intact." The soft-spoken author of *For an Amerindian Autohistory*, a thoughtful call for natives to start chronicling their own history, believes the syndrome is even worse among Québécois elites. Sioui is a respected intellectual in English Canada, where he taught history at the native-run Saskatchewan Indian Federated College, but since his return to Quebec, he's found the difference in attitude striking. "There's a much ampler respect for Indians in provinces such as Ontario and Saskatchewan. There's a limit that Anglo-Canadians won't trespass – the beliefs and spirituality of another people remain sacred for them. The Quebecers still have it present in their mentality that the Indians are not really Indians, which is why they can appropriate things so easily. They do it almost mechanically. They do real old-style anthropology, and they are all over the archeology of the province, calling it their *patrimoine*, their heritage. Those things are just unthinkable in English Canada."

The growing emphasis on Charter-based individual rights and multi-culturalism outside Quebec also contributes to this difference in attitude. English-speaking Canadians are now accustomed to thinking in terms of a framework that guarantees the individual's rights to worship and preserve traditions and culture. Québécois leaders are more apt to value collective rights – which in theory should make them ready to acknowledge the rights of distinct groups struggling for cultural survival within their midst. But their attitude towards natives is strangely inconsistent, a collective failure to recognize the nations within. This intransigence may come from an unspoken awareness that natives have an equal, if not greater, moral right to the territory nationalist Québécois claim as their own.

In their own defence, the Québécois present statistics that show living standards for natives here are higher than elsewhere in Canada. And, in many ways, Quebec's natives are better off: incarceration rates are three to four times lower than in Ontario or on the Prairies, incomes are closer to the mainstream norm, and natives here tend to be better educated than elsewhere in Canada. Politicians point to the model village of Oujé-Bougoumou, built for a band of dispossessed Cree whose living conditions were the worst in the industrialized world until the mid-eighties. Funded by $75 million in grants from the provincial and federal governments, the village, with its sawdust-heated, concentrically arranged buildings, was named one of the world's 50 most outstanding communities by the United Nations. (Before all the attention, however, the Quebec government refused to honour a $6-million payment for joint regional ventures, failed to maintain the road to the community, and defaulted on school-operating fees.)

For Georges Sioui, all this is beside the point: it's the cultural, not material, survival of Quebec's natives that is in danger. "The French are pretty self-assured, and they have a point when they say that they don't practise discrimination in such a blatant way as the anglophones. Deeper down in their mentality, however, they know they really want to achieve complete assimilation of others. Experience tells us that, when the French rule, their only reflex towards our culture is to offer us baptism, to offer us French citizenship. They want a recognition of the superiority of their culture. And it enrages most people in Quebec to think that we would like to remain apart from their great Quebec society."

Encouraging the integration of immigrants might help Quebec become a stronger, more self-confident society. As a means of confronting the distinct nations on their own territory, it's a recipe for disaster. Indians, after all, are anything but immigrants. Used to playing the scrappy, up-and-coming underdogs, Québécois politicians are beginning to realize that opposing the strong moral claims of the natives – based as they are on more than eight millennia of seniority and 500 years of broken promises – can only make them look like hypocrites. It's been said that Canada is a confederation of regions and peoples expert at calling themselves victims – of racism, neglect, and conquest. If so, the natives' tales of victimization blow away the competing victim discourse of Quebec's nationalist elites, making them look like a bunch of whining children. This perhaps explains Québécois politicians' arrogant refusal to grapple with the "Indian fact," and why they still commit the kind of egregious faux pas that are unthinkable in English Canada.

An example of such insensitivity came from the Quebec City offices of the Commission de Toponymie, which celebrated the twentieth anniversary of the Charter of the French Language by bestowing the names of Québécois poems on 101 islands in Eeyou Istchee, the Cree homeland. Never mind that across the province, natives were reclaiming deformed place names: transforming Restigouche to Listuguj, turning Cauhnawaga back into Kahnawake, knocking the Our Lady off Notre-Dame-d'Ivujivik. Never mind that the new islands – among them La parapluie de ma tante (My aunt's umbrella) and La copie carbone – were actually the tips of mountains inundated by a Hydro-Québec dam. "They celebrate their language and culture at the expense of our language and culture," marvelled Bill Namagoose, executive director of the Grand Council of the Crees. "We have names for every bend in every river, every mountain, and every geographic formation." An editorialist in *L'actualité* asked Namagoose what the use of discussion was "since you're sobbing all the time, and at the very sight of the letter *q*, you scramble up your totem poles."

In coming years, there are bound to be more such virulent exchanges. Since the late seventies, Quebec's Indians have enacted a revenge of the cradle as dramatic as the rural French-Canadian population explosion of the nineteenth century. Even as francophone Québécois birth rates became the lowest in the developed world, the province's native population doubled. This was only partly due to a 1985 change in the Indian Act, which with a stroke of the pen turned 9,000 people into status Indians; natives are also having more children. Among the Montagnais and the Inuit in partic- ular, families of nine or 10 children are common, and half the aboriginal population is now under the age of 25. Raised on legends of Mohawk Warriors and sophisticated Cree politicians, these children are coming of age in an era of polarization and militancy. Viewed by Quebecers as quaint anachronisms or scorned as belligerent bandits, the latest generation of natives can't fail to notice they've been allowed little place in Quebec society. While there have been aboriginal ambassadors, lieutenant-governors, sena- tors, and other native politicians in other Canadian provinces and in Ottawa, there are currently none in Quebec. Confined to tiny reserves, increasingly conscious of their power, natives are already manipulating the Quebec government by blockading highways and bridges, always threaten- ing another Oka – an incident that cost the federal and provincial govern- ments $190 million – if their demands aren't met.

What's more, they are in an increasingly strong legal position. Between 1870 and 1923, the Indians of the Prairies and Ontario signed away their lands in a series of treaties, numbered 1 to 11, in exchange for reserves and laughable cash compensation. Quebec, however, like British Columbia and Newfoundland, signed no treaties with natives until late in the twentieth century. The Royal Proclamation of 1763, issued by King George III after the Conquest of New France but before the American Revolution, had serious implications for the former French lands. England, trying to contain colonists straining against the western frontier, proclaimed that all the land west of the American colonies belonged to the Indians unless it had been surrendered to a duly appointed agent of the Crown. Until the James Bay Agreement with the Cree, the Inuit, and the Naskapi, there was no such surrender of land in Quebec. In recent decisions, Supreme Court justices have upheld the principles of the Royal Proclamation, which has come to be known as the Indian Magna Carta. The implications are clear:

most of southern Quebec (not to mention British Columbia, the eastern Arctic, the Yukon, and the Maritimes), from the Gaspé Peninsula to Montreal, is on unceded Indian land.

The sources of native opposition to Quebec sovereignty can be summed up in two little Latin words: *terra nullius*. In 1996 Quebec argued before the Supreme Court that its territory was "land belonging to nobody," and that "no aboriginal right could have survived the assertion of French sovereignty over the territory of New France." Though such an argument has been rejected by the highest courts in both Canada and Australia – because it is based on the racist assumption that aboriginal peoples were too disorganized and uncivilized to be capable of land tenure – there's little doubt that, to prevent the partitioning of its territory, a sovereign Quebec would invoke the principle of *terra nullius*.

"Let there be no mistake about this," said Cree leader Matthew Coon Come, speaking at Harvard University. "The Bouchard government of Quebec has formally advocated the obliteration of the fundamental rights of aboriginal peoples in Quebec, on the basis of the continued application of a discredited, unjust, and discriminatory doctrine." In reality, the Cree, Mohawks, and Innu don't oppose sovereignty because of some sentimental attachment to the Canadian state. They simply suspect that their entrenched rights would have a better chance of surviving in Canada – as slow-moving and underhanded as federal bureaucrats often are – than in an independent, insecure Quebec.

Aboriginal rights are enshrined in Section 35 of the 1982 Constitution – a document Quebec refused to sign (though, as long as it remains a Canadian province, it is subject to the authority of the Charter). In practice, Quebec attempts to subjugate its natives to its own laws – only to be rebuffed by the highest courts in Canada. Georges Sioui underwent the process firsthand when he was arrested for fasting and building a sweat lodge out of alders on traditional Huron land, now a provincial park in the Laurentians. "The judge in the Quebec court actually couldn't keep from laughing," recalls Sioui. "He told us to follow the religion we'd been taught, to be good Catholics, that we didn't need to go to the bush to be in touch with the Great Spirit, since we had the church."

Brandishing a 1760 document signed by British brigadier-general James Murray, seen by the Hurons as a guarantee of the "free Exercise of their

Religion, their Customs, and Liberty of trading with the English," Sioui went to the Supreme Court of Canada and won. Along with the landmark Sparrow and Delgamuukw rulings, which ensure that no development involving aboriginal lands takes place without consultation with, and potential compensation for, the natives affected, such decisions are giving Canada's First Nations the legal tools to win back vast tracts of unjustly appropriated land.

Of course, Quebec is not the only Canadian province unsympathetic to native demands. In British Columbia, provincial supreme court justice Allan McEachern rejected the Gitksan's carefully presented store of oral testimony, adding that pre-contact natives were too uncivilized to hold title to land (the Gitksan later won their case in Canada's Supreme Court). But Quebec is a province that often sees itself as a nascent nation; and while other jurisdictions might deny land claims or pass the buck to the federal government, the province's current policies and actions ominously foreshadow the position a future state of Quebec might adopt towards its natives. So far, Québécois politicians have shown themselves to be arrogant and intransigent, with a tendency to think of their territory as an empty wasteland inhabited by only a handful of residual Indians, not long for this world anyway.

Sometimes it seems the people of Quebec feel the same way. In the summer of 1998, when Mi'kmaqs in the Gaspé Peninsula blockaded a highway after the government prevented them from selling logs to New Brunswick sawmills, a poll showed that 70 per cent of Quebecers believed it was to "blackmail the government to get more money," and not to protect their ancestral rights. Lately, the natives have been getting restless, and, thanks to the autonomy provided by earlier land settlements, they're in a position to fight. In Quebec, which has long got away with ruling its citizens by fiat – whether appropriating farmers' fields to build Mirabel Airport or plugging Côte-Nord salmon rivers to erect another dam – such a turning of the tide may wash away the piles on which the entire society was built.

Every summer, busloads of tourists show up on reserves outside Quebec City and Montreal, expecting to see some of Canada's most "culturally intact" natives. They usually get a nasty shock. In Quebec, natives have been living alongside Europeans for almost five centuries, and even the most remote Inuit now spend the winter in subsidized bungalows rather than igloos. By the late nineteenth century, much of the gross domestic product of the Hurons at Lorette derived from the sale of baskets to American tourists. The Innu still camp on the taiga, but they also maintain a sophisticated, trilingual website at www.innu.ca which proclaims, "Our territory is not the Wal-Mart of energy!" The Inuit, who had largely abandoned their nomadic lifestyle by the early fifties, are now taught by Scandinavian herdsmen to hunt on all-terrain snow machines by chasing caribou into slaughterhouses, for sale to Korean and American gourmets.

Just across the St. Lawrence from Montreal, the 6,700 English-speaking Mohawks of the Kahnawake reserve (not to be confused with Oka-Kanesatake, which is technically not a reserve) have always been at the leading edge of creative cultural survival. With no natural resources on their 5,300-hectare reserve, they've often had to leave Mohawk Territory to make a living. In the nineteenth century, they joined Wild West shows and toured Europe, imitating buffalo-hunting Sioux Indians. Kahnawake warriors, drawing on their experience negotiating the nearby Lachine Rapids, steered rafts through the white water of the Nile on an 1885 mission to rescue General Charles Gordon, under siege by rebel Muslims. They became accomplished ironworkers, specializing in nimble-footed work on the skeletons of such skyscrapers as the Empire State Building. (Since the forties, Brooklyn's Mohawk population has occasionally reached 700, earning it the nickname "Downtown Kahnawake.") Tourism is the latest attempt to bring prosperity to a community with a 35 per cent unemployment rate. Kahnawake's modest Riverside Inn is now advertised in German on Internet sites, and the tip of an ersatz teepee, purchased from the producers of a shot-in-Montreal Pierce Brosnan film, pokes above the fence at the roadside Old Indian Village and Museum.

One midsummer evening, I join a group of Mohawk women, decked out in feathered headdresses and Calvin Klein T-shirts, as they wait for a tour bus outside the Kateri Hall in Kahnawake. Between puffs on cigarettes, they scan the rusting arches of the Mercier Bridge, as an ocean-going cargo ship the size of a cathedral looms behind the steeple of little St. Francis Xavier Church. Thousands of freighters, which pass within a dozen yards of some Mohawk bungalows, yearly ply the main channel of the St. Lawrence Seaway, a water-filled trench dynamited out of expropriated Indian land in the fifties. Only a few weeks before, when the Quebec government proposed a change to tax laws that would put a serious dent in the profits from the reserve's cut-rate cigarette trade, band council leader Joe Norton shot back with a plan to impose tolls on the Seaway and all the highways, bridges, and railways that cross Mohawk land. The band has flirted with high-stakes bingo halls and extreme fighting (a no-holds-barred mixture of martial arts, wrestling, and boxing) as well as the notion of becoming an offshore banking centre – anything to keep the Kahnawake economy independent from Canada and Quebec.

Suddenly, the purple tour bus pulls up, and the woman beside me hurriedly crushes a Player's Filter beneath her moccasined toe. A little boy runs into the hall, screaming to a dancer named Silver Bear, "They're here! They're here!" Forty disoriented tourists from France, most in their fifties, file out of the bus and take the extended hands of children in print dresses, politely muttering, "Bonsoir, bonsoir." Tonight's event has been billed the Mohawk Feast in the Forest, but Kahnawake is a densely packed, semi-urban setting, eroded on all sides by a constant stream of trains, ships, and cars. In the Kateri Hall, where the tourists take their seats at long tables, trees in earthenware pots have been festooned with lights; one of them barely hides a bingo board still covered with numbers from a past tournament. The effect falls somewhat short of sylvan.

I find a free chair next to a woman named Claudette, who's from the Parisian suburb of Suresnes and is travelling with her schoolteacher daughter Françoise and her granddaughter Erica. ("Last year it was Kenya," says Françoise. "This time it's Quebec.") Their brutal touring schedule has already had them wandering the ramparts of Quebec City, watching whales in Tadoussac, and roaming through the Laurentian mountains. Tonight is their one night in Montreal, and then it's off to Ottawa and Toronto – at least 1,700 kilometres in less than 10 days.

The lights dim, and Silver Bear, wearing the kind of head-set microphone Shania Twain favours, solemnly walks to the front of the room, flanked by the women and three prepubescent dancers. Speaking in English, he lifts a peace pipe dramatically towards the plasterboard ceiling, explaining that we are gathered to commemorate the 1535 meeting between Europeans and his

Iroquois forefathers. He calls on Jacques Cartier to approach, and a bearded Frenchman ("C'est Denis!" exclaims Françoise), purple robes dangling towards his tennis shoes, dutifully sucks on the pipe. After a session of rattle shaking during a perfunctory bird dance, the oldest woman dancer explains in thickly accented Québécois French that we're about to enjoy the traditional Three Sisters salad – which turns out to be corn, zucchini, and canned kidney beans covered with a vinaigrette dressing.

The main course, which Silver Bear introduces with an unabashed smirk as "exotic game bird," is actually a fatty chicken breast coated with corn flour. After a chorus of bon appétits, we eat in silence as a 15-minute video called *People of Destiny* explains how the Iroquois, the "Romans of the New World," invented lacrosse, fought with European invaders, and built mighty office towers. Though there's no allusion to Mohawk sovereignty and the most violent aboriginal clash in recent North American history, the video ominously hints that, when challenged, "the Mohawks know how to resist." Françoise looks up from her plate, a little shocked: "Mais, c'est de la propagande!" I ask her whether she's ever heard of the Oka crisis, but get only a blank stare in return. Her mother, however, remembers seeing news reports in the early nineties; she tells me that their Québécois bus driver warned her not to mention the word "Oka" on the reserve. I explain that our hosts are the very Mohawks who armed themselves with AK-47s and armour-piercing machine guns and stood off an entire army. "Ah bon," they reply, and go back to their food. I'd forgotten about the impenetrable incuriosity of the French bourgeoisie.

The evening continues, the meal punctuated by rain dances, smoke dances, and even an alligator dance ("for when our ancestors went down to Florida"). A tiny Mohawk boy in a feathered headdress dances beneath a smoke machine and a strobe light. ("We got the smoke machine at a garage sale," offers Silver Bear, in an aside that goes untranslated. "It used to belong to the Rolling Stones. I feel like Keith Richards here.") To the utter horror of the French, the children select a few audience members and escort them to the centre of the room. A stiff-backed middle-aged man offers a memorable portrait of strained dignity as he's led by a whooping, wheeling child around the chanting Silver Bear.

For the tourists, the evening ends with strawberry mousse and an opportunity to photograph the assembled dancers. The French, forced to eat a meal without a single glass of wine (alcohol is forbidden in the community hall), look like they're in shock. I ask the women how they've enjoyed the show, and they offer a bleary-eyed, noncommittal "C'était bon." They seem relieved to be getting back on the bus that will take them to their Montreal hotel, and perhaps a few hours' sleep before the next instalment of their New World asphalt odyssey.

Perhaps the evening hasn't been a complete waste. Sure, the visitors haven't seen the Survival School, where teachers tell how the Canadian government expropriated 500 hectares of land and evicted six families from their homes to dynamite the trench that would allow Seaway freighters to pass. But at least the French have had a passing glimpse of life on a native reserve, an experience that too few Canadians can say they've shared. And, as tourists, they've contributed, however slightly, to the local economy.

In coming years, the Mohawks hope to tap the lucrative German market. Unlike the restrained French, the Germans – some of whom paint their faces and camp in mock-primitive Indian villages at home – tend to go home with armloads of expensive necklaces and T-shirts. There's every indication that the Mohawks' budding tourism industry will take root, particularly if the Quebec government finds new ways to stem the multimillion-dollar cigarette and contraband liquor trade. The tourist office is already learning to be patient when Bruxellois and Parisians, apparently oblivious to Kahnawake's many satellite dishes and big American cars, ask which part of the St. Lawrence River the Indian women wash their clothes in.

Kenneth Deer, editor of Kahnawake's lively weekly newspaper, the *Eastern Door*, sees tourism as the next economic front for the community, one that could augment tax-free cigarette and alcohol sales. To most Québécois, this is smuggling. Hard liquor and tobacco, purchased in the United States, are brought through the border-straddling Akwesasne reserve and peddled in the dozens of minuscule "smoke shacks" that dot the reserve. The Iroquois, who introduced the French to tobacco in the first place, see it as free trade. When I ask Deer whether the booze gets into the hands of Canadian Mohawks legally, he replies, "Not in Canada's eyes. But don't call us Canadians. Our homeland goes from here, north of the St. Lawrence, and down to Albany, New York. This was always our hunting and fishing territory." Deer continues the long tradition of Iroquois diplomacy by representing the Mohawks before the United Nations Working Group on Indigenous Populations; an upcoming year's trip to Geneva will be his twelfth. Like his Six Nations predecessor Deskeheh – who in 1924 crossed the Atlantic and received the backing of Persia, Estonia, Ireland, and Panama to appear before the League of Nations – Deer travels on an Iroquois passport. He spreads the golden-backed pages on a picnic bench outside his office, showing me stamps from Switzerland, Canada, and Spain. The cover shows a ring of stick-figure Iroquois chiefs, encircling a pine tree with an eagle on its top, poised to cry out a warning if it sees any danger to the Confederacy.

The Mohawks believe their claim to nationhood predates, and even precludes, Quebec's. "It's hypocritical for Quebec to call themselves a nation," insists Deer, "and give themselves the right to self-determination, the right to separate, and not give that same right to people who have been here for centuries before them." Unlike the Québécois, the Iroquois proudly proclaim that they've never been conquered by military force and have never given up their sovereignty. Though Mohawk band council leaders announced before the 1995 referendum that they were against separation, traditionalists like Deer are so highly alienated from both Quebec and Canada that sovereignty leaves them indifferent. "Quebec separation is a fight between brothers, and we shouldn't get involved. Canada has treated us pretty badly too," he says, gesturing towards the tiny swimming pool in his backyard. "We used to be a river people, but since the Canadian government expropriated our land for the Seaway and cut us off from the river, every second house has a swimming pool. Quebec might treat us that badly as well, but why fight for Canada?"

After a hundred betrayals by French and English generals, the deliberate poisoning of Iroquois leaders by missionaries, nineteenth-century raids by Mounties who burned key treaties and documents, and the brutality of the Sûreté du Québec and double-dealing of the Canadian army at Oka, it should come as no surprise that only the most confrontational dialogue between the Mohawks and the governments of Quebec and Canada is the norm these days. As Deer espouses his point of view, speaking from a separate nation within sight of the skyscrapers of Montreal, I'm struck with déjà vu. He's repeating the confrontational, dead-end rhetoric I've heard from many committed Québécois sovereignists, who also tend to insist on the seniority of their claims to the land. "Every day that we exist, it's a political expression that we are a separate nation," Deer says. "Every time an Indian is born, it's a political act. We're giving him a Mohawk name, and we're raising him as a Mohawk person. Our birth rate has gone up, and we intend to continue it. Now the Québécois are importing all these people. The immigrants will be the majority by the time our kids have grown up. Remember, though: to us, you're all immigrants."

A Few Acres of Slush

After the Kamchatka Peninsula in Siberia, the St. Lawrence Valley is the snowiest place on earth. Winter in southern Quebec lasts as long as 160 days, during which more than four metres of snow can fall on the streets of Montreal, Trois-Rivières, and Rimouski.

In January, there are entire weeks when the thermometer seems jammed at 20 below zero, when the snow squeaks underfoot and breath condenses on eyelashes, freezing them into rows of icicles that click with every blink. But Montreal – which is farther south than Seattle and sits on the same latitude as Lyons and Venice – is also one of the world's sunniest winter cities. In this polluted river valley, there are purifying mornings when a citrine sun in a sky of unmitigated azure seems to tamp the plumes of smoke back down towards the factory chimneys.

Before coming to Quebec, I'd pictured the season as a five-month-long sub-zero purgatory, all life constrained by an unyielding straitjacket of snow. In fact, winter here is a volatile season. There are evenings of howling wind and blowing snow that turn a walk to the *dépanneur* into a trek over tundra and make every heated apartment feel as plush as a firelit parlour in a Dickensian December. At least three times each winter, there are the *redoux*, or sudden thaws, when for a few afternoons the mercury shoots up to five above zero, the snow melts, and the smell of thawing dog shit actually makes one long for colder weather. "Here's to the snow over the garbage rotting in the backs of the courtyards!" wrote the Québécois author Roger Fournier. "It resembles a change of government." When you see the flakes settling lazily beneath the street lamps on a windless Sunday night in Old Montreal and glimpse a horse-drawn carriage passing in front of the snow-shrouded stone walls of the Sulpician Seminary, all the cloying tourist-board nostalgia for the idyll of New France is forgiven.

It's a simple reality: if you want to live in Quebec, you have to come to terms with the winter. It's the defining season of the place, the dominating inevitability. Spring is a convulsion, a windy, rainy shudder of cracking ice and meltwater, a brief prelude to a summer that brings waves of sticky heat to the city and swarms of biting insects to the countryside. Fall, shortened by weeks of Indian summer, would barely be noticeable if it weren't for the screeching chlorophyll of the maple leaves. "Mon pays, c'est l'hiver," sang Gilles Vigneault, and he was right: by transforming landscape, culture, and habit of mind, winter really did create a new country, permanently changing a few hundred boatloads of French peasants into a distinct people. Without winter, there would have been no Boom-Boom Geoffrion, no Bonhomme Carnaval, no Bombardier. If the snowfalls along the St. Lawrence had been lighter and the growing season longer, the United States' abortive incursions would certainly have been more frequent and determined. Without the snow, there might have been no *survivance française*, and the people of Quebec would be as integrated into the pan-American melting pot as the Kerouacs and Theroux of New England.

Why, then, have Quebecers declared war on the season that defines their province? After every major snowfall, a peacetime army of snow-removal equipment rumbles through the streets, and convoys of snowplows, front-end loaders, and dump trucks remove every trace of winter from the pavement of even the narrowest sidestreet. A tenth of the population flees south to the guest houses of Key West, the cheap hotels of Hollywood Beach, and the trailer parks of Hallandale. The rest scurry between over-heated apartments and the metro stations and office buildings of Montreal's

Underground City, paying Hydro-Québec and Gaz Métropolitain three billion dollars a year to keep their homes and offices as stuffy as possible. During the ice storm of 1998, when dozens of Quebecers were asphyxiated trying to heat fireplace-free suburban homes with barbecues, newspaper columnists plaintively wondered, How did our ancestors face winter without electricity?

Winter is even beginning to disappear from Québécois myth making. Classic films such as Claude Jutra's *Mon oncle Antoine* – about a mining town on a snowy Christmas Eve in 1940 – and Gilles Carle's *La Vie heureuse de Léopold Z.*, which showed a day in the life of a happy-go-lucky dump-truck driver during a blizzard in the sixties, lingered lovingly on wistful images of snow. More recent movies, from *The Decline of the American Empire* to *El Dorado* and *2 secondes*, take place in a summery Quebec as lush and anonymous as the backdrop to any Éric Rohmer film. Winter, formerly a source of Quebec's pride, of its *différence*, is now viewed as a stumbling block to competitiveness in a global marketplace. Recently, a book-length essay entitled "Abolissons l'hiver!" (Let's abolish winter!) appeared on newsstands. "It's a little worrying," wrote anthropologist Bernard Arcand, "to imagine the future of a country that sings, 'Mon pays, c'est l'hiver' and in the same breath adds that that winter is detestable."

Indeed. In its current denial of nordicity, Quebec has embarked on a social project of breathtaking hubris: the attempt to fool itself, and perhaps even the world, into thinking that technology can overcome the seasons, and life here may one day attain the winterless monotony of southern climates.

It's the end of January, and I'm standing in front of an ice palace, waiting for the fucking Bonhomme to appear. You'll have to pardon my French: it's 15 below tonight, and I'm hemmed in by a crowd of hardy revellers who have gathered on the frozen surface of Place Georges V – renamed Place Lotto-Québec to appease corporate sponsors – just outside the fortifications of Quebec City. We've already listened to an English-only speech by the Swedish ambassador, watched a bare-chested acrobat in electric blue tights being balanced on his partner's feet, and put up with an endless *son et lumière* show and the shrill hijinks of a troupe of harlequin-robed clowns called the Knuks. The temperature is still dropping, and there's no sign of Carnaval's mascot, that mutant Michelin Man, the Bonhomme.

I'm wondering whether one of the early stages of hypothermia is a deep sense of misanthropy. I have to fight back an urge to knock off hats, particularly that drooping, multipointed jester's cap on the guy in front of me. It's really too cold to be standing in one place. When I try to eat a Beaver's Tail, a salty, ovoid Canuck donut, the shredded cheese on top freezes into rigid pencil shavings between my teeth. This small civic square is filled with kids in puffy parkas, blowing piercing fanfares from the thin plastic clarions available in every gift shop in the Old Town. Relief finally arrives in the form of a troupe of dancers in leotards and capes. They begin a Celtic-style dance that involves a lot of prancing in one spot, and the crowd eagerly joins in. "What the hell," I mutter, and jump up and down, giving in to this polar pogo. In a couple of minutes, by God, I can feel my toes again. This must be the origin of the local folk dances: a desperate attempt to stave off a chilly death. When Bonhomme finally appears, a prancing snowman in a multicoloured belt and red cap, I actually cheer the hollow-eyed freak. Later, I realize this evening has taught me a valuable lesson. Curmudgeonly resistance is useless – if you can't learn to love the winter, then you might as well get out of the North.

Quebec City during Carnaval is the perfect place to discover winter, and I spend the rest of the weekend revelling in the unfamiliar triteness. On Saturday, there's a race through the Old Town, and I join in the bilingual countdown ("Trois, deux, un, go!") that sends wildly yapping, slim-bellied dogs pulling riders on sleighs up Rue St-Louis, between crowds pressed against the facades of eighteenth-century buildings. On the Plains of Abraham, carvers from around the world use rasps and spatulas to turn three-metre-high blocks of snow into ephemeral sculptures. There's the *glissoire* on the Terrace Dufferin, a kind of boardwalk suspended from the Upper Town's cliffside; I rent a wooden toboggan for a buck and haul it up a steep staircase to a platform overlooking the clumpers and ice floes on the St. Lawrence. An attendant roughly drops my toboggan into one of three icy grooves, I clamber aboard, and he releases a restraining bolt that sends me plummeting at 65 kilometres an hour. Just as I'm wondering how this rickety death trap is going to stop, the toboggan flies off the ice track and grates to a sudden halt on the wooden surface of the Terrace. Panting, exhilarated, I realize my inner thermostat has undergone some kind of satori: I've forgotten how cold it is.

Over the weekend, I get lost in an ice maze, trade snowballs with the cape-wrapped coachmen on the Esplanade, and ride the sheer funicular to the Lower Town. Most of all, I enjoy roaming within the pseudo-Gothic gates of Quebec City itself, which, as one nineteenth-century traveller put it, looks "like St. Malo strayed up here and was lost in the snow." I'd been expecting a vast binge, the alcoholic fantasyland of New Orleans Mardi Gras in a subarctic setting. The drink of choice here is caribou, a combination of whisky blanc and port, which partiers surreptitiously sip from plastic walking canes topped by a winking Bonhomme. Suggestive of a sangria-and-cough-syrup highball, caribou is one of those deceptively warming, medicinal concoctions whose abuse guarantees a morning-after of cluster headaches. It's probably the source of Carnaval's reputation as a violent hyperborean bacchanalia. In the past, drunken students from Ontario have rampaged through hotels, clashed with Québécois teenagers, and even swarmed the Bonhomme. (Good!) In recent years, however, the city's efforts to turn the 16-day-long Carnaval into a family affair have started to take. There's still the odd patch of frozen vomit among the quaint shops of the Rue du Petit Champlain, but most spectators at the canoe race across the ice-choked river are now parents with young children. It's a question-able deliverance. The world's largest winter carnival, now officially the Carnaval de Québec Kellogg's, was once a freewheeling celebration for the entire society. In coming years it might be Tony the Tiger, not Bonhomme, who bursts from the ice palace.

Quebec's earliest winter carnivals were something else entirely: the spirited attempts of grown-up city dwellers in a marginal climate to turn a gruelling season into a cultural asset. The English-speaking merchants of Montreal launched the prototypical winter carnival in 1883, an event imi-tated by the burghers of St. Paul, Minnesota, Ottawa, and later Quebec City. For a week in February, 25,000 Montrealers and tourists (in a town of only 60,000) cheered at the curling bonspiel, wheeled merrily at the fancy dress carnival on the Crystal Skating Rink, and watched in wonder as Dominion Square was illuminated by electric lights and pyrotechnic dis-plays. Snowshoers met in mock battle, blasting the 15-metre-tall turrets of a castle built from blocks of river ice with volleys from Roman candles. A visiting American travel writer, C.H. Farnham, marvelled at this ice palace in *Harper's New Monthly Magazine*: "It is an opalescent castle intensely brilliant in the sunshine, with walls of translucent shadows edged with prismatic hues. One expects to meet Kubla Khan at every turn." He was equally impressed with the widespread frivolity. "The social season in Montreal is naturally midwinter, and a charming season it is: gayeties, as they say, come and go with the snow."

In truth, there wasn't much else to do. Before icebreakers, navigation on the St. Lawrence stopped dead from November to April. Along with dinner parties and bibulous binges in taverns, bored professionals elaborated a variety of winter pastimes. They twirled rosy-cheeked girls on the world's first covered skating rink, built in Quebec City in 1852. They bet on jockeys who raced horse-drawn sleighs across the ice bridges that spanned vast rivers. And they might well have played the world's first game of hockey on the frozen surface of the St. Lawrence. Adapting the English game of bandy, two teams of eight players descended on the ice in 1837 and used curved wooden field hockey sticks to fight over a ball. Though Dartmouth, Nova Scotia, and Kingston, Ontario, also claim to be the birthplace of the game, Montreal can definitely claim one hockey first: in the 1870s, three McGill graduates published the first set of rules for the game in the Montreal *Gazette*.

Quebec's elaborate winter culture was well known abroad. Charles Smallwood, a professor of meteorology at McGill University, took the first successful photographs of snow crystals. Cornelius Krieghoff, a Dutch immigrant who moved to Quebec City in the 1850s, popularized the Laurentian winter with busy, Bruegel-like canvases of comical French Canadians making merry in snowy landscapes. Paul Blouet, a travel writer from France who visited Montreal in 1890, extolled the vigour of the Canadian character: "In Russia, in the northern parts of the United States, the people say: 'It's too cold to go out.' In Canada, they say: 'It's very cold, let's all go out.'"

Even the gruffest southern curmudgeon betrayed a soft spot for the snows of Quebec. Mark Twain first came to Montreal in 1881, when piratical Canadian publishing houses started mailing cut-rate editions of his books to American customers. In Quebec to establish copyright, he bought a toboggan for his children after sliding down a snowy hill, and marvelled at both the beauty of French-Canadian girls – "it was a kind of relief to strike a homely face occasionally" – and the hardness of Quebec City hotel beds. He also delivered a grouchy monologue at Montreal's Windsor Hotel. Fed up with overzealous local boosters, he blustered, "I have seen the cab which Champlain employed when he arrived overland at Quebec; I have seen the horse which Jacques Cartier rode when he discovered Montreal. I have used them both; I will never do it again. Yes, I have seen all the historical places; the localities have been pointed out to me where the scenery is warehoused for the season." Of Quebec City, he said, "A cabman drove me two miles up a perpendicular hill in a sleigh and showed me an admirable snowstorm from the heights of Quebec. The man was an ass; I could have seen the snowstorm as well from the hotel window and saved my money."

Twain even had a run-in with one of the stranger by-products of the Canadian winter, the Montreal Snowshoe Club. Since pulling on their moccasins in 1840, the manly Tuques Bleues had been rambling over Mount Royal in torch-lit processions, bellowing, "We can beat the fastest engines / In a night tramp on the snow!" When Twain wandered into their meeting hall, they made him an honorary member. As his travelling companion, the novelist George Washington Cable, tells it, "With a roaring cheer, he was laid hold of and walked out into the middle of the floor. Then at the word, 'Bounce um!' he was lifted from his feet in the midst of a tightly huddled mass of young athletes, laid out at full length on their hands and then – what think you? – thrown bodily into the air almost to the ceiling." What Twain thought of this aggressive bonhomie has gone unrecorded.

One has to hand it to the English elite of nineteenth-century Quebec: they were determined to turn the toughest of seasons into a salubrious playground. It's hard, however, not to detect a little condescension in their appropriation of the habitant's hooded capote and sash and the Algonquian moccasin and snowshoe. It was as if a bunch of good ol' boys from New Orleans rubbed on blackface, donned straw hats, and headed down to the bayou on drunken crawfish expeditions. To make matters worse, these pasty city boys were poor losers. During their annual competitions, notes a club pamphlet, "the races were thrown open to all snowshoers, until the year 1874, when Indians were barred from competition with white men, in consequence of their being deemed professionals." Club records reveal the real source of the problem: athletic Mohawks from Kahnawake were consistently kicking white ass, and the French-Canadian snowshoers were so good they had to be segregated into their own club, Le Canadien. Even after the popularity of snowshoeing had declined, these underdogs continued to defeat the Anglos. Members of the club would go on to found the Canadiens hockey team in 1909. (The francophones had to put up with hypocrisy from their own elites. The clerics of Montreal, who never missed a trick, condemned female snowshoers in masculine leggings and blanket coats for indulging in transvestism.)

The chief propagandist of the English-Canadian snowshoers, W. Geo. Beers, in 1883 published a remarkable paean to winter, the lavishly illustrated *Over the Snow*. "Jack Frost means business in Canada," Beers warned, alongside engravings of American tenderfeet falling headfirst into snowbanks. "Nothing astonishes our winter visitors more than the indifference to danger, and the genuine delight in hard, rough pleasure, shown by our Canadian girls." Winter, Beers chides, is no real threat to the constitution. "To any healthy man, woman or child, a Canadian winter, especially that of Quebec and Manitoba, is an exhilarating tonic. Recent years have fully proved that to a certain class of invalids it is a perfect cure!" Two years later, the city's poorest French-Canadian quarters were hit by a smallpox epidemic. In Montreal, 3,000 people died in agony. Grudgingly, the snowshoers of the Golden Square Mile – the richest neighbourhood in what was then the metropolis of Canada – agreed to cancel that year's carnival.

When the French explorer Jacques Cartier first came to Canada in 1534, it was summer, and he found the heat and humidity so oppressive he dubbed the body of water south of the Gaspé Peninsula the Baie des Chaleurs – the Bay of Heat. Recalling these tropical conditions when he returned a year later, he pooh-poohed the warnings of natives who told him he'd better start preparing for winter. After all, this new land lay to the south of his native Brittany, where the winters were mild and rainy. Moored outside today's Quebec City, Cartier watched in consternation as the river started to freeze around the fragile wooden hull of his *Grande Hermine*. From mid-November to April 15, he paced on the decks as more than a metre of snow piled up on the riverbanks, the ship's rails became encased in ice like twigs in amber, and the ship's stock of wine froze in the cask. Of his 110 crew members, 25 succumbed to scurvy, the rest saved only by a vitamin-C-enhancing infusion of cedar bark offered by the local Iroquois. Similar fates awaited the crews of Samuel de Champlain and the founders of Quebec City. "Man's first adaptation to the climate of Canada," the French geographer Pierre Deffontaines dryly noted in 1957, "was to die."

It would have been hard to design a better trap for killing Europeans. The inviting St. Lawrence, where July temperatures can rise to 40 degrees, lies as far south as the Loire River, and its summer heat lingers well into September. But the river offers no hint of an immense inland sea to the north, the southernmost incursion of any arctic ocean into temperate latitudes. This is Hudson Bay, one of the world's coldest bodies of water, which is locked in a constant battle with the Gulf of Mexico, one of the warmest. Quebec is lodged between an icebox and a kettle, whose cold and warm fronts regularly clash over the St. Lawrence Valley, producing prodigious snowfalls. Winter comes with little warning, after a brief fall, and spring appears late. In a good, Eurocentric universe, March 21 would mark the beginning of the planting season. In Quebec, the ground is still frozen at the time of the spring equinox, and the average temperature is minus one Celsius. As a disgusted Samuel de Champlain noted, with only a little hyperbole, this country has six months of winter.

The French colonists had to come up with a new set of words to describe the weather. First there was the *averse*, the little snowfall; then the *bordée* or *abât*, the full-fledged snowstorm, which could drop up to two metres of snow on a village at a time. Between the *pluie verglaçante*, the freezing rain that bowed thick birch limbs to the ground, and the *tempête des corneilles* – the late-winter snowstorm – there were endless *poudreries*, whiteouts of blowing snow. When the flakes were fat and wet, or *pelotants*, it was a *grosse neige*, which dampened one's clothes. Come the debacles of spring – *la mouvance* – when separating ice floes sent thunderlike cracks echoing through the silent St. Lawrence Valley, immense *clefs*, or walls of river ice, raked the banks, wiping away homes and bridges. Even the winds had to be assigned special names: the *surouêt*, the southwest wind that heralded warmer weather, was nothing next to the dreaded *nordet*, from the icy north Atlantic, the wind that brought the worst blizzards.

The winter forced radical changes to centuries-old French traditions. The ill-insulated stone houses of Normandy and Poitou turned out to be disastrous in Quebec. The rock walls trapped moisture, splitting in the bitter cold or shifting with the constant freezes and thaws, making the morning's first task the sweeping up of snow that had blown through the cracks. In the countryside, the farmers started to favour wood-frame houses and barns, raised off the frozen ground by foundations called *solages*. (A 1727 municipal law banning wooden homes, after several disastrous fires, explains why most buildings in Quebec City are made of stone.) They added a *tambour* – a vestibule that can still be seen in most of Montreal's older houses – which prevented heat from escaping when they were shaking off their boots. They eliminated northern windows. Roofs were made of cedar, which kept an insulating layer of snow on the roof. The open hearth of the French farmhouse, great for slow-cooking stews but a terrible source of heat, was replaced by the iron stove, whose snaking pipe conducted heat throughout a house that could now be enlarged beyond a single room. Homes were set at the front of their *rangs* – thin rectangular lots that at first fronted the St. Lawrence – to minimize the shovelling needed to get to the road. Even today, Highway 138, which follows a twisting coach route between Trois-Rivières and Quebec City, is so consistently fronted by homes that it feels like one long main street.

By the time of the Conquest, when the British were moving into the mansions of Quebec City and Montreal, the habitants had got the Canadian climate pretty much figured out. In summer, they worked long into the night, planting and harvesting during a growing season that averaged only 100 days. Given enough firewood, a *cavreau* (root cellar) filled with potatoes and onions, salted pork and cod, and separate farm buildings to house the livestock and grain, most families achieved enviable self-sufficiency. Winter was the time to *s'encabaner*, to hole up, tell stories, fix tools, mend clothes, and smoke pipes by the stove. A good layer of ice and snow facilitated movement between communities, making rivers traversable and normally muddy backlots accessible to horse-drawn sleighs and snowshoes. According to the racial clichés of nineteenth-century novelists, the confrontation with the elements had even calmed the excitable Gallic spirit, making the Canadien soul resigned and peaceful in the face of inexorable nature.

The legend of French-Canadian joie de vivre was also born in the nineteenth century, when Protestant city dwellers, suffering through the seasonal flagging in commerce, looked on in envy at self-sufficient farmers who seemed to relish winter. Between Noël and Mardi Gras, rural francophones enjoyed endless diversions. There was the fur-wrapped sleigh ride to midnight mass, feasts of hare tourtière and doughnut-like croquignoles during the *Fêtes des rois*, and the promise of *veillées*, late-night parties, where the *violoneux* scratched out "Rose du bois" on their fiddles for dancing neighbours. The priests tried to put a damper on it all, but to little effect. English-Canadian observers were shocked to see five-year-old habitant boys sucking on pipes, and household kegs of Jamaican rum drained in a matter of days. The *temps des sucres* – sugaring time – finally came at the end of March; after months in smoky, overheated farmhouses, cabin-feverish families of 15 were grateful to head to the maple groves to suck up ladles of syrup. They finished the winter half-diabetic and stir-crazy, but ready to shake off their confinement and work in the fields.

That, in any case, is the mythic version of winter in French Canada: a timeless idyll, the season when families regrouped to reaffirm language and folk culture in self-sufficient country cabins far from the English interlopers. In reality, of course, Quebec was never spared from history. Starting in the 1830s, rural overpopulation forced older boys to head for work in northwoods lumber camps, New England mills, and Montreal factories. In an effort to stem this migration to America, which was perceived as a letting of racial blood, the clerics urged the colonization of the lands to the north, particularly the Laurentians and the Saguenay. Relentlessly, however, the population shifted to the cities, where self-sufficiency was traded for wage slavery. Worst of all, for most French Canadians, the idle days and pure snows of the backcountry winter were lost forever – to 60-hour work weeks and cinder-blackened slush. The Quebec winter left the farm and settled down in the big city.

These days, a primarily urban Quebec has a new winter vocabulary, characterized by derisory plosives and fricatives, gobbed out in disgust at bus stops and street corners. The *gadoue*, a mixture of tire-melted snow mingled with *gros sel* (rock salt), is cursed as it corrodes the leather of fashionable boots. Puddles of *sloche* hide the curbs and lure pedestrians into ankle-deep quicksands, rimming the hems of trousers with civic guano. The juddering of the one-man *gratte-neige*, or snowplow, skidding over the *grésil* (hardened hail) on a narrow sidewalk, sends panicked pedestrians scattering like rodeo clowns before a maddened bull. City dwellers curse the *crudité*, the humid cold, along with *le calcium*, the chemical de-icer that rusts their cars. In a society that now works year round, winter is vilified as a nuisance, a season to be combatted, carted away, and at best, ignored.

For the local media, the widely hated winter makes an easy target. Itemizing the annual martyrdom of the Québécois, the newsmagazine *L'actualité* reported that the province now spends $90 million a year on cough syrup and vitamins, $290 million on boots, and $460 million on winter coats; that the average age of cars, eaten away by salty slush, is three years less than those of British Columbia; and that cold-buckled roads undergo major repairs every seven years, compared to 15 in Florida. Dailies like *La Presse* keep a running toll of mortal snowmobile accidents (an average of 27 a year) and other winter-related deaths (about 40 a year, from shovelling-induced heart attacks to highway accidents provoked by blocks of ice falling from overpasses). The media rarely mention the positive sides of winter. Criminal activity decreases; theatre, dance companies, and television stations attract their largest audiences; the telephone company records 30 per cent more calls; and lower highway speeds reduce the number of fatal accidents.

Winter is the season the rest of the world associates with Quebec. Europeans are intrigued by vast white spaces; the idea of one day giving up crowded arrondissements for the pristine isolation of *une cabane au Canada* has immense appeal for the world-weary Parisian. They came by the thousands to participate in the eight-day Harricana snowmobile race in the early nineties, and French tourists are a significant presence on Quebec's 30,000 kilometres of snowmobile trails. Shoppers from around the world come to Quebec City's Maranda-Labrecque, North America's oldest fur factory, or browse through the beaver, muskrat, raccoon, and lynx furs at Montreal's annual Exposition nord-americaine fourrures et mode, the continent's largest such fair. (In defence of the 400-year-old activity that built New France, a coat with a lynx collar looks less frivolous on a 30-below morning in Chibougamau than it does at a gallery opening in Paris.)

Millions of tourists holiday at the province's hundred downhill skiing resorts, the most famous of which is Mont-Tremblant. In 1938, a young American millionaire named Joe Ryan convinced then-premier Maurice Duplessis to change a provincial law and sell him part of a protected park – an incident that neatly encapsulates the utter amorality of Le Chef's reign – thus founding one of eastern North America's most popular ski resorts. Popularized by the Norwegian expatriate skier Herman "Jackrabbit" Johannsen, Mont-Tremblant is now a $700-million Legoland of condos painted shades of cotton candy. Skiing, however, was never a native French-Canadian tradition (a group of McGill professors, former Montreal Snowshoe Club members, brought the Scandinavian sport here in 1903), and Mont-Tremblant is now owned by the British Columbia–based real estate company Intrawest. Francophone Québécois are better known for their leadership in other winter-related sectors, among them RPM Tech snow-clearing equipment, Kanuk cold weather clothing, Sport Maska-CCM hockey skates and gloves, and Bombardier snowmobiles.

So Europeans, come from afar to relish this defining season, can be forgiven their surprise at the virtual absence of snow on the streets of the province's major cities. Montreal, a 50-kilometre-long island at the confluence of the Ottawa and St. Lawrence Rivers, gets an average 2.25 metres of snow in at least 10 heavy storms a year – but you'd never know it, because 72 hours after each blizzard, it's virtually gone, systematically eliminated by the world's most aggressive snow removal policy. Starting in early November, the city battens down the hatches: bicycle racks are plucked from the sidewalks, tree trunks are wrapped in protective black sheaths made of recycled tires, and the posts that flag summer bike paths are snatched from the curbsides. When an inch of snow has fallen, and Environment Canada is calling for more, the city goes on alert. Broad-axle pickup trucks roam the streets like panicked rag-and-bone carts, their minatory horns teetering manically between two high-pitched croaks. These are the harbingers of the tow trucks, which haul suddenly ill-parked cars (according to hastily planted street signs) to adjoining sidestreets, leaving $92 tickets on their windshields.

Then the cavalcade begins. The swift spreader trucks, with their slanted blades, push the snow to the side of the road, leaving a mixture of black gravel, Sifto-brand salt, and calcium chloride in their wake. Then come the spindly graders, yellow stick insects with chip-toothed blades that pile the snow into the curb lane in precipitous linear banks. These are followed by convoys of up to 30 vehicles, their ponderous pace determined by the progress of the terrifying front-end loader. The maw of this awesome machine contains an immense horizontal corkscrew that chews up the snow banks, blowing crushed powder through a snaking pipe into the high-walled dump truck that cruises alongside. The convoys rumble through residential streets all night long, rattling windows and casting haunting orange lights on apartment ceilings. As each dump truck is filled, it peels off towards the river, to be seamlessly replaced alongside the snow-blowing loader by another. The truckloads of snow, 300,000 a year, are driven to piers and poured – complete with heavy metals and ground-up bags of garbage – into the St. Lawrence River and the Francon Quarry. *Voilà*: the lucrative transformation of snow into refuse is complete.

Montreal has a snow removal staff of 2,800 workers, who use 1,240 vehicles to clear 42 million tons of snow from 2,000 kilometres of streets. The effort costs the city a million dollars a day, $54 million in an average year (versus $32 million in Toronto, which has almost three times as much pavement). All told, snow removal costs the province half a billion dollars a year. The war on snow has its casualties. Local legend has it that the blades of the front-end loaders have swallowed streetside snow forts, turning the children within into ground chuck. In the winter of 1998/99, seven people were killed by snow removal equipment, including a five-year-old girl who was crushed by a dump truck. Blue-collar workers go flying out of the cabins of their snowplows when they hit manhole covers that have been shaken ajar, and some 300 people a year register complaints about sidewalk plows tearing off fences and exterior staircases. One morning in 1999, the plows' tank-treads lost purchase on sidewalks covered with ice pellets and dented a hundred parked cars.

In spite of it all – the higher taxes, the calcium stains on boots, the fender-benders – Quebec's urbanites believe their taxes have bought them the right to deseasonalized cities. The municipalization of snow removal, the opening of highways to winter traffic in the forties, and the construction of one of the world's most ambitious hydroelectric systems in the sixties have convinced Montrealers that an elusive chimera is within their grasp. One day soon, technology might make it possible to spend a winter in sub-arctic Quebec without noticing that it's cold outside. A suburbanite can begin the day in a toasty four-by-four, started from inside her bungalow with a *démarreur à distance* (a remote control starter) and kept snow-free beneath a Tempo, a Quebec-made, prefab steel-framed car shelter stretched with a roof of lightweight polyethylene. She can flaunt summery skin tones year round, courtesy of the province's 900 indoor tanning salons. Three-quarters of a million Quebecers now sport the carroty hues of the winter tanner – bucking a worldwide trend towards pallor – a phenomenon that's contributed to a 205 per cent increase in skin cancer here in the last decade.

Sometimes these equatorial delusions reach pathological proportions. The longing for a temperate climate has brought an architecture more typical of California or Florida to the suburbs. Many bungalows are now built without *tambours*, the wind-breaking vestibules of the habitants' homes, as though living room doors opened directly onto parrots and palm trees. One of the more pathetic scenes of Quebec's urban winter is the sight of an elegant young woman teetering over sidewalk ice shields on disco heels, like a doe that's strayed onto a frozen lake, to stand in a nightclub line-up with her arms crossed over an unlined leather jacket. This persistent underdressing exacerbates winter flus and colds, turning January theatre performances in Montreal into nonstop, surround-sound choruses of hacking coughs and sneezes. "Public places in Scandinavia," the philosopher John Ralston Saul has noted, "are equipped with enormous coat- and boot-check facilities. People can get in and out of theatres in seconds. In Canada there are sometimes no facilities at all. People are constantly stuffing large winter coats under seats or sitting with them over their knees for hours."

Some people don't bother with winter clothes. They live like troglodytes, rarely emerging from Montreal's interlinked system of metro stations and downtown office towers, which the tourist board boasts is the largest in the world. The Underground City – which in the guidebooks sounds evocative of Roman catacombs and Parisian sewers – is actually more like a cross between a shopping mall and a bomb shelter. Radiating outwards from the Gare Centrale, it's a 29-kilometre network of passages joining two thousand boutiques, seven major hotels, restaurants, department stores, four universities, a museum, the Stock Exchange, the Molson Centre, and virtually every major downtown office building. It links the herborists of Chinatown to the violinists of Place des Arts, the ice skaters at the Bell Amphitheatre's rink to the swimmers on the rooftop pool of the Bonaventure Hotel in one immense, interconnected indoor space. Cast in the stark New Brutalism of the sixties, the Underground City sometimes surprises with its audacity. In the subterranean campus of the Université du Québec à Montréal, you can look up from metro level to find that you're standing beneath a hollowed-out cathedral, whose street-level floor has been removed to create a vast interior space. In general, however, Montreal's underground is an overheated bunker, a Mall of the Americas on the moon. An afternoon in its concrete entrails leaves you feeling that a revival of Inuit igloos and habitant farmhouses might not be such a bad idea.

The most extreme rejection of winter lies on the Cité du Havre, a spit of land in the St. Lawrence River just south of downtown Montreal. On one side of this man-made peninsula, huge freighters from Toronto and Thunder Bay winter in dry dock. On the other side is a pair of architectural follies: Habitat 67, the celebrated housing complex that looks like a vision of an Aztec hill village in concrete; and the infamous Tropiques-Nord, a luxurious residential vivarium for Quebecers who have decided to end their subarctic winter exile.

A blinding snowstorm has hit Montreal, and as I enter the foyer of this white-walled building, the sticky snow that's gathered like moss on my coat instantly liquefies. The building superintendent, in a short-sleeve shirt and faded jeans, leads me through a corridor where bloated ornamental shells cover the wall lights, decor elements created during the last gasp of the *Miami Vice*–era art deco revival. Conceived in more optimistic times by architect Jean de Brabant, the million-dollar condominium units in Tropiques-Nord came up for sale in 1989, just as the bottom fell out of Montreal's real estate market.

I'm given a perfunctory tour of a vacant seventh-floor condo. Stepping onto a broad, tiled balcony spilling over with purple bougainvillea and blood-orange hibiscus, I realize we're above an elaborate oasis of palm and mango trees, separated from the lifeless landscape outside by glass panels that rise 12 stories. Each of the 120 units backs onto this shared courtyard, the stacked apartments rising to form a kind of troglodytes' cliffside village enclosed by a slanted glass ceiling, a residential biodome sustained by natural gas.

Down on the floor of the tropical forest, the superintendent introduces me to Guy Poulin, Tropiques-Nord's overalled horticulturist. Pausing occasionally to put a fallen leaf into a pouch on his belt, Poulin takes me along jungle pathways of imitation flagstones, introducing me to the ecosystem he loves. The branches of *Ficus benjamina* trees droop over a whirlpool bath, whose waters cascade into a swimming pool designed to look as though erosion had carved it into the jungle floor. One unforeseen problem with Tropiques-Nord was the cockroach colony inadvertently imported with the palm trees from Florida; people who had paid $900,000 for a condo became impatient when they found a giant roach in their morning coffee. Poulin, gesturing with clippers towards a digital meter on the trunk of a 20-metre-tall Washingtonia palm, points out that the temperature is 20.2 degrees Celsius, the humidity hovering around 59 per cent, almost the same as today's forecast for Tampa. On our side of the glass, Japanese nightingales flick energetically between the drooping fronds. On the other, threadbare house sparrows, little embers of blood and feathers that have somehow continued to glow through the 20-below-zero January evenings, huddle immobile on the lower branches of a snow-covered apple tree. A tiny, translucent fly hovers around my hand – the first flying insect I've seen in three months.

I scan the rows of broad balconies, trying to glimpse some of Tropiques-Nord's best-known tenants: the singer Roch Voisine now dwells among the hibiscus, in the apartment where his manager's body was found after a cocaine overdose. On this winter afternoon, however, I can only see one woman, wearing shorts and a T-shirt, at a deck table on a second-floor balcony. The kind of people who can afford to live here, I reflect, are either making deals downtown or vacationing in the real south, basking among native palms.

As I walk away from Tropiques-Nord, I'm reminded of the domed garden in a film called *Silent Running*, an ecology-era parable about scientists cultivating a bubble of greenery in outer space after life on earth has been ravaged by nuclear war.

As harsh as winter here can be, it also has its beauties and charms, which reward effort and imagination. The canvases of Ozias Leduc and Paul-Émile Borduas, the novels of Gabrielle Roy and Réjean Ducharme, the poetry of Leonard Cohen and Émile Nelligan are all rich artistic responses to a landscape – inner and exterior – whose central fact is winter. Technological evasive techniques, like the gas-fired Club Med behind me, the Underground City below, and the snow removal trucks all around, somehow impoverish this unique environment. In the long term, I suspect they lessen our ability to make anything meaningful of our winter.

Of course, many Quebecers opt for the most radical solution of all: seasonal expatriation. Somewhere between bohemian Key West, where Michel Tremblay can be seen riding his bicycle, and stinking-rich Jupiter, where Céline Dion has a $10-million mansion, lies "Floribec," a five-kilometre-wide coastal strip that has become a de facto, low-rent suburb of urban Quebec. According to the *Miami Herald*, half a million French Canadians spend more than three months of the year here, making southeast Florida the largest enclave of francophone North America outside Quebec.

I'm starting to believe it. Since leaving Mirabel Airport on an Air Transat charter, I haven't stopped hearing the accents of retirement-age Québécois. The Trois-Rivières couple next to me on the flight to Fort Lauderdale are heading down to Hallandale for a five-week stay in a friend's mobile home. Seventy-year-old Rosaire Arsenault, who worked as a lumberjack after leaving the family farm and his 15 brothers and sisters, is abuzz with news about a retired truck driver from Quebec, shot by a robber who followed him to his North Miami Beach home from the Fort Lauderdale Airport. Just last week, Arsenault confides, a Québécois couple driving to the same airport in their Cadillac were forced off a deserted stretch of highway; they would have been robbed if a line of cars hadn't happened along. "You probably won't have any problem," he says, sighing. "But they see us coming, with our Quebec licence plates and our little grey heads."

I wake up next morning in the Silver Spray Motel to the sound of French-language newscasts and the rolled *r*s of a Montreal accent through thin walls. I've chosen lodgings in Hollywood Beach, a long peninsula separated from the mainland by a waterway full of huge yachts. My motel is run by Gilles and Monique, now American citizens but originally from Drummondville. Walking east to the oceanfront Broadwalk, I discover that I'm on a beach sprinkled with palm trees, separated from the Ocean Drive highway by a stretch of family-run motels. Old men comb the fine-grained sand with metal detectors, as a squadron of prehistoric-looking pelicans sweeps low over a fluorescent Atlantic Ocean. When I left Montreal yesterday afternoon, I was dressed for 20 below zero; this morning, it's 20 above. The contrast between winter austerity and the exuberant greenery almost feels like wilful mockery – as though Florida were laying this great climate thing on too thick. Surrounded by Québécois, I'm in a real-world version of singer Robert Charlebois's fantasy about a tropical Montreal: "O Jacques Cartier / If you'd only steered clear of our wintery ways . . . / Think what we'd have today! / A Sherbrooke Street lined in coconut palms / With flocks of parrots perched in their fronds . . ."

Hollywood Beach is a microcosm of lower-middle-class Quebec. At the Hollywood Food Market, I can pick up yesterday's *Journal de Montréal* and this week's *Allô Police* from an Egyptian counterman who's mastered enough French to steer his francophone clients towards the canned poutine sauce on the shelves. Frenchie's Café – a beachfront bar where oddly relaxed looking bikers suck back Labatt Bleue, play video poker, and smoke tax-free Player's purchased at the nearby Seminole Indian reserve – has put out a lunchtime blackboard advertising "Country-fried steack on a kiaser bun" and Canadian sugar pie. The weak dollar has made this year a slow one for local restaurateurs, and a couple of menu-clutching barkers at rival beachfront canteens get in a shouting match for my lunch custom; I opt for La Belle Gaspésienne, whose New World take on coquilles St. Jacques includes a Caesar salad sprinkled with artificial bacon bits.

Hollywood Beach seems a strange combination of older Jewish retirees, eccentric English-speaking bums, and French Canadians. Come to think of it, that's a pretty good description of Montreal, which might explain why everyone feels at home here. The locals aren't all that thrilled with the situation, judging from the bumper stickers that read, "When I get old I'm going to move to Canada and drive slow." A Fort Lauderdale magazine provoked outrage a few years back when it observed, "The frogs, if not the water lilies, are in bloom again. . . . Here come the oil-slicked, bulging bare midriffs stuffed into swimsuits even a toddler would be ashamed to wear." Apparently French Canadians have a notorious weak spot for minuscule Speedo bathing suits. I recall the character in the popular Québécois film *La Florida* – a comedy about a Montreal bus driver turned Hollywood Beach hotelier – who sits on a bench commenting on the exposed torsos of passersby. "Gall bladder," he mutters, spotting an operation scar. Or, whistling as he notices a particularly worked-over chest, "Triple coronary by-pass."

In a little office near the railway tracks a couple of miles inland, I meet Pierre Vigneault. The editor of *Le Soleil de la Floride*, a French-language monthly with a circulation of 30,000, brushes a portrait of a Québécois bedroom community in beatific tropical exile. The Floribecois, as they've been dubbed, are served by three banks with French-speaking tellers, including the Desjardins Federal Savings Bank and the Banque Nationale (here called NatBank). They can attend mass at the Sanctuaire de Notre Dame du Sourire on Johnson Street, go to one of 17 weekly French-language meetings of Alcooliques anonymes, or join the local branch of Club Richelieu, a kind of francophone Kiwanis Club. Younger expatriates have formed hockey teams, playing on in-line skates or at local ice rinks. And at Hollywood's Greek, Mexican, and Italian restaurants, they can expect to be served in perfect French – because many of the young waitresses have crossed the border illegally to spend a season earning American dollars.

"Life is so easy in Florida," enthuses Vigneault, whose green card allows him to live here year round. "There's nowhere else that people can come so easily and find a place where the cost of living is similar to Quebec's." For most seniors, the only fly in the vitamin E ointment is health care. There are the horror stories: a hospitalization for a heart attack that cost $41,000, of which the Quebec government would refund only $1,650. What's more, staying away from home for more than 183 days means Quebecers lose their right to health care coverage back home, and private premiums for a winter in Florida can cost an older couple thousands of dollars. Vigneault thinks the risks and expenses are worth it. "This is one of the few places where Québécois can come and continue to preserve their culture. You can get four French-language television stations here; you can be connected to everything that's happening in Quebec, while at the same time living far from the winter." Vigneault doesn't miss the snows of Quebec. "It's the whole atmosphere. There are only three colours: white, grey, and black. It's like everything was dead. Me, I like the greenery. Even if it's very hot here in summer, it's enough for me to think that I'll never have to spend another winter in the cold."

Vigneault steers me towards a luxurious mobile home park on Hallandale Beach Boulevard. Dale Village, which lies just past the railway lines and Big Al's Gun Range, is easy to find thanks to the Maple Leaf flying beneath the Stars and Stripes. This is a gated community, albeit on a modest scale: a private security patrol car at the entrance allows seniors to pedal their giant tricycles in peace, even in the midst of rough, all-black neighbourhoods. With 90 per cent of its 330 mobile homes occupied by francophones, Dale Village looks like an obsessively spruce suburb of Chicoutimi, planted with palm trees instead of pines – one that somehow ended up on the wrong side of the American tracks.

Jacqueline and Marcel Grignon are playing shuffleboard next to the swimming pool and *pétanque* pitches. She's 74, he turns 81 tomorrow, and from the way they're turned out for their afternoon game – casually but elegantly, he in shorts and a tropical blue shirt, she sporting earrings like miniature bunches of grapes – I'm not surprised to learn they're newlyweds. "I never liked the cold," says Marcel, the shuffleboard pike leaning on his shoulder giving him the look of a rakish demon who's repaired to warmer climes. "I worked as a prison librarian, and I never had enough money for skiing and skating. What I especially hated in Montreal was the slush. Even when you bought big rubber overshoes, you always got dirty." Jacqueline suppresses a shudder: "In the winter, what's really unpleasant is when you freeze your fingertips or your toes. It's no use having good gloves. They say that if you come and spend the winter here in Florida, it adds 10 years to your life expectancy." Nonetheless, she admits to a bit of nostalgia. "After all, we grew up in Canada, and I used to take my children out in horse-drawn sleighs, all wrapped up in furs. I remember them coming home from school, with their rosy little cheeks, wearing scarves and tuques." Marcel appears unmoved: "I was always sensitive to the cold. Besides, it's harder for older people: slipping on the ice, trying to start the car on a cold morning." But Jacqueline is warming to the subject: "There were good sides to the winter, you know. We'd go tobogganing on Mont-Royal. At home, we hoped it would snow before Christmas; it smelled good, it was pretty. Midnight Mass here in Dale Village doesn't have the same atmosphere." I ask what they'd be doing if they were back in Laval. "We'd be at home, because it was cold out," replies Jacqueline. "Or maybe playing bridge – but inside."

I leave the Grignons to their shuffleboard and the gentle breezes of this February afternoon. I can't blame them for fleeing the Canadian winter. After a few decades of bone-shaking falls on icy sidewalks, chapped lips, and salt stains, I'll probably be tempted to overwinter somewhere warm, too. But there is something limbolike about these tropical Canadas, including the Cuban and Dominican Republic beaches where younger francophones prefer to vacation. It's as though, by centring their aspirations and wisdom – not to mention savings – on months-long seasonal escapes, Canadian snowbirds are somehow draining all the energy from the communities they live in for most of the year, marooning those who winter at home in the emotional doldrums. "Imagine for an instant a country," writes the anthropologist Bernard Arcand, "in which, for five or six months of the year, a very large part of the population would frankly rather be living somewhere else. It's not the kind of situation that bodes well for the general good humour and joie de vivre."

From this perspective, my cut-rate plane ticket is a bit of a devil's bargain, and this charter is beginning to feel like a riveted steel *chasse-galerie*, the airborne canoe of Quebec folklore that whisks the coureur de bois over the woods on a wondrous night flight – a canoe guided, it turns out, by demons. On the way home, I sit next to Jacques, a 50-year-old from Estérel, a village in the Laurentians. One of 25,000 French Canadians who live in Florida year round, he's spent the past 18 years setting up a profitable commercial construction business in Florida. With his fluent, American-accented English, black cowboy boots, and consistent tan, Jacques is every bit the émigré success story, the kind of guy who casually mentions paying a scalper $700 for a pair of Céline Dion tickets in Fort Lauderdale.

Jacques is homesick for the Quebec winter, particularly the skiing on Mont-Tremblant and the hockey games on outdoor rinks. His American wife visited the family home in winter once, but after enduring minus-40 weather, she will now return only in the summer. His six-year-old son speaks no French and shows no inclination to learn it. Suddenly, the wisdom in the old priests' moralizing about the cities of the south being "the cemetery of the race" becomes apparent: in Jacques's case, four centuries of diligently preserved French culture have vanished like a flake of snow in an industrial melting pot, traded for palm trees and lower taxes. When the pilot welcomes us back to Quebec – adding that tonight's low will be minus 15 – the entire cabin of hardy Canadiens lets out a groan.

The culture of winter hasn't entirely vanished from Quebec. Residents of Île-aux-Grues, an island downstream from Quebec City, still break the mid-winter monotony by going door-to-door masquerading as musketeers, mermaids, and harlequins during Lent. In Montreal, people can still be seen carrying cross-country skis, skates, snowshoes, and hockey sticks on the metro and local buses. On the north coast of the St. Lawrence River in the ice-fishing capital of Quebec – a little town called Ste-Anne-de-la-Pérade – I find an entire suburb of miniature wooden shacks set up on the frozen mouth of a river. Heated with gas or wood stoves, supplied with electricity by a network of poles set up on the ice, the 550 chalets beneath the twin steeples of the local church stretch a kilometre and a half from the mouth of the Ste-Anne River.

This year, between Boxing Day and Valentine's Day, 80,000 people will come to sit in rented shacks around trenches cut into the metre-thick ice, baiting hooks with cubes of pork liver and pulling up dozens of sardine-sized *poulamons*. Also called tommycod, the fish are nasty little bottom-feeders with the pallor of cave creatures; they have to be cooked with onions and lard to give them any real flavour. But that's not the point in Ste-Anne: people enjoy spending a cold winter day in toasty shacks, lazily tossing their catch out onto the ice next to two-fours of Molson beer, or finding a clear patch of river to play a casual game of hockey. In a place called L'Escale, I share a bar with an aluminum plant worker making a pit stop for a beer on his weekend snowmobile jaunt between Trois-Rivières and Quebec City. Out here in the countryside, they clearly never got the news about the Montreal-led war on winter. Since there's no hope of carting off the white carpet that stretches to the horizon, they use it for sliding, skiing, and making snowballs instead.

Bernard Voyer, perhaps the Quebec winter's most enthusiastic proponent, firmly believes the city is responsible for killing his favourite season. The arctic adventurer is a household name in Quebec: a cross-country ski instructor and outdoor commentator on French-language television, Voyer was the first person from the Americas to make it to the South Pole unaided. "The problem is, there are two perceptions of the winter in Quebec, and they're completely different," the exuberant Voyer explains in his well-heated office on Montreal's Rue St-Denis. "There's the rural response, which is to continue accepting it, to live with it. The city dweller's response is to completely refuse the winter. For the past 40 years or so, we've been trying to beat it. And that makes me laugh," he says – laughing. "Trying to beat the winter is like trying to stop the wind with your hands," he continues, lifting his broad palms outward above his desk. In his mid-forties, Voyer is what the French approvingly call a *gaillard* – old Brits might say a strapping fellow – with broad shoulders and fine features. A map of Antarctica is pinned to the wall behind his right shoulder, with 66 tiny dots indicating where he spent every night on his journey to the South Pole. He skied 11 hours a day, covering 1,500 kilometres in two months. The average temperature was 25 degrees below zero, and it was uphill all the way.

Winter is the time of the year Voyer loves best. "For me, the winter is actually the softest of seasons. The light comes in at a lower angle, the shadows are longer, the sky doesn't seem quite so high, it's a purer blue. One's gaze is freer to wander, the colours are more pastel. The summer is harder: the contrasts are more intense, the sunlight is blinding." His most vivid childhood memories of the cold are from Rimouski, on the south shore of the St. Lawrence. On the main street, the wind off the Atlantic would blow between the stores that lined the river. "My mother used to say, 'Watch out, we're going to traverse a column of cold air; I don't know if we're going to make it.' She'd build it up, make it sound dangerous, and then we'd run past at full speed. Those were my first expeditions." As a teenager on his first European trip, he spurned Madrid and Rome, instead heading north to Oslo and Stockholm. Though his parents have been wintering in Florida for 25 years, he's visited them only once. "If reincarnation exists," says Voyer, "the thing that would scare me the most would be to come back as a Frisbee. To spend my entire life on a beach, eating sand? *Non, merci.*"

For Voyer, the denial of winter goes hand in hand with what he believes is the gradual disappearance of all that is distinct about Quebec. "Our artistic side, our reflective side, we owe to the winter. When you can't go out because there's a storm, you stay inside with your family, you create, you think, you tell stories, you paint. Winter is enormously inspiring. It's what built our society." In the summer, he says, paraphrasing the singer Félix Leclerc, we used to cut wood and write songs; in the winter, we'd burn our firewood and sing those songs. "There was a richness in that seasonal alternation, but now we're levelling everything. Because we want our culture to be Parisian and our business to be American, we're losing our authenticity. Montreal is the city that experiences the greatest extremes of temperature in the world – 80 degrees Celsius, from 40 below to 40 above. That alternation between extremes has encouraged our fashion industry, engineering, companies like Bombardier, because winter doesn't leave any room for *laxisme*. But the Québécois, judging from their behaviour, don't want the seasons anymore. These days, it's fashionable to hate the winter." Voyer thinks the city of Montreal should relax its frenetic war on winter and leave at least a few sidestreets covered with snow. He also believes that if the snow stuck around longer, society would experience fewer problems – because winter encourages community life over individualism. He dreams of overseeing the opening of a *musée de l'hiver* (a museum of winter), showing the role the season has played in shaping Canadian society. (When next I hear from Voyer, he's atop a place no snowplow will ever scrape clean: Mount Everest.)

There are signs of a backlash against the repudiation of winter. In 1999, a conference on nordicity attracted 900 participants – from countries such as Lithuania, Japan, and Scotland – to Quebec City, where they shared ideas on improving human adaptation to cold climates. The Laval University geographer Louis-Edmond Hamelin, creator of the concept of nordicity – a complex measure of the degree of northernness of a place – has long believed that the province could become a strong, confident society by fully accepting its cold climate. In spite of its title, Bernard Arcand's popular essay "Abolissons l'hiver!" is not a proposal for enclosing Montreal in a giant geodesic dome, but rather a call to reappropriate the season. Arcand would like to see the period from January 2 to the beginning of March declared a national holiday, during which businesses and schools would close. People would spend the darkest months practising winter sports, tinkering around the house, organizing family reunions, or simply lolling about in bed. "Once again, groups of friends would visit one another for the pleasure of eating, drinking, and talking," Arcand imagines. "We could even learn to make music again, and reinvent the art of telling incredible stories. In other words, we'd take the time to reinvent our culture."

It may be a little too late to save Quebec's winter. Nobody likes to talk about it too much, but winter in the northern hemisphere may be an endangered season. Year after year, Environment Canada tells us average winter temperatures are reaching record highs. Spring is coming to the Arctic five days earlier than it did a generation ago, and since the beginning of the century. Montreal's mean annual temperature has increased from 5.2 to 7.4 degrees Celsius. Among the world's scientists – particularly those whose research isn't subsidized by fossil fuel companies – there's a growing consensus that unstabilized levels of greenhouse gases, by raising temperatures, will likely lead to extreme weather events. In Quebec, that means floods, freezing rain, heavy snowfalls. The five-day-long ice storm of 1998 was a national disaster that left 1.4 million Quebecers without electricity in January and cost Hydro-Québec $800 million in repairs. The following winter brought wild temperature fluctuations, from bone-breaking cold to springlike thaws in a matter of hours; the overall temperature, however, was 2.4 degrees warmer than usual. Ice fishers watched their vans crash through the surface of Lac St-Louis, snowmobilers were swallowed up by lakes, and two Montreal children died after falling through the normally solid ice on the banks of the St. Lawrence. During the Fête des Neiges, a family-oriented outdoor festival on Montreal's Île Ste-Hélène, temperatures shot up to eight degrees above zero in early February, transforming an outdoor gallery of ice-framed Monet reproductions into a puddle. Unexpected warm spells have ruined skating rinks, turning the snowshoe tramps over Mount Royal that last century's Tuques Bleues enjoyed so much into slogs. Scientists in 1999 announced that the ice shield over

Greenland – the one that regulates ocean currents, keeping northern Europe's winters warmer than ours – really is melting. Fast.

"Where are the snows of yesteryear?" wondered the Parisian poet François Villon five centuries ago. The French may yet get their medieval snows back, for one of the paradoxical side effects of global warming is to lower temperatures along the north Atlantic coast. And here in Quebec – where nobody knows what to do with the winter anyway – we can look forward to the millennia of lukewarm *sloche*, *grésil*, and *gadoue* we've almost certainly got coming to us.

THE GLOBAL SKI-DOG

Springtime in the Eastern Townships: the road is clear of snow, and the low hillsides and cow pastures are overspread with exuberant greenery, as though, after its winter confinement, the land feels some bumptious obligation to assert its long-stifled fecundity. The villages between Montreal and Sherbrooke, with their neo-Gothic Anglican churches and eclectic Victorian houses, hint at the area's uneasy melding of French and English cultures, as do the road signs: St-Joachim-de-Shefford, Bédard-Landing, Ste-Élisabeth-de-Warwick – Anglo-French toponyms whose like you won't encounter even on the Channel Islands. On the turnoff to Highway 222, the spindly metal cross erected by the local chapter of the Knights of Columbus (here called the Chevaliers de Colomb) suggests that the road is twisting into a predominantly francophone patch of this bicultural counterpane. Apart from the occasional snowmobile-crossing signs, the countryside looks quaintly anachronistic, a throwback to simpler, more pious times.

Just as you're fantasizing about some backroad Brigadoon, the road slams into Valcourt, a hamlet-turned-twenty-first-century company village where the local factory employs as many robots as it does skilled labourers. This is the town Joseph-Armand Bombardier built, and it's hard to escape Valcourt's de facto founding father. The neatly manicured streets bear the names of Bombardier children; the biggest house on the main street is the turreted Bombardier mansion, now a pied-à-terre for executives from around the world; and it was Bombardier who erected the cross visible atop the peak of Mont Valcourt in the Catholic holy year of 1950. Valcourt before Bombardier was a topographical speck, cut off from the world for six months each year, isolated by snow-choked roads and its own obscurity. Valcourt after Bombardier is a key node in a high-tech aviation, mass transit, and recreational empire with assets of more than $14.2 billion and 53,000 employees scattered across Europe, North America, and the Middle East.

Naturally, the town's major museum is devoted to the history of Valcourt's leading export, the Ski-Doo. Located among endless storage yards stacked high with building blocks of crated snowmobiles, the Musée J-Armand Bombardier is built around a little white garage with a brick chimney, world headquarters for the corporation until the Second World War. The Québécois penchant for myth making has found ample material in the story of this small-town *patenteux* (an affectionate term for the handyman-inventor who tinkers with patented housewares). The museum presents Bombardier as a kind of northern Edison, an ingenious conqueror of the winter. The 15-year-old Joseph-Armand, visitors are told, built a snowmobile out of a Model T Ford, a two-man monstrosity on sleds driven by an unguarded red propeller, which whirled right next to the driver. Subsequent contraptions, all lovingly displayed on pedestals, replaced the death-dealing blade with a tanklike tread around the wheels, which came to be driven by a toothed sprocket, a pivotal innovation that is now the company's logo. Especially impressive is the 1936-vintage B-7, a closed-cab seven-person vehicle as endearing, and about as aerodynamic looking, as Citroën's boxy Deux-Chevaux. It was purchased by rural doctors, undertakers, and school boards, opening up villages previously accessible only by horse-drawn calèche. To prove its impressive traction on even the most treacherous surface, Bombardier actually backed a B-7 up the steeply inclined ice slide outside Quebec City's Château Frontenac. With such inspired publicity stunts, the company's order book started to fill, and a slew of eccentric vehicles followed. There was the Mark 1, an armoured pillbox on snow-beating rubber treads sold to the English during the Second World War. And the Muskeg, a twinkle-toed, fire-engine-red tank whose low ground-pressure allowed it to explore swamp and marshland too treacherous even for a man on foot. By the time Bombardier died from cancer in 1964, the debt-free company was putting away a million dollars a year after taxes.

If the inventor's apotheosis into the pantheon of Quebec folk heroes was ever in doubt, it was ensured by *Bombardier: la mini-série*, a 1992 *téléroman*. A sober, bespectacled Bombardier, played by the normally high-spirited actor Gilbert Sicotte, watches in misery as his infant son Yvon agonizes with appendicitis during a snowstorm. "The roads are closed," his brother cries, "it will take two days to get to a doctor in Sherbrooke. We'll never get there in time!" Bombardier runs outside and cranks up the B-7, but the prototype doesn't quite work yet, and the machine gets bogged down in a snowbank. Mad with frustration, he bashes the faulty snow-mobile with a shovel. The next scene is a shot of a tiny cross in a graveyard. Bombardier's motivation for perfecting his machines, the *téléroman* suggests, was a heroic desire to liberate rural Quebecers from their subjugation to the winter.

Throughout the fifties, Bombardier was the definitive francophone business success story. Actually, it was French Quebec's only international success story, and a relatively modest one at that. One of Bombardier's pet projects had been the Ski-Dog, a pokey-looking, canary yellow recreational vehicle with sprocket-driven treads in the back and skis up front. Corporate legend has it that the tail fell off the *g* on the prototype, yielding the doggerel catchphrase Ski-Doo.

Before dying, Joseph-Armand Bombardier named his son-in-law Laurent Beaudoin successor, and this adaptable chartered accountant weathered an energy-crisis downturn in the winter recreation craze by diversifying into subway cars and planes. Bombardier now owns Learjet, makes much of the Montreal and New York subway systems' rolling stock, and is the third-largest civil aviation company in the world. It has spent much of the last decade cheerfully christening new aircraft, including the midsize Regional Jet and the Challenger executive jet, and announcing multibillion-dollar contracts with the likes of Northwest Airlines, Long Island Railways, and, most recently, Delta Air Lines.

In the museum, the tour ends in the tiny garage where the Bombardier story started. My guide has been a diminutive, patient Québécoise with blond curls. I ask her what she thinks about Bombardier CEO Laurent Beaudoin, in semiretirement after a quadruple bypass, handing over the reins of this jewel of Quebec industry to Robert Brown – a British-born, English-speaking Ontarian. She smiles sweetly, resignedly, and with just a hint of a shrug says, "Ah, but Monsieur, Bombardier is a multinational company now." Indeed. I'd forgotten that the quaint B-7 snowmobiles on display belong to a time when the ambitions of Quebecers rarely exceeded the confines of their parishes, let alone the borders of the province. A better symbol for the business aspirations of a rapidly globalizing Quebec would probably be Bombardier's $47-million Global Express Jet, the company's state-of-the-art airborne office, capable of whisking executives from New York to Tokyo at 900 kilometres an hour. And if the best candidate for leading Quebec's fifth-largest employer into the next century happens to be an anglophone, well, so be it. For better – and for worse – Quebec's economy is going global.

Since the sixties, entrepreneurs in Quebec have had a unique status, one closer to the American idolization of enterprise and derring-do than English Canada's dour suspicion of rapid self-enrichment. Local boys who have made good on the world market – such as the late newspaper and printing tycoon Pierre Péladeau, Cascades paper baron Bernard Lemaire, and Softimage founder Daniel Langlois – are larger-than-life folk heroes, championing not only personal initiative but Quebec's fortunes abroad. This is a place where popular *téléromans* are made about guys in suits: *L'Or et le papier*, about the creator of Cascades; *Les Bâtisseurs d'eau*, about the executives and engineers of Hydro-Québec; *Desjardins*, about the founder of Quebec's largest financial institution. A local television network saw fit to interrupt a normally sacrosanct Canadiens game with a press conference on the state of Pierre Péladeau's health shortly before his death in 1997. It's hard to imagine such reverent concern in English Canada, where business titans are respected but rarely admired. At heart (if he has one), the English-Canadian businessman is seen as a ruthless individualist, an arriviste whose balance sheets have no entry for "social responsibility." In Quebec, the successful entrepreneur is more often an unassailable popular icon, symbolizing the growth of a self-made francophone business class, the triumph of underdogs over Anglo capital.

"Businessmen in Quebec are part of the pantheon of heroes, and maybe at the front of it," says Norman Webster, a former editor of the *Globe and Mail* and the Montreal *Gazette*, who now lives in the Eastern Townships, where he manages the affairs of the charitable Webster family foundation. As a *Globe* columnist in the provincial capital during Quebec premier Jean Lesage's sixties Quiet Revolution, and a long-time observer of the Montreal business community, Webster has noticed a change in attitude towards the Québécois entrepreneur. "In the old days, the people that French Quebecers looked up to were much more traditional priests, lawyers, and politicians. And there was not a business class among francophones, certainly not at an upper level. These days, priests are very definitely not part of the pantheon, and the politicians are a bit down on the ladder. When a francophone businessman is doing well, everybody feels pride. He's doing the community proud, and he becomes something of a hero." Surveys tend to back up Webster's observations: an annual poll commissioned by the Conseil du patronat, the province's main business lobby group, shows that Quebecers are two to three times more likely to trust business leaders than politicians.

Such durable esteem must be deep-rooted, because the performance of the Quebec economy for the past decade has been far from stellar. The salad days of Quebec, Inc. – a buzzword for a briefly successful period of Japanese-style state-sponsored entrepreneurship – are long gone. The fall from grace of such eighties golden boys as Bertin Nadeau, Raymond Malenfant, Michel Gaucher, and Bernard Lamarre was rapid and decisive. Since mid-century, Montreal had been losing its status as the financial and business capital of Canada to Toronto, and the nineties exacerbated the gap between Quebec and the rest of Canada. In 1999, *Report on Business* magazine rated Montreal last among 10 major Canadian cities for workers and investors to live in – behind Regina and Winnipeg – on the basis of its high unemployment, low levels of education, and high levels of personal taxation. The province has long been in a battle with Newfoundland as the most taxed region in North America: in 1998, a professional making $65,000 a year in Quebec had a marginal tax rate of 53 per cent (Americans with an annual salary of $375,000 will pay only about 40 per cent of their income in taxes). Sadly, few people here can aspire to such dizzying heights of taxation. Quebec's per capita revenue is only 84 per cent of neighbouring Ontario's, and for much of the nineties, Montreal's unemployment rate was the worst of major North American cities.

For some commentators, Montreal calls to mind a once-strapping lad afflicted with some wasting disease, shrinking within an old varsity sweater. A stroll down what was once St. James Street – Canada's Wall Street before its name was changed to Rue St-Jacques – is a sobering experience. The elephantine columns of the former headquarters of major national banks hide empty shells, and the old stock exchange has been turned into a theatre. (The current Stock Exchange on Victoria Square is definitively switching over to derivatives, making it a secondary node in a Toronto-centred trading system.) In *Titans*, his latest dissection of the Canadian establishment, business writer Peter C. Newman, borrowing a page from novelist Aleksandr Solzhenitsyn, dismisses all of Montreal as a Potemkin village, after the Russian statesman who had false fronts built on impoverished Ukrainian main streets to convince Catherine the Great of the region's prosperity. Major companies like Molson and Seagram, the argument goes, are only nominally based in Montreal; the real corporate business goes on in Toronto or New York.

"You know," says Norman Webster, "the Bank of Montreal's head office is technically here. So is the Royal Bank's. But the truth is, their real head offices are in Toronto now." For Webster, as for Newman, the cause is clear: the first victory of a separatist government in 1976 provoked a letting of capital and talent that's never truly been staunched. "Some of these head offices would have moved anyway, but this massive movement – the Parti Québécois has certainly been an aggressive abettor of the trend. Huge numbers of people have left here. Good ones. And for no other reason than that they didn't feel at home, or because they thought opportunities elsewhere were better because of the Quebec government."

That's the Anglo version of history; most francophones would tell it differently. They'd emphasize the heroic self-invention of a French-speaking entrepreneurial class that, in a single generation, took over an English-Canadian-dominated economy and built its own international business successes, pretty much from scratch. Sure, they'd say, Quebec's economy isn't quite up to the North American standard. But there are good reasons for that, born of corporate traditions of social responsibility only now being called into question. And at least, they'd point out, it's *our* economy.

For most of Canada's history, becoming an entrepreneur wasn't a realistic option for the young man of French descent. The peasants, soldiers, and administrators of New France were discouraged from undertaking any activity that wasn't directly related to the relaying of furs, wood, and fish back to France. The French Crown liked the idea of its coureurs de bois collecting beaver pelts – and its priests Indian souls – but it banned factories in the Laurentian colony on the grounds that they would compete with industry at home. "Some people managed to build fortunes," says Yves Bélanger, a Université du Québec à Montréal political science professor, "but they had to constantly defer to Paris for the proper functioning of their business. At that time – and note that it's still the case – France led a very centralized control of its economy."

Aggressively centralized, in the seventeenth century: when an entrepreneur named Joseph Huppé dared to open a beaver hat business in Montreal, colonial officials raided his store and smashed his fur-dyeing equipment. The more lucrative wholesale operations were controlled by the French; the Canadiens were left to scrape by in retail. Though a tiny local bourgeoisie managed to establish a few tobacco plantations, maple-syrup-refining businesses, and the forges at St-Maurice – Canada's first manufacturing plant – the real French fortunes were being built in Haiti and Martinique, the sugar-and-slave colonies of the West Indies.

Capitalism would really arrive with the English – and in particular, the Scots – who enthusiastically took over the fur trade. As embryonic Anglo old boys' networks started to form, the original Canadiens were left on the margins of trade. Francophone success stories in the nineteenth century were rare. The tycoon Louis-Adélard Sénécal built a significant railway fortune, and a class of small businessmen carved niches for themselves with cotton mills, shoe factories, and grocery stores. A handful of family dynasties were founded, including the paper-making Rollands and Dubucs and financiers such as the Forgets and Beaubiens — names that linger today in the upper echelons of French-Canadian society. By the end of the century, however, the combined worth of the three largest francophone banks – the Banque Nationale, the Banque Jacques-Cartier, and the Banque d'Hochelaga – represented only a fifth of the assets of the Bank of Montreal, an institution founded by English Canadians. The real holders of wealth – the McGills, Molsons, and Holts of Victorian Montreal – were inclined to opine that the French Canadian was inherently predisposed to a life of indolence and economic marginality. Indeed, disdain for material wealth was encouraged by the Catholic elite. "In the nineteenth century," says Bélanger, "there was a whole class of Ultramontane clergymen who basically equated the city with hell and wrote that there was a kind of perversion in making money. For them, money was dirty."

Out of this rural, Catholic suspicion of citified businessmen and bankers was born the Mouvement Desjardins, North America's first credit union. Alphonse Desjardins, a recorder of French debates in the Canadian House of Commons, was struck by a speech in which a Montreal member of Parliament complained that one of his constituents had been forced to pay back a total of $5,000 for a $150 loan. Disgusted by such abuse, Desjardins corresponded with the leaders of European cooperative financial institutions, and in 1900 he opened the first caisse populaire in Lévis, just across the St. Lawrence River from the ramparts of Quebec City. Members would buy a five-dollar share – the poorest could purchase it on a dime-a-week instalment plan – allowing them to borrow money at an advantageous rate and share in their caisse's surplus through year-end *ristournes*, or rebates. The Mouvement's stated goal was "to wage war against usury and to aid the worker who wishes to borrow a small sum." It became a nationalistic movement, aimed at preserving the traditional values of rural society at a time when farmers were being lured to factories in Montreal and New England.

Most important, perhaps, the Mouvement Desjardins was profoundly conservative and Catholic. The opening of a new branch, frequently in tiny villages where the Royal Bank and the Bank of Montreal couldn't be both-ered to go, was often accompanied by the sprinkling of holy water. In 1916 the Vatican itself provided an exemption allowing priests to manage village credit unions. Married women weren't allowed to become full members (it was the husband's duty, in theory if rarely in fact, to manage family finance). And it was policy to turn down applications for such frivolities as carriages (or even cars, as late as the early sixties): loans were only to be granted for serious projects that would advance the prospects of the French race in Canada.

In his biography of the Quebec premier Maurice Duplessis, Conrad Black refers to the Mouvement as "Catholicized socialism," and certainly, the cooperative orientation and democratic structure of the caisses popu-laires led to bouts of communal action that would curl the spats of any self-respecting capitalist. In some communities, for example, members agreed to pay a quarter of a per cent more in interest on a loan to help build a local retirement home. Ultimately, however, the caisses populaires were created to perpetrate the clergy and petite bourgeoisie's nineteenth-century control of rural francophones. Vaunted as a hedge against international trade unions, they often ended up being havens for right-wing nationalists.

To this day, the province's largest financial institution proudly bears the stigmata of its Catholic origins. The Mouvement's constitution is called the Catéchisme, and the branch in my neighbourhood is called the Caisse pop-ulaire Immaculée-Conception, which is also the name of the local parish (in the country, the caisse network was established on a six-by-six-mile grid, the maximum distance a man on horseback could conveniently ride in the winter). Seven out of 10 Quebecers have an account at one of the province's 1,100 caisses populaires, and the Mouvement, the largest employer in Quebec, controls $78 billion in assets, about half the province's savings. The Mouvement is so much a part of the popular heritage of twentieth-century Quebec that when management announced the fusion of a number of branches in 1998, the newsmagazine *L'actualité* ran a cover article titled "La fin de ma Caisse Pop?" (Is my caisse populaire finished?)

For the first half of the twentieth century, the Mouvement Desjardins was one of the few French-controlled outposts in an economy dominated by English-Canadian and American interests. By 1950, there was only one francophone Québécois firm, the shipbuilder Marine Industrie, among the country's 183 largest companies. French-Canadian enterprise was highly circumscribed, limited to small and mid-size businesses centred on forestry, food and dairy, the garment industry, and local transport. It truly flourished only outside the large cities, as in the Beauce, a constellation of small towns bearing saints' names scattered along the valley of the Chaudière River between Quebec City and the Maine border.

In the local mythology, Beaucerons are to Quebec what the Normans are to France: shrewd, independent traders blessed with fertile farmland, too wily to let on how rich they really are. Geographically isolated from power, capital, and ready labour, Beaucerons nonetheless built some of Quebec's enduring fortunes. Rose-Anna Vachon opened a bakery in 1923 so her six sons wouldn't be tempted to settle down in New England, where they worked in lumber camps during the winter. Vachon, now called Culinar, went on to become the Hostess brand of Quebec, the producer of such delicacies as May West and Jos. Louis snack cakes.

Until the end of the fifties, Premier Maurice Duplessis kept himself in office through his *politique de bouts de chemin*, a policy of keeping rural entrepreneurs happy by giving them lucrative contracts to build stretches of road. Local developers signed contracts with secret clauses that guaranteed kickbacks of 10 per cent to Duplessis's party. Meanwhile, the premier ensured a healthy atmosphere for American and English-Canadian investment, using his provincial police to crush strikes in the asbestos, textile, and mining industries. He also nurtured a cadre of paternalistic overlords in outlying districts. "On the one hand," says Yves Bélanger, "Duplessis wanted to develop the economy by relying on big foreign companies. On the other, he needed the rural milieu to ensure his re-election. Under him, we see lots of small companies flourishing, in places like Lac St-Jean and the lower St. Lawrence."

Conrad Black argues that, under Duplessis, Quebec underwent an unwonted period of industrial expansion, its economic growth of 8.2 per cent a year between 1944 and 1959 rivalling Ontario's. Though living standards in Quebec, as in the rest of North America, did increase during the period of postwar prosperity, French-speaking Quebecers, who made up 80 per cent of the population, didn't share in real economic power. Francophones accounted for only 20 per cent of middle management positions and controlled only a quarter of the province's financial institutions,

22 per cent of manufacturing, and 6.5 per cent of the huge mining sector. They were, as the expression had it, *nés pour un petit pain* ("born for small potatoes" might be an English equivalent), destined to be ill-paid clerks and labourers, at best small businessmen.

"Up until 1960, we lived a simple little life," recalled Bernard Lamarre, founder of the engineering company Lavalin, interviewed in *Commerce* magazine. "Our firm built schools, churches, and convents. The English didn't talk to us. . . . They granted their contracts to other English people, and the French did the same with the French. The English contracts happened to be far fatter, of course. But the French Canadians were happy not to be too rich, because they might end up going to heaven! All those English who lived on the mountain were condemned to burn in hell! Then, the Quiet Revolution happened." Lamarre is exaggerating for effect, of course, but not by much. The election of Jean Lesage and his team of young, progress-oriented Liberals produced the first cracks in the facade of the English-speaking business establishment. Winning power under the slogan "Maîtres chez nous" (Masters in our own house), Lesage set about replacing a theocracy with a technocracy, paying $604 million for a network of dams owned by a variety of English-Canadian and American power companies. Lamarre was one of the first to benefit from the creation of Hydro-Québec, his contracts with the state-run corporation eventually making Lavalin one of the top 10 engineering firms in the world.

Tremendous popular pride accompanied the construction of the first big hydro project. The Manic complex was a series of immense dams running from Lac Manicouagan, an almost perfectly ring-shaped lake formed by an ancient meteorite impact on the north shore, to the St. Lawrence River. With Manic, Hydro-Québec briefly became the province's largest employer, and – unheard-of precedent – the language of employment was French. As dam building led to visions of nation building, stirrings of nationalist pride could be detected in such slogans as "Nous sommes tous Hydro-Québécois." Future separatist premier René Lévesque, after all, was the Liberals' minister of natural resources, and in his memoirs he compared the Anglo utility owners to British colonialists who believed the Egyptians were too backward to run the Suez Canal they'd forcibly nationalized. With breathtaking rapidity, the exploited of Quebec in turn became the exploiters of the lakes, rivers, and ancestral hunting grounds of the Cree and Innu. (Popular opinion has long since turned against the utility: in a 1999 *Commerce* magazine survey of the most-admired companies in the province, post-ice-storm Hydro-Québec appeared near the bottom of the list, beaten only by Wal-Mart and Canada Post.)

Nonetheless, the birth of a state-run hydroelectric industry was electroshock treatment for the economy of French Quebec, creating a significant middle class of newly self-confident engineers and entrepreneurs. The state invested heavily in education, and in 1968 Montreal's École des hautes études commerciales, until then a glorified school of accounting, began granting master's degrees in business administration.

While René Lévesque was nationalizing resources, another future separatist premier, Jacques Parizeau, was working as an adviser to the Lesage government to establish some of the key economic institutions of modern Quebec. Scion of a wealthy Montreal insurance family, with a doctorate from the London School of Economics, Parizeau created the capital pools that Quebec entrepreneurs needed to jump-start their businesses. Among them were the Société générale de financement (founded in 1962), a provincial investment body created with funds from the Mouvement Desjardins to aid in the economic development of Quebec, and the Caisse de dépôt et placement (1965), Canada's largest pension fund. Quebec had been collecting its own provincial income tax since 1954, but with Parizeau's help, the province wrested even greater taxation powers from the federal government. Later, as finance minister for the Parti Québécois, Parizeau made use of an alphabet soup of government investment agencies – including Soquip (oil exploration), Rexfor (forestry), Soquem (mining), and the SDI (a general investing body, now Investissements-Québec). Collectively, they aggressively fostered the growth of francophone companies.

The gradual development of a French-speaking business class, dubbed the *émergence*, became a kind of slow-motion storming of the Bastille. By the seventies, however, the Anglos who had long run the place were getting a little weary, and wary, of Québécois nationalism. A few days before the provincial election of 1970, when unfounded fears of an imminent Parti Québécois victory had the English community anticipating anarchy, eight Brinks trucks pulled up outside the Montreal offices of Royal Trust. As newspaper photographers snapped pictures, machine-gun-bearing guards supervised the emptying of the financial services giant's vaults. Mustachioed Royal Trust president Conrad Fetherstonhaugh Harrington had the gold sent down Highway 401 to Toronto, and though the PQ won only seven seats in the subsequent election, the message was clear: Quebec's political instability had spooked the English-Canadian establishment.

When Lévesque, the "Castro of Quebec," as the Anglos called him, swept to victory on November 15, 1976, the "Westmount Rhodesians," as he had once notoriously referred to them, left in droves. Over the next six months, 90 head offices, including those of Redpath Sugar, Northern Telecom, Trizec and Molson, headed off to Toronto. (In the two decades that followed, the cumulative loss of head offices rose to 384.) The enormous insurance firm Sun Life, traumatized by the real Fidel Castro's nationalization of its Cuban assets back in 1959, vacated its 26-storey building on Dominion Square, leaving the skyscraper that was once the largest in the British Empire empty. By the time liquor baron Charles Bronfman was publicly threatening to leave Quebec altogether, Seagram's mock Gothic castle on Peel Street was already a cardboard fortress; the company's Canadian headquarters had quietly moved to Ontario early in the seventies.

From their new boardrooms in Toronto, the ex-Montrealers sat back and waited for the francophone entrepreneurs who were moving into Westmount mansions to fail. It didn't quite happen that way. Lévesque's Parti Québécois actually turned out to be remarkably pro-business, even preferring General Motors to local boys Bombardier in a contract to build 1,200 buses, a clear signal to edgy American investors that Quebec would be no dollar-scorning Cuba. With Parizeau as the PQ finance minister, provincial capital pools started aggressively backing French-Canadian companies. The Quebec Stock Savings Plan, a system of generous tax write-offs for investors (offering 150 per cent deductions on provincial taxes), encouraged the public to sink their savings into Quebec-based companies. In 1983, Quebec deregulated its financial sector – five years before the rest of Canada – turning the Laurentian Group and the caisses populaires of the Mouvement Desjardins into one-stop centres for banking, insurance, and stock transactions. For much of the eighties, Quebec had the fastest-growing economy in Canada, and by mid-decade 40 per cent of Canadian university students taking MBAs were Québécois. They had the encouragement of Canadian prime minister Brian Mulroney, an Irish Quebecer from Baie-Comeau who'd spent his career as a lawyer rubbing shoulders

with the Montreal business community. Quebec overwhelmingly supported the 1989 Free Trade Agreement with the United States, even as
English-Canadian nationalists on the left and right howled in despair.

The eighties were boom years for the entrepreneur hero. Before the
Quiet Revolution, the biggest French-Canadian success story had been
Jean-Louis Lévesque, a financier from the Gaspé Peninsula who had a seat
on the Montreal Stock Exchange, opened his own bank in Paris, and even-
tually bought out stockbrokers L.G. Beaubien. The next wave included
Paul Desmarais of Power Corporation and real estate developer Robert
Campeau, slick Franco-Ontarians who had made their mark – in Campeau's
case, with an unforgettable bankruptcy – in the business world of English
Canada. But the new guys were another breed altogether. There was Bernard
Lemaire of the Kingsey Falls paper giant Cascades (not to be confused with
Bernard Lamarre of the engineering firm Lavalin), a rough-hewn man of
the people who preferred company picnics to the business clubs of
Montreal. The late Pierre Péladeau created Quebecor, now the world's
largest printing company. While the old guard of patrician managers had
been Montreal bourgeoisie, alumni of the Jesuit Collège Jean-de-Brébeuf,
members of the Club St-Denis – and almost always federalists – some of
the up-and-comers didn't see why they couldn't be just as successful in a
sovereign Quebec, particularly now that the economy seemed to be thriving. Through the eighties, they were backed in this conviction by the
knowledge that the managers of Quebec's two largest nest eggs, the Caisse
de dépôt and the Mouvement Desjardins, were ardent separatists.

Matthew Fraser was a Montreal-based correspondent with the *Globe
and Mail* in 1987 when he wrote *Quebec, Inc.*, a panoramic survey of the
thriving business talents of the *émergence*. At the time, the cooperation
between private enterprise and the state appeared to be producing a
booming economy, but only five years later many of the figures Fraser
interviewed were in dire straits. Claude Castonguay's Laurentian Group
of more than 100 companies, crippled by unfortunate real estate investments, had to be incorporated into the Mouvement Desjardins. Bertin
Nadeau's $7-billion Unigesco, which included the Provigo grocery chain,
was overwhelmed by debt and finally bought out by the Caisse de dépôt.
In spite of all the government contracts, even Bernard Lamarre's Lavalin
went bankrupt (it merged with its largest rival to form the engineering

firm SNC-Lavalin, and Lamarre now devotes his time to the presidency of Montreal's Museum of Fine Arts). Overconfidence and overambitious diversification led to the failure of both the Steinberg grocery chain and hôtelier Raymond Malenfant. As had happened in the late fifties, when the rural entrepreneurs encouraged by Duplessis overextended themselves, major Québécois companies were taken over by European, English-Canadian, and American interests. More than a decade after his book appeared, Fraser, now a professor of broadcasting and communications at Ryerson Polytechnic University in Toronto, is philosophical about the fall from grace of the so-called warriors of the *émergence*. "What happened, I think, was that the whole Quebec, Inc. thing was really a flash in the pan, a fireworks display that kind of petered out. There's no question that the country's financial capital is now Toronto, and Montreal is a minor metropolis in comparison."

Not surprisingly, the Quebec, Inc. model, touted as a blueprint for both business success and the high road to sovereignty, has been the subject of intense criticism for much of the past decade. One of the most blistering attacks came in the form of a 1993 book called *Québec Inc. and the Temptation of State Capitalism*. Written by Pierre Arbour, a fund manager at the Caisse de dépôt between 1967 and 1979, it detailed the extent to which the pension fund's investment decisions, as well as those of more than 30 other important agencies of the Quebec government, had been determined by the nationalist agenda of the Parti Québécois.

Arbour is now the manager of a small venture capital company called Alkebec, with offices on the top floor of a squat greystone townhouse just up Rue Drummond from Montreal's Ritz-Carlton Hotel. He's the very image of the bicultural French-Canadian businessman, his manners as smooth as the striped shirtfront beneath his double-breasted blue suit. Tall and classically handsome, with a long straight nose, he peers through rectangular glasses at an open copy of his book. Arbour left the Caisse shortly before Parizeau's 1980 appointment of Jean Campeau, a president whose nationalist convictions would influence most of the Caisse's big decisions.

"I think that Monsieur Campeau had the impression that he would be the economic pope of Quebec," says Arbour, in his precise, virtually Parisian French. "He was more of a politician than a businessman" – in fact,

Campeau became the Parti Québécois finance minister shortly after leaving the Caisse in 1990 – "and he referred back to Monsieur Parizeau a bit more than he referred back to the board of directors." Arbour believes that, for much of the eighties, the investment decisions of the Caisse, a supposedly independent agency, were driven by its political priorities: namely, to keep Québécois firms out of the hands of outsiders.

When Pierre Arbour left the Caisse in 1979, it controlled $7 billion. Today, the figure exceeds $100 billion, making it the largest pension fund in Canada – and the damn thing just keeps growing. The pension fund contributions of just about everybody who holds down a job in Quebec – five million beneficiaries in all – automatically flow into the Caisse (Ontario, in contrast, has two major funds, the Ontario Teachers Pension Plan Board and the Ontario Municipal Employees Retirement Board). The Caisse is not only Quebec's biggest landlord, but also one of the larger real estate owners in France. It was created, in the words of its annual report, "to obtain maximal financial return and to contribute by its actions to the dynamism of the Quebec economy."

According to its critics, however, it was more often used as a bludgeon to beat back encroaching English Canadians – often at the expense of its contributors. A case in point is the Steinberg affair. In 1989, the supermarket chain was owned by the daughters of Sam Steinberg, who were looking to sell. The Caisse backed a bid by local businessman Michel Gaucher, owner of a fleet of buses and oil tankers, blocking an offer by the Toronto-based Oxdon group. Unfortunately, after the Caisse had shelled out $850 million, Campeau and Gaucher discovered that Steinberg was bleeding assets through money-losing stores in Arizona and English Canada. The deal ruined Gaucher, and by 1992, Arbour estimates the Caisse had lost $450 million on the transaction.

Other bad investments, undertaken to keep the Bronfman brothers from buying Noranda Mines and to gain control of the fine-paper and construction products company Domtar, gave the Caisse a below-average return on investments in the eighties. "The Caisse's losses were certainly significant," says Arbour. "Perhaps $1.3 billion altogether. These days, that isn't an enormous sum, but in the context of the eighties, it was a pretty large amount." He believes that, like any pension fund operating in a global marketplace, the Caisse's major goal of looking after the interests of its depositors – the people of Quebec – can't feasibly be subjugated to nationalist goals.

Arbour emphasizes that the current president of the Caisse, Jean-Claude Scraire (appointed by Parizeau in 1995), has assembled a particularly sharp team of in-house investment managers, and decisions now appear to be made according to the interests of depositors. (A recent exception was the Caisse's announcement that it planned to block any attempt by Ontario-based Rogers Communications to buy the Groupe Vidéotron, Quebec's largest cable company.) The Caisse's performance is far better than that of the Canada Pension Plan, which administers the pensions for all the other provinces and is obliged to invest in provincial bonds at an artificially low rate of interest. Nonetheless, Arbour would like to see the massive fund cut down to size. "It's obvious: it would be more effective to split the Caisse in two, creating two teams that would compete. When we're talking about large interventions, in the $10- to $100-million range, if someone isn't too popular with the Caisse – say, for example, that person is too federalist – well, they can complain about the Caisse, but they're going to have to wait until a change of the government to get their money." Like many businesspeople, Arbour is weary of *dirigisme*, the state intervention in the economy that Quebec seems to have borrowed wholesale from France (whose similarly gargantuan pension fund is called the Caisse des dépôts et consignations).

"I think [state intervention] was probably necessary, and beneficial in many ways," says Arbour. "It gave entrepreneurs a push in the right direction. Monsieur Péladeau's Quebecor, for example, probably wouldn't be where it is today if it wasn't for the Caisse. Though it's ironic: the company is now a typical multinational and does most of its investing outside of Quebec." The fundamental problem, for Arbour, is the preponderance of the state in the economy of the province. "Wouldn't it be better to invest more in the responsibilities of government – education, health, roads – and lower taxes so that Quebec becomes a haven of dynamism to attract entrepreneurs? If things were less bureaucratic, maybe entrepreneurs would come themselves without the taxpayers having to subsidize them in all sorts of ways."

It's a valid point. The Quebec economy, the most powerful and central in Canada up until the fifties, is now a strange patchwork, shot through with a rich blend of federal and provincial subsidies. The thriving multimedia sector, whose 600 companies employ just 4,300 people, is a good example. Daniel Langlois, a baby-faced entrepreneur who dresses in black, is often cited as a multimedia success story. He's just opened Ex-Centris, a futuristic cinematic cultural centre among the see-and-be-seen restaurants of Boulevard St-Laurent, and his company, Softimage, makes the computer software that created the special effects for such blockbusters as *Jurassic Park* and *Titanic*. Langlois's former vice-president of marketing, Richard Szalwinski, runs Discreet Logic, another special effects software company, based in a once-neglected warehouse district of Old Montreal. The French computer games company Ubi Soft has taken over a sprawling brick sweatshop in the Mile End neighbourhood, and companies like Matrox (computer graphics hardware) and Locus Dialogue (speech recognition) contribute to Montreal's reputation as a dynamic centre for high tech.

The occupation of old garment factories by tech nerds has incited local boosters to rhapsodize about Quebec's remarkable leap from the Industrial Revolution to the Third Wave "new economy." In reality, Langlois and Szalwinski followed a pattern more typical of Quebec businesses in the fifties: once their companies attained critical mass, they sold out to the Americans. Softimage let itself be gulped up by Microsoft for $130 million (U.S.), and Discreet Logic was swallowed by the Californian firm Autodesk for $400 million (U.S.). What's more, salaries in the industry are so heavily subsidized by the Quebec taxpayer that the multimedia success story might be a pretty fragile one. Until the middle of 1999, the provincial government gave a tax credit of up to 60 per cent of an employee's salary, which meant that multimedia companies could pay fully qualified software engineers as little as $16,666 a year. The government then started a program of what it called "super-deductions," which allowed companies to subtract 460 per cent of their research-and-development expenses. Perhaps the presidents of companies such as Ubi Soft and Motorola really have chosen Montreal for its high quality of life, but if the tax credits and super-deductions dry up, who knows if these highly mobile industries will stick around.

As with multimedia, so with the only areas in which Quebec really leads Ontario – biotechnology, aviation, and international finance. All are subsidized with tax credits. Montreal harbours about 60 international financial centres, essentially the offshore operations of major financial institutions run by skeleton crews who benefit from personal tax credits for their first four years in Quebec and a total tax exemption on profits. The biotech sector is undeniably strong, particularly in research. Laval-based BioChem Pharma developed the widely used AIDS drug 3TC, Quebec City's Æterna Laboratories has gone into the crucial Phase 3 trials of its cancer drug AE-941, and in 1999 Nexia Biotechnologies of Montreal produced a cloned goat whose milk contains a life-saving human protein. Though it lags far behind in the lucrative production of active pharmaceutical ingredients, Quebec's $280-million-a-year biotech sector represents 40 per cent of the Canadian total, placing the region tenth in North America.

Much of this can be explained by the fact that Quebec offers biotech companies a 20 per cent deduction for research and development salaries – 40 per cent if the research is conducted in a recognized research centre – the best tax credit of its kind in the country. In aviation, companies such as Pratt & Whitney and Rolls-Royce (which do their engine maintenance operations here), helicopter manufacturer Bell Textron, and Bombardier have made Montreal the world's largest aeronautics centre after Seattle. These companies too are heavily subsidized. In short, the new industries are often kept afloat by public money from Ottawa and Quebec City, not the inherent soundness of Quebec's economy.

Since the fifties, Ontario's economic stability has been guaranteed by its early investment in heavy industry and its status as a North American production centre for the automobile. Quebec never went through such a profound industrial revolution, and the pillars of its economy remain the natural resource industries. Though nobody talks much about it – software and cloned farm animals are more newsworthy – forestry is still the biggest industry in the province, accounting for $10 billion a year in exports and close to 10 per cent of Quebec's gross domestic product. Hydroelectricity is still another giant industry, one the provincial government has undermined by selling power to aluminum and magnesium companies at half what it costs to produce it. Smelters run by Alcan and other multinationals sit on the great rivers of the Saguenay and Lac St-Jean region, sucking up as much electricity as small cities in the energy-intensive transformation of bauxite ore into aluminum. In naive shared-risk contracts, Hydro-Québec offered to sell its electricity to private companies at about 65 per cent of the already low industrial rate. The utility by its own admission has lost at least $1.5 billion on the deals since the early nineties; even as American states are tearing down dams and restoring rivers, Quebec is announcing new hydro-electric projects. In essence, the cornerstones of the Quebec economy haven't changed much since the nineteenth century, when waterfalls were sold at auction to the highest American and English-Canadian bidders.

Is Montreal's downtown, then, nothing more than a facade of gleaming skyscrapers hiding a couple of regional offices and their bilingual receptionists? Of the top 500 head offices in Canada, only 117 are now located here, versus the 123 corporate headquarters in Alberta and British Columbia, provinces whose combined population is well below Quebec's. What's more, not all companies conduct their business out of their nominal headquarters. Seagram, for example, which still lists its head office in Montreal, employs only a handful of its workforce of 30,000 in Canada. Nonetheless, Quebec still has some stunningly successful entrepreneurs, and in an economy decreasingly hampered by national borders, many of them are succeeding in international markets. Norman Webster is impressed by the ambitions of the current crop of Québécois entrepreneurs. "Bombardier is a good example. Quebecor, which is the biggest printer in the world, is an excellent example. I mean, these are people operating on a global scale, and make no bones about it: they're Québécois, but they're not just in the little pool here. There is a much greater sophistication among francophone businessmen of every sort than a few decades ago. They're taking on the world, and some of them are doing it quite well."

Charles Sirois, the CEO of telecommunications giants Teleglobe and Telesystem, is at the head of the pack of these world-beating entrepreneurs. Born in Chicoutimi, on the remote shores of the Saguenay River, he took over his father's regional telephone paging network when he was only 25. Financed to the tune of $2 million by the Caisse, he bought up paging companies until by 1986 he controlled half the Canadian market and was pulling in $50 million a year in revenues. A year later, his company merged with Bell Canada's cellphone arm. After five years of running the division, Sirois launched a hostile takeover of Teleglobe, a huge but unprofitable company that had the Canadian monopoly on overseas phone service. He laid down transatlantic cable and dismissed almost a quarter of the company's staff, tripling operating income. Late in 1998, Teleglobe merged with Dallas-based Excel Communications, the fourth-largest long-distance carrier in the U.S., which obtains new clients through multilevel marketing – sales reps convince friends and family to become sales reps, the same way Amway sells housewares. With Excel, Teleglobe now has the world's third-largest phone network, and it plans to spend $7.5 billion boosting capacity to become the biggest on the planet. Sirois, an upstart from the Quebec outback, now heads an empire worth $15.8 billion.

Teleglobe is run from a skyscraper on Rue de la Gauchetière, one structure in this Potemkin village that is definitely not a false front. The elevator ride to the twenty-fourth floor of the tallest building in Montreal is a queasy levitation, and the eerily silent reception area of Teleglobe features a disembodied racing helmet in a glass case, a tribute from the British American Racing team – the Teleglobe empire now includes Formula One driver Jacques Villeneuve. The accents in the French-language press's profiles of Téléglobe and Télésystème, I notice, are absent from the companies' annual reports and the corporate logo on the wall behind the receptionist. As with the artist formerly known as Céline, the fragile diacritics of Quebec's distinctness have been quickly eroded by the currents of North American capitalism.

Charles Sirois receives me in a kind of parlour, furnished with plush leather chairs and an old-fashioned globe covered with sea monsters and galleons. A little over six feet tall, with curly hair, laughing eyes, and a beaverlike quality to his eager grin, Sirois looks far younger than 45. He's ebullient about his position as one of Quebec's foremost businessman, as he makes clear in fluent and only occasionally unidiomatic English. "I have started as a regional entrepreneur," says Sirois. "After that, as a provincial, after that, as a national, and then as an international entrepreneur. Right now, more than 75 per cent of the activity of the group is outside Canada. We are now a global company."

He's not alone, either. Since Sirois started in business in the late seventies, he's noticed a change in attitude among his Québécois peers. "In the eighties, the view was Quebec, and then after that Canada, and then the U.S.A., but not too far. But it's obvious that today, Québécois businesspeople are less shy, more risqué. Many of the new generation believe in partnership, almost from day one. Very fast, they see the market internationally. And you have successes that are amazing: Cirque du Soleil – they've completely redefined the circus industry. You have the obvious companies, like Bombardier, Quebecor. Pierre-Karl Péladeau will go where he makes money. He doesn't care whether it's in Ontario, Quebec, or the U.S.A."

In fact, Pierre-Karl Péladeau, the CEO of publishing giant Quebecor, caused a ruckus by announcing plans to spend $45 million on the expansion of a printing plant in the Toronto suburb of Etobicoke because taxes in Quebec are too high. His late father, Quebecor founder and confirmed nationalist Pierre Péladeau, would not have approved. Sirois, too, has complained about local tax rates, and I ask about the consequences for business. "As a state, you cannot afford to have taxation that is higher than your neighbour," he says, spreading his elbows on the sides of his high-backed chair. "I often hear people say taxation in Quebec is not higher than in Germany or in France. I don't give a damn! They're at the other end of the world. I'm worried about Vermont, I'm worried about New Brunswick, I'm worried about Toronto. When your taxes are high, the people who will leave are the ones who have the highest freedom. And who are they? People who have wealth and know-how. So what are you left with? A poorer population. Somebody said to me once that we should tax the wealthy people more. I answered, 'No! We should have more wealthy people to tax!'"

When I point out that he probably wouldn't be here if not for the largesse of the state he's criticizing, he objects that the situation was different in the eighties. "At the time, there was no capital in Quebec. It was all in the hands of the English-speaking community. All the French-based entrepreneurs had small companies, and the venture industry was not as developed as it is today, so it was extremely difficult to get financing. The Caisse de dépôt was the one who invested $2 million in my company in 1984, and it's true, if I didn't have the Caisse, I probably would not have built what I have today. In today's world, though, the role of a government is not interfering to activate the economy. The role of government should be to create an environment that will foster companies and entrepreneurs."

It's not only high taxes that are crippling Quebec, insists Sirois, but also the ongoing political instability provoked by the Parti Québécois. "I think the sovereignty project had some merit back in the seventies and eighties," he says, his argument becoming more complex as he switches to his mother tongue. "There was an inequality, going back to the fifties, that justified the growth of the separatist movement. In today's context, it doesn't make sense. The problem is that the PQ didn't succeed in selling sovereignty to all Quebecers, only the French-speaking ones. So the English community didn't feel they were part of the future of Quebec. We have lost a lot of wealth by having these people leave." Switching back to English, he shrugs. "But you can't rewind the past." Sirois is not much worried about the future. The current premier is also from the Saguenay region – Sirois laughingly calls him a member of the "bleuet mafia," after the nickname for the residents of this area known for its blueberry fields – and he used to work as a lawyer for Sirois's father. "Monsieur Bouchard, don't forget, is a conservative guy. He's not a social democrat. If you just take out the Article 1 of the péquistes' platform, sovereignty, I don't see the difference between them and the Liberals. Monsieur Bouchard knows that he has no choice. We are living in a North American environment which is going more and more into the direction that the state should play a lesser role in our society."

Sirois, a son of the Saguenay – the most separatist area in all of Quebec – is a federalist. In a 1998 *Commerce* magazine survey of 300 Québécois company presidents, only 16 per cent of the francophones said they favoured sovereignty, while 18 per cent of the business leaders said they'd actually leave a sovereign Quebec. Sirois himself volunteered to recruit for Jean Charest's provincial Liberal Party in the 1998 provincial election.

Though optimistic about Quebec's political future, Sirois is a little uneasy about the well-being of the society. "Our standard of living, our level of economic growth is inferior to the Canadian average. Over a year, that's not too bad, but over 20 years, it's enormous. It's led to a serious unemployment rate, which means we're not able to finance our health system or our universities. It means we're beginning a downward spiral, which will be excessively hard to get out of. The biggest argument in favour of the state's intervention in the economy, the basis of the sovereignist project, was that we needed all our taxes in order to build a new country. But the original inequalities, which were the reason we wanted to build a new country, have eroded."

I ask Sirois whether, with the high taxes and instability, he's ever considered packing up for good – after all, only 14 per cent of Teleglobe's employees are based in Quebec. "No. I will never leave. This is my home. When you travel a lot, you come to appreciate that this is one of the nicest cities in the world." He gestures out the window, towards the treed slopes of Mount Royal – we're practically on eye level with the Grand Chalet atop the mountain. "You can look at the bottom line for your companies, but the bottom line for me is not only money. I need to enjoy where I'm living. Besides, Quebec is where I have my roots."

Over the years, such declarations of attachment to Quebec from members of the business elite, whatever their politics, have become almost obligatory. *Quebec, Inc.* author Matthew Fraser remembers hearing similar pledges of loyalty in the eighties: "The Québécois grow up with an abiding sense that they always have to express their allegiance to the Québécois entity. They're all very aware of it. It's very impolitic to say that you don't give a damn."

Two-thirds of young people in Quebec say they'd like to become entrepreneurs. "Entrepreneurs in Quebec have been integrated into the popular imagination in an adoring way," points out Fraser. "Quebec is like a family, and they're sort of like one of the brothers that have made good. It's something you just don't find in English Canada or in the United States, where people look at businessmen simply as being highly successful bank president types. Conrad Black is an intriguing figure, and some people hate him and other people admire him, but it would be difficult to say that people really have feelings of fondness or attachment for him." In English Canada, no one feels particularly betrayed when a member of the business elite confesses he feels just as at home in England or the United States.

The companies that lead *Commerce* magazine's annual survey of the province's most admired businesses almost always have a strong community orientation. The leaders of the 1999 poll were typical. The Groupe Jean-Coutu, a pharmacy chain that's expanding into the eastern United States and eyeing English Canada, is renowned for its avuncular, lab-coat-wearing boss and its community-centre-like presence in small towns. Rona, a group of hardware stores – named after its founders, Roland and Napoléon – was created in 1939 as a cooperative movement to bolster the power of small shop owners. The entrepreneurs who have received the most media attention and popular support since the eighties have been underdogs from modest or rural backgrounds who are perceived as self-made men. Members of Montreal's old middle class, managers of companies like Hydro-Québec and CN, and French-Canadian patrician figures like Paul Desmarais tend to leave the Québécois cold.

While the mythology of the patriotic entrepreneur is well established, the realities of business in Quebec are changing quickly. A striking example was the sell-off of the Provigo supermarket chain to Loblaw's. Created in 1969 from the fusion of three regional grocery store chains, Provigo was heavily backed by the Caisse to discourage the spread of anglophone-controlled supermarkets, particularly Conrad Black's Dominion Stores. The pension fund, which came to own 33.6 per cent of Provigo, became notorious for its meddling in the chain's business: in the mid-eighties, Caisse president Jean Campeau blocked the appointment of the founder's hand-picked successor, naming instead a former Montreal Stock Exchange president who brought the chain close to bankruptcy. In 1998, just before the provincial election, the Caisse orchestrated the sale of Provigo to Loblaw's, an Ontario-based company that now controls a third of the Canadian grocery market. The sale of this jewel in the corporate crown, for $1.6 billion, was finalized on the day of the Parti Québécois's narrow victory over the Liberals.

Only a decade ago, the sell-off of Provigo would have been perceived as the crassest of betrayals; the lack of public outcry in the nineties spoke volumes. Chairman Pierre Michaud was quoted as saying, "A company belongs to its shareholders, and Provigo's shareholders decided to sell because it was in their interest. Provigo doesn't belong to Quebec, no more than the Canadiens belong to Montreal, but many of the so-called managers sitting in the bleachers forget that fact." Heresy! But it's also symptomatic of real change.

Culinar, owners of the sacred Vachon Cakes, in 1999 announced they were selling out to the giant Interstate Bakeries of Kansas City. In the same year as the Provigo deal, Quebec-based Domtar bought the Ottawa speciality paper maker E.B. Eddy, and Quebecor snapped up the Ontario newspaper chain Sun Media. Guy Savard, a former Caisse president and the Merrill Lynch Canada financier who cinched both deals, shrugged: "Sometimes we sell to Ontarians, sometimes we buy from them. It has to work both ways." Meanwhile, the current leadership of the Caisse emphasizes its apolitical investment strategies and expresses frustration at federal regulations that restrict investments in foreign companies to 20 per cent of its total holdings. Even the Mouvement Desjardins, headed by the nationalist Claude Béland, seemed to be acknowledging the brutal realities of globalization, closing 400 caisses populaires in small communities across the province to compete with the large Canadian banks. Norman Webster sees such changes as profound and durable: "The Parti Québécois still has some of those old reflexes — we can't let terrible Loblaw's take over the collectivity's food supply – however, it's just fine if Bombardier goes out and beats the world in everything else. Which is just nonsense. Fortunately, I think Quebec has become a relatively sophisticated society. Most people have realized that if you're going to take on the world, the world is going to be here too."

Quebec, like the rest of Canada, is becoming enmeshed in a worldwide economy whose borders, we are told, are being erased to make the world safe for multinationals. (Some of this is hyperbole: a 1999 article in the *Canadian Economic Review* shows that Quebec still trades with the other Canadian provinces 22 times more often than it does with the United States.) In some ways, Quebec is well situated to take advantage of the situation. The *émergence* really did work. Francophone Quebecers now control at least two-thirds of the province's economy, with foreign investment accounting for more than half the remainder. A class of francophone businessmen, supported by capital pools amassed by the government – which in theory means the people of Quebec – occupies a milieu that had for generations been the preserve of an English-speaking elite. True, the new entrepreneurs haven't restored Quebec's title as Canada's economic centre of gravity, but the movement of capital to Ontario had already begun in the twenties and was merely hastened by the rise of the separatists. The people of Quebec really have built an economy of their own, an achievement of which they are justifiably proud.

It's not an economy without problems, of course. A corollary to the collective spirit that identifies with the entrepreneur-hero is the absence of the tradition of individual initiative that would lead to the creation of more such entrepreneurs. The work ethic associated with immigrants and Protestant enterprise in the rest of North America has always been a little diluted in Quebec. For much of the nineties, more than half the active population of Montreal depended on government support. Quebec's high unemployment, typically 50 per cent higher than Ontario's, doesn't include the hundreds of thousands who have stopped looking for work. One in 14 Quebecers works for the government, and 42 per cent of workers belong to a labour organization, the highest unionization rate in North America. Some estimates place government participation in the economy at 45 per cent. Add the continent's highest taxes, and you're getting dangerously close to a statistical portrait of one of the sclerotic societies of western Europe, where a generation of chronically unemployed young people has become fatalistically reconciled to a future bound by bureaucratized institutions and well-established, unionized baby boomers. In Quebec, they used to jokingly refer to the *État-providence* (the welfare state) as the État-Provigo. That was before Provigo itself was sold to a company from Ontario. If Quebec is a supermarket, it may soon have fewer people stocking the shelves than clearing them.

In the snowmobile museum in the Eastern Townships, one wall is covered with a few lines from Joseph-Armand Bombardier, uttered as he lay dying on a hospital bed in 1964. "Never forget that our company saw the light of day in a small garage in Valcourt," he reminded his children, "and it was the people of our village and the surrounding areas who always helped me make it what it is today." Such sentiment was at the heart of the singularity of Québécois entrepreneurship: real success was meaningless unless it was used to enrich the community. That was then; the neoliberal values of success for its own sake, and at all costs, have long since won the day. As a cutthroat business philosophy, it's produced some real successes. But it has also produced a tendency to embrace individualism, globalization, federalism – whatever philosophy serves an elite increasingly contemptuous of the collective good.

EXTINCT SOCIETY

The bells are tolling from towers named Perseverance and Temperance, and the flocks are gathering in front of Notre-Dame, as they have every Sunday morning for more than three and a half centuries. Montreal's first church, which started as a bark-covered chapel in the corner of a fort in 1642, is now a proud basilica, a stately pile of grey stones that boasts one of the largest bells in Christendom. The Gros Bourdon, as it's called, can apparently still muster a respectable crowd. Ten minutes before high mass, three tour buses are idling on the Place d'Armes, in spots normally reserved for the big-hoofed calèche horses. Beneath the portals, out-of-towners wearing ponchos emblazoned with maple leafs seek shelter from the rain. The panhandler outside the church door, taking note of the crowd's demographics, switches to soliciting spare change in English.

Within the basilica, the pews are filling up. Like much of Montreal, Notre-Dame is a hybrid, an English superstructure subsequently embellished to suit the tastes of the French-speaking population. The sober exterior, designed by the Irish-American architect James O'Donnell in the 1820s, is in the British Gothic revival style, but the interior is a burst of French neo-Gothic exuberance. Bundled columns of pine rise through wooden galleries, parting like the ribs of a parasol to expose a canopy of turquoise, a ceiling spangled with 22-karat-gold fleur-de-lys. The nave, following the natural slant of the terrain, drops towards the altar, which then rises in gleaming steeples, a gilded church-within-a-church peopled by the holy family and its retinue. Henry David Thoreau, wandering into a Montreal church in the middle of the last century, confessed that he was "impressed by the quiet religious atmosphere of the place. It was a great cave in the midst of a city; and what were the altars and tinsel but sparkling stalactites. . . . Such a cave at hand, which you can enter any day, is worth a thousand of our churches which are open only Sundays." (A New England Transcendentalist, he was unable to resist adding, "I am not sure but this Catholic religion would be an admirable one if the priest were quite omitted.")

This morning, the cave seems to be overrun with Neanderthals. A paparazzi assault of camera flashes, illuminating every sculpted martyr, ends only when two church elders are pushed out in wheelchairs and parked on the side of the choir. The ceremony that follows bewitches the senses. In the aisle, the hypnotically swaying censer spills the sweet smoke of incense, and the pipes of a huge organ fill the vaults with portentous notes. But few people are following the French prayer books, because few people here are francophone Quebecers. The whispered remarks in the pews are almost entirely in English, and the priest kicks off the service with a bilingual preamble. If the attendance at Notre-Dame-de-Montréal this morning seems to contradict reports of Catholicism's decline in Quebec, it's only because it's the height of summer tourist season. Subtract visitors from the United States, Japan, and Ontario, and the 3,500-seat basilica would be practically empty – except, of course, for the usual sparse sprinkling of little grey heads, the rapidly aging core of the dwindling congregation, all that remains of the faithful hordes in contemporary Quebec.

A generation ago, you would have been hard pressed to find a vacant pew. In the fifties, close to 700,000 of Montreal's 1.4 million citizens – virtually the entire French-speaking population of the island – attended mass regularly. The province also boasted 43,000 nuns and more clergymen per capita than any other part of the Catholic world. Daily life was stitched together by rituals: baptism, confirmation, catechism, confession, the reciting of the rosary, the days of obligation. The good sisters ran the province's hospitals and the institutions for unmarried mothers, the blind, and the orphaned. Priests registered marriages and deaths, taught in schools, and oversaw trade unions and insane asylums. As official registrars of births, they also made sure that generations of rural French Canadians bore such resound-ingly antiquated names as Épiphane, Onésime, and Zacharie, chosen from the calendar of the saints. From first communion to last rites, it was virtu-ally impossible to be born, study, marry, get sick, or die in French Quebec outside the Catholic church.

A decade later, Quebec was on its way to becoming the most impious region in North America. Today, only 15 per cent of Quebecers attend church regularly, versus 21 per cent of Canadians and 40 per cent of Americans. Nine-tenths of the province's 3,300 remaining priests are over 50, and clergymen from Rwanda and Burundi have to be recruited to fill the ranks of a church that once sent missionaries all over the world. It's as if Quebec had been hit by an unreported neutron bomb – one that acted on the soul rather than the flesh. In a single brilliant flash, it incinerated the Catholic faith, leaving the man-made structures intact. The spires are still here, jutting out of the province's 280 remaining Catholic churches. So are the crosses: 2,965 of them in Quebec, bristling from hilltops, listing along-side rural routes, often hung with the hairless, baby-pink body of a painted plaster Jesus. The local road maps still read like hagiologies, while the monasteries, convents, and presbyteries of Montreal and Quebec City squat, unprofitably, in the shadows of the skyscrapers. But the temples of fran-cophone Catholicism are being handed over to Vietnamese and Latin-American congregations, and they've started paying their bills by renting their steeples to Bell Canada for its cellular phone antennas. Filled with a haunting absence, Quebec sometimes feels like a house forsaken by its ghost.

At the same time, Quebec has transformed itself from one of the most morally oppressive, ethnically homogeneous, and backward corners of the continent into a modern and relatively diversified society. It's among the most tolerant and liberal parts of North America. Common-law couples are the norm here, and the provincial government in 1999 gave wide-ranging rights to gay and lesbian couples, affording them the same status as heterosexuals. The child mortality rate, driven down by free and widely accessible health care, is the lowest in Canada and among the lowest in the world. Babies born in Quebec, according to *Archives of Environmental Health*, are the least likely to show the effects of pollution, and the province's high school students, profiting from free and universal education, consistently get some of the highest scores on international math and science tests. Juvenile incarceration rates are low, and in a place with phenomenally little violent crime, the chances of being assaulted or murdered are remote.

That's the good news. The list of modernity's bad points is somewhat lengthier. The suicide rate is the highest of any Canadian province. One in 10 Quebecers now collects welfare, a further half-million are unemployed, and salaries are among the lowest in North America. All told, more people live beneath the poverty line here than anywhere else in Canada. Quebec has the highest illiteracy rate in the country, the worst high school drop-out levels, and the lowest percentage of personal computer ownership and Internet use. The men of Quebec commit suicide five times more often than women, they leave school earlier, are three times more likely to have a drinking problem, and have the lowest life expectancy in the country. In Quebec, you're more likely to grow up poor, in a fatherless family, than in any other province. If your parents are married, which is unlikely, there's a fifty-fifty chance they'll get divorced – another Canadian record. The suicide rate among youth is one of the highest in the world.

Chronic poverty and unemployment, broken homes, hopelessness, suicide: it looks as though the Pandora's Box of social ills the priests railed about for decades has been opened. In the absence of a unifying religion, the default values of North American neo-liberalism – self-fulfillment, mercantilism, and individualism – have driven a wedge into a society that once saw itself as the continent's beachhead against crass materialism. In an abrupt act of will, one of the most hermetic parts of North America came out of its cloisters, demanding its fair share of the pleasures and satisfactions of modern life. It's an apostasy Quebec is paying for, if not with its soul, then at least with its distinctness.

>‹

In his home on a shady side street of the Town of Mount Royal, a quiet bedroom community on the island of Montreal, Jacques Henripin, the province's leading demographer, is poring over a graph charting the population of Quebec. When he was born in 1926, women of his mother's generation were averaging more than five children each, versus fewer than three per family in neighbouring Ontario. During the Depression, the birth rate dropped, as it did elsewhere in Canada, briefly rebounding during the postwar baby boom. In recent decades, however, Quebec's birth rate, once the highest in the industrialized world, has dipped to record lows. In the late eighties, when women in the rest of Canada were averaging 1.9 babies each, Quebec's mothers were giving birth to only 1.35 children. "You need 2.1 children per woman to ensure that one generation will be replaced by the next," says Henripin. "For the past 20 years or so, most young women in Quebec have been averaging only 1.6." In 1998, there were fewer than 80,000 registered births in Quebec, the same number as in 1937, when the population was less than half what it is today. Henripin believes that in 35 years, a quarter of all Quebecers will be senior citizens. When the last of these baby boomers die off, with no significant cohort to replace them, the population will decline by one per cent every year for decades to come. He runs a pen along a line that peters into oblivion towards the end of the next century. "By the year 2081, we'll go from a population of seven million to four million." Kids under 15 already make up less than a fifth of the population, the lowest proportion in any Canadian province. Compared to the United States and France, which have had relatively high birth rates in recent years, the playgrounds and parks of Quebec are strikingly quiet.

With his Amish-style beard, Henripin is evocative of a northern Everett Koop. He's rather conservative in his outlook, but conservative in a distinctly Québécois way: though he was opposed to the recent granting of equal rights to homosexual couples (on the ground that society's priority should be rewarding people who produce children), he's an agnostic. When his much younger wife walks into the room, she introduces herself with her maiden name. Their seven-year-old daughter – Henripin's sixth child – is an adopted Chinese girl who bears the hyphenated surnames of both parents.

Unlike most English-Canadian conservatives, Henripin is an enthusiastic supporter of immigration, which he believes is the solution to Quebec's
demographic crisis. Unfortunately, the province has a lot of catching up to
do. "The rest of Canada, where 16 per cent of the population was born elsewhere, is an extremely welcoming place for foreigners," he says. "Quebec,
with eight per cent immigrants, is two times less inviting. We don't refuse
immigrants, but we have trouble keeping them. We've been getting only
30,000 a year recently, and over the long term, half of them leave for other
provinces. And when it comes to migration between provinces, Quebec
also comes out the loser; we give far more people to the rest of Canada than
the world gives to us." Since 1972, Quebec has suffered a net loss of almost
half a million people to other provinces. Ironically, the chief contributors
to population growth in Quebec these days are anglophones, immigrants,
and natives. The revenge of the cradle, once the hallmark of francophone
Québécois, is now being re-enacted by *eux autres*.

At Confederation, I remind Henripin, Quebecers accounted for a third
of Canadians, but the province's share of the population dropped to less
than a quarter in the 1996 census. The provincial government, in an effort
to boost the birth rate, has offered baby bonuses of up to $7,500, and
Premier Bouchard notoriously lamented that the Québécois were "one of
the white races that have the fewest children." Henripin, while deploring
such language, admits that he's a little perplexed about the causes of the
phenomenon himself. "How is it that, after having a fertility rate that was
the double of Ontario's at the beginning of the century, we dropped so low,
so fast?" he wonders. "I think it's because we discovered what freedom was,
especially in relation to the bishops and the clergy."

Henripin believes that the sudden withdrawal of a once-pervasive religious framework from daily life has had dramatic effect. "Belief, and obe-
dience to the clergy, did come with certain advantages. It probably wasn't
the best moral atmosphere you could imagine – it was a little narrow – but
at least there was something. Men didn't leave their women after fathering
a child, to go off and 'find' themselves. I've got the feeling there's a refusal
of long-term commitment among a large fraction of young adults, and it's
worse here in Quebec than elsewhere. There is, after all, a fundamental
moral framework that's useful for a society, and it's weak in the French-
Canadian context."

In the rest of Canada and the United States, changes in traditional patterns of community, religion, and family life came gradually and were reflected by a slow transformation of laws and mores. In Quebec, modernity came like a dam burst. The opening proclamation of the Quiet Revolution, spoken by Premier Paul Sauvé on Maurice Duplessis's death in 1959, was the prophetic "Desormais . . ." ("From now on . . ."), which presaged that nothing in Quebec would ever be the same. Through the sixties, when Quebec and the entire industrialized world were profiting from unprecedented economic growth and low unemployment, reform after reform swept society. Universities were opened; hydroelectric dams were nationalized; the health system was revamped; an elaborate system of social services (and with it the beginnings of a huge bureaucracy) were put in place. Young priests, newly defrocked, married ex-nuns and became government ministers, joining in the optimistic reform of the sclerotic institutions they'd quietly struggled against during the bad old days of political patronage and clerical control. The idea of being Québécois, as opposed to French-Canadian, became fashionable, as did the notion of forming a distinct nation, one defined by language and culture rather than religion. Future prime minister Pierre Trudeau observed that "a new clericalism appears to be taking hold of Quebec. For our mother the Holy Church, we're substituting our mother the Holy Nation."

According to the standard trope, the province, after a century-long dark age, was suddenly flooded with the light of openness, joie de vivre, and tolerance. In fact, Quebec in the fifties was more urbanized than most of Canada, and the wave of consumerism that swept the continent with televisions, cars, and appliances after the war certainly didn't circumvent French-speaking Quebec. Arguably, the leading lights of the Great Darkness – people like Trudeau, Gérard Filion, André Laurendeau, Gérard Pelletier, reformers drawing on a rigorous classical education – set an intellectual standard in public debate that hasn't been surpassed since. And the church was hardly a monolithic bastion of backwardness. There were radical priests, among them the socially committed Jesuits. The lower clergy, unlike their bourgeois peers in France, usually came from the same social strata as their parishioners and were often the most obstinate advocates of change. Archbishop Joseph Charbonneau of Montreal defied Duplessis by organizing collections to support striking asbestos miners (and was exiled to British Columbia by the church elders for his pains). The Jeunesse étudiante catholique became a rallying point for well-read and reform-minded Catholic youth.

Meanwhile, as crucial as the Quiet Revolution was for the advancement of Quebec, it proved an aesthetic disaster. The urban "planning" of Montreal mayor Jean Drapeau, which gutted elegant Sherbrooke Street and put a bunker on the nineteenth-century Carré St-Louis (two minor incidents in the carpet bombing of the most architecturally rich city in Canada), can hardly be considered an improvement over the churches of Ozias Leduc. To this day, when the doors of Montreal's sixties-vintage metro trains close, the first three notes of Aaron Copland's "Fanfare for the Common Man" echo through the fluorescent-lit, concrete stations. It's a representative touch of democratic idealism, but a reminder that, for all the good it brought, Quebec's Great Leap Forward was also the triumph for economies of scale and the lowest common denominator. The Quiet Revolution did indeed renew, in the late sociologist Fernand Dumont's words, the "poétique collective" (the communal sense of poetry) of the Québécois. Unfortunately, it also produced a soul-crushing, take-a-number bureaucracy which, as in many modern states, tends to view the populace not as a citizenry to be fostered but as a clientele to be served. Slowly.

There's no denying that Quebec had to change. In particular, the lot of French-speaking women was enough to warrant the loudest of revolutions. While English-Canadian suffragettes won the right to vote in 1918, the women of Quebec had to wait until after the Second World War to vote in provincial elections. Until the mid-fifties, an unconscionable double standard was enshrined in the Quebec Civil Code: while a man could obtain a legal separation if he could show that his wife was having an affair, a woman had to prove her husband's paramour was actually living under the same roof. Only in 1964, almost a century later than in the rest of Canada, were women declared adults; until then, they had the same legal status as minors and the insane, which meant a grown woman could not borrow money from a bank, sign a contract, or have surgery without her husband's approval.

Renée B.-Dandurand, an authority on the social anthropology of the family in Quebec, recalls having to visit a notary before her 1959 marriage in order to set up the division of property that would prevent her from automatically having the legal status of an eight-year-old child. A couple of years after she was married, everything started to change. "There was a kind of historical acceleration that was very significant in Quebec," she recalls. "Before 1968, you had to present a private bill in the federal Parliament to obtain a divorce. And that meant you needed a lot of money." Quebec, in fact, didn't even acknowledge the existence of divorce: for most of the fifties, the provincial censor board wouldn't allow the word to be uttered in movies. Since couples had to go to Ottawa and appear before a Senate committee with a private detective in tow to end their relationship, it tended to be Protestants and Jews who made the trip. The apparent stability of French-Canadian marriages often masked relationships marked by endurance rather than domestic bliss. "Women didn't have the choice to leave a relationship," says Dandurand. "The few who left did so at their own risk and peril, and they usually ended up exposing themselves to the greatest misery." Separated from their children, discouraged from working by the clerical elite, such women were ostracized. Outside the cloisters and the brothels, there wasn't a lot of social space for an unmarried woman in fifties Quebec.

"The changes in English Canada were much more gradual – certainly on the judicial front," says Dandurand. Within a decade, the women of Quebec went from a virtually feudal regime of institutionalized repression to near-complete legal control over their bodies and lives. The first family planning centres were introduced in 1964, the same year women lost their minor status; common-law couples were accorded legal rights in 1965; civil marriage was allowed in 1968; and Trudeau's omnibus bill legalized divorce, contraceptives, and therapeutic abortions nationwide a year later.

Dandurand is astonished by the change she's witnessed in her lifetime. "Look at Louise Arbour," she says, referring to the Québécois prosecutor for the International Criminal Tribunal who now sits on the Supreme Court of Canada. "Or Thérèse Paquet-Sévigny, the first female under-secretary in the United Nations. Or the senior ministers in the Parti Québécois like Pauline Marois and Louise Harel." Compared to most places, Quebec – where, until the late sixties, unmarried mothers needed a certificate of good conduct from a local notary before they could pick up their monthly support cheques – is now a Brave New World of equal opportunity. After the Ministry of the Status of Women, headed by Lise

Payette, was founded in 1976, large swaths of social policy were created by progressive-minded feminist ministers, including the unique system of $5-a-day daycares, largely conceived to lighten the burden of working women. The majority of university and high school degrees now go to women, and 44 per cent of the Quebec workforce is female. Unlike in the United States and France, where old boys' clubs still dominate national politics, one in five candidates in Quebec's provincial elections is female.

This reversal of several centuries of tradition in less than 40 years hasn't come without trauma. Fifty-five per cent of Québécois children are born out of wedlock, a statistic that inspired the newsmagazine *Alberta Report* to call Quebec a "province of bastards." In a place where a quarter of all couples now live in common-law relationships, the Civil Code actually requires a special procedure for a married woman to adopt her husband's name. Not that many marriages are happening here: only 37 per cent of Québécois women under fifty are or have been married, versus 61 per cent of women in the rest of Canada. Dandurand isn't particularly surprised. "I don't think there's a crisis of the family," she says. "Or if so, only indirectly. What we've lived through, in fact, is a crisis of marriage. It's an important institution that's going through a period of transition. But I think it's normal. Before, women didn't have access to the work market – and then all of a sudden, they were allowed in. Why not have a kind of rejection of the family for a generation?"

It's a good point, but not much consolation for the child born into what everyone hopes is merely a "transitional period." Though Dandurand insists that common-law relationships in Quebec are becoming more stable and long-lived, they're far more likely to end in a break-up than traditional marriages. Quebec now has the most single-parent families in Canada, and in most cases they're run by a young mother living below the poverty line. In interviews, sociologists find that men are confused by the enlarged social roles of women – and that women are getting tired of confused men. Influenced by a North American culture that values romantic passion over pragmatism as the basis for a couple, encouraged by liberal Quebec's ready acceptance of the relatively weak bonds of the common-law relationship, men often throw up their hands and say, "Go ahead. You can have your job and your kid – I'm taking off!" This shows up in the cinematic and television paradigms of Quebec manhood, particularly *l'homme rose* (the pink man), a strident supporter of feminism with a penchant for breaking into tears and confessing his vulnerability. The Hyde counterpart to this liberated Jekyll is *l'homme fuyard* (the runaway mate), who welcomes gender equality because it gives him the freedom to abandon a relationship when passion wanes or problems arise. This would be just part of the ongoing tragicomedy of embattled free spirits, one certainly not limited to Quebec, if it weren't for the children left behind. "There's one value that I find important, which I think has been lost," says Dandurand. "It's that when you bring a child into the world, having a certain amount of stability as a couple is very desirable."

Such problems, and the rhetoric that accompanies them, are found in most of the industrialized world. Once again, however, Quebec is unique in that it has had to face the traumas of modernity far more abruptly. It's probably no coincidence that, in a province hearteningly free of serial killers, the one significant episode of mass murder in the past 20 years was directed at women. On December 6, 1989, Marc Lépine, a 25-year-old student fascinated by war movies and guns, walked into Montreal's École Polytechnique with a high-powered rifle and shouted, "I want the women. You're all a bunch of feminists. I hate feminists." Forcing the men out of classrooms at gunpoint, he murdered 14 women and injured 13 others before turning the gun on himself. Lépine had been beaten severely as a child by his Algerian-born father and for most of his adolescence had lived with his mother, a lapsed Catholic nun who in 1972 had taken advantage of Quebec's new divorce laws to break free of her hellish relationship. The people of Quebec went into shock after the unheard-of massacre, closing ranks like a giant wounded family. Students from the École Polytechnique, few of them practising Catholics, spontaneously wandered to the nearby Oratoire St-Joseph to mourn the dead in candlelight vigils. Dandurand is still troubled by the implications of the incident. "It was a crime against women," she insists. "He shot the girls, who, from his point of view, shouldn't have been admitted to the school. Obviously, Lépine was a sick person. But we get the kind of sick people who correspond to our society. I think it's an event that made us ask ourselves, Have the changes in society been too quick for men?"

There's some evidence that they've been too quick for just about all Quebecers. The overall suicide rate in Quebec is now 19.4 per 100,000, more than twice as high as in Ontario. Among young Québécois men, the figure is an astonishing 33.8 per 100,000, a rate surpassed only in the turbulent countries of the former Soviet bloc. In other words, about one person in the 15-to-24 age group succeeds in committing suicide every day; and for every one that succeeds, there are at least 40 who attempt it. The reasons people end their lives, of course, are notoriously diverse and resist simple explanations. However, the peak in youth suicide does coincide with a time when it's not particularly propitious to be young in Quebec. In a society that was once remarkable in North America for the durability of its community and familial ties, such age-old institutions as marriage, religion, and parenthood itself are in a phase of fragmentation and redefinition. For people on the brink of adulthood, the increasingly familiar North American perspective of a working life of instability and part-time jobs is exacerbated by Quebec's history of structural unemployment. For the young, there are few solid career options and little hope for secure posts in universities and government. Shortly before he died in 1997, the sociologist Fernand Dumont, noting that 40,000 students a year were dropping out of school without high school diplomas, told an interviewer, "If I were 20 years old today, on the one hand I wouldn't feel very much solidarity with my elders, and on the other I'd probably have the feeling that I was living a situation that was unjust and inequitable. . . . We could at least suggest to the older generation that they share [their privileges] a little."

The education system, the chief locus of reform during the Quiet Revolution, probably deserves some blame. Until the beginning of the sixties, the educational careers of most Quebecers tended to be rather short; more than half of francophones over the age of 25 hadn't completed seventh grade. (To this day, 21 per cent of Quebecers, versus 12 per cent of Ontarians, have less than Grade 8.) A small elite went to the private collèges classiques, and these lucky few often received an extraordinary education in which increasingly open-minded priests offered an introduction to Latin and Greek classics, in the rigorous French style. To cope with the immense demographic bulge of baby boom teenagers moving through the school, the Liberal government of Jean Lesage established the Ministry of Education in 1964 and set up the Parent Commission, whose epoch-making reforms were implemented under later administrations. It led to the creation of the first cégeps (collèges d'enseignement général et professionel), postsecondary institutions that correspond to the last year of high school and the first year of university in the rest of Canada. The Université du Québec, the first real institution of higher learning not founded by the Catholic church, was opened in 1968, with campuses in Chicoutimi, Rimouski, Trois-Rivières, and Montreal. Education was democratized, and school attendance rates in Quebec shot up.

Strangely, while more people were getting educated than ever before, it became harder to get a really good education. To house this vast cohort of thirsty young minds, the education ministry built the *polyvalents* – massive blockhauses in the worst Bauhaus-derived style – which typically boasted three or four thousand students, often bused absurdly long distances. To combat elitism, academic and technical currents were wrapped into a single mainstream program, which accommodated underachievers but left bright students bored. By the nineties, the average length of time a Quebecer spent in school – about 12.3 years – had surpassed the average in most European countries. But analyses of the quality of the education suggested there were serious deficiencies. While students in France's university-oriented lycées attend school for 42 hours a week, Quebec's equivalent cégeps impose only 20 to 30 hours. The school year here, at 180 days, is the second-shortest in the industrialized world. The laissez-faire, child-centred teaching styles of the sixties and seventies consistently downplayed the teaching of history and grammar, and critics point out that the ministry is still obliged to dumb down its year-end French exams, allowing dozens of faults in passages of only a few hundred words. The severest critics say that Quebec's educators, terrified of producing more dropouts, are producing illiterates incapable of conjugating the verb *être* or using the *passé composé*. Young Quebecers, on the other hand, say there isn't much point in living up to such high demands, since an older generation, among them the more vocal critics of the school system, is blocking most of the positions that demand an education.

"When I look around me," says Helene Jutras, a 24-year-old Québécois writer from the Mauricie village of St-Edouard-de-Maskinongé, "I realize there are lots of people who were trained to form an intellectual elite. They went to university, they got doctorates. But there's no room for a renewal of the intelligentsia in Quebec, because there's a kind of ceiling blocking them." I've met Jutras at a noisy café on Montreal's Rue Ste-Catherine.

My first impression is that she's like a lot of Québécois her age – determined to be a little *flyée*, or wild. Jutras confesses that she omits the accent marks from her given name, Hélène, because they remind her too much of raised eyebrows. Her hair is died mauve, her ears are pierced three times each, and rings stick out of her right brow and nostril. She's also highly articulate and very well read. She finished high school at one of Quebec's most prestigious private schools, Montreal's Collège Jean-de-Brébeuf, and went on to take law at McGill. If she'd graduated with similar credentials a generation ago, she would probably be on track for an academic teaching position by now. This being the end of the nineties, however, Helene – no accents – spent the summer broke in a cabin on Quebec's isolated Côte-Nord, working on her first novel.

To tell the truth, I'm surprised to find Jutras in the country at all. In 1994 she became notorious for writing a couple of letters to *Le Devoir*, subsequently published in a book called *Le Québec me tue* (translated into English, by Jutras herself, as *Québec is Killing Me*), in which she threatened to leave Quebec for good. "It was during the 1994 campaign, when Jacques Parizeau was elected," she recalls. "I was on summer break, after finishing cégep, before starting McGill. I just sat down in front of the computer one morning and wrote it. I'd never done anything like it before." The letters expressed her weariness with the debate over independence, her disgust with the education system, and her desire to start life afresh in a place where social progress wasn't blocked by incessant infighting. "My well-being takes precedence over a country that refuses to be a country," Jutras wrote. Quebec's problem was that "we bring things down to the level of the least accomplished and the weakest, and make no provision to enhance the advancement of those who aim to succeed." She added that she had no intention of voting in the coming election. This was one disgusted-sounding young woman, and radio commentators and columnists, baby boomers all, reacted with condescension and outrage. "They called me a spoiled little girl from McGill," she recalls. *Maclean's* blundered in, hailing her as a spokesperson for a new generation that saw separatism as "outmoded." Actually, Jutras is still a firm believer in independence for Quebec. At the time, she was just a little sick of hearing about it and thought it was time to talk about issues she considered more pressing.

Like, I suggest, the state of education? "Oh, *mon Dieu*," she says, rolling her eyes. "The only reason I heard about the Second World War was because I took an optional course." As for French, "there were a lot of experiments in the seventies – just a little before my time – where they tried to teach us French orally. It doesn't work! There are tons of letters in the French language that you don't pronounce. They'd give us books that were supposed to be appropriate for seven-year-olds, which would have been about right for five-year-olds. They never encouraged us to read, to go farther. I've got friends who make tons of errors when they write; they're aware of it, and they're ashamed of it. I remember meeting someone, in the second year of cégep, who was incapable of telling the difference between *j'ai été* and *j'ai eu*" (rather like being unable to distinguish between "I was" and "I had"). An obsessive reader and writer, Jutras says she eventually managed to teach herself French grammar in spite of the school system.

With her prematurely disillusioned voice, Jutras scared a lot of older Quebecers. "The attacks were very personal," she says. "Columnists like Nathalie Petrowski and Pierre Bourgault said how much I discouraged them. For other people, it was like a pretext for feeling good about taking an interest in young people. They made a big deal about me, and then they could forget about the whole thing for a few months because they'd spent a little time thinking about the younger generation." The baby boomers of Quebec, fond of seeing themselves as the most revolutionary contingent in the history of the province, were particularly upset at being cast as forces of stagnation and oppression. "We're never going to have the jobs that they had," says Jutras. "After getting a master's degree, we're not going to get a job with tenure and all that. We'll never have the house in the suburbs with the swimming pool and the two cars. It's just not part of our reality." I ask what her parents think of all this. "They're separated," she replies. "My mother agrees with me. But I don't know what my father thinks. I haven't talked to him for the past eight years."

In the wake of Douglas Coupland's demographic-defining *Generation X* and the experiences of millions of kids worldwide who've grown up with history's most self-indulgent cohort of parents, Jutras's complaint may not sound particular to Quebec. Once again, however, the singularity of Quebec lies in the intensity of its response to modernity. What's more, as pollster Michael Adams remarks in his book *Sex in the Snow: Canadian*

Social Values at the End of the Millennium, the baby boomers of Quebec differ from those in the rest of the country. Ontario has a disproportionate number of what Adams calls Disengaged Darwinists, middle-class, individualistic boomers who tend to be suspicious of hippie hedonists and support the neo-conservative swing towards Premier Mike Harris. In contrast, Quebec is full of Connected Enthusiasts, passionate, gregarious children of Woodstock with a penchant for following New Age trends, buying new-generation Volkswagens, and doing things en masse. (A single statistic speaks volumes about the difference in mentality between the two provinces: Quebecers are four times more likely than Ontarians to have casual sex when vacationing abroad.) Ironically, as Adams points out, "though they harbour many of the values associated with youth, most Connected Enthusiasts do not regard young people as their equals."

English Canadians were memorably exposed to Quebec's boomers in Denys Arcand's *The Decline of the American Empire*, the popular, Rohmer-esque film that showed a group of child-free academics talking about a lifetime of free-spirited sex and broken commitments as they sipped imported beer in a sprawling house in the Eastern Townships. For Anglos who had seen themselves reflected in *The Big Chill*, it was a delightful introduction to a particularly light-hearted and articulate group of French-Canadian soulmates. For a younger generation, however, one that would later recognize itself in the film *Trainspotting*, it was a chilling portrait of insufferably smug and privileged yuppies. Pathetically attached to their long-gone youth, the Enthusiasts of *The Decline of the American Empire* seemed to spend the film mocking the students they had marginalized.

François Ricard is in some ways the Québécois baby boom incarnate. We sit down on the summery terrace of a French restaurant in Outremont, and he orders the classic drink of the carefree yuppie, a glass of white wine. Playing the part of the hard-bitten post-boomer, I order a businesslike espresso. Born in 1947, Ricard remembers Montreal's Expo 67 as being the chief fête of his youth. With his full head of hair, his round brown eyes set in an unlined face, his knee-length shorts and sports sandals, Ricard looks considerably younger than his half-century. With my dress shirt, pocket watch, and black boots, I suspect I look considerably older than my third-of-a-century. If our conversation doesn't lapse into the usual exchange of intergenerational resentment and suspicion, it's mostly because Ricard is so damn gracious. He proffers an Export A, in the French way, with one cigarette drawn from the pack, and when I refuse, he asks – in the Canadian way – whether the smoke will bother me.

As biographer and confidant of the late Gabrielle Roy, a novelist who began her writing career in the forties, Ricard has spent a lot of time thinking about the lost values of a bygone Quebec. And though he's a full member of the baby boom, he's also one of its chief critics. His book *La Génération lyrique*, which appeared in 1992, was less a celebration than an excoriation of his peers. In an act widely perceived as a betrayal, he accused them – at length – of being self-obsessed, addicted to novelty, and ludicrously attached to their fast-fading youth.

Though *La Génération lyrique* was more literary essay than sociological treatise, the book was also informed by Ricard's historical research on contemporary Quebec in the French studies department at McGill. Demographers say the increased birth rate between 1945 and 1970 added 900,000 more children to the Quebec population than would have been born if prewar fertility rates had remained constant. I ask him whether there was anything unique about the baby boom in Quebec. "It's true that it was a Western phenomenon," says Ricard. "In France, there was the New Wave and May '68, the United States had the hippies and Woodstock. But it was very particular in Quebec, because Quebec was a very conservative society. It wasn't just a question of religion, but also a certain vision of culture, an attachment to the past, to traditions. There was a kind of marginality, of mistrust, in relation to the modern world. So when the youth arrived, in the sixties, it was really a deflagration, an explosion."

The Quiet Revolution, according to Ricard, was no less than the baby boom's triumphant arrival on the stage of modernity. The older, frustrated reformers – Trudeau, Laurendeau, Lévesque – who had been kids in the Depression and come of age in the last years of the Great Darkness, were finally free to change society in the name of a vast cohort of fresh-faced youth. "You have to imagine Quebec in 1955 or 1960," Ricard points out, "and realize that in the space of four or five years, everything collapsed. It had never happened so quickly anywhere else. The United States had the hippies, but there had been beatniks before them. English Canada also had a tradition of protest, going back to the CCF. These were societies that were rather Protestant, capitalist, modern. In Quebec, the change was really brutal. Personally, I'm a partisan of slower reform. I think these changes left terrible scars. There was a kind of joy in the rupture, in the devastation."

The children of the Québécois baby boom saw a world that changed around them, and for them, with every new step in their life. Ricard calls the first-born of the boomers, his peers, the lyric generation, a reference to Czech novelist Milan Kundera's notion of "lyricism" in which the world appears as a vast open field, free of obstacles, burdensome only in its "unbearable lightness." "Belonging to the lyric generation," wrote Ricard, "meant being at once the first and the last: the last of the old world, whose stability we knew without having to suffer the oppression, and the first of the world to come." It also meant, in his memorable phrase, "breaking down doors that were already open." In other words, the older generation gave up its power to the young without much of a struggle, in spite of the boomers' claims that they won everything through committed protest.

Ricard himself recalls growing up to see all the old barriers crashing around him. Raised in small-town Shawinigan, he nonetheless went to a good collège classique and was taught by priests. "The collège classique that I knew was in transition; it was extremely open. We read Sartre, Camus, the journal *Parti pris.*" Only a decade before, the Catholic church's Index of Prohibited Books would have made such liberties unthinkable, but Ricard got to take advantage of a rigorous education in a newly liberal context. Upon graduation, he set off for Europe. "If I'd been born 25 years earlier, I would have worked in a big company like Shawinigan Water and Power. Like my dad." Instead, when he got back from the continent, he had his choice of well-paid academic positions.

Brought up in relative prosperity, used to seeing the world changing to suit its needs, Ricard's generation set about brushing aside the old standards. "We rejected all the values, all the traditions, so much so that the world appeared like something malleable to us. We could change anything – laws, behaviour, morals – it was enough to want to change it." In Quebec, that meant dispensing with the tiresome rules of French grammar, European culture, Catholicism, and Cartesian traditions of rational argument. In its place came the fractured, Americanized diction of joual, child-centred learning, and playful flirtation with Marxism, Maoism, and pop psychology. Gone were the cultural tours of *la vieille France*; Québécois hippies instead hitchhiked to Woodstock and Haight-Ashbury. "The whole idea of Americanness, of California," says Ricard, "is a simple way of not having any model at all. 'America' represents space, total openness, the end of neurotic complexes. In fact, however, it's more a refusal of standards, of challenges. At heart, the idea of 'America' isn't a challenge. In the Quebec context, it's just a form of francophobia, of revenge against the European tradition that was imposed on us."

The baby boomers, while very good at kicking apart all the old values (and in Quebec, there was a lot to demolish), didn't leave much of value for generations to come. No literature, certainly. The best writers of modern Quebec, including Jacques Ferron, Réjean Ducharme, Michel Tremblay, and Anne Hébert – most of them products of the collèges classiques – were born before the boom. Instead, boomers embraced their own disposable form, the *téléroman*, whose infancy coincided with their own. (The same is true of American boomers. The real writers of the counterculture, Kerouac, Pynchon, Salinger, Burroughs, Kesey, and company, were already at work while the future hippies were still watching *Howdy Doody*.) The manifestos of Québécois student revolt were shameless echoes of the futurists, the surrealists, and the Marxists who'd said it all – better – decades before them. "Virginia Woolf once said that, when one is a young writer, the simple fact that the work of a Flaubert, a Chekhov, a Thomas Hardy exists means that one's hand trembles," says Ricard. "In Quebec, there haven't been a lot of trembling pens lately. It's characteristic of my generation: a kind of navel-gazing, of easy complacency about oneself. Because if we start to look outside Quebec, we'll not only realize how privileged we were, we might also notice that we weren't very original or brilliant."

What does make the baby boomers of Quebec unique is their omnipresence. An immense government and academic bureaucracy was not only created for these people; they now occupy its leading positions and refuse to make room for the young. "We dress like young people," says Ricard, plucking a little sheepishly at his own polo shirt. "We act like young people, at work and in our relationships. The result is, there's no more room for young people in society. Go to the Jazz Festival, and you'll find it's full of people my age. A lot of the daughters of my female friends have had to compete for men with their own mothers in the cruising bars of Montreal."

By the time he was my age, Ricard points out, he'd already been in a full-time teaching position for seven years. I suggest that, as a professor at McGill, he must have watched young Quebecers develop coping strategies. "As a matter of fact, four of my students have committed suicide over the years. It was no use for them studying, getting doctorates – everything was blocked. Life definitely wasn't a question of 'lightness of being' for them. At a profound level, I see a sort of moral despair. The kids of my friends have problems with drugs, depression, suicide. I think it's because my generation refused to be parents. We didn't want to play the role – rarely brilliant or glorious, often disagreeable, thankless, dull, and especially old – against which young people rebel, but which also gives them a framework in which to grow. It was our generation, after all, that invented divorce."

I have to give him credit. Ricard, who never had children himself, has mastered the art of the elegant *mea culpa*. I ask what the future holds for his generation. "Oh," he sighs, taking a final sip of wine, "death will come, sickness will come." As usual, however, many boomers will face the final novelty by failing to accept the gravitas of the situation. "I'm playing the prophet here, but I think we're going to see a huge wave of assisted suicides. They'll have the laws changed" – and in liberal, boomer-dominated Quebec, it won't be that hard – "so that their suffering can end as quickly as possible."

When the time comes, I suspect that much of Quebec will greet the news with a long-awaited, sincerely expressed *bon débarras* – which I'll be happy to translate, for the benefit of all the similarly embittered post-boomers in English Canada, as good riddance.

As a demographic cohort, the baby boomers were crucial in creating the contours of modern Quebec society by ushering North American values of consumerism and self-fulfillment into a traditional society. But other, sometimes deeper, issues go just as far towards explaining the challenges facing Quebec. The province's leading intellectuals, who grapple to find the sources of the current malaise, point to the failure of the sovereignty movement, the growing alienation from history and tradition, and the spread of the more egoistic varieties of North American individualism.

Unfortunately, their analyses often go unheard. Québécois society is genuinely egalitarian and displays a kind of honest disgust with the behaviour of flashy arrivistes. The unfortunate flip side is a widespread suspicion of intellectuals and an aversion to any discourse that starts to sound complex. For much of its history, francophone Quebec had no intellectual or social elite – the educated priests and lords went home after the British victory on the Plains of Abraham, leaving a fast-growing populace of habitants whose clergy was drawn from the ranks of farming families. Premier Duplessis, who boasted of never reading books, dismissed intellectuals as "pelleteux de nuages" (shovellers of clouds). Even apart from its Index of Prohibited Books, the mainstream Catholic church spent much of its history waging war against the free dissemination of ideas. Though philanthropist Andrew Carnegie repeatedly offered to establish a lending library in Montreal, as he had in other major North American cities, the church blocked his every move. The public library, wrote nationalist pamphleteer Jules-Paul Tardivel in 1890, was "a pestilential spot . . . where the public goes to poison itself." It wasn't until 1959, the year of Duplessis's death, that a law establishing a network of libraries was adopted.

Even today, book reading is not deeply entrenched in Quebec. The central branch of the Montreal public library allows patrons to take out only four books at a time and imposes a $4.50 charge to "rent" recent bestsellers for three weeks – an innovation that would arouse indignation anywhere else in Canada. While people in British Columbia borrow 11.2 library books per year, Quebecers average only 4.9, the lowest number of loans per capita in the country. And it's not just a question of libraries going unpatronized: 43 per cent of Quebecers say they rarely or never read books, while 21 per cent of the population is functionally illiterate, the highest rate in Canada (the figures are dramatically higher among men). On the other hand, there's no shortage of writers in the province. Quebec has more than 200 publishers, and 6,000 new titles appear every year. Informed by European currents little known elsewhere in North America, Quebec's intelligentsia produce an astonishing array of books and essays. The problem is that few people read them.

One of the favoured cuckoo-lands of Quebec's "cloud shovellers" is the Olivieri bookstore, in the multi-ethnic Montreal neighbourhood of Côte-des-Neiges. The Jehovah's Witness at the metro station, a Caribbean woman, has spread the steel surface separating the escalators with magazines; the title *Awake!* appears translated into Cyrillic, Arabic, and Chinese characters. The street is full of Russians, Algerians, and Vietnamese, which makes the presence of a bookstore that looks as though it belongs in Paris's Latin Quarter a little disorienting. In Olivieri, the shelves are filled with books by leading French authors, and intellectuals sip café au lait from bowls and debate ideas in the best Left Bank tradition. The place is elitist, highbrow, and profoundly un-Québécois – and Jean Larose, whom I find hobnobbing with other writers on the backstore terrace, looks right at home there.

"The word 'intellectual' is an insult in Quebec," says Larose, lighting a Matinée Slim. "Intellectual always means *too* intellectual here. That's exactly why, in my books, I make a point of presenting myself as an intellectual." Larose, in his beige suit, with his neatly trimmed hair, his rapid-fire diction – and his slightly perverse delight in provocation – brings to mind a Parisian. In fact, he's a real Québécois baby boomer, born in rural Valleyfield just after the war. A Université de Montréal professor, he did his doctoral work in literature at Vincennes, in France, in the seventies. A product of the traditional collège classique, Larose is notorious for writing books criticizing what he sees as the poverty of thought and the low standards of education in Quebec. I suggest that he's adopted a position that must make him unpopular among the more ethnocentric Québécois nationalists. "I *like* being poorly thought of," he snorts. "And there are more and more of us who don't mind being poorly thought of either. Quebec is no longer a monolithic place. It's enough to look around Côte-des-Neiges to realize that. My wife is Cambodian; my niece is Chinese; my landlord last year was Bulgarian; my neighbours are Russian and Sri Lankan."

One of the recurrent themes in Larose's essays is the *esprit de clocher* (spirit of the belltower), a deliberately cultivated sense of parochialism that he sees pervading even Quebec's educated classes. When he returned from France in 1979, he found "the progress of populism in the intellectual world had become really significant. It was like an ideological constraint, weighing down the entire culture." He wrote a book, *La Petite Noirceur*, which argued that the Great Darkness of the past had continued in a rejection of all things European and a too-easy embrace of all things Québécois and North American. "In the seventies, we started to say, 'We're a small people – and we're perfect that way.'" Larose admits that such an attitude makes him worry about the future of Quebec. "We've destroyed the institutions, like the church, that meant we were less advanced than the rest of the world. But they were also the ones that kept us together. These days, the churches are empty. They're *really* empty. Quebec hasn't become independent, and we haven't replaced Catholic morality with any kind of civic morality. Nationalism served as a kind of social cement for a while, but it's starting to wane too."

Larose sees Quebec society as increasingly atomized, with people growing more and more cut off from one another. Though he's not a practising Catholic, he believes that Quebec's religious heritage should be stressed in the schools. A recent government report advised presenting Catholicism from a sociological perspective and teaching it in schools as just one of the world's many religions. Larose sees this as a slide into relativism, dangerous for Quebec. "Religion is there to give meaning to what's most mysterious, what's most unanswerable, in human life," he insists. "Now we say we're going to present a kind of catalogue of possible responses to these questions and let people make their own choice. Once again, we're giving up our position of authority in favour of being merely a kind of guide or host."

Larose's position is similar to that of novelist and multiculturalism critic Neil Bissoondath, who believes it's essential for Quebec and Canada to assert their identities and traditions – religious, linguistic, and cultural – as a way of coping with the challenge of immigration. "In my opinion," says Larose, "teaching religion like that leads to the New Age, the Solar Temple, and other sects. It's the same position that leads to suicides among the young. Nobody wants to assume the role of the father." Larose, in his early fifties, has finally assumed the role of father himself by having a child with his Asian wife. "Like a lot of people in my generation, I thought it would never happen," he laughs. "I've got a 16-month-old boy. I suppose he's half Buddhist and half ex-Catholic." I ask how he's going to help his son navigate through the Quebec he sees as increasingly rudderless. "One thing is certain," Larose replies, with the kind of unapologetically elitist edge you hear more often in France. "I'm going to send him to a private school. And I'll make sure he travels a lot."

Among intellectuals of all generations, there's a recognition that, though the Quiet Revolution brought necessary changes to Quebec, much has been lost along the way. What surfaces most often is an impatience with the self-satisfied acceptance of literary and artistic mediocrity, and a kind of despair over the erosion of shared values and common goals. Jacques Godbout, the celebrated author of *Salut Galarneau!* and a long-time documentary filmmaker for the National Film Board of Canada, is the contemporary of Mordecai Richler and Jean Paré and part of a generation that François Ricard calls the Frustrated Reformers, the overseers of the baby boom. Godbout welcomes me into his high-ceilinged, hardwood-floored office in the Boréal publishing house on Montreal's Rue St-Denis and gestures for me to sit down next to a table piled with galleys and catalogues. He's tall, clean-shaven, white-haired, broad-shouldered, and a master of the pronunciamento. Given his magnificent, gravelly voice and almost papal manner, I get the feeling that interruptions are poorly received in this room. Fortunately, I don't have to formulate too many questions. Godbout has a tendency to ask and then answer them for me.

"One of the great sicknesses of the Québécois," he intones, "is that we believe everybody has to be the same, equal, and that we have to get rid of our elites. If, for example, you correct a student in school, or demand a high-quality text, you're guilty of elitism. If you look at the immigrants learning French in our schools, they tend to speak better French than young Québécois. Why? Because the immigrants are being taught French, while we don't dare tell our young Québécois that they don't know how to speak French: that they don't know the meaning of words, that they have no vocabulary and no idea of linguistic structure. And why is that? Because we no longer give *dictées* or make them learn anything by heart."

I ask whether he's concerned about the state of the family in Quebec. "Perhaps men are a little less responsible than they should be. Women tend to believe happiness is something that's due to them, that can't withstand difficulty. If things go badly, they rapidly abandon the relationship. I think that we haven't taught our children that a couple is first a relationship based on love, but it's also a social and economic enterprise. We've probably accorded sexuality a role that's far more important than it actually occupies." It's an old-fashioned outlook, but I suppose I shouldn't be surprised; Godbout once dismissed the Internet as a "CB radio with a keyboard," and there's definitely something of the nineteenth-century *littérateur* in his style. I remark on the lack of a computer in the office, and he tells me his old Waterman pen is his only writing instrument.

I ask Godbout for his take on the disappearance of religion from society. "At the age of 15, I stopped going to church," he recalls. "And when I stopped, my father told me, 'I was waiting for you to do that, because I didn't want to go anymore either.' I imagine it happened like that in a lot of families. If the only reason you go to mass is because the priest tells you God will punish you if you don't, and the priest loses his authority, then why go? Nonetheless, religion has remained in our society. It's remained in a certain kind of nostalgia, our gregarious way of doing things, the way we seek consensus."

The Quiet Revolution, Godbout believes, was largely a success. "When the objectives of independence were being formulated in the early sixties, there were three of them. One: Take charge of the economy, which was controlled by Anglo-Americans. Done. Second objective: Get rid of the Catholic church. Done. Third objective: Distance ourselves from France so we weren't always dependent on Paris. That's been done too." Quebec, then, has gained the more positive attributes of nationhood, if not the actual status. "In my opinion, the political program of the Parti Québécois doesn't stand much of a chance. It's a vision of the world that's been bypassed." He says that he sees young Quebecers, the ones born after the baby boom, demonstrating a new openness towards the world. "My generation, the generation of the collèges classiques, went to Europe and came back with European ideas about national independence – 'The Swiss have a country, why not us' – that kind of thing. The baby boomers went to Big Sur, to California, and came back with ideas about feminism and sexual liberation. People of your generation tend to go to Africa, to Asia, to the Third World. On my last film crew, there were a half-dozen people your age, and their girlfriends and boyfriends were all foreigners: Japanese, English, Vietnamese, French. In my time, it was always French-Canadian Catholics marrying French-Canadian Catholics. Québécois society is becoming more diverse. It's neither good nor bad; it's just part of a worldwide trend."

What has come to obsess Godbout lately is the way history is taught in Quebec. His last NFB documentary was the controversial *Le Sort de l'Amérique*, in which he suggests that the notion of the Conquest of 1759 may be a sort of historical fraud. According to Godbout, the Plains of Abraham – generally viewed as the definitive tragedy in the history of Quebec – was actually a battle between distant colonial powers, one that left the habitants at the time relatively indifferent. There's evidence that most Canadiens, who after a couple of centuries of Laurentian winters were no longer calling themselves Français, greeted the arrival of the efficient British as a relief after the neglectful French regime. "When the film came out, there wasn't a single history professor who publicly dared to contradict the idea that this had been a war between France and England, and that the Canadiens were only victims by accident – which isn't what they teach in the schools. In the schools, it's our 'Defeat,' it's the 'Conquest.' You see, history has always been poorly taught here. Before, it was taught from the perspective of the French-Canadian Catholic, with the perspective that we were victims. This was a country founded by Jesuits who went out into the woods to be cut into slices by the Iroquois. Now, it's taught with a nationalist perspective, to put us in the situation of the victim. So we can claim the right to take revenge or blow the place up."

Quebec's politicians are notorious for portraying the Québécois as the victim of Anglo machinations; western Canadians, meanwhile, have become equally adept at adopting the aggrieved victims' role in relation to the perceived indifference of the Quebecers and Ontarians who run Canada. John Ralston Saul has referred to this as the Lord Durham syndrome, after the British colonial administrator who in 1839, invoking the "irremediable inferiority" of francophones, advised establishing structures to encourage their assimilation. It didn't happen, of course – the revenge of the cradle saw to that – but Durham's outrage became the prototype for a long tradition of resentment.

"Our most basic myth of victimization unites all regions, languages, and classes," Saul writes in *Reflections of a Siamese Twin*. "It is, in short, that Canada exists only because it did not wish to be American. In other words, that our existence is an artificial construct based entirely on a negative. That therefore there is no real purpose, content, or agreement on a project." In fact, as Saul stresses, Canada is a rather miraculous and complex project, and the relatively peaceful coexistence of immigrants – in a matrix of French, natives, and English – on this New World soil can be seen as a hopeful template. It's certainly a project that Quebec has helped to create and sustain; but it's one that requires continuing goodwill and imagination, qualities that have been lacking among political elites, Canadian and Québécois, for the past couple of decades. For both John Ralston Saul and Jacques Godbout, the myth of victimization is a way of avoiding the real challenges facing Quebec and Canada.

Godbout resists the idea that there are significant problems with Quebec, dismissing the suicides, unemployment, and dropout rates as not significantly worse than those elsewhere. Perhaps I should have expected this. If a young Québécois journalist showed up in the office of an Albertan intellectual, with a notepad full of statistics about social problems like Indian-bashing and redneck racism, he'd probably be run out of town on a rail – particularly if, like Godbout, the intellectual was an elder who felt partly responsible for creating that society. When I mention the high suicide rate among young men, I'm surprised to hear him dismiss it rather lightly. "In my opinion, if boys kill themselves more than girls, it's because girls read more novels, and boys don't read at all. And when you read novels, it means you're capable of having an imagination and thinking that something might happen in your life. After all, why not go on living until a Prince Charming arrives." I mention that it's not just boys who are killing themselves, it's adult baby boomers as well. "Ah!" he laughs. "To make some room for everyone else."

The chief project of modernity, the logical momentum of the Quiet Revolution, is one I've deliberately avoided: the sovereignty of Quebec. In a sense, this void has been as artificial as the one the French author Georges Perec subjected himself to in *La Disparition*, a 312-page novel written entirely without the letter *e*. Like the most common letter in the alphabet, however, separation is an issue that recurs in every discussion in Quebec, and I must now type the missing *e*. After all, it was virtually the destiny of the massive demographic wave born after the war to create a new nation. "Independence appeared to them like an immense party," François Ricard wrote in *La Génération lyrique*, "similar to those of their youth, where the people united, released from all constraint, sang the same song and thrilled to the same joy: that of discovering themselves to be unanimous, similar, unique, and beautiful." In other words, national liberation as blissed-out rockfest, a seventies-vintage commercial for the Pepsi Generation. By all logic, the baby boomers of Quebec should have had their country, just as the hippies of California should have had their Republic of Love. The numbers were right, the will was there, the weed was good.

Too bad they got distracted, tempted into Buddhism, sensual massage, Solar Temples, sabbatical years at Berkeley. The future of Quebec is now in the hands of another generation, the young people the boomers refuse to see as young. From what I can tell, the latest cohort is too concerned with survival to devote serious energy to nation building. Many Quebecers my age, the ones who aren't crippled by their own generational victim mentality, take off for a dose of reality in Asia, South America, or Africa. As it was for the artists who penned the *Refus global* manifesto in 1948, exile from a sclerotic, bureaucratic society sometimes looks like the only decent hope.

Significant Others

When the French historian and sociologist Alexis de Tocqueville came to Lower Canada in 1831, he praised the Canadiens' open-heartedness and their lack of religious fanaticism and base mercantile motivations, traits he saw as distinguishing them from their American neighbours. He predicted a bleak future for the democratic United States: "I see an innumerable multitude of men, alike and equal, constantly circling around in pursuit of petty and banal pleasures with which they glut their souls. Each one of them, withdrawn into himself, is a stranger to the fate of all the rest. Mankind, for him, consists of his children and his personal friends. As for the rest of his fellow citizens, he is close to them, but he does not see them; he touches them, but he does not feel them; he exists only in himself and for himself alone; and if his family still remain to him, he may be said at any rate to have lost his country." This is a pretty accurate portrayal of an anomic America of gated communities, daycare massacres, deep-seated suspicion of government, and minimal voter turnout. It's coming to be a good description of large swaths of Canada, too, where crocodile-eyed downsizers have convinced many people that, since there are no longer any jobs and no social classes, there can be no solidarity of interests either.

It might also help to explain what's happening to Quebec, a place where modernity, if it arrived late, also hit particularly hard. Since the Quiet Revolution, Quebec's distinctness, once unassailable, has been undergoing a nefarious erosion from within, one that probably started around the time many baby boomers decided they felt more at home on the beaches of Florida and California than in the cafés of Paris. The Montreal-led refusal of winter, reflected in suburbs filled with Hollywood-style bungalows laughably ill-suited to these subarctic climes, is just one sign of the relentless drift into American consumer culture. The certainties of the old parishes haven't proved much of a match for modernity's allures. The move towards individualism, one of the hallmarks of the modern age, doesn't always mean a decline into egoism and atomism – provided it's undertaken with some grace, imagination, and a will to reinvent community and family ties. It rarely happens that smoothly, however, and Quebec's suicides, ruptured families, and high unemployment are signs of a society riding the rapids from a community-oriented past to a more atomized North American future. The canoe, it seems, is hitting a lot of submerged rocks along the way.

In both heritage and thought, the distinguished philosopher Charles Taylor is a product of Quebec's defining contradictions and compromises. His father was an anglophone who came to Canada's metropolis from what was then the boondocks – Toronto – at the turn of the century. Taylor's French-speaking mother was one of the Beaubiens, a family that owned much of Outremont and produced some of Canada's leading senators and stockbrokers. Taylor, born in 1931, grew up in a household where the cohabitation of English and French allowed him to harmonize two sometimes contradictory world views. One of the world's leading authorities on the philosophy of Hegel, he ran for political office against Pierre Trudeau as a federal New Democrat in 1963 and served as the Chichele Professor of Social and Political Theory at Oxford in the seventies. His speciality is identity, particularly in relation to the varieties of human communities. In Quebec, he's found rich terrain.

Taylor's cramped office is lined with shelves sagging under the weight of bulging file folders, volumes by Locke, Heidegger, and Mills, and the

Spanish, French, and German translations of his 700-page opus *The Sources of the Self*. I find him hunting-and-pecking over a computer keyboard in the midst of this genial disorder, his long back held straight. Taylor is tall and erect, casually dressed in a yellow polo shirt. Striped white socks droop beneath loose trousers. He looks at once authoritative and approachable, an impression heightened by his mad scribble of eyebrows and his breathless, enthusiastic way of talking, in which syntax is often left tangled in the rush to convey an idea.

We're on the ninth floor of the Stephen Leacock Building on the McGill campus, and I suggest that most of the skyscrapers I can see over his shoulders weren't around when he was a young man. Taylor agrees that the changes in his hometown have been pretty astonishing. "I describe it to my grandchildren, and it's just inconceivable what Quebec was like before. It's a million light-years away," he marvels. "If you take American society, the changes begin slowly with Henry Ford at the beginning of the century and gradually take in more and more people. At any one moment, however, it's not terribly abrupt. In Quebec, however, it was contained, and then suddenly burst its bonds. So what the Americans did over the whole century – and this is only slightly exaggerating – we did in 10 years. We went screaming to the other end of the spectrum." A practising Catholic, Taylor agrees that the decline of religion was one of the most dramatic changes. "It was very much part of people's identity here, and now it's gone. You had to see it to appreciate how important it was. People used to go up the stairs of the Oratoire St-Joseph on their knees, performing *les sacrifices*, saying a prayer at each step. I knew people who did these things, and it was not trivial or external. It was very deeply ingrained in their souls. So there's been a real shift in what's important."

Taylor believes modernity generally brings with it three malaises, and Quebec hasn't escaped any of them. First, individualism, a hallmark of the modern age in the industrialized world, tends to become trivialized into an egotistical search for self-fulfillment, which leads to a loss of meaning and a fading of moral horizons. This is often accompanied by the primacy of what Taylor calls "instrumental reason," in which efficiency becomes the measure of success and economic standards of cost-effectiveness are applied to almost all endeavours – from downsizing a company to rationalizing government services. Finally, in a society in which individualism and instrumental reason hold sway, the connections within communities and between individuals fray, producing a "flattening and narrowing" of human relations – a social predicament often referred to as anomie or atomism. This is the dystopia de Tocqueville warned about, a mass of disconnected people so obsessed with their pursuit of banal pleasures that they become strangers to the fates of their fellow citizens.

The positive side of individualism, according to Taylor, is the quest for authenticity – for example, the kind of self-realization undertaken by the poet Émile Nelligan and other exemplars of the Romantic tradition. Often it involves a rebellion against restrictive morality. The negative side is narcissism and self-indulgence accompanied by a flight from responsibility and community ties. In Quebec, this is what the essayist François Ricard pinpoints as the chief characteristic of the lyric generation, the cohort that brought modernity to the province: their refusal to be parents or even adults, in favour of a never-ending quest for youthful self-fulfillment. "This culture of consumerism-slash-authenticity-slash-hedonism," says Taylor, "puts a tremendous responsibility on people to find a way of bringing stability and order to their lives. They have to discover ways to believe in long-term relationships. And if they can't, it's just terrible for the children. Where there's no stability, they really suffer."

Quebecers, and Canadians in general, tend to be more resistant to extreme individualism than their American neighbours. "We in Quebec are very much more like English Canada than either of us is like the United States," says Taylor. "The Americans have ideological quirks that even English Canadians find strange. This gun business, for example. And the way they are highly individualistic and tremendously suspicious of government." In other words, Canadians have trouble understanding why American society enshrines one's absolute freedom to possess semi-automatic weapons – but not to buy an aspirin that contains a couple of milligrams of codeine.

Taylor believes that Quebecers, more so even than other Canadians, disdain the violent solutions that tend to go with individualism. "So many people shrink from violence here. We're at the antipodes of the United States in that regard. I remember back in 1970 there was some sympathy for the FLQ members who kidnapped Pierre Laporte, but as soon as they killed him, there was a wave of horror. There's a strong sense that we've got to resolve things peacefully. Though we've got our share of racists here, they're more reluctant to move to some kind of action, more so even than people would be in Toronto or Vancouver. And these kinds of feelings are never translated into political positions – not like in France. Nobody would dare."

The problem, of course, is that the deep-set differences of this once cohesive, Catholic society have been challenged by its enthusiastic embrace of modernity. "We entered modern consumer society with a bang after 1945, and it had a tremendous dissolvant effect on the structures that existed before. It's the turnover that produced the Quiet Revolution in 1960. We really went overboard, too, because we came from somewhere that was way outside. We're like a lot of other Western societies that way: no matter what our long-term cultural tradition, there's a veering towards this individual kind of behaviour." Outside Quebec, Taylor sees the Charter of Rights and Freedoms, with its emphasis on individual rights, diluting the country's traditional respect for collective rights, steering Canada towards an American model in which social issues are confronted by legalistic appeal to a constitution, rather than legislation. "American judges have taken incredible powers upon themselves," emphasizes Taylor. "In the case of affirmative action, for example, they determine exactly how and what percentage of jobs are going to people. In Canada, the judges used to believe in the tradition of legislative superiority. The question is, How much will the new Charter go to their heads and make them become like American judges? The jury is still out."

Canada is now the terrain of confrontation between two different models of what constitutes a decent, workable society. There's the viewpoint of many English Canadians that, in a multi-ethnic society of immigrants, all citizens ought to be equal members of a mosaic, their rights protected by the Canadian Charter of Rights and Freedoms. A newly arrived immigrant from Pakistan equals an Inuit from Nunavut equals a francophone Québécois equals a Manitoba Mennonite. Quebec is just one of 10 provinces, with the same status as Prince Edward Island.

On the other side is the notion, common in Quebec, that assuring the collective rights of minorities sometimes ought to take precedence over individual liberties; that a community has a right to take legal measures to ensure the survival of its language and traditions. The former, individualistic approach, according to critics, takes little account of Canada's two-pronged history of European settlement and its record of cautious alliances and treaties with Indian nations. In practice, too, we end up blindly following the American model. The detractors of the collective-rights approach, by contrast, say it gives some groups "extra" rights and "special" status – which they find deeply unfair.

For Taylor, the failure of the Meech Lake Accord in 1990 was also a failure to reconcile, or even acknowledge, these different conceptions of society. In Quebec, where English- and French-speakers have lived side by side for centuries, accepting the existence of a significant other, one with a cohesive and distinct world view, has been a civilizing influence. "The idea that you work it out between different communities is very much the Québécois way," he says. "The whole idea of the rights of the minority, the English minority for instance, is profoundly entrenched. Most Quebecers think, *Il y a des Anglais, il y a des Québécois*. It's just evident. That's a primacy of collective rights on an unthought level. And the idea that you can put the two in a big steamroller just isn't accepted by the majority in Quebec. The distinct society is a great reality. Among the people of Quebec, there's a sense that this society is different and a puzzlement that the rest of the country doesn't see this." Taylor confesses his own exasperation over the issue. "It's just so obvious. Sometimes you feel like taking people in the rest of the country and shaking them. 'What's the matter with your head?' " he says, raising the spread fingers of his large hands in mock entreaty.

Since Quebecers, and most natives, resist being declared uniform patches in the Canadian mosaic, Taylor believes that the idea of second-level or "deep" diversity is the only solution to the current conundrum. "Someone of, say, Italian extraction in Toronto . . . might indeed feel Canadian as a bearer of individual rights in a multicultural mosaic," Taylor has written. "His or her belonging would not 'pass through' some other community, although the ethnic identity might be important to him or her in various ways. But this person might nevertheless accept that a Québécois or a Cree or a Dene might belong in a different way, that these persons were Canadian through being members of their national communities. Reciprocally, the Québécois, Cree, or Dene would accept the perfect legiti-macy of the 'mosaic' identity."

Taylor likens this approach to the way people once carried Soviet pass-ports with Ukrainian or Russian stamped on them, indicating their "deep" belonging to a particular unit within a larger political union. "So what do we do here in Canada?" he asks. "We either break up or we accept that a real multinational society allows people to belong through different kinds of formulae. That's what I call deep diversity. It's diversity at the level of how you understand belonging, as against simply diversity between people who belong to a country in the same way but are diverse in other ways."

Such a formula would undoubtedly be advantageous for Quebec and Canada, but it's also one that Quebec resists applying within its own boundaries. The francophile political elites – though usually not the people – too often betray a streak of Jacobinism, the extreme, French-born republicanism that suppresses local cultures in favour of a strong national identity. In France, this led to the eradication of the Breton and Provençal languages through extreme policies of cultural assimilation, and the perception of the wearing of the hijab, the Muslim veil, in schools as a threat to the separation of church and state. Many Québécois politicians have demonstrated such leanings, particularly in their refusal to acknowledge the sovereignty of First Nations or their outrage at the suggestion the province could be partitioned in the event of separation. While deep diversity would be advantageous for the Canadian status quo, one suspects that the politicians of a sovereign Quebec, eager as they are to be received as equal in the diplomatic quarters of Paris, would strenuously resist acknowledging deep diversity within their own borders.

Strangely enough, in spite of Quebec's official policies of integration and interculturalism, this is one of the few places on the continent where day-to-day, de facto deep diversity can be said to exist. Quebec was settled by people from the west and centre of France, whose family structures were inherently egalitarian. In such families, property was divided among sons – a measure later formalized in the Civil Code – and the organization of the early colony, with land divided into *rangs*, or long, equal strips, is a geographic manifestation of this deeply ingrained sense of equality. The Americans, noted for their facade of equal opportunity, were in fact the most inegalitarian of people. As in Britain, property in New England was passed on to the oldest son. As long as there was a frontier and new land to settle, younger sons could set out to find virgin territory on which to start new families. As the country filled, however, the old resentments – the sense of inequality and unacknowledged social divisions – became woven into America's fabric. And of course the United States was founded on slavery, the idea that some people are inherently inferior to others, and the legacy can be seen in the country's bizarre myopia over its apparently permanent underclass of blacks and Hispanics.

"All men are created equal in the United States, but after that, it's every man for himself," the French demographer and historian Emmanuel Todd wrote in an essay in *Newsweek*. "French culture is complex and heterogeneous, but at its heart there is this idea of the rightness, the necessity of equality." A savvy debater would object that France is the home of Jean-Marie Le Pen's Front national, the racist anti-immigration party that often gets 15 per cent of the vote in French national elections. Todd responds that while the French can be accused of xenophobia, the real test of their egalitarianism is in their willingness, on the most fundamental level, to recognize the humanity of outsiders. Mixed marriages between the French and North Africans, the target of Le Pen's rage, are widespread. In contrast, mixed marriages between whites and blacks in America are rare. Such deep acceptance of the other is also one of the singularities of the French in America. When de Tocqueville was riding through the woods of Michigan in the 1830s, he was astonished to meet *bois-brûlés*, the "burnt-wood" offspring of the coureurs de bois and the Indians, men who paddled canoes in moccasins while singing the songs of seventeenth-century Norman peasants. The Americans and English Canadians preferred genocide and segregation on reserves to any significant mixing with the natives; the French took them as lovers and mates, producing an important community of Metis in the process.

Later, when Irish immigrants arrived en masse, another significant mixing of blood took place as French-speaking Quebecers welcomed the newcomers. Interestingly, modern Québécois attitudes towards outsiders tend to be similar to those of the French. They initially demonstrate a superficial xenophobia, which in Quebec's case is really more a question of a minority society's fear of losing its identity, traditions, and language. But once the initial reticences are overcome, they are remarkably relaxed about entering into real relationships with outsiders. Witness the demographer Jacques Henripin's Chinese daughter, the intellectual Jean Larose's Cambodian wife, or the intercultural liaisons in Jacques Godbout's young Québécois film crew.

It's true, French Canada didn't experience the Revolution that brought egalitarian ideas to the mainstream of political thought in France. But while the French waited until 1792 to decapitate their aristocrats, Canadien society had lost its head some 30 years earlier, when most of the colonial elites – the soldiers, seigneurs, and curés – went home after the British took power. Though the habitants who remained came to be dominated by the English and an extremely hierarchical church, day-to-day life in the villages and farms tended to be egalitarian and community oriented. For much of its history, English Canada, with its Old World Tory-derived belief in good government and its willingness to acknowledge group rights, as well as its prairie-born cooperative traditions, shared these values. "Egalité, Solidarité, Survivance" would have been an appropriate motto for Quebec – and, in translation, for the rest of Canada – reflecting values that fostered a conservative but humane society. It still sums up what distinguishes Quebec from much of the rest of North America, where the unspoken corporate slogan – in spite of all the professed ideals of equality – is increasingly "Corporatism, Competition, and Conquest."

Quebec was originally a colony of peasant farmers with profound collective traditions, abandoned on the most ruthlessly individualistic continent on the globe. This contradiction has provoked a durable cleavage within French-Canadian society itself. From the start, there was the coureur de bois, the lone adventurer and fortune seeker, an exemplar of individual freedom, whose culture and blood sometimes melded with those of the Indians he met as he roamed the woods. His very existence threatened the curé, who remained behind in the village, preaching the purity of the race, the continuity of traditions, the need for *survivance* – a collective vision of society. The historical tension between the priest and the coureur de bois is very much present in contemporary Quebec. We see echoes of the coureur de bois in people like Richard Martineau, the editor of *Voir*, and François Girard, the director of *The Red Violin*, who believe in cultural cross-breeding and the value of international collaborations. The modern-day priests are people like *Elvis Gratton* director Pierre Falardeau and his apologists, who are suspicious of what they consider the modern-day "cultural potlatch" and believe Québécois language and culture is self-sufficient and need not concern itself with outside, "cosmopolitan" standards.

Neither side is entirely right or wrong, but their discourses tend to slide towards negative extremes. The blindly accepting coureur de bois loses all sense of continuity, tradition, and even language, finally to be swallowed up in the wilds of the north woods, the beaches of Florida, or the bland McWorld of a globalized culture. The thundering preacher of survival tends towards xenophobic nationalism, convincing his flock that outsiders represent a threat to the parochial standards he defends. (For the artist, of course, the answer to this apparently insoluble conundrum is simply to make good art. Director Robert Lepage, at his best, renders Québécois stories universal by filtering them through his eminently cosmopolitan imagination.) At worst, such demagogues encourage Quebecers to march up Rue St-Urbain with swastikas on their sleeves or blame their electoral defeats on "money and the ethnic vote." Happily, the mainstream of Quebec rejects these extremes. For the most part, the American business gurus who preach savage capitalism find their messages received with blank stares in a society that still believes solidarity is an important value. Meanwhile, the historical *métissage* between Québécois of French-Canadian origin and natives, English-speaking Canadians, and immigrants is too widespread to allow the xenophobes' *pure laine* diatribes to make much headway.

Quebec's profound distinctness on this continent, its continued – though increasingly diluted – defiance of the Anglo-American notion of individualism at all costs, means that Canada has available to it a different way of looking at society, an original blueprint. In other words, English Canada has a significant other, and its lifelong dialogue with Quebec has made it a richer place. (The United States, in contrast, seems to be engaged in a narcissistic monologue, gazing at itself in a mirror as an increasingly disgusted world looks on.) The continuing dynamic with significant others – francophone Québécois and natives – is what makes English Canadians more than just unarmed Americans with health cards. To the extent that English Canada impatiently cuts off dialogue with these groups when their demands are perceived as too extreme, it risks losing its own distinctness. "People in western Canada will be furious about this," says the bicultural, bilingual Taylor, "but people like me, who are very profound federalists, believe that we *are* Canada. Canada is a kind of mélange of alliances, of two languages. We who are at the heart, where those two met, in Quebec – we *are* Canada. That's why there's such a difficulty leaving the Canadian identity in Quebec – the feeling is, we made this, it is our country. We essentially defined it."

As someone who grew up in British Columbia, a place that periodically toys with the idea of merging with Washington and Oregon and calling itself Cascadia, I don't feel insulted by such an outlook. I didn't begin to understand Canada until I started understanding Quebec. This is truly the heart of the nation, where the French, the natives, and the English came together. It's also the place where the three groups have coexisted, with improbable civility, for centuries. Hence the panic before the 1995 referendum, the planeloads of earnest federalists who flooded Montreal with an embarrassing gush of unrequited love: deep down, many English Canadians realize that if they lose their significant other, Canada will start to lose its identity.

Unless there's a backlash against economic globalization, however, all this talk of distinctness and dialogue might become a historical footnote. The Québécois, who until recently considered themselves *Canadiens français*, shed their Catholicism, one of the key pillars of their identity, in only 40 years. The French of Quebec is becoming homogenized under the influence of television; joual and regional dialects are disappearing. Quebec's business elite echo the rhetoric of the big-picture, factory-closing, bottom-line capitalism perfected in the United States. To distance themselves from English Canada, Québécois nationalist politicians are encouraging trade with the United States, going so far as to promote the adoption of the American dollar as the official currency.

If there's a country more Jacobin than France, though, it has to be the United States – as evidenced by the fate of the French in New England and Louisiana. English Canadians, the world's most accomplished observers of the world's most powerful nation, have always had a pretty good idea of how different they are from their southern neighbours. The Québécois, on the other hand, shielded by language, are starting to display a distressing enthusiasm about their affinities with *les Américains*. Many have taken to referring to themselves as *Français d'Amérique*. Forget Meech Lake, the Charlottetown Accord, and referendums. The real challenge to Quebec's distinctness will happen as the baby boomers, the most Americanophile, ambitious, and materialistic generation ever, assume full political and social power.

After three years of getting to know one of the most liveable, civilized, and intriguing parts of North America, I can assure Quebecers of one thing: they don't know how much they have to lose.

INDEX

The text of this book is set in Minion. Inspired by the beauty and elegance of classical, old-style typefaces of the late Renaissance, Minion was designed in 1990 by Robert Slimbach.

Book design by Sari Ginsberg